The best of **Britain**

D1628477

Norfolk and Suffolk

SUSAN GRIFFITH

Contents

The Guide

Photo Essays – in the centre of the book
The best of... Suffolk
The best of... Norfolk
The best of... Cambridgeshire

Introduction

If Dr Johnson was right when he said, 'The great source of pleasure is variety', East Anglia can provide boundless pleasure. A motorist in a hurry can travel from top to bottom (Ipswich to Cromer) and side to side (Cambridge to Lowestoft) in little over two hours. But what a wealth of landscape and human history would be missed. The same distances could enjoyably occupy a month of pottering around ruined abbeys, riverside hamlets, wild sea coasts, perfectly preserved medieval churches and village pubs turned gastronomic paradises.

Take just one example: within a 35-mile radius of the glorious medieval cathedral in Norwich, you can tuck into a seafood feast for £8 in a garden overlooking the coastal marshes of the north Norfolk coast, or travel south to the grassy heathland of the little-known Brecks. For the children, just a short distance east from Norwich is a magical adventure playground on Hoveton Little Broad, or west is a dinosaur adventure park in a Norfolk woodland. A little further west you can eat in a top organic restaurant favoured by Stephen Fry in the market town of Swaffham, and further east, you can walk for miles along beaches

colonised by seals in the winter breeding season. The concentration of pleasurable places of interest and beauty in such a small area is astonishing.

The theme of the region is water. The shifting coastlines draw many, who come to walk, swim, birdwatch and contemplate. The fascinating maze of meandering waterways in the region is an essential element in its uniqueness. Because there are so few bridges, the parishes and districts have retained their individuality far longer than they might have: for example the River Yare has only one crossing place between Great Yarmouth and Norwich, and that isn't a bridge but a ferry at Reedham. There are no motorways to ravage the coastline, partly because of all those rivers, marshes and estuaries which guarantee that the coasts have remained mostly unspoiled.

The English imagination has been formed by certain iconic images of the countryside, some of which can be attributed to the paintings of Suffolk-born John Constable and Thomas Gainsborough. Those contented cows grazing in river meadows in an idyllic rural landscape represent an uncomplicated past. Only a little exploring along the River Stour will show how little has changed here as in so much of East Anglia – one of the least industrialised parts of the British Isles.

Praising the vast skies over the flatlands and seascapes of East Anglia has become a cliché, but that doesn't mean that they don't deserve praise and wonder. Another cliché that doesn't hold up to scrutiny is that a flat and empty landscape is boring, an old chestnut that deters some people from heading east. In fact the East Anglian landscape offers a raw and unconventional beauty. Much of the hinterland is untamed, unmanicured. And what is wrong with an empty landscape anyway if it allows the imagination to soar and brings a feeling of freedom and tranquillity to people usually hemmed in by buildings and timetables? Overgrown hedges and twisted pine trees evoke an ancient landscape perhaps best appreciated when shrouded in mist. This is a storied and magical landscape trodden by ghosts.

The East Anglian coastline is always in flux, with the unpredictable tides filling and emptying estuaries and reedbeds, marshes and mudflats. A region that might at first seem uneventful will slowly reveal unexpected wonders of Man and nature. It turns out that following roads that go nowhere in particular and losing track of time is immensely rewarding.

The mention of East Anglia has at times prompted a metropolitan sneer. If holding onto old-fashioned values of community and resisting unwanted make-overs deserves to be mocked, then let them. One of the most remarkable aspects of East Anglia, especially in the remoter corners of the Fens, the Broads and the Heart of Suffolk, is how successfully the social traditions and culture have been maintained despite their proximity to the south of England. Many rural North Folk (from Norfolk) still speak with a 'Naaarfuk' accent, in contrast to other regions of England where accents have become diluted more quickly because of a more mobile population.

It's comforting to know that we have on our doorstep a place that proudly maintains its differences. The continuity with the past is sometimes astonishing. It feels as though this is an area where the oral tradition is still alive, where bakers and pub landlords have handed down secrets to their successors, like the recipe for butter buns in Southwold or for Nelson's Blood bitter fortified with rum, served in Horatio Nelson's old local in Burnham Thorpe. Suffolk, Norfolk and Cambridgeshire have been more successful than most regions at following the mantra 'Keep it local' as illustrated by the large swathe of Suffolk that is the only Tesco-free area in the country. As a result, farmers selling direct to the public have flourished and the quality of the food and drink throughout East Anglia would justify a trip in itself. Alongside the old-fashioned charms a sophisticated infrastructure has grown up including state-of-the-art museums, Blue Flag beaches, boutique hotels, cutting-edge kitchens, and all the things that discerning tourists now expect.

Unmissable highlights

01 Holkham Beach

The staggering vastness of the white sands of this five-mile stretch of the North Norfolk coast make this arguably the most beautiful and unspoiled beach in Britain, p. 182

02 King's College Chapel

The magnificent fan vaulting of the roof seals this building's status as one of the most glorious Late Gothic buildings anywhere. The choir, known around the world, from their broadcasts every Christmas Eve, performs a sung service daily in term time, open to the public and free of charge, p. 307

03 Butley Oysterage, Orford

Feast on freshly caught crabs and oysters served plain at this no-frills café run by a fisherman, p. 98

04 Norfolk Broads

Hire a motor cruiser for a day or a week at Potter Heigham to mosey through the Northern Broads, mooring at riverside hostelries beloved of boaties, p. 251

05 Blythburgh

The magnificent medieval church overlooking the Suffolk marshes has a door bearing the claw marks of the Devil who once visited in the form of a black dog, p. 68

06 Wicken Fen

This National Trust nature reserve with boardwalks and a windmill is the last remaining fragment of fenland wilderness as it was before the fens were drained in the 17th century,

07 Blickling Hall

This great Jacobean house not only has a marvellous interior and parkland, but offers cycles for hire and a wonderful food shop in the estate barn,

08 Constable Country
Constable Country

After looking at some famous paintings by Constable and Gainsborough, marvel at how few incursions the modern world has made on the picturesque water meadows at Sudbury or the river scene at Flatford Mill, p. 130

09 Elm Hill, Norwich

This historic cobbled lane is lined with more timber-framed Tudor buildings than survive in the whole City of London, p. 230

10 Coastal Walks

It isn't easy to choose between Areas of Outstanding Natural Beauty. The North Norfolk coast between Wells and Blakeney has unrivalled scenery but then so does the Suffolk Coast & Heaths Path, especially between Dunwich and Minsmere Bird Reserve, p.71–73 and p.193–200

Secret
East Anglia
Local Recommendations

01 Norwich Puppet Theatre

Much better known in the city of its origin, these endlessly inventive puppeteers often use music, digital projections and animation to bring to life classic stories and more modern tales, p. 239

02 Cycling in the Saints

In a remote wooded part of the Waveney Valley, there is a group of 13 villages known as the 'Saints' which conceal a fantastic brewery, lovely churches and one or two ruins, p. 114

03 Blakeney Hotel

The upstairs lounge at this old-fashioned harbourside hotel has huge picture windows with a perfect view of the sun setting over the marshes, p. 210

04 Walk the Devil's Dyke

Locals know where to get a wonderful view over the gallops at Newmarket and the Fens. This seven-mile embankment, built as a defensive earthwork in the Dark Ages, finishes at a lovely brew pub, p. 324

05 Fish shacks, Southwold

Several huts along the Blackshore between Southwold and Walberswick sell fish, but the best one allows you to bring your own bread and wine to accompany a mouth-watering choice of seafood platters, p. 65

06 Architectural conversions, Norwich

Norwich architects have worked miracles in redundant churches and merchants' houses to create chic cafés, restaurants, bars and most recently, a spectacular cinema, p. 228

07 Little Ouse Headwaters Project

Footpaths beside the River Little Ouse lead to the headwaters on the Suffolk/Norfolk border where wetland habitats are being created out of neglected farms, and all kinds of wildlife is returning, p. 299

08 Railway Farm Shop, near Saxmundham

Like a shop attached to a giant allotment, this wonderful farm shop sells its own as well as its neighbours' produce and offers old-fashioned personal service, p. 80

09 Institute of Astronomy, Cambridge

Every Wednesday evening in winter, Cambridge University astronomers invite the public in to look through their telescope, and point out stars and constellations of interest, p. 313

10 Out-of-season visiting

In coastal places, the locals seem to prefer the off-season when they can draw up to the open fire in their local pub and congratulate themselves for having beautiful beaches and cliffs all to themselves, p.17

Factfile

01 East Anglia has the lowest rainfall of any UK region.

02 The region of Cambridgeshire, Suffolk and Norfolk is 85 miles east to west (Aldeburgh to St Ives) and 72 miles north to south (Wells next the Sea to Sudbury)

03 The 326 surviving windmills (excluding new offshore wind farms) give East Anglia the largest number in the country by far.

04 The lowest point in the British Isles is at Holme Fen in Cambridgeshire, which is up to 5 metres below sea level, due to the shrinkage of the peat fens after drainage in the 17th century.

05 Apart from the M11 to Cambridge, no motorways scar East Anglia, which is partly why it retains its rural atmosphere despite proximity to the capital.

06 East Anglia has more than 400 Sites of Special Scientific Interest, from ancient oak woodland to seaside marshes, fritillary meadows to Anglo Saxon dykes.

07 The rivers Waveney and Little Ouse separate Norfolk and Suffolk, and form the county boundary for most of its length.

08 After reaching dangerously low numbers in the 1960s and 70s, otter numbers in East Anglia have risen dramatically following a successful programme of re-introduction.

09 Suffolk and Norfolk have more than 1,200 medieval churches, said to be one in eight of all in the British Isles.

10 Although there are no official National Parks in East Anglia, the Broads Authority has had the status of a NP since 1989, and looks after more than 200 miles of rivers and broads.

THE FACTS

WHEN TO GO

By British standards, East Anglia is dry, with the driest part of the country falling in the region of Breckland on the Norfolk-Suffolk border. Surprisingly, the driest month in Norwich is February, with less than 3cm of rain, and the wettest is October, with just over 5cm. Of course showers and grey skies can intrude on holidays at any time of year, but you would have to be particularly unlucky not to enjoy some fine weather on a week or fortnight's holiday in the east of England. If it does rain, you are never far from cities and other places with indoor attractions.

Popular tourist centres like Wroxham in the Norfolk Broads or coastal resorts like Hunstanton and Southwold can get extremely crowded on holiday weekends and in July and August. Although the beaches and restaurants can usually cope, the limited car parking facilities sometimes struggle. If you are visiting in high summer and find heavy traffic on the main approach roads like the A149 Norfolk coastal road or the A12 along the Suffolk coast, you can usually find an alternative route along back lanes that might by chance take you past a village fete or appealing country pub.

Many locals profess that their favourite time of year is winter when the crowds disperse. It is hard to beat a bright frosty day for crunching along a shingle beach or strolling through a nature or bird reserve. Venturing out into a storm can be exhilarating as you watch wild winds paint swooping and swirling clouds on the canvas of a vast sky. Every season brings its particular rewards. On a misty autumn day on the Fens, a lonely farmhouse or hunting barn owl will loom in the distance, creating a delightfully spooky atmosphere. On a fresh spring day, the meadows of mid-Suffolk are full of glorious wild flowers. On a rainy summer's day, friendly local museums or bookshops provide refuge.

Travelling out-of-season can also bring financial rewards. Some of the most lauded hotels and restaurants in the region offer amazing weekend deals in November, January and February. As long as you are going for the great outdoors rather than the stately homes, most of which are closed from the end of October until Easter, you can really indulge yourself at reasonable cost. Self-catering cottages on heath and farm, riverside and woodland, are often a steal on either side of the school holidays.

GETTING THERE
By car

Motorways will get you only so far, that is to Cambridge from London. Beyond that and for drivers coming from the Midlands or the north, there are the trunk roads that often lapse into single carriageway – it isn't unusual to find yourself following in the wake of a tractor or horsebox. If road rage looms and you aren't obliged to get to your destination along the most direct route, simply turn off. The A14 that links Felixstowe with Huntingdon via Ipswich, Stowmarket, Bury St Edmunds and Cambridge is the principal east–west route for lorries to and from Felixstowe docks, which at least means that it is dual carriageway for its whole length.

Roughly it should take just over three hours to drive from London to the north Norfolk coast, two and a half hours to Norwich, an hour and three-quarters to Ipswich, and an hour and a quarter to Cambridge. If you are heading to some remote holiday cottage in the wilds of Suffolk or the Fens, it's best to have your own transport. But if you are planning a city break in Norwich, Cambridge or Ipswich, consider depending on public transport.

Parking your car may present problems in a busy resort such as Orford. Most coastal places make provision for cars, and there are huge car parks at popular places such as Dunwich and Holkham. Since some of the coast is in the care of the National Trust, members are sometimes permitted to park free, for example at Blakeney Harbour.

By train

Rail services to and within East Anglia are mainly provided by the train operating company National Express, East Anglia which operates two routes out of Liverpool Street Station to Norwich, one via Cambridge and Ely, the other via Ipswich. The trip to Norwich takes less than two hours and if proposals to build a high-speed link go ahead, travel time could be reduced to one hour. For the range of lines and destinations within East Anglia, see the next section on Getting Around.

The rival service on the very busy London–Cambridge route is run by First Capital Connect from King's Cross to King's Lynn via Ely and Downham Market. Travel times on their fast trains are less than an hour to Cambridge, with half-hourly departures, and just over an hour and a half to King's Lynn, with hourly services in the daytime.

Access by rail from the Midlands and the north usually depends on a change at Peterborough on the main line to Newcastle and Edinburgh, and sometimes a second change in Ely, though services are frequent.

Rail fares are much higher than coach fares as usual, but prices can be reduced by canny early booking. Sometimes an annual railcard, such as a Family Railcard for £24 or a Network card costing £20, will pay for itself in the savings on one return journey. For example a Saver Return from London to King's Lynn costs £38 per person, but only £25 with a Network card.

To check times and fares, ring National Rail Enquiries (☎ 08457 48 49 50) or visit www.thetrainline.com or www.qjump.co.uk, where tickets can be purchased. Otherwise call the individual train companies:

First Capital Connect (☎ 0845 026 4700; www.firstcapitalconnect.co.uk).
National Express, East Anglia:
(☎ 08457 484950;
www.nationalexpresseastanglia.com).

The policy on carrying bicycles is improving and both companies claim to be committed to making it easier to take cycles, although First Capital Connect imposes restrictions at rush hours in London and Cambridge. There are no charges for conveying bicycles, though National Express limits the number of cycles on local trains to four and asks cyclists to make an advance reservation to guarantee space on trains in Suffolk, Norfolk and Cambridgeshire. This can be done on the telephone number above.

Check out special deals pitched at tourists. For example Londoners heading for the Norfolk Broads can buy a special Broads Boat Train fare of £40 from Liverpool Street which covers return rail fare plus a cruise on the Broads (£20 child fare).

By bus

National Express coaches link London to the main cities of East Anglia, though the necessity of thrashing through the London traffic makes the journey by road much slower than the equivalent by train. For example the coach from Victoria to Cambridge never takes less than two hours (except a couple of late evening services) compared with the fast train from King's Cross taking 50 minutes.

The quickest journey by coach from London Victoria to Norwich via Thetford is three hours and a bit, four to five hours to Great Yarmouth. Non-stop coaches ply this route four or five times every day. The return fare to Norwich is £28 unless you book in advance for fares from £20, or even less if you can get a funfare, from £7 one way. Unfortunately megabus.com, famed for its supremely cheap fares, does not yet serve destinations in East Anglia, except for Cambridge from Oxford; fares of £1 for this route are easy to find if you check its website a week or two in advance.

From other parts, the coach is usually a non-starter since journeys involve complicated changes, often in London. For full details call 08717 818181 or check www.nationalexpress.com.

GETTING AROUND

Car

A few roads are designated tourist routes, signposted with the come-hither brown signs, such as the A1120 which cuts a direct swathe between the A14 at Stowmarket and the Suffolk coastal highway, the A12. Most scenic shortcuts will not be so direct, but this one happens to follow the course of an old Roman road. Some touring motorists have been known to indulge in 'brown-signing' which means driving around at random and turning off at any brown tourist sign spotted. Readers of this book can plan their itineraries in a less haphazard fashion. However, it's fun to get off the through-routes and lose yourself in a tangle of remote villages. If the weather is good and you spot a footpath sign, why not follow your impulse?

Public transport

Traveline East Anglia is a one-stop travel advice service for anyone wanting to plan a journey by train, coach or bus. Traveline assistance is available seven days a week between 7am and 9pm; call 0871 200 2233 at 10p per minute or use the journey planner facility on www.travelineeastanglia.co.uk.

Rail

East Anglia has done better than some regions at protecting its rural rail routes, and several branch lines still run, involving changes at obscure stations such as Mark's Tey. Fanciful names have been assigned to some of its routes aimed at the leisure market. Among its 'Tourism Trails' are the Gainsborough Line to Sudbury (http:/www.esscrp.org.uk/gainsborough_line.php), the Wherry Line to Lowestoft and Great Yarmouth (www.wherrylines.org.uk) and the Bittern Line through the Norfolk Broads (www.bitternline.com). On the latter two lines, day passes cost £6, children's tickets cost £3 and a family ticket costs £14. The ticket allows integrated travel on either line plus BroadsHopper and CoastHopper buses (see below). It is worth browsing the rail route map to work out the possibilities.

Some of the services are infrequent; for instance the East Suffolk line connecting towns between Ipswich and Lowestoft runs at two-hourly intervals.

Special fares for exploring East Anglia by rail represent good value, especially if used with a bicycle, and a railcard to give a further third off. National Express sells a one-day 'Anglia Plus' ticket for £12 that allows unlimited hop-on hop-off travel within its network. For £24, you can travel for three days anywhere in the region. The days don't have to be consecutive but have to be within one week. Up to four children can be added to the ticket for just £2 each, provided they travel with the ticket-carrying adult. Anglia Plus ticket holders can also use local buses free of charge to travel from the stations to the city centres in Norwich, Ipswich, Great Yarmouth and Bury St Edmunds. Also check two-for-one deals at www.visiteastofengland.com.

Norfolk appears to be well supplied with steam train enthusiasts, judging from the number of light railways and narrow-gauge lines on which restored locomotives trundle. The following trains operate under steam or sometimes diesel:

Poppy Line (Sheringham to Holt) (www.nnrailway.co.uk).
Wells to Walsingham Light Railway (www.wellswalsinghamrailway.co.uk).
Wells Harbour Railway – narrow gauge, open-sided train between the resort and the water's edge.
Bure Valley Railway (Wroxham to Aylsham via Coltishall in the Broads) (☎ 01263 733858; www.bvrw.co.uk).

Bus

Buses and coaches are rarely the best way to get from one point to another, but the delights of travel by country bus with their meandering routes and sociable passengers have been celebrated in an excellent book: *Great British Bus Journeys: Travels Through Unfamous Places* (David McKie, Atlantic Books, 2006). On some obscure routes, services operate only once a week, almost always on market day.

The old Eastern Counties bus company has been swallowed up by the **First Group** which still offers decent coverage of the region. Visit www.firstgroup.com for relevant services and timetables at the Eastern Counties part of the website. For fare information call 08456 020121.

Among the most useful routes for visitors are:

X1 – Peterborough to Lowestoft via King's Lynn, Norwich and Great Yarmouth
X2 – Norwich to Lowestoft via Beccles
4 – King's Lynn to Hunstanton via Castle Rising and Sandringham
50 – Norwich to Sheringham via Cromer
54 – Norwich to Stalham via Wroxham
63 – Ipswich to Framlingham via Woobridge
64 – Ipswich to Aldeburgh
99 – Southwold to Lowestoft

But the real gem of a service is the **Coast Hopper** bus operated by Norfolk Green based in King's Lynn (☎ 01553 776980; www.norfolkgreen.co.uk). Between Hunstanton and Sheringham, hourly services operate in summer, with some services connecting to King's Lynn, and two-hourly in winter. This award-winning service was set up 12 years ago and wins praise for its reliability. Timetables are posted along the coast and with a little research you can spend half a day walking along the coast and then get back to your base in 10 minutes. (The prices of a one-day unlimited Rover ticket are: adults £5, under-16s £3, families £11; combination tickets with the Bittern rail service to Sheringham and Cromer from Norwich to Sheringham adds only £1 to the adult fare and £3 for a family.)

Other useful bus services operated by Norfolk Green include the X8 Fakenham to King's Lynn service every two hours and the X6 hourly service Fakenham to Cromer. The Norfolk County Council website also has links to public transport information (www.norfolk.gov.uk).

The BroadsHopper is another brilliant service for tourists. It travels four times a day from Salhouse to Aylsham via Wroxham/Hoveton and Coltishall. An all-day ticket costs only £3 per adult, £4 for a couple and £6 for a family. Bicycles are free, which makes one-way cycle rides easy to organise. Unfortunately the service operates only Monday to Friday. Blickling Hall is added in the summer.

For Suffolk, the County Council posts up-to-date timetables of local routes (www.suffolk.gov.uk) whether the X16 from Sudbury to Bury St Edmunds or the 521 Aldeburgh to Southwold via Halesworth. A range of destinations can be reached from the Old Cattle Market bus station in Ipswich; ring 0800 919390 or check www.ipswichbuses.co.uk /suffolkbus.html for ideas. A Sunday Rover ticket is valid on all cooperating bus and train services all day at a cost of £6 for adults, £4 for the under-16s and £12 for a family. For details call the Traveline on 0871 200 2233.

THE COASTAL ENVIRONMENT

The East Anglian coast is faced with an enormous problem – it is slowly disappearing. The inexorable assault by the beating waves and sucking tides of the North Sea means that the fringes are being washed away, cliffs are crumbling and shingle is dumped on once-sandy beaches. Geographers and politicians must contend with scary processes such as 'littoral drift', which simply means movement of sand due to waves breaking at an angle. This could see all the beautiful clean sand of Lowestoft's Blue Flag beaches being carted away to the south. The erosion issue is of huge importance to coastal residents. Visitors to affected communities will soon notice posters for emergency meetings of the council and campaigns to raise money for sea defences. And of course when the sea levels rise with global warming, the risk of flooding will increase.

Impending danger lends a fascination, albeit a melancholic one, to these coastal landscapes, as does erosion's impact on the history of the region. While contemplating the salt marshes around Cley on the

The best... regional specialities

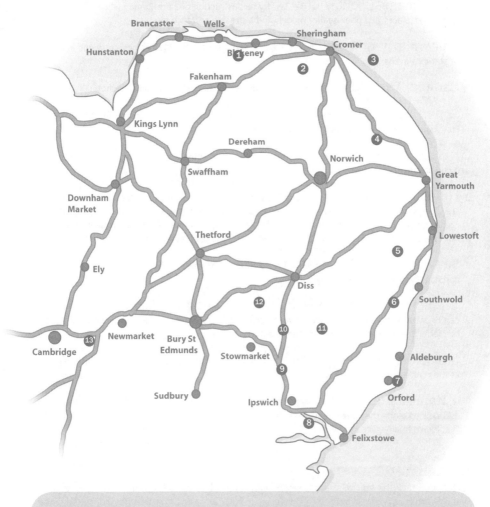

1. Mrs Temple's Cheeses, Wighton, p.208
2. Bread from Letheringsett Water Mill, p.198
3. Cromer crab, p.222
4. Woodforde's Brewery, Woodbastwick, p.258
5. St Peter's Brewery, St Peter South Elmham, p.112
6. Suffolk Black Ham (Emmett's of Peasenhall), p.171
7. Orford oysters, p.96
8. Jimmy's Farm Sausages, Wherstead, p.125
9. Alder Carr Farm Ice Cream, Creeting St Mary, p.169
10. Palmers Bakery cakes, Haughley, p.171
11. Aspall Cyder, Debenham, p.173
12. Wyken Vineyards, Stanton, p.156
13. Fitzbillies' Chelsea buns, Cambridge, p.318

10... places to avoid in East Anglia

1 Iceni Village, Cockley Cley Tawdry reconstruction of a pre-Roman village with no genuine artefacts, just poor quality models and a sizeable entrance fee

2 California, near Great Yarmouth Tacky resort with video games, crazy golf and acres of static caravans

3 Cardinal Park, Ipswich Tends to be where the chav set congregate to shop

4 Soham This Fenland town was thrust into the public eye during the tragic murders of 8-year-old Holly and Jessica, and has been the unwilling recipient of 'grief tourism'

5 Hunstanton Pier Destroyed by storms in 1972 and subsequent fire, the pier is a ruin guarded by an arcade of coin-operated games

6 Linton Travel Tavern, Linton The fictional inn where Alan Partridge had an extended stay. The website www.kost.co.uk/linton_travel_tavern describes the facilities. Ben the Cuisine Facilitator (waiter) finds the time to create delicious snacks for guests, such as sandwiches with a hot egg, crescent of crisps and a side clump of cress. (Average preparation time 10 minutes.)'

7 Sealand, North Sea (6 miles off the Suffolk/Essex coast) Principality with its own currency and flag that consists of a rusting gun platform

8 Stretch of the A11 between Norwich and the M11 is almost all dual carriageway except for the stretch between Barton Mills and Elveden where horrendous bottlenecks can form. If you are subject to road rage, avoid it!

9 Smithy Fen, Near Cottenham, Cambridgeshire Travellers' site which has been at the centre of nasty hostilities

10 Happisburgh Cliffs These are among the fastest eroding parts of the East Anglian coast and walking along the edge might make the ground under your feet collapse. Last year Cliff House Tea Rooms finally gave up the struggle and closed for good.

Norfolk coast or the tiny village of Dunwich on the Suffolk coast, it's difficult to believe that both of these were once important European ports. Much more recently, high dramas took place during the great floods of 1953 when more than 300 people were drowned in Britain and many more had to be rescued from rooftops and upper storeys by boat. With this in mind, the authorities can't be blamed for the cautious approach in November 2007 when thousands of residents in endangered areas between Great Yarmouth and Ipswich were evacuated.

Indeed, tides at Yarmouth on 9 November, 2007 were the highest they had been since 1953, but the level of the water was 20cm lower than predicted and, apart from minor breaches, disaster didn't strike. At least not on that occasion.

The Environment Agency uses reassuring terms such as Shoreline Management Plan (SMP) and Coastal Strategy policies, which might lull you into thinking that the government is tackling the problem. In fact its policy is one of 'Managed Realignment' or 'Managed Retreat', which basically means allowing nature to take its course, because it's stopped allocating funds to maintain and build new sea defences. The only exceptions are in a few places such as the high-profile resorts of Cromer and Sheringham and the nationally important gas terminal at Bacton. Even in places where buildings are at urgent risk, nothing is being done. This has been most controversially illustrated in Happisburgh on the Norfolk coast between Cromer and Great Yarmouth. No modern sea defences are in place for more than a mile, and the resulting erosion has been dramatic. Last year the owners of the tea shop decided that they could no longer risk opening it since it's teetering so close to the edge. For visitors, it is disconcerting when a clear path ends at a barrier before a cliff edge, but it's a stark demonstration of how quickly this coastline is changing.

The threat isn't confined to the coasts. If the defences at Sea Palling and elsewhere on the Norfolk coast are breached, an inundation of saltwater would flood low-lying villages and contaminate the Broadland system, wreaking environmental havoc.

The people of Southwold, Walberswick and Dunwich are running an energetic campaign that in 2008 included about 1,500 people gathering on Walberswick beach to form themselves into a giant SOS. They want the government to know that they need urgent funding to repair and maintain sea defences. Without help, they claim, the Blyth estuary is in danger of being washed away within 20 years.

Green tourism

East Anglia is one of the least polluted parts of the country. With the exception of the sugar refinery at Bury St Edmunds and a few factories in the main cities, heavy industry is rare. On a stroll along the estuary on the Shotley Peninsula or along the banks of the River Cam or through woodland and heath in mid-Norfolk, you will feel a million miles from the 'dark satanic mills' in Blake's famous phrase. East Anglia is an ideal destination for people interested in pursuing a green holiday agenda.

ACCOMMODATION

From the £1 tent pitch on an organic farm in the Waveney Valley to the most chic and exclusive country house hotel, East Anglia runs the whole gamut of holiday accommodation for all tastes and pockets. But if you had to come up with a description of a couple of quintessential places to stay, they might be a holiday cottage in a converted windmill or a farm bed and breakfast, near an unpretentious village pub and a maze of cycle lanes. Because East Anglia is such a deeply rural region and because so many farmers have been diversifying over recent years, the choice of farm bed and breakfasts is almost inexhaustible. Outside the honeypot coastal resorts, you can always find vacancies in places that will be only a short drive away.

In this book we have singled out the unusual, the unique and the boutique accommodation options that East Anglia has to offer. But we've been selective rather than comprehensive, and there are plenty of useful accommodation resources online. The website, www.farmstayanglia.co.uk for example, lists some out-of-the-way farms that offer self-catering, camping and/or B&B accommodation. Just Suffolk (http://justsuffolk.com) lists individual owners and independent agencies, and offers local knowledge within Suffolk. And the selective B&B group, Wolsey Lodges (www.wolsey lodges.com), has about a dozen places in East Anglia.

Self-catering

It isn't so easy to find guidance when choosing a holiday cottage, especially if you start with nationwide agencies such as Country Holidays (☎ 0870 078 1200; www.country-holidays.co.uk), English Country Cottages (☎ 0870 238 9922; www.english-country-cottages.co.uk) or The Holiday Cottages (☎ 01749 685153; www.theholidaycottages.co.uk). More selective companies cut down the choice for you, such as Rural Retreats (☎ 01386 701177; www.ruralretreats.co.uk) and Premier Cottages (☎ 0114 275 1477; www.premiercottages.co.uk).

10... most eco-friendly destinations

1 The Greenhouse, Norwich city centre Vegetarian café, organic/Fairtrade shop and environmental centre, all heated by solar power and with a strong recycling policy, p. 246

2 Cley Marshes Visitor Centre Newly built centre powered by wind and sun, with displays about the fragility of the north Norfolk coast and the potential impact of climate change, p. 197

3 Assington Mill near Sudbury Remote water mill and private nature reserve where weekend nature courses are held, for example on mushroom identification and hedge laying, p.139

4 Courtyard Farm, Ringstead Fully organic farm, owned by Lord Melchett of the Soil Association, that welcomes visitors to see the animals, walk in the grounds and visit the farm shop, p.182

5 Deepdale Backpackers Hostel & Campsite Eco-conscious owners rent out Sioux-style tipis, p.188

6 Scroby Sands off Great Yarmouth With 30 offshore turbines, this is the biggest wind farm in the region, p.219

7 Barton Broad boat trip *Ra* is a solar-powered boat that takes up to a dozen passengers on a gentle tour of this recently restored broad, p. 252

8 The Great Fen Project Woodwalton Fen is in the process of being returned to the wildlife-rich habitat that it would have been before the draining of the Fens in the 17th century, p.352

9 Green Quay, King's Lynn Environmental education centre overlooking the River Great Ouse with displays about The Wash, including a freshwater aquarium with lizards, p.275

10 Stratton Hotel Shortlisted in 2007 for a 'Green Hotel of the Year' award, this boutique hotel in Swaffham serves only organic food, recycles all hotel waste and gives a discount to guests arriving without a car, p.295

For holiday accommodation that will be a talking point for years, the Landmark Trust's portfolio of unique historic buildings can't be rivalled (the sumptuously produced handbook costs £11.50 including UK postage; call 01628 825925 or visit www.landmarktrust.org.uk). Their collection includes the Ancient House in Clare, Freston Tower near Ipswich, the Martello Tower in Aldeburgh and the Water Tower at Sandringham. The National Trust has also turned some of its properties into holiday accommodation which is more modestly priced (☎ 0844 8002070; www.nationaltrustcottages.co.uk).

In the most popular areas, such as the Heritage Coasts of Norfolk and Suffolk, specialist agencies list scores of cottages in a small geographical area in a range of prices, and the staff in these offices will be happy to advise on any specific requests. For Suffolk try www.suffolkcottageholidays.com, www.heritagehideaways.com in Beccles; Best of Suffolk in Woodbridge

The best... boutique hotels

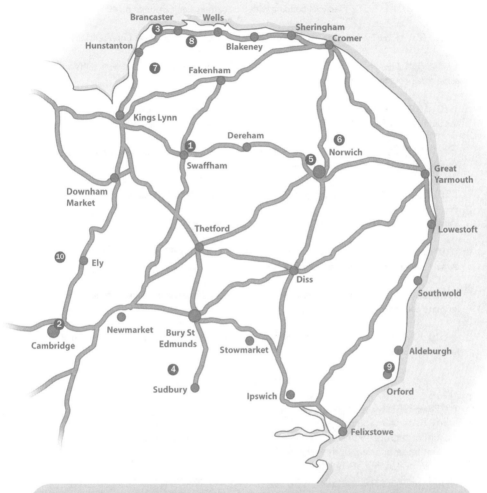

① Strattons, Swaffham. Luxurious independent hotel committed to green values and serving magnificent organic food, p.295

② Hotel du Vin, Cambridge. Supremely sophisticated destination hotel with quirky individualism, intelligent service and superb restaurant, p.316

③ Titchwell Manor, near Brancaster. Family-run hotel with a much-praised kitchen, ideally situated beside the famous RSBP bird reserve at Titchwell near the sea, p.187

④ Black Lion Hotel, Long Melford. Individual rooms named after great wines, some of which are served in the top-rated restaurant, p.140

⑤ By Appointment, Norwich. Eccentric layout over several late medieval merchants' houses in the city centre, with ambitious dining room, p.242

⑥ Broad House, Wroxham. Newly opened hotel occupying a Broadlands mansion with extensive grounds, p.259

⑦ King's Head, Great Bircham. Luxurious touches such as fresh flowers and a decanter of port in this contemporary pub-hotel, p.277

⑧ Hoste Arms, Burnham Market. 17th-century coaching inn which annually wins prizes for its restaurant, p.187

⑨ Crown and Castle, Orford. Perfectly judged service without losing the human touch at this hotel with a superb restaurant and wine list, p.93

⑩ Anchor Inn, Sutton Gault. In a middle-of-nowhere location, this inn has cosy rooms and a menu based on brilliant local ingredients, p.339

10... East Anglia B&Bs

1 Lavenham Priory Medieval building with Elizabethan wall paintings, p.140

2 Byfords, Holt By declaring itself a 'Posh B&B' it proves it is original yet unpretentious, p.205

3 Cranmoor House, Ipswich Owners of this small B&B are chefs and wine buffs and will serve three-course dinners on request, p.124

4 The Stables, Henham Park Complimentary home-made brownies can be walked off in the landscaped park, p.64

5 Bodgers Farm, Fens Rural retreat and pottery studio where badgers (but not bodgers) are occasionally seen in the grounds, p.349

6 The Hall, Milden Imaginative, child-friendly place that lends free bicycles, p.140

7 West Lodge near Norwich Victorian village serving all-vegetarian food, p.243

8 Rumburgh Farm, near Halesworth Top-notch breakfasts served in the old dairy by owners who are Rick Stein food heroes, p.109

9 Waterside, Ely Two 18th-century workmen's cottages have been knocked through, with an intimate courtyard garden, p.339

10 Old Cannon Brewery, Bury St Edmunds Characterful accommodation in the old Brewhouse, p.154

(☎ 01728 638962; www.bestofsuffolk.co.uk); or Suffolk Secrets in Southwold (www.suffolk-secrets.co.uk). It sometimes seems that three-quarters of the houses on the north Norfolk coast are holiday cottages. Try Norfolk Country Cottages (www.norfolk cottages.co.uk), Sowerbys Holiday Cottages in Burnham Market (www.sowerbysholiday cottages.co.uk) or the specialist Blakeney Cottage Company (www.blakeneycottage company.co.uk). For inland properties, try Coast & Country Holidays in Wymondham (www.coastandcountryholidays.co.uk).

The difference in prices between high and low season can be colossal: for example a charming house in Southwold that sleeps eight, costs £1,400 a week over the New Year but just £380 in November and February Cottages can easily cost three times more in August than mid-March, so avoid the school holidays if you can.

Camping

The scenic coasts of East Anglia have their fair share of massive caravan parks, especially in and around Great Yarmouth. The website of *Practical Caravan* magazine (www.practicalcaravan.co.uk) has a searchable database of campsites that includes links to more than 200 in the East of England. The website www.ukcampsite.co.uk includes reader reviews of hundreds of sites, so if you want to know how big the shower cubicles are or what the children's playground is like at a site you are considering, this should be your first port of call.

10... East Anglia campsites

1 Clippesby Hall With swimming pool, tennis courses and on-site pub, you would expect it to feel more suburban than it does, p.259

2 Highfield Farm Touring Park Excellently maintained site in one of Cambridgeshire's prettiest villages, with farm walks (good for picking blackberries) and a good children's play park

3 Harbour Caravan Park, Southwold Just on the other side of the dunes, with unimpeded views of the town and a rabbit population of almost Hitchcockian proportions

4 Deepdale Campsite and Hostel, North Norfolk Tipis sleeping up to six come equipped with pot-bellied stoves and wind-up lanterns, p.188

5 Kelling Heath Holiday Park With its own halt on the North Norfolk steam railway line, this is more like a resort than a humble campsite, p.205

6 Deer's Glade Inland from Cromer, with its own fishing lake and is adjacent to a deer park, p. 221

7 Orchard Camping Bounded by a river and with the remains of an apple orchard, you can learn about the night that space aliens landed in nearby Rendlesham Forest, p.95

8 The Old Hall & Cow Shed near Beccles Organic smallholding that especially welcomes cyclists and charges tent campers £1, p.109

9 Brighthouse Farm Campsite Buried in deep Mid-Suffolk, the family who own this farm campsite with B&B have mapped out lovely local walks for the benefit of guests, p.154

10 Pinewoods Located right on the seaside at Wells-next-the-Sea, this site has beach huts on stilts that can be hired by the day, p. 205

Back-to-nature tent campers are also well provided for in East Anglia. Only four campsites make it into the seductive *Cool Camping England* (Jonathan Knight, Punk Publishing, 2007) but individual campers might argue that the lavishness of the facilities matters less than the location so would stick up for more ordinary campsites such as Waxham Sands or High Sands Creek in Stiffkey or Harbour Park in Southwold. But there is no doubt that hilarious weekends in magnificent locations are only a tenner away if you are prepared to sleep in a tent.

FOOD AND DRINK

While Britons have been holidaying in Sardinia and Slovenia, a revolution has been taking place in their absence. The food culture in holiday destinations throughout Britain has improved exponentially. In 1982, the American travel writer Paul Theroux walked around the perimeter of the British Isles to write *Kingdom by the Sea*. The sneering description of a typical East Anglian seaside resort provides a useful marker of how much has changed over the past quarter century: 'There was always an

Indian restaurant and it was always called the Taj Mahal... Of the three fish-and-chip shops, two were owned by Greeks and the third was always closed... There were four pubs, one was the Red Lion, and the largest one was owned by a bad-tempered Londoner.'

How things have changed. Nowhere in the country are 'locavores' (those who use locally grown and seasonal ingredients) better catered for than in East Anglia, where a wealth of vegetables and animals is grown and raised and where so many outlets sell direct to the public.

You can still find traditional dishes like fish and chips or pie and mash, but they are far less likely nowadays to be out of catering packs from industrial food manufacturers. At the other end of the eating-out spectrum, hundreds of restaurants and gastropubs, not just the handful run by celebrity chefs, feature dishes such as carpaccio of venison and crayfish and onion risotto. The holidaying clientele has become much more discerning, forcing the quality up. The chapters that follow include foodie recommendations that could take a lifetime of holidays to sample.

Dairy farming has not traditionally played a key role in East Anglian farming; however, in recent years some independent cheese makers and a number of superb ice cream makers have set up shop in countryside locations. Suffolk and Norfolk lamb and other meats have always been of the highest quality with a recent revival of old breeds such as Red Poll cattle. Enterprising little companies such as Tasty Tavern Meats (www.taverntasty.co.uk) in north Norfolk specialise in rare breed butchery. Artisan sausage-and-pie makers are dotted around the region too.

With nearly 150 miles of North Sea coastline and a long history of fishing, the choice of fresh seafood is often dazzling, whether from humble sheds on the beach to destination restaurants. Some of the very best food producers are listed in the *Guardian's* Food Directory (http://lifeandhealth.guardian.co.uk/fooddirectory). And it's also worth seeking out the winners of food competitions run by local newspapers such as the *East Anglian Daily Times* and the *Eastern Daily Press* in which categories are judged from 'Best Farmers' Market' to 'Chef of the Future'. See also Gary Rhodes' Local Food Heroes at http://uktv.co.uk/food/localfoodhero.

Tastes of Anglia is the regional food and drink marketing group, and its website (www.tastesofanglia.com) features links to farmers' markets and individual food producers in the region. The annual food festival organised by Tastes of Anglia takes place in March (www.feasteast.co.uk). Two other excellent special foodie events are the Aldeburgh Food & Drink Festival (www.aldeburghfoodanddrink.co.uk) in the latter half of September, and the Bidwells Norwich & Norfolk Food Festival in mid-October (www.visitnorwich. co.uk/food-festival.aspx).

Drinking

Brewing in East Anglia is flourishing, partly assisted by the climate (East Anglia receives more sunshine and less rainfall than the rest of the British Isles), partly because of the quality of malting barley grown in the region, and partly because of judicious investment from the East of England Development Agency. The East Anglian Brewers' Association has links to its more than 40 member breweries (www.eastanglianbrewers.com). For a complete selection of these beers in bottled form, the Real Ale shops near Wells in Norfolk or Wrentham in Suffolk are the places to go (www.therealaleshop.co.uk).

FESTIVALS AND ANNUAL EVENTS

Traditional summer seaside carnivals held in resorts from Felixstowe to Hunstanton feature parades, fancy dress and fireworks. The atmosphere at these events is usually fantastic, with residents and visitors equally enjoying the spectacle and competitions. Even some brand new events like the Latitude Music Festival in Suffolk's Henham Park have caught on with surprising rapidity. The premier arts festival of the region is the

The best... farm shops & markets

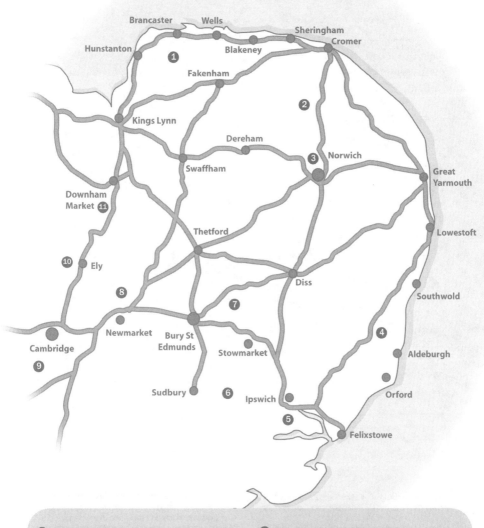

1. Courtyard Farm, Ringstead, p.182
2. Samphire, Blickling Hall, p.222
3. Norwich Market, p.244
4. Railway Farm Shop, Benhall Green, p.80
5. Suffolk Food Hall, Wherstead, p.125
6. Hollow Trees, Semer, p.138
7. Wyken Farmers' Market, Stanton, p.156
8. La Hogue Farm Shop, Chippenham, p.155
9. Burwash Manor Farm Larder, p.318
10. Ely Farmers' Market, p.340
11. Dent's of Hilgay, p.280

The best... restaurants

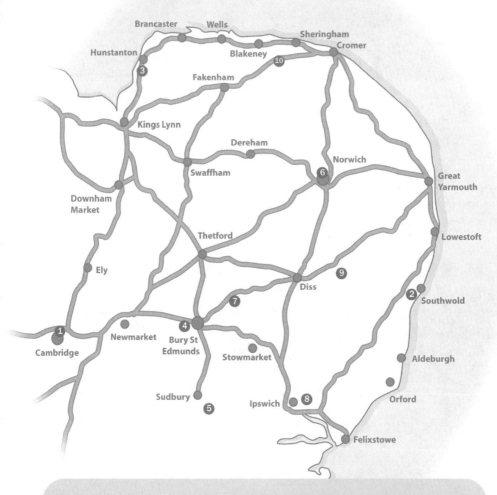

① Alimentum, Cambridge. One of the *Independent's* top 10 restaurants of the year, the ingredients aren't only ethically sourced but beautifully prepared, p.319

② Sutherland House Hotel, Southwold. Housed in a Tudor townhouse, this boutique B&B has a superb dining room and a menu which records the number of food miles involved, p.66

③ The Mulberry, Heacham. Fine dining based on quality, locally-sourced food, p.190

④ Maison Bleue, Bury St Edmunds. Lavish seafood platters served in elegant surroundings, p.156

⑤ Case Restaurant with Rooms, near Sudbury. Deep in rural Suffolk, memorable meals are lovingly prepared, p.142

⑥ Elm Hill Brasserie, Norwich. Unpretentious French-influenced food in a prime Norwich location, p.245

⑦ The Leaping Hare, Stanton. Suffolk pigeon, lamb and vegetables, much of it from the estate, are featured at this country restaurant in an airy barn conversion on a vineyard, p.156

⑧ Bistro on the Quay, Ipswich. In a converted warehouse looking over the docklands, this casual restaurant serves eclectic, well-presented dishes, p.126

⑨ Fox and Goose, Fressingfield. Creative dishes served in this high-end pub-restaurant are displayed to great effect in their multi-course taster menu, p.172

⑩ Byfords, Holt. This self-styled 'posh' place serves unfussy affordable dishes in its casual oak-beamed, brick-walled dining room, p.209

10... East Anglian seafood outlets

1 Butley Oysterage, Orford Family-run smokery located beside its own oyster beds on Butley Creek produces range of fish that can be eaten at rough and ready tables or taken away, p.98

2 Cookie's Shack, Salthouse Fantastic value seafood salads served from a humble wooden hut, p. 208

3 Aldeburgh Fish & Chips Queues on the high street are the giveaway, p.80

4 Sole Bay Fish Shed, Southwold Harbour Friendly, modest restaurant overlooking the River Blyth with six choices of seafood platter, p.57

5 World of Fish, Lowestoft Huge range of wet fish and shellfish, next door to a traditional smokehouse, p.110

6 Willie's Seafood Caravan, Blakeney or Morston Quay Summer-only mobile purveyor of superbly fresh dressed crab, p. 208

7 River Farm Smokery, Bottisham Hot-smoked trout and mackerel are among the many delicious products smoked slowly in brick kilns, p.318

8 Flora Tearooms, Dunwich Famed for its fresh fish and chips, particularly skate, p.81

9 Davies' Fish Shop, Cromer Legendary family of lifeboat men sell Cromer crabs caught that morning by their own boat, p.222

10 Gurney's Fish Shop, Burnham Market Upmarket fishmonger selling Thai fish cakes, chowder, wild smoked salmon and its famous potted shrimp, p.189

Norwich and Norfolk Festival where mainstream and cutting-edge music, theatre and other performances are scheduled (www.nnfestival.org.uk). July is one of the best months to be in Cambridge when the annual film festival takes place, artists open their houses for Open Studios on weekends, the City Council sponsors Summer in the City with free entertainment, and the famous Cambridge Folk Festival is held at Cherry Hinton Hall (though you have to be very well organised to get tickets).

TRAVELLING WITH CHILDREN

Seaside resorts like Cromer and Sheringham, Great Yarmouth and Lowestoft have been honing their child-friendly entertainments since the Victorian period. The bucket-and-spade loving child will happily potter on the perfect sands at Wells-next-the-Sea, and marvel at the way everything changes with the movement of the tides. In most places the water shelves gently and the waves are benign, though parents should always remain watchful of young children, since tides and undertows can

CALENDAR OF TOP SPECIAL EVENTS

January – New Year's Day Swim in the Sea, Hunstanton
February – Lambing at Baylham House Rare Breeds Farm
March/April – Re-creation of Tudor life at Kentwell Hall (Easter)
May – Norwich and Norfolk Festival (first two weeks)
June – Strawberry Fair, Cambridge (first Saturday)
June – Aldeburgh Festival of Music (last two weeks)

July – Rose Fair, Wisbech (Flower Festival, first week)
July – Snail race, Congham (third Saturday)
August – Cromer Carnival (third week)
September – Festival of the Broads (third week)
October – Apple Day at Gressenhall (last Sunday)
December – Christmas lights switch-on Southwold (first Friday)

change quickly. Whereas some resorts go in for candy floss and boisterous entertainment, others feel quieter and more old-fashioned, where the great excitement is crabbing from a pier or taking a boat trip to see seals.

Inland, the region abounds with family-friendly farms that encourage young children to cuddle lop-eared rabbits and see new-born lambs, to run through a maze made of maize or go for a pony ride. For thrill-seekers the region offers theme parks and high-ropes adventures. But most of the attractions for children in the east of England are gentle and rural. The new BeWILDerwood park in the Norfolk Broads manages to encompass both excitement with its vertical slides and zip-wires, and a back-to-nature emphasis on fort-building in the woods.

WALKING AND CYCLING
Cycling in East Anglia

Cycling in parts of East Anglia is as idyllic as it gets. It is wrongly assumed that the region is entirely flat and therefore potentially dull. In fact areas of Mid-Suffolk are picturesquely rolling so the experience of free-wheeling at speed down to a valley floor isn't out of reach. It is precisely because of the absence of hills and mountains that East Anglia (like the Netherlands) is ideally suited to leisure cycling for adults and children.

Roads in East Anglia are hardly ever straight, unless they're old Roman roads and probably now A roads which you will want to avoid in any case. Back lanes twist and turn, sometimes into the wind, but soon enough with it behind you. Even on flat terrain as on the Fens, roads have great kinks so the view is always changing (unlike in the Netherlands). Hedges inhabited by nesting birds in spring or laden with blackberries in autumn will suddenly clear to allow sweeping views up to a country house or church steeple. Even when the scenery isn't particularly dramatic, there will be plenty of interest to enjoy. Country folk often sell their potatoes or honey, flowers or eggs from little unmanned roadside stands which operate on the honesty principle, and at which car drivers rarely stop. If the weather turns nasty there is always a medieval church in the next village where you can do a little impromptu sightseeing, or a welcoming hostelry where you can rest until the shower passes.

The three county councils of the Eastern region all have cycling teams to promote cycling and to publicise cycling routes. Councils working with local tourist authorities publish leaflets (sometimes downloadable) suggesting itineraries with tempting names such as 'The Painters' Trail' (a 69-mile route through Constable Country), 'Churches, Copses and Country Lanes' (24 miles between Lowestoft and Southwold), 'The Lost Villages of Breckland' or 'The Two Rivers Route' (King's Lynn to Lowestoft via Diss). Other routes are shared online, for example on www.cycle-route.com where enthusiastic individuals describe their favourite rides. To take just one example see 'A Cyclist's Guide to the Peaceful Lanes of West Norfolk' at www.peacefulbyways.co.uk.

East of England Tourism (☎ 0870 225 4852) has a campaign to promote the eastern region as 'England's Cycling County' and has a wealth of information on long-distance, circular and traffic-free

The best... things to do with children

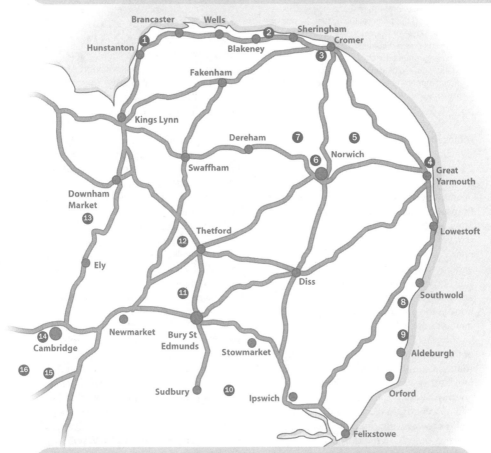

YOUNG CHILDREN

4 Sea Life Centre – Marine world with a walk-through underwater tunnel, tropical shark display and a flourishing colony of breeding seahorses, p.219

5 BeWILDerwood – Fantasy land that features aerial walkways, painted treehouses, rope tunnels and zip-wires, in the marshlands of the Norfolk Broads, p.257

8 Crabbing at Walberswick, p.60

9 Peter Pan Island on Thorpeness Meare – paddle a canoe and feed the swans, p.76

16 Wimpole Home Farm (Cambs) – Charming rare breeds farm with a thatched great barn, adventure playground and seasonal events, p.325

OLDER CHILDREN

3 Surf lessons at Cromer, p.219

6 Norwich Castle (Norfolk) – Ancient castle where you can take a tour of the dungeon, especially scary when they turn out the lights, p.232

11 West Stow Anglo Saxon Village – Reconstructed village of life in the sixth century AD, p.159

12 Thetford Forest – Home of Go Ape, a high-wire forest adventure across rope bridges to 40ft above the forest floor, p.291

ALL AGES

1 Hunstanton (Norfolk) – Fabulous broad beach beneath red and white striped cliffs as well as a traditional seaside resort with candy floss and funfair rides, p.178

2 Morston to Blakeney Point boat trips to have a picnic near the seal colony, p.195

7 Dinosaur Adventure Park at Lenwade for a woodland encounter with T-Rexes and pterodactyls, p.238

10 The Hall organic farm near Lavenham where the owners facilitate pond dipping and scavenger hunts, p.140

13 Welney Wetland Centre – 1,000-acre floodland nature reserve that hosts thousands of migratory swans from Arctic Russia, p.286

14 Punting in Cambridge – Punt trips along the River Cam through college gardens can be self-propelled or chauffeured, p.309

15 Duxford – Huge aviation museum, part of the Imperial War Museum, with a collection of WW1 bi-planes and regular air shows, p.326

MAPS

The possibilities for cyclists and walkers are infinite. The only essential ingredient for a cracking day out is an Ordnance Survey map, always a wise investment for anyone who likes exploring off the main routes by foot, bicycle or car. The whole of Cambridgeshire, Norfolk and Suffolk is covered in nine Ordnance Survey Landranger maps (scale 1:50,000). In their characteristic pink livery, you can buy these maps from any good bookshop or from the Ordnance Survey Map Shop (http://leisure.ordnancesurvey.co.uk).

routes. Its 'Cycling Discovery Maps' give directions and describe points of interest on 28 routes of between 13 and 30 miles; these are all freely downloadable from www.visiteastofengland.com. Discovery Touring Maps are being developed to cover longer rides of up to 100 miles. So far the three regions covered are the Suffolk Coast, the Fens and Constable Country. For free maps and packs ring East of England Tourism (EET) on 01284 727470. Cycle-hire addresses are provided throughout this book in the Visitor Information listings. For a directory of cycle-hire outlets follow the Cycling link from www.visiteastofengland.com. The CTC (formerly Cyclists' Touring Club) has collected links to many providers of route information; for Suffolk go to www.ctc.org.uk/resources/touring_other/CAWSuffolk.pdf and for Norfolk to www.ctc.org.uk/resources/touring_other/CAWNorfolk.pdf.

More mainstream routes are designated National Cycle Routes. NCR1 links Kent with Edinburgh and enters Suffolk at Hadleigh before continuing north via Framlingham and Beccles to Norwich, then Fakenham, King's Lynn and Wisbech and on into Lincolnshire. You can get a copy of the route from the national cycle campaigning organisation Sustrans (☎ 0845 113 0065) or from www.sustrans.org.uk. NCR51 links Newmarket and Felixstowe. Signposting isn't always complete, so you should have a good map. Regional cycle routes are being added to the Sustrans network. The Norfolk Coast Cycleway from King's Lynn to Cromer and on to Great Yarmouth is

Regional Route 30; two maps cover the route and can be bought from Sustrans for £2 each. An inland route connects King's Lynn with Lowestoft via Diss.

Walking in East Anglia

Almost the entire coastline of East Anglia and dozens of rivers are lined with public rights of way. Many pass through Areas of Outstanding Natural Beauty. The two main ones are the Suffolk Heritage coast between Ipswich and Kessingland, and almost the entire North Norfolk coast. The possibilities for anyone who likes to lace on some boots and stride out are endlessly appealing. Walking is the way to experience the magnificent bird life of coast and wetland, and to observe and enjoy the minutiae of nature.

All walks in East Anglia are categorised as easy, although people walking along the coast and estuaries should be aware of the tides. It isn't unusual for walkers to find that their return journey along a footpath they have blithely followed at low tide has been covered by tidal waters in the meanwhile. Be aware that walking on shingle is hard on the calf muscles, though often a clifftop or inland alternative is available. Ongoing deterioration of sea defences means that coastal paths can be precarious. For example popular footpaths were flooded and boardwalks were damaged by the tidal surge of November 2007. The classic coastal walk from Dunwich to Walberswick, is suffering the effects of erosion and great care should be taken if undertaking this walk.

At least a dozen long-distance footpaths criss-cross the region. Besides the famous coastal paths, others trace ancient droving routes. The Peddars Way stretches from the Suffolk border to Holme-next-the-Sea to connect with the Norfolk Coast Path. From Castle Acre, the Peddars Way follows a dead straight Roman road for about 20 miles. Some long-distance tracks are recent creations of tourist boards to boost neglected regions. These also have their charms: the Weavers Way (54 miles Cromer to Great Yarmouth) and the Wherryman's

Way (34 miles Norwich to Great Yarmouth). Mostly these routes for walkers pass through villages where you will find food and accommodation but a little research will pay off. For example the 93-mile Peddars Way passes through only six villages, three of which don't have a shop/pub, so you will need to carry water and provisions along some segments. The excellent website www.nationaltrail.co.uk/PeddarsWay has up-to-date information about the walk and might, for instance, inform you that a walkers' pub is temporarily closed after a fire.

FURTHER INFORMATION

The regional tourist board, East of England Tourism, covers Norfolk, Suffolk, Cambridgeshire, Essex, Hertfordshire and Bedfordshire. It is always worth calling into the local visitor information centre to pick up a town trail leaflet or to find out what's on at the moment. Apart from the busy offices in Cambridge and Norwich, many tourist offices in places such as Sudbury and King's Lynn aren't mobbed, and the staff will be happy to take some time to get you oriented or to point you in the direction of your special interest. As usual, they are supposed to be impartial but you can still ask for guidance.

The main website www.visiteastofengland.com has links to all the tourist offices in the region (listed throughout this guide as well) plus an easily navigable wealth of background information. The searchable databases of attractions and accommodation including campsites are particularly useful. The sister site www.letsgoeastofengland.com operates in conjunction with National Express and carries special visitor offers. Related websites maintained by county and district councils for their regions can also help: for example www.west-norfolk.gov.uk; www.visit-ipswich.com; www.visitsuffolk.org.uk; and www.visitnorthnorfolk.com; www.northnorfolk.org.

Local newspapers

Norfolk has a long and distinguished history of independent print journalism. The Norwich-based company Archant publishes the *Eastern Daily Press* in Norfolk (the biggest selling morning regional daily in the country), the *East Anglian Daily Times* and the *Suffolk Evening Star* (voted Britain's best daily newspaper of 2007). The group also publishes magazines including the glossy *Suffolk* magazine (www.suffolkmagazine.co.uk) which in the issue in print at the time of writing featured articles called '30 of the most attractive people in the county' and 'Our sexiest hotels'. These publications champion local enterprises (such as the 'Shop Local' campaign mentioned above) and sponsor events of interest to tourists such as the Suffolk Food & Drink Awards, and you can access the winners via their websites (http://new.edp24.co.uk; www.eadt.co.uk; www.eveningstar.co.uk) where you may also find restaurant reviews and other information of interest.

Local Radio Stations

BBC Radio Norfolk (Norwich) 95.1, 104.4 FM (www.bbc.co.uk/norfolk/local_radio)
BBC Radio Suffolk (Ipswich) 95.5, 95.9, 103.9, 104.6 FM (www.bbc.co.uk/suffolk/local_radio)
BBC Radio Cambridgeshire 96, 95.7 FM (www.bbc.co.uk/cambridgeshire/local_radio)
Broadland FM (Norwich) 102.4 FM (www.broadland102.co.uk)
KLFM (based in King's Lynn) 96.7 FM (www.klfm967.co.uk/home.html)
North Norfolk Radio 96.2 & 103.2 FM (www.northnorfolkradio.com)
SGR FM (Ipswich and Bury St Edmunds) FM 96.4, 97.1 (www.sgrfm.co.uk)
The Beach (broadcasting to Great Yarmouth, Lowestoft and Southwold) 103.4 & 97.4 FM (www.thebeach.co.uk)
Vibe FM (Bury St Edmunds) 105-108 FM (www.totalkiss.com)
Fen Radio (Wisbech) 107.5 FM (www.klfm967.co.uk/fenradio)
Hereward FM (Peterborough) 102.7 FM (www.hereward.co.uk)
Q103 (Cambridge, Newmarket, Haverhill) 103 FM (www.q103.co.uk)

The best... coastal and country walks

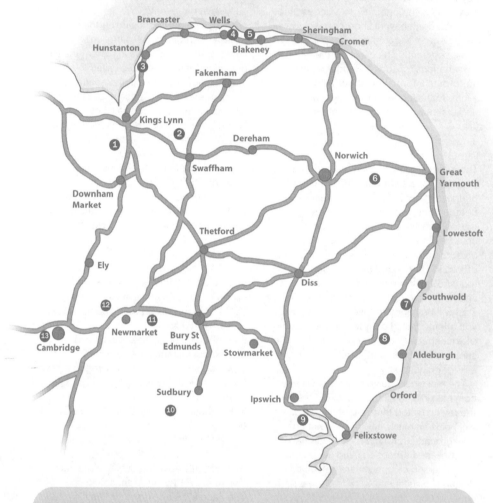

1. Wiggenhall St Mary Magdalene to King's Lynn, p.282

2. Nar Valley (Narborough to Castle Acre), p.294

3. Snettisham to Hunstanton, p.179

4. Holkham Beach, p.182

5. Stiffkey to Blakeney, p.194

6. Wherryman's Way, Norfolk Broads, p.255

7. Dunwich to Walberswick, p.63

8. Snape to Iken, p.75

9. Woolverstone to Pin Mill, p.129

10. Clare to Cavendish, p.136

11. Three Churches Walk near Newmarket, p.163

12. Devil's Dyke (Newmarket Heath to Reach), p.324

13. Cambridge to Grantchester, p.309

THE BACKGROUND

HISTORY
The mists of time

The building material most closely associated with East Anglia today is flint, an almost black form of quartz that can be found in chalky ground. Flint was being mined at the end of the Stone Age at Grime's Graves in the Brecks to be made into axes and tools for clearing trees. After the Neolithic period came the Bronze Age when mysterious structures such as Seahenge (older than Stonehenge) were created. The timbers have survived for more than 3,000 years because they were submerged in water, off the north coast in the case of Seahenge, and in the waterlogged fen soil at Flag Fen.

Much later the conquering Romans subdued the local tribes and hunkered down for the next 400 years. Their first capital in Britain was at Camulodunum (now Colchester) and they built their trademark straight roads, at first for trading, and then when the locals became rebellious, for military purposes. Some of these roads have turned into main arterial roads today, but others survive as walking routes, most famously the Peddars Way, slicing a straight north–south line through Norfolk, as part of the original road linking Colchester with Norwich. The Roman colonists imposed a harsh regime which enraged the locals. In AD62 the Iceni tribe rose under Queen Boudicca and destroyed Colchester. But their victory was short-lived since the disciplined Romans imposed a cruel and crushing defeat on the rebel army. The site of the battle and of Boudicca's final defeat isn't known but legend has it that she swallowed poison rather than face capture.

After the withdrawal of the Romans in AD406, the region was invaded by Anglo-Saxon tribes from the continent, and the region was named after the East Angles. A ruling dynasty emerged that took its name from the early East Anglian king Wuffa; his descendants, treasure was discovered at Sutton Hoo in the 1940s, roughly 13 centuries after it had been buried. About this time Christianity made an appearance, with the arrival of St Felix and a little later St Botolph who might have landed on a spot on the River Alde in AD645. Even if he didn't a visit to St Botolph's church at Iken in Suffolk where there are the remnants of a Saxon cross evoking those ancient times.

Invasions from the continent continued, resisted by the Wuffing kings. In 869 the young King Edmund was killed by the Danes under Ivar the Boneless, and was venerated as a martyr, is still patron saint of Suffolk (see the chapter on Bury St Edmunds). The very oldest remains of churches in the region date from this period. The Anglo-Saxons remained vulnerable to attack for centuries and so built earthwork defences, like the Devil's Dyke in Cambridgeshire, which survive. The museum curators at West Stowe near Bury St Edmunds have done a splendid job of re-creating what it might have been like in the Dark Ages at the end of the first millennium.

The Middle Ages

Following the arrival of the Normans in 1066, the great age of castle-building began, with Norwich Castle getting underway in 1067 and Orford, Framingham and Bungay in the years that followed. Dunwich, King's Lynn and Ipswich became international ports. The whole region at that time looked outwards to the sea, rather than inwards to London or the Midlands. The rivers were navigable and began to carry cargo to and from their hinterlands. Wisbech, Beccles, Norwich and many other places that are now inland were bustling river ports. For example the beautiful white Caen stone used in the building of Norwich Cathedral arrived from France by river barge. The supremacy of water transport lasted well past the Middle Ages.

The best... country houses and castles

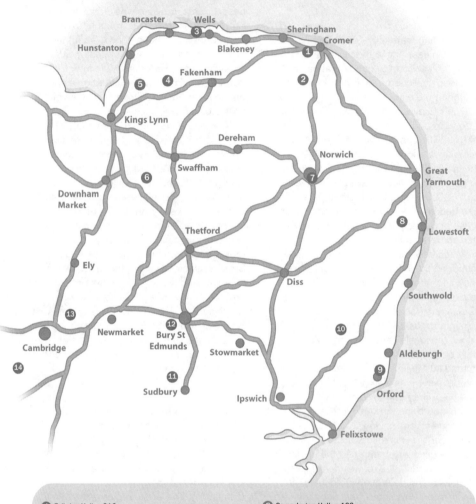

1 Felbrigg Hall, p.216

2 Blickling Hall, p.216

3 Holkham Hall, p.183

4 Houghton Hall, p.284

5 Sandringham House, p.284

6 Oxburgh Hall, p.290

7 Norwich Castle, p.232

8 Somerleyton Hall, p.103

9 Orford Castle, p.86

10 Framlingham Castle, p.165

11 Kentwell Hall, p.137

12 Ickworth House, p.158

13 Anglesey Abbey, p.323

14 Wimpole Hall, p.325

The unique selling point of East Anglia in the 15th century was its superior quality wool, much of it from flocks of sheep belonging to monasteries. The cloth trade brought astonishing prosperity which manifested itself in ways that can still be admired, in the riverside warehouses at King's Lynn, the merchants' houses of Norwich and the great wool churches of Lavenham and Long Melford. At first just the raw material was exported to be woven on the continent, mainly in Flanders. But Flemish weavers also migrated to England and a local cloth-making industry grew up.

Churches

Many people are unaware of what treasure houses churches are. Many are ancient and beautiful buildings containing splendid examples of medieval and later art, and they are freely open (or at least most of them are). Even the country churches that have no outstanding architectural features will convey a sense of the life (and death) of the local people over many centuries. Several Suffolk and Norfolk churches are simply magnificent. Many were built in the heyday of the wool trade and employed craftsmen of the highest skill. An absolutely wonderful encyclopaedic resource are Simon Knott's easy-to-use websites www.suffolk churches.co.uk and www.norfolk churches.co.uk. These include not only informative entries about individual churches but a personal response to the places themselves.

Tudors to the Civil War

Henry VIII's break with Catholicism and resulting decision to suppress the monasteries in the late 1530s had an enormous impact, still visible today. The great monastic estates were broken up almost overnight and granted to wealthy families and allies of the king. A typical example can be found in Leiston Abbey near Saxmundham: following the Dissolution Act of 1536 it was given to the Duke of Suffolk (brother-in-law to Henry VIII). Over the centuries the abbey buildings decayed and later farm buildings incorporated the ruins.

During the Reformation wholesale destruction was wreaked on the parish churches of England. Any carvings or pictures considered 'idolatrous' or 'superstitious' were hacked to pieces by the dreaded Captain Dowsing and his henchmen, who toured most of the

EAST ANGLIA AS WITCH COUNTRY

A failed lawyer from Manningtree on the River Stour, Matthew Hopkins, was put in charge of rooting out the scourge of witchcraft wherever it could be found and he acquired the dreaded title Witchfinder General. It's estimated that Hopkins is responsible for the execution of about 400 women (and a few men) accused of witchcraft in 1645. His methods of extracting confessions make it easy to understand why his legal practice hadn't flourished. He kept the accused in solitary confinement, left them tied up cross-legged, and walked them up and down for days without rest, until they confessed. The other useful method was to tie the person's hands to her feet and throw her into water. If she floated, that meant that her master the devil had saved her; if she sank, she was innocent and of good character.

The key to detecting a witch was to discover that she kept a 'familiar', a hellish imp in animal form. Matthew Hopkins illustrated a book himself showing bull-headed dogs, black rabbits and other witches' familiars to watch out for. Keeping pets was a dangerous practice, especially if you were a lonely old woman. A woman called Faith Mills in Fressingfield, Suffolk confessed that her three pet birds had forced a cow to jump over a stile and a horse to throw its rider into a stream. Not only did witches keep familiars but they suckled them with blood as well. Hopkins had a special line in detecting a third nipple in accused women who were unlucky enough to have an unfortunately positioned mole or mosquito bite.

The Witchfinder General was invited into various Suffolk and Norfolk towns to rid them of witches. He was paid £15 by the worthy burghers of King's Lynn and a colossal £23 in Stowmarket. So even when people finally began to have doubts about his methods he retired back to Manningtree a rich man. The 1968 film The Witchfinder General with Vincent Price in the starring role is truly terrifying.

The best... medieval churches

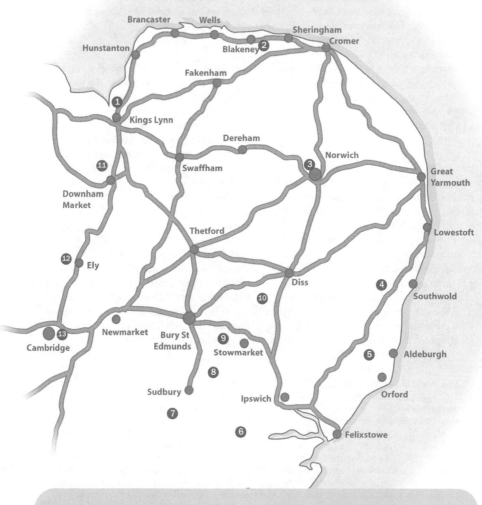

① St Nicholas Chapel, King's Lynn, p.273

② St Margaret's, Cley, p.272

③ St Peter Mancroft, Norwich, p.236

④ Holy Trinity, Blythburgh, p.68

⑤ St Botolph, Iken, p.37

⑥ St Mary's, Stoke-by-Nayland, p.131

⑦ Holy Trinity, Long Melford, p.130

⑧ St Peter and St Paul, Lavenham, p.135

⑨ St Mary's, Woolpit, p.160

⑩ St Mary's, Thornham Parva, p.166

⑪ Hare Chapel, Stow Bardolph, p.285

⑫ Ely Cathedral, p.332

⑬ King's College, Cambridge, p.307

10... great East Anglian museums

1 Kettle's Yard, Cambridge Unpretentious 20th-century collection of paintings donated by the artists, pebbles, driftwood and furniture harmoniously arranged, p.308

2 RNLI Henry Blogg Museum, Cromer New museum which celebrates the courage of the lifeboat crews and in particular the local hero who gives his name to the museum, p.217

3 Museum of East Anglian Life, Stowmarket Open-air collection of buildings bringing to life the social history of old Suffolk, with trails and rare-breed animals, p.165

4 Gressenhall Museum of Norfolk Life, Dereham Reconstructed House of Industry (workhouse) for the local poor, workshop for the blacksmith, school and chapel, p.250

5 Collectors' World, Downham Market Amusing collection of kitsch and curiosities made by eccentric owner, p.285

6 Christchurch Mansion, Ipswich Set in a magnificent urban park, this Tudor mansion contains the best collection of paintings by Gainsborough and Constable outside London, p.122

7 Air Defence and Radar Museum, Norfolk Broads Hands-on recreation of Second-World-War operations, p.256

8 Moyse's Hall, Bury St Edmunds Rare survival of a Norman house, the museum contains a fascinating local history collection which includes displays about women accused of witchcraft and about the trial of William Corder who killed Maria Marten, p.150

9 Sutton Hoo, near Woodbridge Site of a buried ship and accompanying treasure belonging to an Anglo-Saxon king of the 7th century, p.91

10 Wisbech and Fenland Museum One of the oldest museums in the UK with an intriguing collection of Fenland curiosities displayed in the original Victorian cases, p.347

churches of East Anglia. Beautiful angel roofs, exquisite statues of saints, carved fonts and screens, tomb effigies, all were defaced. A few survived, of course, since resourceful parishioners managed to hide or disguise some of their treasures. But the Puritan terror of the 1640s was also wickedly effective. But that was not the only terrible thing about this decade. For just over one year in 1645, witch fever gripped superstitious East Anglia.

The witch hunts went on in the middle of the Civil War. Oliver Cromwell was a Fenman himself (see chapter on the Fens) and most of East Anglia supported the Puritan cause, though King's Lynn remained loyal to the Crown.

The modern period

Norfolk and Suffolk ports remained important into the 18th and 19th centuries, though the silting up of the rivers and harbours was making transport more difficult. With the coming of the Industrial Revolution, East Anglia began to fall behind, because it had no coal reserves. Of course the absence of industry is one of its glories for today's visitors. The coming of the railways prompted a further economic decline in an area that had depended on its network of waterways for so long. But before that it produced the hero of whom the county is still so proud, Horatio Nelson (see *Coastal Norfolk*).

GEOGRAPHY

The prevailing winds affecting the British Isles are from the Atlantic Ocean to the west and south-west. The precipitation they carry tends to fall on the west side of the country which means that East Anglia is the driest part of the UK. In fact it receives a third of Scotland's annual rainfall and less than half endured by Cornwall and Devon in the south-west. So cycling, walking, even swimming in the sea become more attractive propositions. Of course biting winds sometimes arrive from the arctic north or the east with nothing between Siberia and East Anglia. The inevitable difference of temperature over land and sea causes sea breezes along coasts that usually reduce the temperature by a few degrees.

The geography of Suffolk, Norfolk and Cambridgeshire has its fascinations but there is no denying that the area lacks the drama of mountains and caves, gorges and ridges. However the eye soon attunes itself to the more subtle gradients, and begins to focus on what makes this region so special, which mostly has to do with water and sky and the interplay between them.

Wildlife

Even the casual visitor who wouldn't know which end of the binoculars to look through may catch some of the excitement of seeing unusual birds such as avocets with their upturned bills or oystercatchers or terns. If you go for a walk in the vicinity of any of the famous bird reserves such as Snettisham, Titchwell, Cley Marshes or Minsmere, you will see phalanxes of people with impressive hardware and tripods. If you spot a group peering expectantly into a bush, it's difficult to resist tiptoeing up to share in their excitement. Recently sighted birds will be chalked up on a blackboard at the visitor centre so you will know what you are looking for.

Coastal birds that you have the best chance of observing include the avocet, the oystercatcher (which eats cockles not oysters), redshanks, whose white-edged wings you can see when they are in flight, grey plover and pink-footed geese which travel in gigantic flocks. Marsh harriers and bitterns are harder to spot.

If you are particularly lucky, you might witness one of the great spectacles of nature, if a flock of wading birds flying past. In certain conditions, for example at Snettisham on The Wash, the flock feeding on the mudflats will be forced by an incoming high tide to abandon their breakfast *en masse* and take to the skies. The best chance of seeing such a sight is very early in the morning. At peak times, up to 300,000 birds visit The Wash, some of them *en route* from their breeding grounds in the Arctic, including dunlin, knot and Arctic skuas. Other birds that are attracted to the sand flats and salt marshes of the North Norfolk coast are sanderling, redshank, plovers and godwits, oystercatchers, shelducks and Brent geese. Bird lovers are anxious that a rise in sea level will destroy these rare coastal habitats. The monthly web magazine *Birds of Britain* has useful summaries and contact details for all the key bird-watching places county by county; see www.birdsofbritain.co.uk/reserves/norfolk.asp and www.birdsofbritain.co.uk/reserves/suffolk.asp.

The stone curlew is the prize for bird-watchers at the heathland habitat in Breckland (see chapter on West Norfolk and the Brecks). Inland habitats attract many birds, dragonflies, butterflies and insects.

Apart from birds, the other coastal creature that causes excitement is the seal. Seal watching trips to Blakeney Point and Scroby Sands are described in the chapter on Coastal Norfolk, as is the amazing experience of visiting Horsey Beach in the winter when the seal pups are born. Until a few years ago, you could visit a centre near Bungay run by the Otter Trust and admire the clever playful creatures lying on their backs and juggling pebbles just for fun. The

10... unique geographical features

1 Intertidal mudflats and salt marshes that make up the Area of Outstanding Natural Beauty around Blakeney on the north Norfolk coast, p.195

2 Collapsed cliffs at Dunwich, Mundesley and other coastal places where the ravages of erosion are plain to see, p.72, 212

3 Orford Ness The largest vegetated shingle spit in Europe, 10 miles long, p.87

4 Hunstanton Cliffs Curious multilayered cliffs of red and white chalk and carstone, p.178

5 The Norfolk Broads Vast network of shallow lakes and channels created in the Middle Ages as a result of our ancestors digging for peat, p.251

6 Breckland Dry sandy heath covered with gorse that attracts unique flora and fauna, p.267

7 Holme Fen Post near Peterborough A post that shows the level of the land as it was 150 years ago, a full 15 feet higher than it is now. The drainage of the Fens resulted in dramatic shrinkage of the peat, p.353

8 Wicken Fen Rare, undrained fenland with a boardwalk over the reed-filled bog, p.343

9 Pingo Ponds, Thompson Common, Norfolk Brecks Few words in English derive from Eskimo but pingo is one, referring to a donut-shaped mound left by retreating glaciers, that encloses a shallow pool, p.295

10 The Wash The largest tidal estuary in England providing an ideal habitat for birds, especially waders, p.179

centre is now closed for the best of reasons, that the Trust feels that their mission is accomplished and the otter no longer requires a breeding sanctuary. Otter numbers have escalated since their low point in the 1960s when English rivers were full of farmers' chemicals. So now you have a sporting chance of seeing an otter in the wild.

CULTURE

Writers and musicians, painters and photographers inevitably gravitate to the sea and to beautiful evocative landscapes, so it's no surprise that East Anglia is full of artists. From potters to abstract oil painters to escapees from the big city honing a craft, Suffolk, Norfolk and Cambridgeshire are hives of creative activity. One of the artistic hotbeds is Southwold together with Walberswick on the Suffolk coast, which has been attracting artists and theatrical people for generations. The Norfolk coast also has its hives of artistic activity, places such as Burnham Market and Holt have some marvellous galleries and workshops selling everything from glass jewellery to art photographs. Local arts centres have busy programmes in unexpected places such as The Cut in Halesworth and the Quay in Sudbury.

The best... coastal highlights

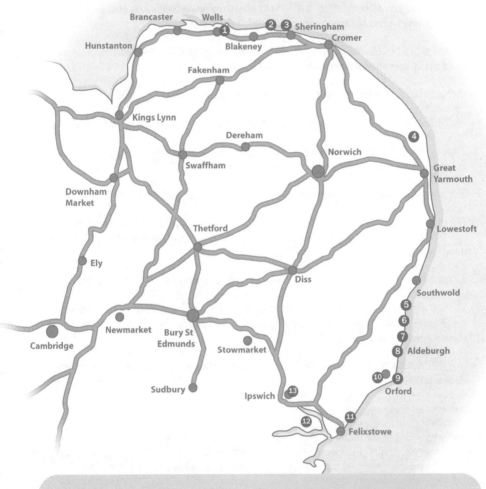

1 Holkham Beach, p.182

2 Blakeney Point, p.195

3 Cookie's Crab Shop, Salthouse, p.208

4 Horsey Gap (breeding colony of seals on beach), p.215

5 Southwold Pier (Laugh-out-loud amusement arcade by English eccentric), p.55

6 Minsmere Reserve (birds), p.72

7 House in the Clouds, Thorpeness, p.78

8 Aldeburgh (Shell Sculpture), p.74

9 Orford Ness (ruins of secret Cold War testing facility), p.87

10 Butley Oysterage, Orford, p.98

11 Felixstowe Ferry (ferry across the mouth of the River Deben), p.88

12 Pin Mill (traditional boatyards and great pub), p.129

13 Ipswich waterfront & yacht harbour (trendy restaurants), p.120

Art

Outstanding art collections of international importance can be visited in Norwich (the Castle Gallery and the Sainsbury Centre for the Visual Arts), Cambridge (the Fitzwilliam) and Ipswich (Christchurch Mansion). Two of England's greatest artists, Constable and Gainsborough, famously captured the beauty of the ancient countryside of Suffolk's Stour Valley (see *Constable Country*). J M W Turner took himself on a walking tour of the Suffolk coast between Orford and Lowestoft in about 1830 in order to paint and sketch. More than half a century later, Philip Wilson Steer settled in Walberswick, bringing with him the spirit of Impressionism he had imbibed in France, and spent eight summers painting the Suffolk coast, honing his own version of English Impressionism. He owned a house next to the pub in Walberswick which he later rented to Charles Rennie Mackintosh. Unfortunately his tenancy was short-lived. Mackintosh aroused suspicion among the locals by going out on the beach at night with a lantern. Because they assumed he was a spy signalling to the Germans, they clapped him in jail for one week in 1915 until he was able to prove his innocence.

The Norwich School of Artists was a remarkable flowering of homegrown talent in the early decades of the nineteenth century, and was the first school of art to flourish in the provinces, largely independent of the London art world. These artists painted exactly what they observed, and many paintings are of everyday scenes in and around Norwich, in the tradition of Dutch genre painting. The two leading lights were the two Johns of their day, John Sell Cotman and John Crome, many of whose paintings can be seen in the Norwich Castle Museum.

Among contemporary East Anglian artists, Maggi Hambling is probably the best known woman artist in the country. Her sculpture of a scallop shell installed on Aldeburgh beach has attracted national attention. She was born in Sudbury in 1945, attended school in Hadleigh and studied art at Benton End and then the Ipswich School of Art. She spends part of the week in Suffolk in a cottage with water meadows that was bequeathed her by an admirer Lady Gwatkin in 1994. Recently she has been painting the North Sea near her cottage, and her recent exhibition in London 'Waves Breaking' attracted favourable notice.

Another important female sculptor comes from Suffolk. Elisabeth Frink's most famous sculpture is probably Shepherd and Sheep, recently installed in Paternoster Square near St Paul's Cathedral in London. Among her work on display in Suffolk, one that stands out is her 1976 bronze sculpture of a young and sensitive looking King-turned-Saint Edmund in the great churchyard near the ruined abbey in Bury St Edmunds.

Music

Maggi Hambling's Scallop Shell is a memorial to the composer Benjamin Britten who was born in Lowestoft but settled in Aldeburgh. Some of his music incorporates the sounds of the sea in various moods and snatches of re-worked sea shanties. Ralph Vaughan Williams, whom some consider the pre-eminent English composer, travelled to King's Lynn when he was a young man to collect the folk and fishing songs that had been passed from father to son. The vicar directed him to the Northend fishermen's

A 20TH-CENTURY ARTIST

The 20th century has seen a continuation of the artistic life of Suffolk with painters such as Sir Cedric Morris who first set up a school of painting in 1937 in Dedham. After it was destroyed by fire he moved to Benton End, a Georgian mansion with a huge garden, in Hadleigh. Here the bohemian residential East Anglian School of Painting and Drawing counted Lucian Freud and Maggi Hambling among its students. Many of Morris's paintings are on country themes such as a basket of eggs and a poignant painting from about 1960, now in the Tate, called *Landscape of Shame* depicting a vast unending field with dead and dying birds in the foreground, the artist's angry response to the effect of pesticides so liberally applied in the 1950s. The jays which dominate the foreground of his earlier painting of Stoke-by-Nayland Church are very much alive.

watering hole, the Tilden Smith public house (now the Retreat). Fortunately he visited in a stormy January when the fishermen were shorebound and amusing themselves with song. The composer recorded 61 songs, some of which later influenced his Norfolk Rhapsodies and Sea Symphony.

At the other end of the musical spectrum, some successful bands have emerged from East Anglia such as The Darkness from Low-estoft, and Cradle of Filth, a genre-busting heavy metal band that formed in Suffolk in 1991 and are still making records. Norfolk has produced Beth Orton and, like her, big names often come to play at the University of East Anglia.

Cambridge offers an amazing range of music, especially during term-time. The stan-dard of student musical groups is exceedingly high, and yet tickets are cheap.

Literature

The creative writing course at the University of East Anglia is probably the best in the country, with a dazzling list of graduates including Ian McEwan, Kazuo Ishiguro, Trezza Azzopardi, Tracy Chevalier and Toby Litt. The well-respected author of reflective travelogues, W G Sebald, taught at the uni-versity. His book *The Rings of Saturn* records a journey on foot that he made through coastal East Anglia, though he uses this as a jumping-off point for reflecting on farflung historical events. Norwich has a vig-orous independent publishing industry. Black Dog Books, for example, specialises in literature and the arts related to the east of England including three volumes of *Stories from East Anglia*. The most recent volume *Dead Men Talking* not only includes short stories by contemporary writers such as Rose Tremain and Susan Hill, but col-lected old stories from the oral tradition, such as those by Chafer Legge originally published in *Tales from the Fens*.

Among the luminaries of letters in the region today is the novelist and critic D J Taylor, a native and resident of Norwich. His novel *The Comedy Man* is partly set in Great Yarmouth and he has written a number of stories with an East Anglian

setting. Trezza Azzopardi's *Remember Me* is a beautifully constructed novel set in Norwich about an elderly homeless woman trying to recover her memories of the past.

Cambridge has more than its share of writers and poetry readings, story-telling evenings and appearances by famous writers at Heffers Bookshop take place all the time. One recent title set in Cambridge which became a surprising best seller was Alexander Masters' *Stuart: a Life Back-wards*. The literary festival in early April has quickly established itself as a fixture in the calendar and promotes local writers such as Michelle Spring whose crime fiction is often set in the city where she lives. Ruth Rendell also writes detective novels, some of which are set in East Anglia, as does P D James. Suffolk and Norfolk settings have inspired plenty of authors, for example Dodie Smith who had once seen a medieval moated castle partly in ruins with a Victorian house built on to one wing. That image was the starting point for her first novel *I Capture the Castle*.

As for literary figures from the more distant past, there are too many to mention. For a start Cambridge has nurtured a great many poets and writers including Byron (who is said to have kept a bear in his rooms in Trinity), Wordsworth and Tennyson. The second-hand bookshops scattered over the region must be some of the most atmos-pheric in the country, such as the ones at Westleton, Halesworth, Holt, Norwich and (of course) Cambridge. You can find a list at www.2nd-hand-books.co.uk/guide/guide.html.

LOCAL HEROES

Henry Blofeld or 'Blowers', the cricket com-mentator, was born at Hoveton Home Farm in the Norfolk Broads in 1939. His nephew is Tom Blofeld, owner and creator of the new children's attraction BeWILDerwood in the same location. The story goes that Ian Fleming (who went to Eton with Henry's father) borrowed the name for James Bond's arch enemy, the evil genius Ernst Stavro Blofeld.

ITV racing commentator and former

10... film & TV locations

1 Felbrigg Hall and Park After filming *A Cock and Bull Story* (2005) here and at nearby National Trust house Blickling Hall, Steve Coogan claims to have fallen under the spell of Norfolk with its magnificent sunrises and sunsets. The film's director, Michael Winterbottom, describes Felbrigg Hall near Cromer as one of his favourite locations, p. 216

2 Northern Fens The scene in *Atonement* (2007) in which James McAvoy stumbles upon the corpses of some massacred children near Dunkirk was filmed in an orchard at Walpole St Andrew, North Cambridgeshire with a gaggle of girls from a local acting academy

3 Elveden Hall, Thetford This Georgian country house (once owned by a maharajah) has seen filming for Kubrick's *Eyes Wide Shut* (1999), *Gulliver's Travels* (1996) for TV with Ted Danson, *Lara Croft: Tomb Raider* (2001) in which Elveden Hall is used as Lady Croft's ancestral home, and *The Living Daylights* (1987), in which Timothy Dalton plays James Bond, p.292

4 Deepdale Farm, Burnham Deepdale Scenes from *Die Another Day* (2002) were filmed here where surrounding fields doubled as a North Korean paddy field, p.181

5 Holkham Hall *The Duchess* (2008) stars Keira Knightley as Georgiana the Duchess of Devonshire, and Ralph Fiennes. Much of the filming took place at the grand Palladian hall at Holkham. Nearby Holkham Beach was famously used in the final scene of *Shakespeare in Love* (1998) with Gwyneth Paltrow, p.183

6 Swaffham, Norfolk The pleasant market town serves as Market Shipborough in *Kingdom* (2007), the ITV comedy drama starring Stephen Fry, p. 289

7 Wisbech, Cambridgeshire The sweeping Georgian terraces of Wisbech and 18th-century Peckover House have often been used in costume dramas, for example *Martin Chuzzlewit* and *David Copperfield*. It is also used in the 2008 film *Dean Stanley*, a surreal Edwardian comedy centred on a canine reincarnation, p.344

8 Orford Castle The violent finale of the 1968 film *The Witchfinder General* starring Vincent Price was filmed in the castle, p.86

9 Great Yarmouth *Cuckoo* (2008) a film about a female medical student who is losing her mind was filmed here and also at UEA where the lead character's tutor is played by Richard E Grant, p.215

10 Norwich The fantasy film *Stardust* (2007) transformed the historic café The Briton's Arms in the centre of the city into the 'Slaughtered Prince Inn', p.246

Formula 1 competitor himself, **Martin Brundle** was born in King's Lynn. He started his racing career age 12, driving a Ford Anglia grass track car that he had built himself near his West Norfolk home. Demolition derby seems to have been one of the main hobbies of **Michael Carroll** also from King's Lynn. Former dustman Mike came to national attention when he won £9.7 million in the National Lottery in 2002, all of which he has since spent on the usual vices such as a personalised number plate 'King Chav' plus old scrap cars for trashing in the field next to his home near Swaffham. At last report (according to the *Sunday Mirror*) he had served a prison sentence for affray in Downham Market and was dating a 17-year-old waitress in a greasy spoon café in King's Lynn.

The inventor and millionaire **Sir James Dyson** was raised in Holt and attended the prestigious local public school Gresham's where he studied Latin and Greek rather than science. The first invention to which he contributed when he was a student at the Royal College of Art in the 1970s may have arisen out of his seafaring place of birth, Cromer. The Sea Truck is a flat-hulled fibreglass high-speed watercraft which is still manufactured in Bath.

The successful comedy duo from Norwich the **Nimmo Twins** have appeared on BBC One's *Stand Up Show* and been frequent guests on Radio 4's *Loose Ends.* In their native city, they are best known for their annual sell-out Christmas sketch show called *Normal for Norfolk* at the Norwich Playhouse. The locals seem to enjoy hearing them poke fun at the local football club, media and politics. One of the 'twins', Karl Minns, writes regularly for the *Norwich Evening News.*

Tricia Goddard hosts a confessional chat show on Channel 5 while living in Norwich and writing for the local papers. She is patron of the charity Mind in Norwich.

Cambridge launched **Pink Floyd**, who met when they were at school, Dave Gilmour at the posh private school 'the Perse' and Roger Waters at the High School for Boys (now Hills Road Sixth Form College). Former lead singer Syd Barrett died at age 60 in the summer of 2006 at his mother's home in Cambridge where he had lived as a recluse for 30 years after he had a break-down and left Pink Floyd.

Other famous names associated with Cambridge are Professor **Stephen Hawking** who is occasionally seen in his high-tech wheel chair attending concerts in the university. **Clive James** and laddish comedian **Rory McGrath** have homes in Cambridge. Another Cambridge graduate who retains a connection with the region is **Griff Rhys Jones** whose second home is near Holbrook on the Shotley Peninsula near Ipswich which gives him access to his 45ft, 50-year-old wooden sailing yacht *Undina* which he restored himself. A couple of years ago he participated in a demonstration in Cambridge to protest against the proposed closure of the school of architecture where his son was a student.

Jeffrey Archer and his fragrant wife Mary have lived in the Old Vicarage in Grantchester near Cambridge since the 1980s.

Plenty of media people have homes in and around Southwold, including the Freud dynasty: Clement and his daughter Emma and her husband Richard Curtis (see chapter on Southwold).

10... great historical figures

1 Sir Isaac Newton Considered the most influential scientist of all time for having 'discovered' gravity and the laws of motion. You can see his statue in the chapel of his old college, Trinity, and books from Newton's library are on display, in the college's beautiful Wren Library, p.308

2 Admiral Horatio Nelson Norfolk's most famous son was born in Burnham Thorpe where he lived until he was 12 and joined the Royal Navy. When he called into the port at Great Yarmouth in 1793 he met Lady Hamilton, the love of his life. The story of his heroic defeat of Napoleon at the cost of his own life is well told in the Nelson Museum in Great Yarmouth, p.218

3 Thomas Paine Son of a corset maker in Thetford, Thomas Paine is known as the 'Father of the American Revolution' for his free-thinking pamphlets published in the American colonies in 1776. These argued passionately for independence from royal rule. He is best remembered now for his book *The Rights of Man* and is commemorated with a statue in the place of his birth, p.292

4 Sir Robert Walpole Although the term 'prime minister' was not used in the 1730s, Walpole is recognised as the first *de facto* prime minister of England. He was born at Houghton Hall in Norfolk, which is open to the public, p.284

5 John Milton The great 17th-century poet and Puritan essayist, author of *Paradise Lost*, graduated from Christ's College, Cambridge. A tree in the garden is popularly referred to as Milton's Mulberry since it is said to have been planted in the year of his birth, p.308

6 Thomas Clarkson The campaigner for the abolition of slavery was born in Wisbech. When still a young man, he became devoted to the cause and was instrumental in assisting William Wilberforce persuade Parliament to pass the Abolition Bill. The 2007 film *Amazing Grace* brings the story to life, and made use of Peckover House, Wisbech's finest building, p.345

7 George Vancouver The name of this Royal Navy officer from King's Lynn is immortalised in the city and island on the west coast of Canada. The five-year long Vancouver Expedition in the 1790s was one of the great round-the-world expeditions of exploration, p.270

8 Edith Cavell During the First World War, this nurse and humanitarian assisted hundreds of soldiers in their escape from occupied Belgium. She was executed by the Germans in 1915. A memorial bust to her as 'Nurse, Patriot and Martyr' can be seen outside Norwich Cathedral, p.231

9 Howard Carter In 1922 this archaeologist from Swaffham discovered the tomb of Tutankhamun in the Valley of the Kings in Egypt. The town museum in Swaffham has exhibition rooms dedicated to Carter's life and discoveries, p.292

10 Harriet Martineau Feminism was unusual in the Victorian period but Harriet Martineau from Norwich wrote books and pamphlets throughout her life arguing for women's rights. Her views were applauded by the philosopher John Stuart Mill. You can visit the historic Octagon Unitarian Chapel in Norwich which she and her family attended, although she had lost her faith by the end of her life, p.234

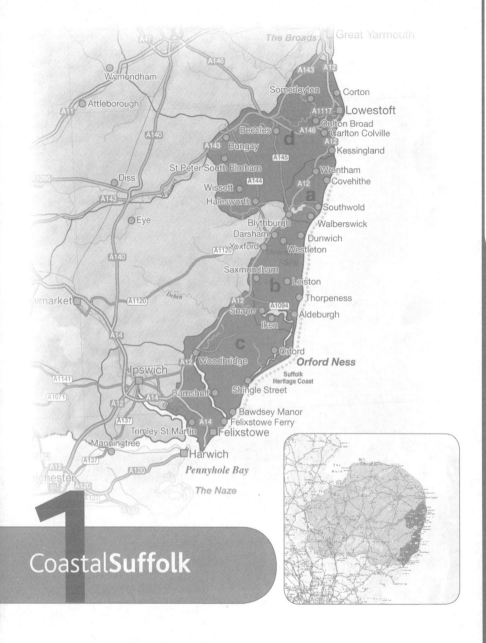

Coastal**Suffolk**

a. Southwold and Walberswick

b. Dunwich to Aldeburgh

c. Orford to Felixstowe

d. Lowestoft and the Suffolk Broads

Unmissable highlights

01 Catch crabs in Walberswick and eat oysters in Orford, p.60, 96

02 Discover why an Anglo-Saxon warrior king's ship was buried at Sutton Hoo, p.91

03 Laugh out loud at the wacky amusements on Southwold Pier, p.55

04 Visit Blythburgh Church as the sun sets over the marshes, p.68

05 Join the queue at the fish and chip shop on Aldeburgh High Street and take your purchase down to the beach, p.82

06 Stay at the House in the Clouds in Thorpeness or the Martello Tower in Aldeburgh, p.78

07 Browse among the posh kitchenware or listen to the haunting music of Benjamin Britten at Snape Maltings, p.76

08 Get lost in the Victorian maze at Somerleyton Hall, p.103

09 Browse in eccentric bookshops in Westleton or Halesworth, p.82, 108

10 Ramble around Orford Ness, the secret military test site turned nature reserve, p.87

COASTAL SUFFOLK

Between the two busy shipping ports of Lowestoft in the north and Felixstowe in the south, some of the loveliest coastal landscapes of East Anglia can be found, not to mention resorts and towns. Access to some of the most beautiful spots is only on foot. Often, the beaches of sand and shingle (or a combination) are invisible from a coastal road, separated by a precious ridge of grassy dunes and salt marshes that protects the inhabited places from the sea. Although this coastline has few bays and inlets, variety is provided by fishermen's huts, estuary openings, promenades and fishing boats. Marram grass, gorse and yellow ground lupins flourish in the dunes and their roots help to repel the voracious North Sea which is always trying to reclaim the sands that it laid down several million years ago.

On a sunny day, there is nothing nicer than to stroll for an hour along the beach and then arrive at a kiosk selling mugs of tea or delicious fish and chips. The scene is benign, reminiscent of perfect seaside holidays from childhood. But in other weathers, it soon becomes apparent that this is a battered coast. Coastal erosion has taken great bites out of many coastal communities. Plucky Suffolk folk wage an ongoing battle with the sea (and the Environment Agency) to maintain their sea defences.

Even if you bridle at the label 'Heritage Coast', you can't deny that a coast so close to London that has almost completely escaped urban encroachments and developments is a marvellous thing. One minute you are on the busy A12 whizzing past Ipswich and the next you are among grazing marshes, estuary bridges, tidal lagoons, woodland and reed beds, all forming a 150-square mile Area of Outstanding Beauty. It can be a magical world when the sun sets scarlet behind a lighthouse and the harsh sea crashes in on a wild and desolate stretch of coast.

But the wildness and desolation never last long, because this coast is favoured with a charming series of villages, towns and resorts, all with individual character and a satisfying old-fashioned atmosphere. The freshness of the seafood is sublime and the unhurried service in shops and pubs unrivalled. With one or two exceptions this coast has avoided the ruination that relentless tourism has brought to so many British seaside resorts.

SOUTHWOLD AND WALBERSWICK

Southwold is a town full of one-off shops and pleasures, of picturesque yards and passages, of unforced nostalgia. The brightly coloured, much-loved beach huts are iconic, as is the pier, rescued from dereliction and turned into something unusual and wonderful. In both Southwold and Walberswick, there is a jumble of architecture, houses of flint and brick, stone, colour wash and weatherboard, at odd angles, as though they have grown organically over the centuries with no particular design. Yet they manage to create a harmonious whole.

Some say that Southwold has kept the modern world at bay and retains a 1950s innocence. Others think it's so popular among London media types who own second homes hereabouts that it might as well be labelled Hampstead-on-Sea. Neither of these does it justice. It does have more than its fair share of old-fashioned pleasures, including the regulation boating lake with quaint tea pavilion, the Sailors' Reading Room (state-of-the-art in 1864) and a 66-seater Edwardian-style cinema. And it can't be denied that a host of actors, authors and media personalities have connections with Southwold and environs. But Griff Rhys Jones is definitely exaggerating when he says that people who visit Southwold and Walberswick can pretend that they are attending a Channel 4 script meeting.

A hasty glance at a map will lead you to conclude that Southwold and Walberswick are adjacent towns, which they are, but only if you are a crow. There is no road bridge across the River Blyth between the A1095 and the sea and the round trip by road is 16 miles. Pedestrians must walk about a mile inland to cross the river on the sluice bridge. Fortunately visitors can cross easily from Southwold to Walberswick in a couple of minutes by ferry rowboat. In high season two of these long skiffs (one is aptly called *Halcyon days*) operate throughout the day, ferrying no more than a dozen people at a time plus a couple of dogs, for a cost of 80p each way. Only one family is licensed to operate the ferry service and has done so since 1942 (see local knowledge box).

Whereas Southwold is a living breathing productive community, Walberswick seems a little as though it has been caught in aspic, with postcard-pretty cottages, perfectly picturesque fishermen's cottages, houses on stilts and wedding parties being photographed on the green. But some of the genteel retirees and artists who populate Walberswick have recently turned militant against a government policy to subject their coast to 'Managed Realignment', which means giving up on investing in the expensive sea defences and putting properties at risk if the North Sea were to invade.

For now, the sandy beach is intact and the maze of footpaths, walkways over mudflats, marshes and creeks and bird-filled hinterland of outstanding natural beauty are a delight to explore.

WHAT TO SEE AND DO

 ## Fair weather

Strolling and browsing, paddling and swimming can occupy hours and days. Most visitors make a comfortable little encampment on the beach and sit awhile and watch the children build their sandcastles. At some point, you will want to explore the town, which has a spacious feeling because of the several attractive green spaces, said to have resulted from long-ago fires that burned down houses that were never replaced.

If you want to walk the length of the beach and start at the northern end on Sole Bay (opposite the boating lake), it will take about half an hour to walk to the mouth of the River Blyth. Much effort has been invested in tasteful sea defences to complement the wooden groynes, so that large black boulders of mica schist have recently been installed. If your legs tire of walking on sand you can climb one of the many sets of steps to the promenade just above the beach. If you want to stride out, you can walk along the river harbour to the bridge near the sluice then either head back around the back of Southwold (towards the water tower) or cross the bridge to the Walberswick side and walk across the Common to the village of Walberswick.

Anyone who dabbles in photography or painting will probably be inspired by Walberswick, which has always attracted artists. Charles Rennie Mackintosh and English impressionist Philip Wilson Steer were part of a utopian seaside artists' colony here nearly a hundred years ago and there is still a very spirited community of artists today who are attracted to the open skies, haunting light and shimmering sea.

Southwold Pier

Southwold Pier
Southwold Pier is a revelation. A genius has taken the British seaside pier,

which might be considered past its sell-by date, and breathed new life into it. One of the stated aims of the new owner of the pier, Stephen Bournes, is to discard anything that has the whiff of tackiness. The shops are tasteful and not franchised, the café and restaurant appealing and the Under the Pier arcade games (actually located on top of the pier) a whimsical marvel.

Amusement arcades are as necessary an ingredient of English resorts as rock candy and a chilly wind. This one has been created by Tim Hunkin who is usually described as an artist-cum-engineer, but primarily he is a humorist. His inventions are part Heath Robinson, part Wallace & Gromit, with moving parts and recorded video. (A foretaste is available at www.underthepier.com and www.timhunkin.com.)

The rest of the pier is also full of surprises. In his guise as a 'horological urologist', the irrepressible Tim Hunkin has created a water clock which puts on a show on the hour and half-hour (roughly) in which a male and female figure sharing a bath squirt each other through their cigarettes, and the short trousers worn by two lads drop on cue before they proceed to relieve themselves to the detriment of the tulips below.

Beach huts

The pastel-painted and decorated beach huts of Southwold are classic. No one can resist peering into the open ones and admiring the doll's house lace-curtained neatness of some of them. All proudly sport name plaques. Although Southwold itself does not seem unduly 'chocolate box', one of its pretty beach huts has called itself just that. Although the prices are plainly absurd – upwards of £30,000 for a shed-on-a-beach where overnighting is forbidden – you will inevitably find yourself wishing that you could brew up your tea in 'Linga Longa' or wondering what on earth is behind the name 'Aunty Bing-Bong'. It is possible to hire one costing from £20 a day.

DURRANTS HOLIDAY LETTINGS, 98 High street, Southwold IP18 6DP; ☎ 01502 723292; www.durrantsholidaycottages.co.uk; Holiday letting agent for beach huts and cottages.

Southwold's famous beach huts

The Visitors' Book

Autumn break in Southwold

'Meandering eastwards along the A1120, signposted 'Scenic Route', we (a group of women friends from Cambridge) anticipated the weekend with relish. Coastal Suffolk lay invitingly before us, all tangly and wild, like a dishevelled wood sprite.'

'We found the Harbour Campsite (Ferry Road) just a dune away from the beckoning sea. Unable to resist, half of our group rushed off for an exhilarating plunge, whilst we ambled along the sandy beach, past colourful beach huts, into Southwold, picturesque and timeless. Were I to win the lottery, here on its gorgeous green is where I would buy my dream cottage, casement-windowed and quintessentially English, with hollyhocks at the door.'

'Years ago, I heard Brian Johnston drooling over a local speciality and so, popping into a seductively stocked delicatessen, I was delighted to learn that butter buns are still to be had, but alas, not at weekends. This disappointment was soon forgotten upon discovering, on the pier, the unforeseen delights of the quirky arcade games. My favourite was the hilarious 'Bathyscope' which offered a surreal voyage to the bottom of the sea where Robert Maxwell's skeleton frolicked amidst amorous nuclear canisters!'

'Gastronomic highlights were an excellent supper of fresh wild bass with seasonal vegetables, at The Lord Nelson, and a sublime selection of lobster and crab platters at the unpretentious Sole Bay Fish Shed, on the harbour, where we experienced the unexpected excitement of watching the fishmonger-owner feeding the lobster, crabs and fish in his giant aquarium.'

Claire Russell, October 2007

Southwold Lighthouse

The black fishermen's huts set among the grassy dunes in Walberswick form a photogenic little enclave and with luck you will catch a glimpse into the neat-as-a-pin interior of one or two.

The harbour and lighthouse

Southwold's harbour is some distance south of the town, along the estuary of the River Blyth, and it is still the bustling home of fishing boats and fishmongers. An early morning potter will take you past a flurry of marine activity. Boat stages line both sides of the river upstream to the sluice footbridge. The locals constantly battle the silting up of their harbour, and sailing into the narrow river mouth is tricky whatever the tidal conditions.

The white-painted circular lighthouse vies with the water tower and the church tower to dominate the skyline of Southwold, and rises from among sea-facing terraced houses in the centre of the town. Built in the 1880s, its light was visible 17 miles out to sea. The keepers of the lighthouse (until 1938 when the beacon was electrified) slept in a service room but never lived there. At the time of writing its light was dimmed by scaffolding, but when restoration is finished tours will be available (☎ 01502 722576).

St Edmund's Church

Some consider the Church of St Edmund the finest late mediaeval church in the county. Like the better known Suffolk churches at Lavenham, Long Melford and Blythburgh, Southwold's church is on a vast scale, quite out of proportion with the small population of what was a fishing village in the late 15th century. This solid flint-clad, copper-roofed church has many interesting features including a screen depicting 36 carved and painted prophets, disciples and saints, and carved armrests in the choir, some based on the mediaeval bestiary, e.g. a beaver biting its privates. The original of the logo of Adnams' brewery can be found in the porch: Southwold Jack uses his axe to strike a bell to summon people to a service.

 ## Wet weather

Southwold isn't a resort which boasts a number of indoor tourist attractions. It is a place of simple pleasures, with some small museums within walking distance of one another.

The **Southwold Museum** of local history is housed in two Dutch-gabled cottages, knocked through and refurbished and extended with a lottery grant for 2008. All exhibits have been found in the immediate area, including things from the sea or washed up on the beach. Various exhibits and old photographs cover (among other things) the story of the town's fishing industry, its railway link (which closed in 1929) and the 17th-century battle of Sole Bay against the Dutch.

SOUTHWOLD MUSEUM, 9–11 Victoria Street, Southwold IP18 6HZ; ☎ 01502 726097; www.southwoldmuseum.org; free; open daily 2–4pm, Good Friday to end Oct; mornings also in Aug; donations welcome.

The **Sailors' Reading Room** is a left-over from the Victorian self-improvement and temperance movement. The widow of a naval officer was worried that local fishermen and sailors were spending too much time in the pubs, so she built this rival attraction, which is still open today. You aren't obliged to stick to literature good for the soul, so feel free to take the Sunday supplements in if you like. The room displays some model ships and seafaring lore, and it's near the tea kiosk on the beach.

SAILORS' READING ROOM, East Cliff, Southwold IP18 6EL; free; open daily 9am–5pm Good Friday to end Oct; otherwise 9am–3.30pm.

Like all British coastal places, Southwold has its **RNLI Lifeboat Station**. Next door, near the harbour mouth, is a museum devoted to Southwold's most famous lifeboat. The *Alfred Corry* saved dozens of lives between 1893 and 1918. Afterwards it changed hands many times and eventually, in 1976, was ignominiously abandoned by its owner. The grandson of the original heroic coxswain of Southwold bought and restored it before returning it to Southwold Harbour. It is still being restored but can be visited in a 1920s lifeboat shed floated in from Cromer in 1998.

ALFRED CORRY MUSEUM, Ferry Road, Southwold IP18 6NG; ☎ 01502 723200; http://freespace.virgin.net/david. cragie; free; opening times vary; closed Wed.

 ## What to do with children...

Southwold is a natural playground where running on dunes and watching the pleasure craft negotiate the harbour and playing in the sand provide the chief entertainment. For a treat take them to the old-fashioned sweet shop for some retro sherbet lemons or check out the **Southwold Summer Theatre** children's productions on weekdays at 5.30pm and Saturdays at 2.30pm. Also, old-fashioned Punch and Judy puppet shows are performed on the promenade in summer.

CELEBRITY CONNECTIONS

One travel writer has identified Walberswick as the haunt of WORCs (Well-Off Retired Celebrities). And it's true – you can't even venture to the pub without tripping over some well-heeled media type. **Michael Palin** has been associated with the area for a very long time; it was while he was on holiday in Southwold with his parents that he met his future wife to whom he is still married 41 years later. He owns a house in Walberswick and actively supports the Electric Picture Palace in Southwold.

Other actors and directors known to haunt this part of the coast include **Geoffrey Palmer**, **Liz Smith** (of *The Royle Family*), **Richard Curtis** (director of *Four Weddings and a Funeral*), **Bill Nighy** and **James Nesbit**. **Anna Freud**, the daughter of Sigmund, acquired a house in Walberswick in the 1930s, and it has remained in the family ever since with her son Clement and his daughter **Emma**, and her husband **Richard Curtis** (scriptwriter of many films including *Notting Hill*). Other media personalities who favour the area include **Libby Purvis** and husband **Paul Heiney**. Politicians have also been associated with Southwold: you would be unlikely to miss **Martin Bell** because he would be wearing his trademark white suit. **P D James** is Baroness James of Holland Park, of Southwold in the County of Suffolk and sets many of her detective novels in the region, notably *Death in Holy Orders*. Other writers include **Esther Freud** (cousin of **Emma**), who presented the prizes at last year's crabbing championship.

Crabbing

Every child who has ever been to Southwold and Walberswick remembers it for the crabbing. Beaches you can find in lots of places, but the footbridge over the creek near the harbour on the Walberswick side must be one of the few places in the world that every child (and grown-up child) is virtually guaranteed a catch. Set-up costs are minimal. You need a line with a weight on it, bait (usually bits of raw bacon) and a water-filled bucket to keep the crabs alive until you get round to turning them back into the creek. Children find it endlessly fascinating watching the little crabs scuttle down the bank back to safety, only to be caught again a few minutes later (they never learn).

Once a year, children can enter a crabbing competition, held on a Sunday in early August (see Crabbing link on www.explorewalberswick.co.uk for exact date). Entry costs £1 with the proceeds to charity.

Local knowledge

Southwold native **Dani Church** is the ferrywoman on the River Blyth linking Southwold and Walberswick. A ferry crossing has been here since 1236, and members of Dani's family have been rowing the ferries since the late 1800s. In 1942 her great grandfather obtained sole rights to the service, which then passed to her great uncle, then her father, and now her.

Best walk: Starting from either of the car parks in Dunwich Forest, you can walk down to the beach via Dingle. You don't see many people on the forest paths and now that I have Charlie I like the fact that the paths are suitable for pushchairs.

Secret tip for lunch: The Tearoom next to the chandlery on the harbour serves unpretentious food like sausage rolls and jacket potatoes and their home-made cakes are really good too. Children and dogs are always welcomed, even when they arrive cold and dripping wet.

Favourite pub: A real locals' pub with a great garden is the Star in Wenhaston (pronounced Wennist'n), 7 miles inland from Southwold. They do great home cooking using local game and other produce.

Most fun thing to do with children: The Crabbing Competition held every August in Walberswick is fantastic for kids. I used to compete when I was growing up but for some reason it was always a non-local who won. The music, stalls and prize make it a brilliant occasion.

Favourite Shop: I have to choose my mother's shop Daddy Longlegs which is mainly a shoe shop but sells men's clothes and other things. It's at 84 High Street.

Favourite Takeaway: The Shoeme Balti House opposite the fish and chip shop at the top end of the High Street has been there for ages and serves superior Indian food.

Best thing to do on a rainy day: It might sound perverse, but I always like to be outdoors and so would probably go for a walk in the woods where you are a bit sheltered.

Ruined St Andrew's Church, Covehithe

Boat trips

Any boat trip called 'The Blast' is bound to appeal to children, and the 30-minute 'Sea Blast' around Sole Bay is no exception. The New Zealand-designed speedboat zooms out to sea and back again, and the trip costs £18 per adult and £9 for the under-13s; the aspirational email address is thrills@southwold.ws (☎ 07887 525082; www.coastalvoyager.co.uk). They also run more sedate cruises along the River Blyth and excursions to see as many as a hundred grey and common seals basking at nearby Scroby Sands, two nautical miles off the coast of Great Yarmouth, especially interesting in July when the pups are born.

Aquariums

If you have a late lunch at the **Sole Bay Shellfish** eatery on the Blackshore, you may be present when the fish in the giant aquarium are fed. Local children bring in bucketsful of live crabs which are tipped from a stepladder into the aquarium, followed by dessert of chopped-up squid. It is fascinating to see the giant blue-tinged lobster come to life and try (not always successfully) to pincer a crab, and to watch the very large Colin the Cod try (not at all success-fully) to hide vertically among the fronds of greenery. Almost better than a rerun of *The Blue Planet*.

... and how to avoid children

Southwold is an excellent place for highbrow shops including antique shops, bookshops and delicatessens. Another good grown-up haunt is Adnams' Wine Shop on Pinkney's Lane, which specialises in bin ends of quality wines; check their bargain basement. Also try Adnams' newer and more spacious shop behind the Crown Hotel, which sells classy kitchen equipment as well as wine. Among the most interesting antique shops is Southwold Antiques Centre

(Buckenham Mews, 83 High Street; ☎ 01502 723060), which provides a showroom for 20 dealers.

Most cinemas cater to children, but not Southwold's **Electric Picture Palace**. Opened in 2002 by local resident Michael Palin, but emulating cinemas of 90 years earlier, it puts on seasons of films more for film buffs than for Disney fans. Its target audience is local, so tickets are sold to visitors only after residents have had a chance to book. It is also necessary to become a member (only £5 a year, or £2 for a season) before you can attend this gem of a place (☎ 07815 769565; www.southwold.ws/electric_picture_palace).

Gazing at **George Orwell**'s former house at 36 High Street, you can imagine how relieved he must have been in 1929 to move back in with his parents after his grim experiences in London and Paris that resulted in his book *Down and Out in London and Paris*.

Energetic adults can enjoy a strenuous 10 mile round walk to **Covehithe,** north of Southwold. This may involve contending with mud on the inland path and incoming tides on the walk back along the coast (or vice versa). St Andrew's Church is remarkable for having a small church housed inside the ruined shell of a much older church; neither is likely to survive the encroaching sea beyond the next few decades.

Entertainment

Special events

The **Southwold Summer Theatre** on Cumberland Road in Southwold (☎ 01502 722389; www.southwoldtheatre.org) is supported by lots of well-known 'luvvies', and puts on quite lavish productions that are usually well reviewed in the national papers. Tickets often sell out so should be bought from late May if possible through the Tourist Office.

After just two years, the **Latitude Music Festival** has become enormously popular, partly because of its rural setting and also for the impressive line-up. Specialising in indie and alternative rock, this medium-sized festival takes place in mid-July in Henham Park, 5 miles inland from Southwold (www.latitudefestival.co.uk).

Relaxing at Latitude Festival, Henham

The best... PLACES TO STAY

BOUTIQUE

Blyth Hotel

Station Road, Southwold IP18 6AY
☎ **01502 722632/0845 348 6867**
www.blythhotel.com

Richard and Charlie Ashwell renovated an Edwardian property last year, decorated it in the muted colours of the seaside and opened their stylish hotel. All the rooms and suites have different features from a corner bath to French doors leading to a private balcony. In October 2007, the restaurant was runner-up in the 'Best Restaurant' category of the *Suffolk Magazine* Food & Drink Awards.

Prices: B&B from £100 for a double. Special packages include dinner (£20 for two courses, £25 for three, with coffee).

HISTORIC HOTEL

The Swan Hotel

Market Place, Southwold IP18 6EG
☎ **01502 722186**
www.adnams.co.uk/stay-with-us/the-swan

Long famed as the most civilised place to stay in the centre of Southwold, this handsome Adnams-owned hotel is laid-back in its pursuit of good style (i.e. some bits are a little dog-eared). Some of the rooms have superb sea views; the Admiral suite even has a telescope.

Prices: B&B from £152 for a double. Dinner in the acclaimed restaurant adds only £15 per person.

INN

The Bell Inn

Ferry Road, Walberswick IP18 6TN
☎ **01502 723109**
www.thebellwalberswick.wordpress.com

This centuries-old pub with its uneven flagstone floor and tales of being haunted is in a prime beachside location near the village green. The Bell has five double rooms – all en suite and with views of the sea – plus a four-person family suite. At weekends and throughout the summer, there is a minimum stay of two nights.

Prices: B&B £60 (Sun to Thurs) or £70 (Fri and Sat) for a single; £80 (Sun to Thurs) or £90 (Fri and Sat) for a double.

B & B

Amber House

North Parade, Southwold IP18 6LT
☎ **01502 723303**
www.southwold.ws/amber_house

At this old-fashioned roomy Victorian seafront guesthouse, three of the five bedrooms have uninterrupted sea views. Amber House is a two-minute walk to the pier and five minutes from shops and pubs. Children have to be over 5 to stay.

Prices: B&B from £70 to £100 for a double/twin.

The Stables

Henham Park, Beccles NR34 8AN (6 miles from Southwold)
☎ **07939 566714**
www.stablesathenhampark.com

These converted red brick stables have three rooms with exposed beams and vaulted ceilings, and set in lovely parkland with great views. An enticing organic breakfast is served and complimentary homemade chocolate brownies are offered at reception. The isolated location means that Henham Park is suitable for car drivers.

Prices: from £80 to £100 for a double.

SELF-CATERING

Poplar Hall

Frostenden Corner, Frostenden, near Southwold NR34 7JA
☎ **01502 578549**
www.southwold.ws/poplar-hall

Comprising a converted loft and stables and cottage, both these self-catering properties share the grounds with a 16th-century thatched cottage, Poplar Hall itself. While the loft house sleeps up to six, the cottage for two makes a cosier retreat. Both allow guests to make ample use of the acre and half of grounds.

Prices: from £190 to £480 for a week.

The priceless **British Open Crabbing Competition** is described above. A wackier competition takes over Southwold on the fourth Sunday in September: the **Flying Egg Competition** (www.flyingegg.co.uk) invites anyone to invent alternatives to everyday objects. The most recent theme was umbrellas, all of them displayed on Southwold High Street, including one planted with mustard and cress.

The best... FOOD AND DRINK

Eating well in Southwold is a given. The high point of eating (out or in) is the fish and seafood, mainly because a handful of longshore fishermen continue to brave the elements and European Union (EU) regulations to bring in a daily catch of herring, Dover sole, plaice, skate, cod, crabs and lobsters. Small-scale fishermen go out in 'punts' (small open motor boats) and sell what they can from their boats, from fish sheds along Blackshore and through local pubs and restaurants.

A Southwold speciality from the opposite end of the food group chart is the butter bun. Southwold butter buns are a traditional sticky yeast bun that can still be sourced in the most unexpected place – the butcher – and only with advance planning. Not too long ago the local bakery sold the secret recipe to Hutson Ltd, the butchers on the Market Square who continue to oversee the baking and selling of the legendary pastry. These must be pre-ordered (available only Mon/Wed/Fri; ☎ 01502 722104).

▶ Staying in

If you happen to be in Southwold on the last Saturday of the month, you can visit the **Farmers' Market** on the Pier. The **Black Olive Delicatessen** in the High Street (☎ 01502 722312) has an enticing range of foods for a holiday larder such as marinated sardines, exotic salamis, freshly baked bread and custom-made sandwiches, as well as local produce such as Suffolk Gold cheese and local honey. **Nutters Cheese Shop and Deli** at 11 East Street has lots besides cheese, including home-made cakes and excellent jams.

If you want to buy the catch of the day for home barbecuing or preparation, visit the fishmonger's along Blackshore, preferably in the morning. They will pack the fish in ice for you on request. You can sometimes even buy fish direct from the boats, for example from **John and Geoff Palmer**, who are licensed to sell from their boats. Note that fishing boats that don't have numbers painted on them aren't licensed to sell fish. **Samantha K's** near the sailing club (☎ 01502 672400; www.samanthaksfreshfish.co.uk) sells a selection of fresh and

EATING OUT

FINE DINING
The Crown Hotel
High Street, Southwold, Suffolk IP18 6DP
☎ **01502 722275**
crown.hotel@adnams.co.uk;
www.adnams.co.uk/stay-with-us/
the-crown

Like its sister hotel, the Swan (see p.74), the Crown is owned by the Adnams company. Although its atmosphere is more informal than the Swan's, the cooking is seriously good. The words 'Suffolk' and 'local' appear all over the menu, and its excellent wine list benefits from Adnams' reputation as a superior wine importer.

Sutherland House Hotel and Restaurant
56 High Street, Southwold IP18 6DN
☎ **01502 724544**
www.sutherlandhouse.co.uk.

Winner of the 'Best Use of Local Produce Award' in the *Good Food Guide 2008*, this restaurant (housed in a 15th-century townhouse) takes its carbon footprint states so seriously that it broadcasts the number of food miles beside each dish on the menu. Since the owners have an allotment in Southwold, some ingredients have travelled less than one food mile. Interesting (and distinctly un-Spanish) tapas bar serves fritters made from ox tongue and home-made black pudding. The hotel is a venue for Summer Theatre lunchtime performances (no booking). The restaurant is closed Sun evening and all-day Mon during winter.

PUB
Lord Nelson
East Street, Southwold IP18 6EJ
☎ **01502 722079**
www.thelordnelsonsouthwold.co.uk

In October 2007 the gimmick-free 'Nellie' was placed fifth in the *Good Pub Guide's* annual competition for the best pubs in the country, not that they need the extra custom. They don't take bookings so get there early. The blackboard specials usually include a seasonal fish dish with vegetables for a very reasonable £8.

CAFÉ
Trinity's Tearoom and Café
54 High Street, Southwold IP18 6DN
☎ **01502 722888**

Open daily 10am–5pm. Cosy in winter and with a garden for summer visits, Trinity's serves decent coffee and fine teas with homemade cakes as well as daily lunch specials such as seafood salads.

FISHMONGER
Sole Bay Shellfish Eatery
22E Blackshore, Southwold Harbour IP18 6ND ☎ **01502 724241**

This fishmonger selling its own-caught fish and shellfish now doubles as an eatery serving seafood platters (mixed, smoked, crab and lobster) that cost between £9.50 and £16.50. Customers are expected to supply their own drink and bread, an unusual DIY idea borrowed from the famous Company Shed on Mersea Island in Essex, from where the proprietor hails.

prepared fish and shellfish as does the **Sole Bay Fish Company** closer to the sea (see *Eating out*).

Fish and chips

Superb fresh fried fish is sold with chips from Christine Cara's outlet in one of the fishermen's huts on the River Blyth. Cara's also smokes kippers and other delicacies on the premises.

The Promenade Café on the Pier has an attractive glassed-in area outside as well as counters inside at which you can eat superior cod and chips. In July and August, between 5pm and 7pm, they dispense fish and chips in paper to be taken away and eaten on the beach or prom.

 ## Drinking

Southwold is blessed as the home of the **Adnams' Brewery** and every single one of the six pubs and several hotels in town serves Adnams' bitter (tasty), Broadside (strong) and Explorer (citrusy). Until September, 2006, beer was transported from brewery to local pubs by two well-loved dray horses called Sam and Monarch; this tradition ended when a new eco-friendly distribution centre was opened in Reydon a couple of miles inland.

The Lord Nelson, described above, is just as good for a drink as a meal, especially in the lovely enclosed garden behind. **The Harbour Inn** on Blackshore is a much loved boozer which is also praised for its fish and chips (though not at bargain prices). Try to find a table in the old multi-level side of the pub instead of the modern conservatory extension. If you fall into conversation with locals you may be told how the pub was cut off by the great flood of 1953, forcing the landlord and a few customers to hole up in the attic with no more than a bottle of whisky and a rabbit pie.

A more trendified pub is **The Sole Bay Inn** at the base of the Lighthouse, whose renovation has seen the installation of lots of blond wood and chrome. In fact all the pubs of

Sole Bay Inn and Lighthouse

SOUTHWOLD AND WALBERSWICK

REAL ALE SHOP, Priory Farm, Wrentham, Near Beccles NR34 7LR; ☎ 01502 676031; www.thereal aleshop.co.uk/suffolk; open Tues to Sat 10am–6pm (4pm in winter), Sun 12–4pm.

Southwold have their merits, and all can be impossibly crowded in the busy season. Wine drinkers are well served because of Adnams' other hat as a classy wine merchant. And most pubs serve the tasty Aspall Cyder made in the Suffolk town of Debenham.

Just opened, the **Real Ale Shop** housed in a redundant barn at Priory Farm in Wrentham on the A12 (4 miles north of Southwold) sells beer brewed locally from barley grown on the farm. Like its sister shop in North Norfolk (see p. 210) it also sells a range of bottled beers from Suffolk microbreweries.

FURTHER AFIELD

Blythburgh

At some point you must tear yourself away from the evocative sea and head back to the busy A12. But there is a fantastic consolation prize in **Holy Trinity Church**, Cathedral of the Marshes, in Blythburgh. If you are lucky enough to have time, weather and energy on your side, it is possible to walk the 4 miles from Walberswick across Tinker's Marshes, though the dotted lines on the Ordnance Survey map may well mislead you into thinking you can walk on water, since they may date from a time when the Blyth Estuary enjoyed more protection from the sea than it does now.

Because the parish has been relatively impoverished and shrinking for a long time, the church was not subject to any makeovers in the 19th century. Its unaltered windows allow the light to stream in even on days that aren't particularly sunny. The bleached wood of the delicate angels hovering along the central span of the vast roof is aesthetically pleasing to a modern eye. The painted angel over the door illustrates how the angels would once have been coloured and seems almost garish. The medieval carvings on the bench ends are worth puzzling over, since they represent the Seven Deadly Sins (only Gluttony with his fat belly is easy to identify), the Seven Works of Mercy and the four seasons (the headless figure is reaping the autumn harvest).

With any luck the doors to both tiny spiral staircases will be open, one beside the undistinguished rood screen, and the better one just to the left of the main door up to small low-ceilinged Chapel of the Blessed Sacrament, and on a little higher to an old wooden door that (miraculously) opens onto the roof. Health and safety monitors would certainly disapprove of stepping out, however the view over the beautiful combination of estuary marshes, woods, heath and pasture is exceptional. If you miss the day or the dusk, the church is floodlit at night.

Visitor information

Tourist Information Centres:
69 High Street, Southwold IP18
6DS, ☎ 01502 724729;
southwold.tic@waveney.gov.uk;
www.visit-southwold.co.uk; open
daily from 10am in summer (11am on
Sundays); shorter hours and closed
Sundays between 1 November and
Easter. www.suffolkcoastal.gov.uk –
the Suffolk District Council website
has good tourist info including a
downloadable visitors' guide to the
Suffolk coast.

Hospitals: Ipswich Hospital has the
nearest 24-hour A&E department,
Heath Road, Ipswich IP4 5PD; 2
miles east of Ipswich town centre on
the A1189 (Heath Road); Minor
Injuries Unit, Southwold Surgery,
York Road, Southwold IP18 6AN, ☎
01502 722326.

Supermarkets: The food shops and
delis of Southwold persuade most
people that they don't need to travel
to the nearest Sainsbury in Ipswich
or Tesco's in Lowestoft or Beccles;
Somerfield, 2 Market Place, Southwold IP18 6EE, open daily 8am–8pm
except Sun 10am–4pm.

Bike rental: Walberswick Cycle
Hire, Ilanga, Lodge Road, Walberswick, ☎ 01502 724070,
www.walberswick.ws/cyclehire/inde
x.php, £12 per day, £40 per week for
an adult bike, £9/£30 for children, £5
extra for a tandem, bicycles can be
delivered and collected in the
region; Byways Bicycles, Priory
Farm, Priory Lane, Darsham IP17
3QD, ☎ 01728 668764,
www.bywaysbicycles.co.uk, closed
Tues, £15 per day, £30 for 3 days,
£40 per week, route information
given including off-road; Darsham
Country Centre in the old Darsham
Station house (☎ 01728 668736;
darsham@woodcraft.org.uk) is run
by the Woodcraft Folk who sometimes let out the 22-bed
accommodation to private users or
hire out their 10 bikes.

Taxis: Southwold Taxis, ☎ 01502
723400/07737 139853; A to B Taxis,
Reydon, ☎ 01502 722111.

Local legends: beast of Blythburgh

On 4 August, 1577, Holy Trinity Church suffered a terrible visitation. As a storm raged, the devil in the guise of a massive black dog known as **Black Shuck** – a figure common to many East Anglian legends – swung down from the rood screen, slew a man and a boy, and left other worshippers 'scorched and hysterical'. In a trice, the monstrous Baskerville-like creature with red eyes fled from the church through the door, as the church spire and bells crashed down into the nave. The door is said to bear the marks of burning claws, though it was not until 1933 that the marks appeared when the door was cleaned, and these can be seen today. There have been sightings of a dog 'as big as a pony' loping over the marshes as recently as 1973 by a man repairing the sewers and in the 1980s by a policeman patrolling the A12.

Other tales that have attached themselves to Blythburgh have more historical respectability. **Toby's Walks,** as marked on the Ordnance Survey map just south of Blythburgh, are named after Tobias Gill, a strapping black musician who was stationed with a regiment in the 1750s. He had the misfortune to be found dead drunk next to the dead body of Anne Blakemore from Walberswick and was promptly arrested for her murder. Despite vehemently protesting his innocence and despite a complete absence of signs of violence on Anne's body, Tobias was hanged, tarred and left to rot in public. His restless ghost is said to haunt the spot still, though visitors in spring have more chance of hearing the first nightingale hiding in the dense vegetation, bracken, conifers or marshes.

Twilight over Blyth River estuary from the roof of Blythburgh church

DUNWICH TO ALDEBURGH

The straight shingle coastline stretching south for only 10 miles from Dunwich to Aldeburgh has virtually no buildings and therefore remains in its natural state unspoiled by development. On a summer morning when fresh sea air fills the lungs and the clouds scud across an arching sky, this coast seems like a wild paradise. The nautical flotsam and jetsam of fishing and boating activity is always picturesque. The heathland, marsh and estuary walks in the vicinity, as well as lovely pubs, restaurants, places of interest and musical events have attracted generations of loyal visitors. Just inland is the characteristic landscape of coastal Suffolk known as the Sandlings, comprising dry heaths and bright yellow gorse in season.

Dunwich is a fascinating place – the once-great port reduced to a mere hamlet cowering atop the low crumbling cliffs. Where seven centuries ago there was a thriving town the equal of Ipswich, with eight churches, 80 ships, a market, hospitals, windmills and a guildhall, now there is a single pub, a fish and chip tearoom, one undistinguished Victorian church and a museum to remind you of the glorious past. There is a melancholy fascination with the notion that the sea has claimed one church after another over the centuries; the ruins of All Saints survived into the 20th century but have now been swallowed up too. All that remains is the occasional human bone from a drowned church graveyard sticking out of the dunes, plus a legend that the bells of All Saints can be heard tolling under the waves (which the curator of the museum says only happens at pub closing time).

Aldeburgh is perfectly intact and is a charming seaside town with enough good restaurants and cafés to keep discerning holidaymakers returning again and again.

WHAT TO SEE AND DO

 ### Fair weather

This atmospheric stretch of Suffolk's 'Heritage Coast' is ideally enjoyed on a bright breezy day when you will want to explore on foot the low cliffs, reed marshes, lagoons, pebble beach, warrens and coverts. This area is part of the Suffolk Coast and Heaths Area of Outstanding Natural Beauty. Depending on your route, you might want to look up the tide tables because some footpaths become submerged at high tide.

Grassy dunes at Dunwich Beach

Dunwich

All who live in Dunwich can hear the death knell of their village, which is being eroded at a rate of about a metre a year. The Roman settlement on this coast is now a mile and a quarter out from shore under the North Sea, so it will be far less than a millennium before the pub, museum and chip shop disappear.

The beach is reinforced with extra shingle but this can't prevent ongoing erosion and occasional breaches after tidal surges. Signs warn walkers away from the edge: 'Cliff Edge Can Give Way Without Warning'; though leading off the main footpath heading south of the village, small dead-end paths lead through the dappled woods to excellent secluded picnic spots overlooking the sea.

Dunwich Heath, south of Dunwich, is very carefully managed by the National Trust. Footpaths run round the perimeter and bisect the heath which is gloriously carpeted with heathers in late summer. To the north of Dunwich, excellent walks can be taken across **Dingle Marshes** in the direction of Walberswick, a mere 3 miles away, though inlets and marshes mean that you can't walk in a straight line. A good day's walk can be based on a figure of eight, starting in Dunwich using the inland path heading north and returning along the beach. Sand martins have recently colonised the cliffs at points and the pockmarked cliff face indicates their nesting tunnels.

To find the path heading south, walk away from the beach car park and bear left past the ruined gatehouse of **Greyfriars,** the last remnant of medieval Dunwich. As long ago as 1289 the friary had to be moved inland to escape the ravages of the sea.

Cyclists can approach Dunwich by a beautiful minor road from Wenhaston past 'Newdelight Walks' and through **Dunwich Forest** (a sea of bluebells in spring).

Minsmere

The heathland south of Dunwich gives way to the reeds of Minsmere, an important RSPB nature reserve providing a precious habitat for rare birds. This is an excellent place for rookie birdwatchers to catch the excitement of a sighting of a rare bird from one of the many hides equipped with informative bird charts. Wading birds like avocet and spoonbills are easier to spot than the rare bittern.

RSPB MINSMERE,
Dunwich, Saxmundham, Suffolk
IP17 3DJ; ☎ 01728 648281;
www.rspb.org.uk;
minsmere@rspb.org.uk; adults £5,
children £1.50, families £10.

Thorpeness

House in the Clouds, Thorpeness

Less than a hundred years ago, it was possible to buy a great swathe of this coastline, and that is exactly what a wealthy Scottish barrister called Glencairn Stuart Ogilvie did. Among his schemes was to build a model holiday village using ye olde Englande architectural styles, mainly mock-Tudor and weatherboard. It sounds more kitsch than it is, and it is an attractive place with a large artificial boating lake, the Meare. Amusingly, the intention was to satisfy the needs of the refined classes in contrast to the more vulgar Southwold with its pier, 10 miles up the coast. Now groups are bussed in huge numbers to experience this eccentric seaside resort. The restored windmill is perched on the point of a peaked roof below and looks like it might overbalance at any minute. Next door is the amazing **House in the Clouds** (see *The best... places to stay*) overlooking the Meare (see *What to do with children*).

Aldeburgh

The defiantly old-fashioned seafront evokes the Victorian and Edwardian period when Aldeburgh became a genteel seaside resort. The town (pronounced as two syllables 'Orld-Brerr' or even 'All-Bra') also has much that appeals to a 21st-century visitor. The High Street runs parallel to the sea behind rows of cottages and boarding houses, and has both quaint and contemporary shops and galleries among historic buildings such as the **Old Custom House** whose front door is positioned six steps above the footpath in case of flooding. Aldeburgh's pastel coloured buildings, some with Dutch gables, make for an attractive ambience (apart from some graceless new blocks of flats at the north end of the beach). At one time the half-timbered Elizabethan **Moot Hall** (assembly hall) was located in the centre of town. Due to

Maggi Hambling's Scallop Shell sculpture, Aldeburgh Beach

erosion it is now stranded on the shore not far from the fish stalls on the beach. The lovely little building with its Jacobean chimneys houses the town council and the local museum (open summer season only).

Sand castles are not on the agenda since the shoreline is almost exclusively shingle, but the north end of the beach does offer Maggi Hambling's intriguing scallop shell sculpture. This controversial installation has been defaced a few times but with luck you won't see any rude words, only the intended quotation from Britten's opera Peter Grimes: 'I hear those voices that will not be drowned.'

Benjamin Britten memorial plaque

Aldeburgh's most famous resident was Benjamin Britten who, with his life-long partner Peter Pears, set up the Aldeburgh Music Festival not long after the Second World War. This flourishing arts festival takes place over the last two weeks of June. The annual influx of creative people and their audiences has brought a wealth of restaurants, book-shops and other amenities to the area. Restaurant tables and parking are at a real premium from June to August.

Martello Tower, Aldeburgh

The River Alde

After some strenuous crunching through the shingle of the exposed beach at Aldeburgh, it is lovely to turn inland along the sheltered estuary. Lovely walks can be done from Aldeburgh or Snape. Cars can be left opposite the snooty looking 1920s Aldeburgh Golf Clubhouse on the A1094 or in the free car park at the Snape Maltings. From the Maltings, a footpath heads south and follows the edge of the estuary, perhaps past a rigged sailing barge or two, to the picturesque little thatched church at **Iken** (wellies can be useful at high tide). Wonderful views over the tidal estuary can be had, perhaps with a couple of Aberdeen Angus cattle grazing in the foreground, next to the church.

Some believe that one of the early Christian saints, Botolf, landed and founded a monastery at Iken in AD645. The base of a Saxon cross (probably ninth century) was recently discovered lurking in the fabric of the tower. The 15th-century font bears carved figures of angels, holding different symbols of the Passion of Christ, such as a fistful of nails and a spear.

Wet weather

Dunwich Museum

This small but perfectly formed museum is housed in an old cottage. The exhibits were completely revamped a decade ago with lottery money. Its star attraction is a huge model of mediaeval Dunwich showing the impact of the

DUNWICH MUSEUM,
St James' Street IP17 3EA; ☎
01728 648796; www.dunwich
museum.org.uk; free; open daily
Apr to Sept 11.30–4pm; Oct
12am–4pm

shrinking coastline from the 12th century to the present day. It also explains why there is a Bishop of Dunwich when the population is just 88. Having had no bishop since AD871, the position was reinstated in 1933 when the Bishop in Bury St Edmunds decided he needed a deputy.

Snape Maltings

This very upmarket retail park is housed in some wonderfully converted buildings with their striking roofscapes. The combination of nearby barley crops and river access to the sea made this the obvious place in the 1860s to develop a maltings industry which lasted for a hundred years. Spotted by Benjamin Britten, the redundant malt kiln was turned into a concert hall in 1967 with attendant tea and gift shops.

What to do with children

Any children interested in nature and wildlife will have a field day along this coast. Special 'Explorer' packs with binoculars, bug box, activity booklet and colouring pencils can be borrowed free from the visitor centre at Minsmere and a programme of guided walks is run year-round for both children (£2.50) and adults (£5).

A little way inland from Aldeburgh, the owners of the **Friday Street Farm Shop** (see below) create a different maize maze every year; this is open between mid-July and October. Children can pick up a quiz whose answers are hidden in the five acres of paths.

Feeding the swans and hiring canoes, punts or rowboats on **Thorpeness Meare** is always popular. The artificial lake features islands with names such as Peter Pan's Island and Crocodile Island, inspired by the stories of J M Barrie, personal friend of Thorpeness's founder.

Ogilvie had a vision of making Thorpeness a holiday village for the upper middle-classes of the early 1900s. Holiday homes were built and a 64-acre lake, The Meare was dug. The lake was themed around J M Barrie's children's story *Peter Pan* (Barrie was in fact a family friend). On the lake are numerous islands, Crocodile Island, Peter Pan's Island and The Fort. Children are as captivated by the place today as they were in the early 1900s.

Concert hall, Snape Maltings

Entertainment

Concerts

An eclectic programme of concerts and performances is put on in the superb 832-seat **Snape Maltings Concert Hall,** converted from the cavernous space of the old maltings. You can choose to hear anything from ragtime to Rachmaninov. The more intimate space of the Britten Pears Recital Room is more suited to music, and other venues are used such as the Jubilee Hall in Aldeburgh and its lovely church. In August, prom-style concerts take place at which the 'cheap seats' consist of a BYO cushion on the floor. Information about the year-round programme is available at www.aldburgh.co.uk (☎ 01728 687110).

Aldeburgh Cinema

Aldeburgh is blessed with an independent cinema housed in an 18th-century house on the High Street which seats almost 300. At the end of November each year, the cinema hosts a

ALDEBURGH CINEMA
51 High Street, Aldeburgh IP15 5AU; ☎ 01728 452996; www.aldeburghcinema.co.uk; adults £7; evening programmes Mon to Sat plus Wed matinees.

The best... PLACES TO STAY

BOUTIQUE

Brudenell Hotel

The Parade, Aldeburgh IP15 5BU (on the seafront at the southern end of the town)
☎ **01728 452071**
www.brudenellhotel.co.uk

This gracious Edwardian seaside hotel is decorated in blue and yellow (useful in counteracting possible grey skies). A flash menu is served either in the dining room, with huge its picture windows, or on the terrace in summer.

Prices: £100+ per person in doubles.

INN

Eel's Foot Inn

Eastbridge, Leiston IP16 4SN
☎ **01728 830154**
www.theeelsfootinn.co.uk

The odd name is said to have derived from the substandard work of a pub sign painter trying to depict a devil in a boot. This is a much favoured Adnams' pub with six en suite rooms in separate building. The sea is less than an hour's walk away via a bridleway and footpath past Minsmere. Folk music jam sessions are held every Thursday. The pub no longer has a campsite but nearby Eastbridge Farm (☎ 01728 830729) operates a family campsite with very basic facilities and a tent charge of £5.

Price: £55 for a single; £80 for a double plus £25 for extra child or adult.

B & B

Ocean House Aldeburgh

25 Crag Path, Aldeburgh IP15 5BS
☎ **01728 452094**
www.oceanhousealdeburgh.co.uk

This long-established B&B on the Victorian seafront with bay windows overhanging the beach, was listed by *Independent Travel* in 2007 as one of its top ten B&Bs by the sea. Guests may use the grand piano in a studio with uninterrupted views.

Price: B&B £40 pppn for a double.

SELF-CATERING

Coastguard Cottages

Dunwich Heath c/o National Trust Holiday Cottages, Holiday Booking Office, PO Box 536, Melksham, Wiltshire SN12 8SX. ☎ **0844 8002070 (National Trust Booking line) www.nationaltrust cottages.co.uk/nt.asp?p=81&c=137**

One of the old coastguard cottages sleeps four, while two others sleep two. All in smart white and blue livery, the cottages offer wonderful views and birdwatching opportunities.

Price: from £274 to £840 per week.

UNUSUAL

House in the Clouds

Uplands Road, Thorpeness IP16 4NQ
☎ **020 72243615**
www.houseintheclouds.co.uk

This iconic landmark in the 1920s fantasy village of Thorpeness is visible from miles around. The building – a former water tower disguised under wooden cladding – sleeps 12 on four levels with the large top storey having been converted to a games room. Huge private grounds are adjacent to the Meare.

Price: from £520 for one night in winter to £3,200 per week in summer.

Martello Tower

Slaughden, Aldeburgh (on the beach past the sailing school)
c/o The Landmark Trust
☎ **01628 825925**
www.landmarktrust.org.uk

This unusual fort was originally built to defend England from Napoleon. The structure appears somewhat squat and ugly from the outside but the exposed whitewashed brick inside, refectory table and lantern lighting make it an appealing place to stay, with magnificent views from the roof.

Price: from £567 for three nights in winter to £1,143 per week in summer.

weekend documentary festival with the participation of local celebrities such as Libby Purves.

Special events

The **Aldeburgh Festival** is one of the pre-eminent summer music festivals in the country. The **Aldeburgh Summer Theatre**, affiliated to Southwold Summer Theatre, may not be as famous but is great fun. The **Aldeburgh Food & Drink Festival** in late September lasts 10 days with cookery demonstrations, tastings at restaurants and delis, and farm walks throughout East Suffolk.

- **Aldeburgh Festival**, Snape Maltings Concert Hall, Snape, IP17 1SP (☎ 01728 687110 Box Office; www.aldeburgh.co.uk). Festival dates are over the last two weeks of June each year.
- **Aldeburgh Summer Theatre**, Jubilee Hall, Crabbe Street, Aldeburgh IP15 5BW (☎ 01728 454022).
- **Aldeburgh Food & Drink Festival** (☎ 01728 688303; www.aldeburgh foodanddrink.co.uk).

The **Aldeburgh Carnival** on the third weekend of August involves fireworks, a Chinese lantern procession and merry-making .

The best... FOOD AND DRINK

 Staying in

Due to a concerted local campaign, a proposed Tesco was kept out of Sax-mundham a few years ago, and this whole area of East Suffolk is still a supermarket-free zone, principally due to the efforts of Lady Caroline Cranbrook, President of the Aldeburgh Food & Drink Festival. According to her, 'In the absence of a large supermarket, a thousand flowers are blooming, referring to the proliferation of independent food producers and shops, including her own Alde Valley lamb. Tesco disagrees of course.

Inshore trawling fishermen still push off from the shingle at Aldeburgh and sell their catch of sole, plaice and cod from sheds on the beach. The best time of year for catching sprats and herring is November and December though the season extends a month on either side. Shrimps, lobster and crab are available year round but at their best in spring, summer and autumn. Lobster goes for £10 a kilo, which is the weight of a good-sized lobster (sold cooked with its pincers in rubber bands).

The specialist deli **Lawsons** at: 152 High Street, Aldeburgh sells an impressive range of cheese, hams and local produce (open daily; 10am–2pm on Sun). Note that it is attached to an excellent unpretentious restaurant 152 Aldeburgh. A very good food shop can also be found in the bigger town of Saxmundham, 7 miles inland, attached to the Bistro (see Eating out).

Farm shops and markets

Two excellent farm shops flourish within a mile or two of each other, just off the A12 at the turn-off for Aldeburgh. The **Friday Street Farm Shop** stocks produce from as many as 100 local suppliers, with a range that includes fruit preserves, chutneys, smoked fish, organic vegetables, duck eggs, ice-cream from three local farms, and so on. In season you can pick your own courgettes, sweetcorn and soft fruits. The **Railway Farm Shop** not only sells wonderful home-grown produce from its own and neighbouring farms but gives old-fashioned personal service too.

- **Friday Street Farm Shop and Tearooms**, Farnham, near Saxmundham, IP17 1JX (☎ 01728 602783), open 7 days a week.
- **Railway Farm Shop**, Benhall Green, Benhall, near Saxmundham, IP17 1HU (☎ 01728 605793).

The **Riverside Farmers' Market** is held at Snape Maltings on the first Saturday of the month (9.30am–1pm). Stock up on Suffolk beef (Red Poll breed), organic salmon and produce from inland farms along the valley of the River Alde, and pick up some locally made pasta sauces and dips from **Purely Pesto**. Look out also for the stall from **Maple Organic Farm** in Kelsale which is owned and run by the man who rescued Green & Black Chocolate from financial disaster. His products are sold at the best food shops in the region such as **Salters Butchers** (107 High Street, Aldeburgh). **Simply Delicious** (70 High Street, Leiston) and he stocks produce from 80–100 local suppliers, ranging from organic beef to premium chutney in clay pots, hand-painted by a local artist. The choice is impressive: you can buy local eggs, quail eggs or duck eggs, and local ice cream from three farms.

Takeaways

In a survey of top chefs for *Observer Food Monthly*, queuing for fish and chips at **Aldeburgh Fish & Chips** was voted number 30 on the list of top 50 things for foodies to do before they die. Needless to say the fish is fabulously fresh. You can try to eat it by the sea wall but will probably encounter competition from brazen seagulls. The rival on the other side of the street, the fish takeaway **Golden Galleon**, is also superb and has a smart sit-down restaurant upstairs called the Upper Deck.

EATING OUT

FINE DINING
Regatta Restaurant
171 High Street, Aldeburgh IP15 5AN
☎ **01728 648941**
www.regattaaldeburgh.com

This popular restaurant in Aldeburgh High Street has been run by a couple for 19 years; (the chef's wife is the niece of Ruth Watson, Hotel Inspector.) The lobster, halibut and smoked trio of fish are all highly praised, but fairly pricey. An unusual flavour of ice cream is served: fudge and Malteser.

Wentworth Hotel
Wentworth Road, Aldeburgh IP15 5BD
☎ **01728 452312**
www.wentworth-aldeburgh.com

At first it might seem a little crusty, but you don't have to be a retired colonel to enjoy this place. Instead of the formal dining room, you can eat by the cosy coal fire in the bar serving an Adnams and excellent range of wine by the glass. The family, which has owned the hotel for generations has connections in Kenya so you will find a little Swahili on the menu: *kwanza* and *kubwa* mean small and large portions of, for example, roast Suffolk lamb and Mrs Campbell's fish pie. The view would be better if the eating areas were on the upper floors, but these are for guests' rooms.

TEASHOP & CAFÉ
Dunwich Heath Tea Rooms
National Trust Coastal Centre and Beach, Dunwich IP17 3DJ
☎ **01728 648501**

In October 2007, this teashop and restaurant was rewarded for its food-sourcing policy of using regional and seasonal food by gaining first prize in its category at the East Anglian Food and Drink Awards. After

a blustery walk or patiently time spent, in a nearby bird hide, a pork and apricot casserole with dumplings, or stilton and leek quiche can hit the spot.

Flora Tearooms
Beach Road, Dunwich
☎ **01728 648433**

Most people know it as the fish and chip shop in Dunwich since it's famous for its superb quality fish (particularly skate) and chips. It would never be caught dead with a frozen product. The shack-like restaurant seats over 100 and many more on the trestle tables outside; in high season there can be quite a crush. The tearooms are closed in winter.

Bridge Nurseries
Bridge House, Dunwich IP17 3DZ
☎ **01728 648850**

This garden centre not only specialises in clematis, but serves excellent cakes in its friendly café.

BISTRO
The Bistro at the Deli
26a, High Street, Saxmundham IP17 1AJ
☎ **01728 605607**
www.thedeli.biz

This bistro offers imaginative menus plus great cakes to accompany coffee at any time of day. The signature dish is christened the Black Slate, combining tapas-style selection of complementary tastes. Apparently broadcaster and journalist Libby Purves is a regular at this place.

- **Aldeburgh Fish & Chips**, 226 High Street, Aldeburgh IP15 1DJ (☎ 01728 452250).
- **Golden Galleon**, 137 High Street, Aldeburgh IP15 5AR (☎ 01728 454685).

The quality of ice cream and choice of 60 flavours served at Ives Ice Cream Parlour (160 High Street, Aldeburgh) is unbeatable. You can also indulge in a tasty cone of locally made ice cream down at the boating pond, available from the cappuccino hut.

Drinking

Adnams is still the dominant force on this stretch of coast and in many of the inland pubs too. The atmospheric **Mill** in Aldeburgh (opposite the Moot Hall) attracts colourful locals and is busy year-round. The restyled **Plough and Sail** (Snape Maltings, Snape Bridge IP17 1SR; ☎ 01728 688413; www.debeninns. co.uk/ploughandsail/index.html) attracts a more trendy crowd but is attractive and welcoming with an excellent menu featuring seafood dishes such as seared trout with Chinese greens and steamed fillet of sea bass.

For a cosy cluttered village local away from the tourist crowds, go to the **Lion Inn** in Theberton (IP16 4RU; ☎ 01728 830185) which has pub games, a garden and good value food.

FURTHER AFIELD

Westleton

Just over two miles from Dunwich, Westleton is a quintessentially English village. Built round a pretty village green with a duck pond, it has a good mixture of typical Suffolk houses, one with Tudor gables, a thatched church, a tearoom, and a village store-cum-post office that sells homemade cakes. The excellent **Crown** is a possible place to stay and there is a good second pub too, **The White Horse**. Eighteen lime trees surround the pond – planted to represent the 18 men of the village who died in the First World War.

The crowning glory of Westleton is its second-hand bookshop. It occupies a former Methodist chapel on The Street and is officially called **Chapel Books**, though it is more often referred to as Bob's Books after the affable eccentric who runs it. If you want assistance you are invited by a scribbled notice to pick up the

CHAPEL BOOKS, The Street, Westleton IP17 3AA; ☎ 01728 648616; open every day; erratic hours.

Visitor information

Tourist Information Centres: High Street, Aldeburgh IP15 5AQ ☎ 01728 453637, atic@suffolk coastal.gov.uk, open daily 9am–5.30pm in summer (Apr to Sept), closed Sun in winter; the community website www.onesuf folk.co.uk has links to many villages and events.

Hospitals: Ipswich Hospital has the nearest A&E department, Heath Road, Ipswich, IP4 5PD, 2 miles east of Ipswich town centre on the A1189 (Heath Road); the Minor Injuries Unit at Aldeburgh Hospital has recently been closed.

Supermarkets: Sainsbury, Ipswich IP4 1DR, Tesco, Martlesham Heath near Ipswich IP5 3RU; Somerfield, Church Street, Saxmundham IP17 1EP.

Bike rental: Avocet Sport, ☎ 07706 479965, pre-booked hire bicycles can be made available from Snape and can be delivered to surrounding villages including Aldeburgh and Thorpeness.

Taxis: Book in advance; may not make late night collections; Oscars, Knodishall near Leiston, ☎ 01728 830614; Miller's Taxis, Kelsale near Saxmundham, ☎ 01728 603279; Squirrel's Taxis, Saxmundham, ☎ 01728 602344; Amber Taxis, Leiston, ☎ 01728 833621.

broken wooden spoon provided and bang it on an upturned Carr's biscuit tin, but be prepared to find Bob wearing pyjamas (two pairs in winter). Most visitors are content to browse at random among the towering mountains of books, covering everything from East Anglian birds to old films. Sit on one of the collapsing sofas and you may even be offered a cup of tea if Bob happens to be brewing one.

Like many villages on or near the Suffolk coast, Westleton hosts special events such as the **Wild Flower Festival** at the end of July and the **Barrel Fair** on the third Sunday of August when barrel-pushing competitors race up and down the green. Also St Peter's Church acts as an attractive rural concert venue, holding monthly chamber music concerts featuring musicians of international repute.

Chapel Books, Westleton

ORFORD TO FELIXSTOWE

Driving east from the busy A12 brings you to peaceful outposts that some-times seem so secret that they can't have been discovered by the outside world. A perfect example is the tiny road that leads down to Ramsholt, on the estuary of the River Deben, which consists only of a pub, a church and a thatched farmhouse. Car access to the waterside is limited and just a few roads peter out at tiny settlements that feel wild. But footpaths reward walkers with magnificent views of sparkling river estuaries lined with pine woods, colourful heathland and sandy beaches. The Suffolk Coast & Heaths Path links Orford with Felixstowe via Shingle Street which has no church, no pub and few houses but an interesting history. Bawdsey Quay is another unusual little place at what would be a dead end if there weren't an escape route by foot ferry across the mouth of the river to Felixstowe.

By contrast the main towns of Orford and Woodbridge are bursting with wonderful places to eat and stay, shop and visit. By far the biggest town in this part of Suffolk east of Ipswich is Felixstowe with a population of 30,000. Despite its Edwardian gentility, Felixstowe remains resolutely unfashionable, probably because of its mighty container docks.

This part of the coast has punched above its weight militarily ever since Martello towers were built in the first decade of the 19th century to protect England from Napoleon. The coast, especially around Bawdsey, is still littered with the decommissioned furniture of war, pillboxes and bunkers, some of which have slid into the sea with the relentless erosion. The most fascinating left-over is the mysterious Orford Ness, once a top-secret weapons testing site now turned National Trust nature reserve.

WHAT TO SEE AND DO

 Fair weather

Orford

Oozing charm and individuality, Orford makes a fine destination for a day trip. It is even better as a base to stay. Because it sits behind the massive shingle spit of Orford Ness, it is no longer on the coast and therefore has no beach, and yet there is plenty of boating activity because it is at the mouth of the River Ore. It may now have a tiny population of just 700 (nearly half of whom are second-home owners) but it offers architectural variety, from the substantial

Local knowledge

Owner of the renowned Crown & Castle Hotel in Orford, **Ruth Watson** is a successful hotelier, restaurateur, cookery writer and most recently television presenter. After fronting Channel 5's *Hotel Inspector* she has moved to Channel 4 to film a behind-the-scenes series about country houses that can benefit from her expertise in the hospitality business.

Favourite café: The Wild Strawberry Café in Woodbridge serves excellent cakes all baked on the premises along with good Illy coffee, Innocent smoothies and original lunches.

Best view: I love looking over Orford at night especially out of season when every-body else is indoors. In the day, the light over the sea and river is endlessly changing. The best view is from the top of the castle tower.

Favourite deli: Patrick Hockley and Tish Goodwin run an excellent deli – the Wood-bridge Fine Foods Company. They bake pork and stilton pies (among others) on the prem-ises, and sell everything from locally caught crab to blueberries grown near Aldeburgh.

Favourite restaurant: The Regatta Restau-rant on Aldeburgh's High Street. My niece Johanna Mabey and her husband Robert have run it for more than 15 years. Their dishes using game from estates in the neigh-bourhood are especially good.

Favourite pub: I would have to choose the King's Head in Orford which we also run. When we took it over we were careful not to put the prices up and to keep it an honest local pub serving Adnams bitter and plain but delicious pub food like properly battered scampi and doorstop sandwiches.

Best walk: One of my favourite places is The Thicks at Staverton Park just near Butley along the B1084. This is a fantastic place in winter when, devoid of leaves, the gnarled old trunks of ancient oak trees are revealed in all their glory. The site includes an area of old holly trees that is said to be the largest in the country.

Best kept secret: The Railway Farm Shop just near the A12 opened two years ago and is quite special. It is basically a big allotment where they grow most of the vegetables and flowers they sell, plus they buy in free range chickens, bantam eggs, local chutneys, and lots of other things.

red-brick Georgian cottages that line Quay Street to the black-tarred shack that famously serves as a smokery to the imposing tower keep of **Orford Castle,** built in the 1160s and almost perfectly preserved and run by English Heritage.

The panoramic view from the battlemented roof of the castle over the estuary and Orford Ness are sensational, though it can be astonishingly windy up there. The castle was built by Henry II to display his wealth and power as well as to defend against mercenaries from the Continent who came to assist his enemies, the rebel-

Orford Castle

lious barons of inland Suffolk and Norfolk. Sure enough the 10ft-thick walls successfully repelled attack (by his eldest son) in his lifetime. Visitors can explore the multiple spiral staircases in each of the three turrets, and the labyrinth of chambers and passageways, some not recommended for the claustrophobic. Movie buffs may be interested to know that the gruesome finale of the superior British horror movie *The Witchfinder General* made in 1968 starring Vincent Price was filmed in the castle.

ORFORD CASTLE, Orford, IP12 2ND; ☎ 01394 450472; adults £5.60, children £3.40, families £14.60; open daily 10am–5pm Apr to Jun/Sept, 10am–6pm Jul to Aug, 10am–4pm winter but closed Tue/Wed.

Lovely walks and cycle rides start at the Castle and proceed alongside Gedgrave Marshes to the foot ferry across Butley Creek about two miles from Orford. **The Butley Ferry** (c/o Butley Pottery, Mill Lane, Butley IP12

Local legends: the wild man of Orford

Two years after building work began on the castle, fishermen returned one day excited at having netted something bizarre. The creature was naked and bald but with a shaggy beard and much body hair. They turned him over to the castle for safekeeping where the man (some said merman) was fed and periodically beaten for refusing to speak. He was no more obliging when forced to sit through church services. Curious to see him back in the element from which he had emerged, the local people decided to let him swim offshore but first of all erected several

3PA; ☎ 01394 450843) is the smallest licensed ferry in Europe and saves a 6 mile detour (£1.50 per person, £1.50 per bicycle; book in advance except in high summer, (no scheduled timetable) and does not operate in winter.

Orford Ness

A 'ness' is a promontory, cape or headland. In the case of Orford Ness, the promontory does not stick out into the sea but is a 10-mile elongated piece of land running parallel to the coast, comprising silt dumped by the rivers, shingle (rounded pebbles) deposited by the sea, and water marshes which over time have been colonised by plants and migrating birds. A perfect habitat for a nature reserve you might think, which is indeed what it is now. But between 1913 and 1983 this uninhabited place, with limited access from the mainland, was used by the military to develop radar and later as a secret testing site for nuclear weapons. The derelict concrete buildings and the forest of broadcasting aerials remain as an eerie reminder of the ness's secret history. Some years ago the National Trust bought the land from the Ministry of Defence and opened it to the public by running a boat service from Orford allowing people to explore the whole sinister site on foot. The circuit is over 5 miles and involves a short but strenuous stretch of walking on shingle.

Lighthouse on Orford Ness

The other secret work associated with Orford Ness used the code name Cobra Mist and was intended to be a key spying operation during the Cold War. In the late 1960s the Americans were looking for bases in Europe to install sophisticated radar equipment for monitoring aircraft movements as well as Russian and possibly also Chinese missile testing. Construction of a huge steel

barriers of nets. These proved no barrier at all since almost immediately he could be seen repeatedly diving down and bobbing up for air well past the nets. But the call of the open sea was not sufficiently strong to keep him there and he voluntarily returned to land where interest in him flagged. Eventually it is said that he returned to the water and disappeared for good, apart from his spirit which is still said to haunt the castle. The sign above Orford's famous Oysterage depicts a bearded fish-tailed creature holding a fish and a plate of oysters in his hands.

building at the north end of the ness began in 1967, and was completed four years later, at a cost of up to £150 million. But the surveillance was not effective because the engineers could not solve the problem of noise interference. The whole project was a white elephant and closed in 1973. Later the BBC World Service adapted the building as a medium wave transmitter for its English language broadcasting service to Eastern Europe, a function it still fulfils under contract.

ORFORD NESS NATIONAL NATURE RESERVE, Quay Office, Orford IP12 2NU; ☎ 01728 648024/01394 450900; orfordness@nationaltrust.org.uk, www.nationaltrust.org.uk; adults £7.50, children £3.75 (less for National Trust members); open July to Sept: Tues to Sat, plus Sat Apr to June and Oct.

A small ferry *Octavia* leaves from Orford Quay about three times an hour between 10am and 2pm (the distance can be covered in five minutes), and the last return of the day leaves the ness at 5pm.

HAVERGATE ISLAND RSPB RESERVE, bookings ☎ 01728 648281; www.rspb.org.uk/reserves/guide/h/havergate/index.asp; members £12, non-members £15; boats leave Orford Quay at 10am on first Sat of every month, special events on selected weekends.

Havergate Island

Another short hop by boat from Orford Quay will take you to the bird reserve of Havergate Island nestling between Orford Ness and the marshes south of Orford. Boat leaves Orford Quay at 10am (20-minute journey) and returns at 3pm. The most common species seen in spring are the lovely black and white avocet with their turned-up bills, and sandwich or common terns. Even without a keen interest in ornithology, this makes for a good trip because of the views back towards Orford's castle, church and environs.

Felixstowe

Four miles of beachfront and well-maintained seafront gardens at the end of the beach make this resort at the end of the Felixstowe peninsula a surprisingly pleasant destination. Lovely views can be had from near the Cliff Road car park and you can walk all the way from the Martello Tower near the tip of the peninsula to the tiny satellite village of **Felixstowe Ferry** at the mouth of the River Deben. In the other direction, the **Trimley Marshes** wetland reserve (☎ 01473 710032), only 2 miles from the Port of Felixstowe, is a top spot for birds.

Yet Felixstowe struggles to attract enough tourists to keep it vibrant. After a long struggle, the pier is due to be demolished just over 100 years after it was built, and a proposed casino development on the disused Palace Cinema site has been rejected by the council.

Trinity Container Terminal at Felixstowe is the largest container handling facility in the UK. The terminal is so named because much of the land is owned by Trinity College, Cambridge. Due to a canny investment by a college bursar in

The Shingle Street myth

Caught between marshes and the stony windswept shore is the almost non-existent community of Shingle Street. With no pub, no church and only a handful of holiday houses, it has a surprisingly controversial history relating to the Second World War. The population of this fishing hamlet was much larger in 1940 when the Ministry of Home Security gave the inhabitants three days to evacuate and find alternative accommodation inland, but before this took place there were burnt bodies washed ashore. The sudden evacuation was puzzling at the time and has continued to puzzle, especially since the relevant documents were classified for 75 rather than the usual 50 years, leading some to speculate that a top-secret operation had been involved. Rumours continued into the 1990s that the Germans had tried to invade the Suffolk coast but were repelled by a wall of fire from petrol poured on the sea just off Shingle Street or even by a mustard bomb. In fact historians have shown that the one or two bodies that came from the sea belonged to German flyers whose plane had crashed in the North Sea a month earlier. The rumour mill took over, and may have instilled some fear in the Germans that the coast was defended far more vigorously than it in fact was.

After the fall of France in the summer of 1940, the British Government pursued a policy of creating a Defence Area from Essex to The Wash. As a result, the beach at Shingle Street was heavily mined which accounts for the evacuation. Naturally the inhabitants wanted to reclaim their properties as soon as the war ended but the ministry dragged its heels about carrying out promised mine clearances. Furthermore, the houses that had been vacated so hurriedly had been looted (possibly be the sequestering soldiers) and blasted by the weather. Anyone interested in this story should be sure to visit Shingle Street and to read a balanced account of the events in James Hayward's book *The Bodies on the Beach: Sealion, Shingle Street and the Burning Sea Myth of 1940.*

the 1960s, the college continues to be hugely enriched by this investment.

Apart from the excellent sandy beaches, the chief attraction is the **Landguard Fort** and nearby bird observatory. Although the fort does not look too ancient, it has seen a great deal of action over the centuries, most famously in 1667 when 400 English soldiers successfully defended the fort against several thousand Dutch invaders. It is now gently dilapidating, as it was left by the military in the 1970s, but you can still explore its network of tunnels.

LANDGUARD FORT, View Point Road, Felixstowe, IP11 3TX; ☎ 07749 695523; www.languard.com; adults £3.50, children £1; open daily Apr–Oct, Jun–Sept 10am–6pm, Apr, May and Oct 10am–5pm.

Bawdsey

As mentioned, a little ferry (Deben Ferry, Old Felixstowe IP11 9RZ; ☎ 01394 270106/mob 07709 411511) shuttles foot passengers between Felixstowe Ferry and Bawdsey Quay on either side of the Deben river mouth (cyclists £2.60; runs Apr to Oct 10am–6pm). If it isn't in evidence when you arrive, you are instructed to wave a bat at the ferryman. If you miss the last ferry, it is a 40-minute journey by car via Woodbridge, so don't believe maps and sat navs that erroneously indicate a road bridge across the river.

> **BAWDSEY TRANSMITTER BLOCK**, Bawdsey Manor; ☎ 07821 162879; www.bawdseyradargroup.co.uk; adults £3, children free; open on selected Sun, Easter to Sept 12.30–4.30pm (see website).

RAF Bawdsey played a key (and underestimated) role in the defence of Britain during the Second World War. Although radar development began on Orford Ness in 1937 after six months it moved to Bawdsey where four 350ft-high transmitter towers were built; the last one was demolished in 2000. The story is told in the Magic Ear exhibition at the **Transmitter Block**. You can still see bullet holes on the southern side of the building where German fighter planes strafed it during one of their 11 attacks on the station between 1940 and 1943.

Woodbridge

This market town with a population of 7,400 people is instantly likeable. Its prosperous looking shops, pubs and lanes are immaculately kept, and of course its situation beside the lovely River Deben (opposite Sutton Hoo) helps. Restful hours can be passed watching the busy

> **WOODBRIDGE TIDE MILL**, Tide Mill Way, Woodbridge Suffolk IP12 1AP; ☎ 01473 626618; adults £2.50, children £1.50; open daily May to Sept, weekends only Oct; museum open for 2 hours on either side of low tide.

yachts come and go. The streets are lined with Dutch-influenced gabled buildings, some decorated with pargetting (inscribed plaster drawings and patterns). The quayside has just been attractively redeveloped and is a big improvement on the old gasworks that was here. Among the town's features are two working mills, one a six-storey windmill named after the last miller, a Mr Buttrum, and the distinctive white-boarded tidal mill, the only one in the country that has been restored to working order. The ability of the 20ft water wheel to turn depends on the pull of the River Deben, as the tide changes. The dramatic retreat of the water at low tide can be seen at nearby Ramsholt where huge swathes of mudflat are exposed in just over a quarter of an hour. The tide mill was in commercial operation from when it was built in 1793 up until 1957.

> **BUTTRUM'S MILL**, Burkitt Road, Woodbridge IP12 4JJ; ☎ 01473 264755; adults £2.50, children free; open May to Sept, weekend afternoons subject to change, ring before visiting; shop sells flour and bread mixes.

Sutton Hoo

This mass cemetery for the 7th century Anglo-Saxon Kings of East Anglia should spark your imagination. 'Hoo' is a Saxon word meaning the spur of a hill. This important archaeological site slumbered peacefully until 1938 when the landowner could no longer contain her curiosity about the grassy mounds and commissioned further investigations. To everyone's astonishment, the most priceless hoard of Anglo-Saxon objects ever found was discovered buried in the largest mound; it included a huge buried ship containing gold and silver treasure, which scholars now think belonged to King Raedwald, ancestor of King Edmund (venerated in the West Suffolk town of Bury St Edmunds). Like an Eygptian pharaoh, he was buried with things needed for the afterlife, including his weapons, purse with 37 gold coins, a drinking horn, a lyre and a board game. Visitors can wander around the large site with many burial mounds alongside the River Deben, on which the king's ship once sailed. The exhibition hall brings the history of this little-known period of England's pagan past to life, with a life-size reconstruction of part of the ship, some genuine artefacts and many copies of originals now in the British Museum, including the instantly recognisable masked helmet.

Burial mounds, Sutton Hoo

SUTTON HOO, Tranmer House, Sutton Hoo, Near Woodbridge, IP12 3DJ; ☎ 01394 389700; sutton hoo@nationaltrust.org.uk, www.nationaltrust.org.uk; adults £7.20, children £3.75 families £18.20 (if gift-aided); reductions for arriving on foot or bicycle; open 10.30am–5pm daily in high season/school holidays; Mar, Wed to Sun; weekends only (11am–4pm) in low season.

☂ Wet weather

If the weather is discouraging, the best idea is to head for one of the scores of cosy pubs and cafés. In Woodbridge, head for **Browsers Bookshop and Café** on The Thoroughfare (see Café listings below) to browse the shelves, read the paper, make use of their free wifi or just indulge in cake. Nearby at number 33 they have a dedicated children's bookshop.

Of course there are small museums dotted about, including in the upper hall of Orford Castle, with a collection of local finds such as Roman jewellery and coins. The small town museum in Woodbridge is worth a stop as is the intriguing **Suffolk Punch Museum**, which is neither on the theme of seaside puppet shows nor a history of local pugilism, but focuses on the breed of heavy working horse called the Suffolk Punch used in agriculture. All Suffolk Punch horses can be traced back to one stallion called Crisp's Horse born in 1760.

SUFFOLK PUNCH HEAVY HORSE MUSEUM, Shire Hall, Market Hill, Woodbridge IP12 4LU; ☎ 01394 380643; www.suf folkhorsesociety.org.uk; adults £2, children £1.50; open Easter to end Sept: Tues/Thurs/ Sat 2–5pm.

 ## What to do with children ...

Sutton Farm is a great place for children to be entertained while parents shop in the farm shop or relax with a coffee. The farm features a maize maze, gold-panning, pitch-and-putt and the chance to become a pretend fireman, plus free activities for young children such as ride-on pedal tractors and a bouncy castle. They also run guided bug walks and have picturesque way-marked farm tracks leading to Sutton Hoo.

SUTTON FARM, near Melton (Farm office at Fir Tree Farm, Blax-hall, IP12 2DX); ☎ 01728 688984; http://www.sutton-farm.co.uk; from £1 for gold panning to £4.50 for bug hunt (children; adults free); bug hunts on Tues/Wed/Fri at 10.30am and 2pm (up to 10 children).

Opportunities to go crabbing are plentiful, such as from Orford Quay and Bawdsey Quay. Bawdsey has a sheltered sandy beach on the estuary which is safer than the shingle beach facing the sea where a strong current runs close to the shore.

Older children who are into mountain biking should know about some exciting off-road opportunities in Rendlesham Forest. The enter-

RENDLESHAM FOREST CENTRE, Tangham, Rendlesham Forest, near Woodbridge IP12 3NF; 4 miles from Woodbridge just off the B1084 to Orford; ☎ 01842 816031; e.anglia.fdo@forestry.gsi. gov.uk; occasional cycle events for cyclists over 8; helmets compulsory.

prising people at the **forest centre** organise various events in the summer including UFO walks (see box) and guided trail bike rides from Rendlesham to Tunstall Forest.

 ## ... and how to avoid children

Brunch and cocktail cruises on the *Lady Florence* boat accompanied by a commentary on wildlife and history are unlikely to appeal to children. This former Second World War supply boat has had a chequered history but is now a floating restaurant carrying up to 12 passengers upstream and downstream on the sheltered waters of the rivers Ore and Alde including Havergate Island. Options include a two and a half-hour morning

LADY FLORENCE River Cruise Restaurant, Orford Quay; ☎ 07831 698298; www.lady-florence.co.uk, Price for lunch cruise:£10–£15 depending on season plus a meal from the menu; operates year-round; coal fire in winter.

cruise where an American-style brunch is served for £22, an evening cruise with à la carte menu, and a longer lunchtime cruise. The food served is local (e.g. smoked fish is from Orford, and fruit is supplied by High House Farm near Aldeburgh).

Entertainment

Theatre

Like all old-fashioned resorts, Felixstowe has a seaside theatre with the usual exuberant programme of tribute shows, nostalgia programmes of war music and musical comedies (Spa Pavilion Theatre, Undercliff Road West, Sea Front, Felixstowe IP11 2DX; ☎ 01394 282126; www.thespapavilion.org).

RIVERSIDE THEATRE & RESTAURANT, Quayside, Woodbridge, IP12 1BH; box office ☎ 01394 382174; restaurant: ☎ 01394 382587; www.theriverside.co.uk.

Woodbridge supports an unusual restaurant-cum-theatre at the **Riverside**. Up-market *après et avant* theatre meals are served in this Quayside complex. The theatre is mainly used for films but it also puts on a winter pantomime. Imaginative combination tickets are available, for example tapas and a film matinée for £18, pre-pantomime two-course dinner for £15 and a full dinner and evening film for £30. The quality of the Sunday lunches is renowned.

Special events

The famous **Aldeburgh Festival** every June has always used several venues in this part of Suffolk, principally St Bartholomew's Church in Orford which was such a favourite of Benjamin Britten so that he chose to premiere his opera about the Flood *Noye's Fludde* here in 1958 (five years after the devastating floods of 1953 when many homes along Quay Street were flooded more than two feet). The church is still a popular venue during the festival. A much more avant-garde part of the festival is an electronic musical event mounted an atmospheric remote corner of the Bentwater Airbase.

Felixstowe mounts a colourful annual carnival on the second weekend of August (www.felixstowecarnival.org).

Shopping

Woodbridge has many independent and arty shops. The main shopping street is the narrow and bustling thoroughfare which has a chocolate shop and a contemporary art studio among the staple fashion and stationery shops.. You might like to have a peek at the prints and photographs for sale in the brand new Gallery at the **Crown and Castle Hotel**. One of the proprietors, David

Local legends: UFOs in Suffolk

Rendlesham Forest covers a vast area of coastal heathland known as the Sandlings inland of Orford. Its acres of coniferous trees and wetland have almost no habitation and just on its northern edge is the old US Air Force base at Bentwaters. Late on Boxing Day 1980, a local man and a couple of security men patrolling their patch saw a flashing airborne object come down in the forest and assumed it was a crashed plane. They reported there had been so much electricity in the air that their hair had stood on end. They claim to have seen an object floating just above the ground but before they could get near enough to examine it properly, they saw it rise quickly and disappear in a flash of light.

The next day a party of men returned to the spot to find three matching depressions in the ground and trees with broken tops and burn marks. They tested for radiation and the Geiger counter readings showed levels 10 times above the average. The next night a seasonal party for officers at the base was interrupted by a report that further strange things were happening in the forest. They hurried out armed with lights (which malfunctioned) and recording equipment, but nothing was seen except by two patrolmen deep in the forest who saw a light on a pillar of mist and gave chase for more than an hour until again the craft rose and disappeared. Hundreds of base personnel and one local woman reported seeing strange lights that night. Because of the large number and general reliability of witnesses, the sighting was taken very seriously and of course made for exciting tabloid headings. More sane and sober people think that the flashing of the Orford Ness lighthouse might have confused the men. The Rendlesham Forest Centre on the B1084 distributes a leaflet and has signposted a trail to the mysterious spot.

Rendlesham Forest was the real setting for the 2005 Channel 4 reality-comedy programme *Space Cadets* in which contestants were persuaded by means of an elaborate hoax that they were being trained in Russia to become the first space tourists.

Watson, is an Associate of the Royal Photographic Society and takes stunning pictures in both local and foreign locations (www.davidwatson.org.uk).

Shopping in Felixstowe isn't all about the chain multiples. The new gift shop **Glyph** at 70 Hamilton Road (☎ 01394 274134) has a quirky, ever-changing stock of jewellery, cards, pottery and so on that recently earned it a Great Gift Retailer prize.

The best... **PLACES TO STAY**

BOUTIQUE

The Crown & Castle

Orford IP12 2LJ
☎ **01394 450205**
www.crownandcastle.co.uk

The unmistakable stamp of proprietor Ruth Watson's big personality and penetrating intelligence is in evidence everywhere. The Crown & Castle is almost a textbook example of how a hotel should be, except nothing is from a textbook or rule book since nothing is cloned. The standard of cooking and wine is superb, and the service informal yet attentive.

Prices: B&B from £90 for a double or £145 including dinner mid-week in the most basic room; guests must stay at least two nights at weekends.

Chequers B&B

220 High Street, Wickham Market IP13 0RF, ☎ 01728 746284
www.chequerssuffolk.co.uk

Each room has individual décor with luxurious bathrooms and all mod cons such as free internet and flat screen TVs. Huge leather beds are made up with superior cotton sheets and, unusually for a B&B, delectable breakfasts of, for example, Orford smoked salmon are served in the rooms.

Prices: from £85 for two in the Garden Room and £120 in the premier Hayloft Suite.

INN

Ramsholt Arms

Dock Road, Ramsholt, near Woodbridge IP12 3AB, ☎ 01394 411229

In one of the loveliest waterside situations imaginable, this isolated Suffolk-pink pub has two spacious bedrooms affording superb views of yachts under way and coastal birds. The half-mile walk across the marsh to the round-towered All Saints' Church is rewarding. The pub serves seasonal wholesome food, including fish and game.

Prices: From £80 per double.

B&B

Hill House Bed and Breakfast

30 Market Hill, Woodbridge IP12 4L
☎ **01394 383890**
www.hillhousewoodbridge.com

This ancient house with an attractive Georgian facade is known architecturally as a 'wealden hall', a timber-framed building with an open hall which in this case has Tudor wall paintings. Overlooking the broad piazza-like market place, the house has a cosy ambience with wood-burning stoves.

Prices: from £55 for a single, £70 for a double, £75 for a twin and £120 for a family suite.

CAMPSITE

Orchard Camping

Spring Lane, Wickham Market IP13 0SJ
☎ **01728 746170**

The friendly owners run a very attractive site with large pitches set among trees and meadows, still in walking distance from the town with its decent pubs. Most campers prefer to stay round their campfire (wood is sold by the wheelbarrowfull). Occasional 'Alien Encounter Weekends' are organised since the location of the UFO sighting of 1980 isn't far away (see panel).

Prices: £16 per pitch all-inclusive.

SELF-CATERING

The Old Granary Cottage

Tide Mill Way, Woodbridge IP12 1BY
☎ **01394 383793**
www.theoldgranarycottage.co.uk

The big windows of this converted quayside cottage provide plenty of light and give wonderful views over the marina. Two double rooms and an open-plan living area comfortably accommodate four on three levels.

Prices: from £695 for a week; B&B available in the same property at £90 per night.

The best... FOOD AND DRINK

Staying in

On a busy weekend in the luscious village of Orford, it seems that every other car parked along the verges of Quay Road has come for the seafood. The **Butley Orford Oysterage** (Market Hill, Orford, IP12 2LH; ☎ 01394 450277; www.butleyorfordoysterage.co.uk) with its deli counter just next to its unpretentious dining area (see below) incites a fish frenzy in most seafood lovers. In addition to oysters, smoked fish of all kinds is the speciality. It all comes from the Pinney family's own smokery situated next to their oyster beds on Butley Creek (confusingly, not from their back yard where there is an unrelated and also excellent smoking house called Richardson's). The oysterage makes its own taramasalata from cod roe and pickles its own herrings to make roll mops, plus you can buy smoked trout, various kinds of salmon, fish pâtés, etc. **Richardson's Smokehouse** uses a slow-smoking technique over oak to prepare smoked ham, pheasant, garlic, Stilton and other foods.

> **RICHARDSON'S SMOKE-HOUSE**, Baker's Lane, Orford, IP12 2LH; ☎ 01394 450103; www.richardsonssmokehouse.co.uk; open daily 9.30am–5pm.

Not surprisingly Orford also has a superb butcher, (which doubles as the post office) and a good greengrocers, **Orford Supply Stores** on Pump Lane. Down on the quay in Orford you can buy fresh fish from decaying tarred huts.

Woodbridge is also favoured with marvellous food shops such as **Les Chocolats Belges** (45 The Thoroughfare). The **Woodbridge Fine Food Company** (2a New Street ☎ 01394 610333) has been called the Harrods of Woodbridge. It prides itself on stocking unusual items, though the prized food of the region (lobsters, blueberries, etc.) are all on offer, as well as pies baked daily on the premises. The acclaimed deli, **Loaves & Fishes** (52 The Thoroughfare) has recently been bought by the Framlingham deli Carley & Webb, so the quality of fish in season and range of wonderful olives, cheese and vegetarian food is unlikely to drop. Among many local products, it sells organic fruit and vegetable juices from James White in Ashbocking. Look out everywhere for the Stokes range of real sauces including tomato ketchup and brown sauce, made by Ess Foods in Rendlesham (it isn't known if the 'S' is for the founder Rick Sheepshanks or for Suffolk).

Because of the agricultural richness of this region, farm shops abound and there are two farmers' markets, every other Saturday in Woodbridge, and in Felixstowe on the first Saturday morning of the month, where you can be sure

Felixstowe Beach

of finding a stall selling Suffolk Red Poll beef and another stocking delicious Suffolk Meadow ice cream from Rendham. To illustrate the vitality of the local food movement in these parts, all the food grown at **High House Farm,** 2 miles north of Orford, is sold within a 12-mile radius of the farm (apart from apples).

The **Grange Farm Shop** in Hasketon (just west of the A12 from Woodbridge) carries Italian sausages, organic beers and seasonal plums and blackcurrants (☎ 01473 735510). Prize-winning bacon and smoked meats can be bought from the **Five Winds Farm Smokehouse & Butchery** next to the railway station in Melton just outside Woodbridge (☎ 01394 386116). **Garnett's Garden Nursery and Farmshop** in Hacheson (north of Wickham Market; ☎ 01728 724589) is certified organic and offers PYO raspberries among many treats.

🍷 Drinking

Although Suffolk is a flourishing brewing county, most beer-and-cider-makers are located elsewhere, so the majority of pubs serve Adnams or Green King beers. Assuming you can resist the seductive menus posted by many of the classic pubs in this neighbourhood, it is perfectly feasible to enjoy a simple drink, whether sitting outside at **The Ferry Boat Inn** at Felixstowe Ferry or next to a roaring fire at **The Maybush** in Waldringfield gazing out at the flotilla of yachts on the River Deben. In the off-season, friendly landlords will tell you tales of how their hostelries were used by smugglers, as at **The Jolly Sailor** in Orford (where the landlords of 41 years have just retired). One of the most charming pubs in Suffolk is **The Oyster Inn** in out-of-the-way Butley. If you are tired of tasteful contemporary décor, head for **The Wilford Bridge** in Melton at the head of navigation on the Deben, where the distinctly unflash interior means that the braying classes are usually not tempted to come for the well-priced beer and good fresh food.

EATING OUT

FINE DINING
The Captain's Table
3 Quay Street, Woodbridge IP12 1BX
☎ **01394 383145**
www.captainstable.co.uk

Considered the best restaurant in a town full of good ones, this pricey restaurant delivers excellent quality, from the bowl of toasted almonds to munch while you wait (£3.50) to one of the house specialities, a starter of twice-baked goat's cheese soufflé (£6.50). Everything is homemade including the sorbets (£2.95).

RESTAURANT
Butley Orford Oysterage
Market Hill, Orford IP12 2LH
☎ **01394 450277**
www.butleyorfordoysterage.co.uk

This always busy dining room, small and unpretentious with formica tables, serves some of the best fish platters you will find anywhere. The massive oysters are less salty than elsewhere since they grow in the estuary not the sea. Alongside the mixed selections of smoked fish, blackboard specials might feature griddled squid (£7) or salmon fillet with oyster sauce (£9).

GASTROPUB
Froize Inn
The Street, Chillesford, Near Woodbridge IP12 3PU (4 miles from Orford on road to Woodbridge). ☎ **01394 450282**
www.froize.co.uk

In a region full of gastropubs, this chef-run pub stands out. Not only is the food of the highest standard, but the prices aren't too astronomical. The two-course buffet lunch with an impressive choice of hearty dishes is especially good value. The friendly service contributes to this pub's popularity so it is wise to book ahead. It is open for lunch daily except Mondays and for dinner on Thursday, Friday and Saturday only.

King's Head Inn
Front Street, Orford IP12 2LW
☎ **01394 450271**
www.thekingsheadorford.co.uk

This sister eatery to the famed Crown & Castle is under the same management but has a completely different vibe. It remains an honest pub for locals as well as visitors, serving a plain but impeccably prepared menu, such as prawn cocktail with granary bread (£6) and steak and ale shortcrust pie (£10).

CAFÉ
Waterfront Café
Woodbridge, The Granary, Tide Mill Way, Woodbridge IP12 1BY. ☎ **01394 610333**
www.thewaterfrontcafe.co.uk

Top-quality food is served in a four-star location next to the Tide Mill. This upmarket café serves organic food, from crab sandwiches up to venison dinners, accompanied by fine wines. Since it is run by the same pair who run the Woodbridge Fine Foods Company, there is no doubt about the provenance of the ingredients. Although it calls itself a café, tables should be booked in advance and wallets should be checked. Orders placed between noon and 3pm must be for at least £6.

Oaks Tearoom
1 Crescent Rd, Felixstowe IP11 7BY
☎ **01394 273444**

Proving that good places can exist in unlikely places, this café takes pride in its carefully prepared snacks and dishes. A chocolate is served with a chocolate milkshake. Traditional sardines on toast are tasty, but the afters are really worth visiting for, including knickerbocker glories and Eton Mess (meringue with red fruit and cream).

Wild Strawberry Café
Woodbridge, 19A Market Hill, Woodbridge IP12 4LX
☎ **01394 388881**

Delicious and original lunches that change constantly are served in this central location. The irresistible cakes are all made at the café, which has a good atmosphere and free wifi.

Visitor information

Tourist Information Centres:
Woodbridge Tourist Information
Centre, Railway Station, Station
Road, Woodbridge IP12 4AJ,
☎ 01394 382240, wtic@suffolk
coastal.gov.uk, open daily in the
summer, from Easter to Oct, Mon to
Sat; Felixstowe Tourist Information
Centre, 91 Undercliff Road West,
Felixstowe IP11 2AF, ☎ 01394
276770; ftic@suffolkcoastal.gov.uk,
open daily 9am–5.30pm (closed on
Sun – Oct to Mar).
Hospitals: The nearest A&E depart-
ment is at Ipswich Hospital, Heath
Road, Ipswich, Suffolk IP4 5PD.
Websites: http://woodbridgesuf
folk.info; www.visit-woodbridge.
co.uk; www.visit-orford.co.uk.
Supermarkets: Tesco, Anson Road,
Martlesham Heath, Ipswich IP5 3RU,
☎ 0845 6779456; Morrisons,

Grange Farm Avenue, Felixstowe
IP11 2XD, ☎ 01394 671333; Solar
Supermarket (Coop), Hamilton
Road, Felixstowe IP11 7DT,
☎ 01394 272331.
Bike rental: Friend's Garage, Front
Street, Orford IP12 2LP, ☎ 01394
450239; Avocet Sports, ☎ 07706
479965, stevenedwards69@btinternet.
com/www.eastcoastmountainbik
ing.co.uk, pre-booked bicycles can
be collected at Snape or Rendlesham Forest Centre; £12 a day, £50
a week; Alford Bros,119 Hamilton
Road, Felixstowe IP11 7BL, ☎ 01394
284719.
Taxis: Atlas Cars, Melton/Wood-
bridge, ☎ 0800 074 7094; Coastal
Taxis, Felixstowe, ☎ 01394 277777;
1st for Taxis, Felixstowe,
☎ 01394 270078.

The River Waveney

LOWESTOFT AND THE SUFFOLK BROADS

Like a statue in New York harbour dedicated to something other than liberty, the Suffolk Broads have an uphill struggle to achieve any recognition. Even the tourist literature uses the tag 'forgotten broad near the sea'. The Norfolk Broads are a household name but outside the Waveney Valley the Suffolk Broads are nearly unknown – which of course is a large part of their appeal. After visiting them, Virginia Woolf concluded that it was a kind of lotus land: 'It seems to lull asleep all ambition. Don't you think they have discovered the secret of life? I thought it wonderfully harmonious.'

The Waveney River cuts a meandering course through once-flooded water meadows and marshlands, that might flood again one day if sea levels rise. Like most of the rivers that drain East Anglia, the Waveney used to be navigable much further inland than it is now. Ten miles inland from Lowestoft, Beccles was once a significant port, trading in herring, wool and agriculture. Now the traffic is purely for pleasure, and the river can be pleasantly bustling in summer, without being a madhouse as on some of the most popular Norfolk Broads.

This region of northeast Suffolk is notable for having three delightful market towns: Beccles is the largest with a population of nearly 10,000, while Bungay a few miles upriver and Halesworth 10 miles inland have half as many. Yet they provide a range of shops, restaurants, arts events and an ambience far in excess of what might be expected in such small places.

Lowestoft is a different kettle of fish. As an important fishing port since the Middle Ages, it is still the place from which fish vans scatter to many inland cities and towns on market days. Because of EU fishery policies and market changes, the commercial fishing fleet is a shadow of its former self. Yet the seafront remains a vibrant place where early in the morning you can still see small fishing smacks and anglers' charter boats making ready to set out to sea.

WHAT TO SEE AND DO

 ## Fair weather

Boat trips

From Beccles or Oulton Broad, you can hire a boat to potter on the gentle **River Waveney**. Some families prefer DIY exploration and will hire a Canadian canoe for the day (from £25) or a motor cruiser (£100–140). Others are content to have someone else navigate them and simply take a short cruise, for example on the Edwardian-style *Liana* from Beccles Quay. This is hardly a white-knuckle ride – the speed limit on broads rivers of 3–6mph is to minimise bank erosion and disturbance to nesting birds – but the commentary by a Broads Authority Park Ranger conveys some of the area's interesting history (fishermen, thatchers, smugglers) and natural history. Because the floodplains on either side are too wet for any development, the views of grazing marshes and reedbeds are completely unspoiled. It's an hour and a quarter trip upriver to Geldeston or downriver to Worlingham Staithe, depending on the tides.

- *Liana Boat Trips* The Quay, Beccles, NR34 9BH (☎ 01502 713196; www.broads-authority.gov.uk/broads/live/visiting/activities/boat-trips-1.html); price: adults £4.50, children £3.50, families £11; June to Sept daily at 11am/2.15pm/3.45pm; Apr/May/Oct same times Sat/Sun only.
- **Waveney River Tours** Mutford Lock, Oulton Broad NR33 9JU (☎ 01502 574903; http://mysite.wanadoo-members.co.uk/waveney_rivertours); price: adults £4–8.50 depending on length of trip; daily Apr to Oct.

The **Waveney River Centre** half-way between Beccles and Lowestoft is located on a sleepy loop of the river where all sorts of boating activity takes place. It will take an hour and a half to reach Beccles, less than an hour to Somerleyton and about 20 minutes to Oulton Broad, a popular destination – on some days too popular – for sailors, windsurfers and powerboat racers (see '*Special* *events'*). On the edge of Bungay, **Outney Meadow Caravan Park** also hires out canoes and written directions for the three-hour 'Bungay Loop'.

- **Waveney River Centre** Staithe Road, Burgh St Peter, near Beccles NR34 0BT (☎ 01502 677343; www.waveneyrivercentre.co.uk). Canoes, row-boats and day cruisers for hire.
- **Oulton Broad Day Boats** 1–4 The Quays, The Boulevard, Lowestoft NR33 9JS (☎ 01502 513087).
- **Outney Meadow Caravan Park** Bungay NR35 1HG (☎ 01986 892338; www.outneymeadow.co.uk). £20 for half a day, £30 for full day 9am–6pm.

Lowestoft

With the decline in fishing and related seagoing activities over the past decades, much investment has gone into preventing Lowestoft from sliding into decrepitude, including land-scaped gardens, improvements to the promenade and a new fountain artily lit at night. The new yacht-filled marina has a Heritage Vessel Mooring where you might see a traditional sailing trawler or a Lowestoft sidewinder fishing trawler like the *Mincarlo*.

Lowestoft Pier from South Beach

Energetic beach maintenance has won not just one, but two Blue Flag awards for Lowestoft's beaches, a rare accolade. The fine sandy **South Beach** offers lifeguard coverage all day in June, July and August and is lined with brightly coloured beach huts that can be hired by the day or week via the tourist information centre (☎ 01502 533600) for very reasonable rates: from £10 a day in summer, £5 otherwise. The Euroscope at Britain's most easterly point, Lowestoft Ness, indicates the distance to various scattered points, demonstrating that you are only 120 miles closer to Land's End than to John O'Groats.

Any fans of the now defunct glam rock band The Darkness might like to make a pilgrimage to **Kirkley Community High School** on the south side of town, the school attended by three of the four local heroes who founded the band, and also the setting for Channel 4's *Rock School* where Kiss' Gene Simmons launched the musical career of pint-sized Lowestoftian Lil' Chris.

Somerleyton

Just a short walk from Somerleyton railway station, **Somerleyton Hall and Gardens** reflect the glory of the man who brought the railway to Lowestoft, just a short drive away. The wealthy Victorian entrepreneur and philanthropist, Sir Moreton Peto, had this country house recast according to his own extravagant tastes (and the tastes of his age) for Neo-Italian architecture and lavish décor. The highlight is the walled garden, adorned with a pergola draped with wisteria and roses, a pond, greenhouses and best of all a yew maze planted in1846. The hall is owned by the descendants of Morton Peto's friend Sir Francis Crossley, to whom he sold it in 1866, and is now a hotel with a conference centre, gastropub (see *Eating Out*) and tea room.

> **SOMERLEYTON HALL**, Near Lowestoft NR32 5QQ; ☎ 01502 734901; www.somerleyton.co.uk; adults £8.95, children £4.95, garden only £5.50/£3.50; garden open 10am–5pm, tours of the hall 11.30am–3.30pm (last tour), Apr to Oct Thu/Sun plus Tue/Wed in July/Aug.

Beccles

At the time that Horatio Nelson's parents were married in Beccles (1749), boats could tie up to the wall behind **St Michael's Church**. The river is now a long way down the escarpment. When the belfry tower was due to be added to the church in the early 16th century, the ground to the east was too soggy, so they built a grand tower nearly 100ft high quite separate from the church to the west, a landmark that can be seen from far and wide. The view is bound to be magnificent from the top but unfortunately the tower is locked to the public except on special occasions such as the Beccles Festival. Beccles has always been a centre for clockmakers who proudly installed clocks on the north, south and east faces of the tower, but not the west. It is said that this was because after the great fire of 1540, the north folk on the other side of the Waveney would not donate anything to Beccles in its hour of need, so the town elected not to give the people of Norfolk 'the time of day'. Another interesting feature is the blocked-up doorway part way up the tower that served as an outdoor pulpit for preaching to lepers.

Beccles town centre

A walk around the town will reveal many fine buildings, some with a Dutch influence but more with elegant Georgian façades. The spacious and gracious **New Market** leads to Ballygate which is lined with historic buildings, the best of which is the old school, now the town museum. The Quay is a second hub of activity in Beccles, about a kilometre from the church, where you should head for the tourist office, for boat trips and a choice of riverside walks where you can spot wetland birds and wild plants.

Bungay

Another sleepy market town straddling the Waveney is Bungay. The ruined Norman castle is contemporary with Framlingham Castle and has an interpretive centre for visitors. Old inns such as **The Fleece** and **The Butter Cross** enliven a visit. The domed Butter Cross, built in 1689 the year after a fire destroyed the town, is surrounded by stalls on Thursdays, market day.

The East Anglian demon dog, Black Shuck, visited Bungay one stormy day in 1577, the same day he visited Blythburgh (see p.212 and 350). While people prayed in the church for mercy from the vicious storm, the belfry tower and clock were shattered, and the deranged hell hound bit and clawed members of the congregation. In fact the official records show that two men died in the belfry, so the black dog may have been the people's version of a lightning strike. So ingrained is the story into the local psyche that the black dog has given its name to the local football side and appears on the town's coat of arms.

Halesworth

Completing the trio of eminently liveable market towns in this area is Halesworth, 9 miles south of Bungay via a straight Roman road, or a couple of hours by bicycle using the lovely winding lanes, or 15 minutes on the occasional trains that run along the East Suffolk line. Whereas Beccles is on a hill, Halesworth is secreted away in the Blyth Valley. The clear spring waters that drain into the Blyth were an essential ingredient in malting and brewing which were the mainstays of the town three centuries ago.

This is yet another town that has resisted the cold dead hand of the supermarket (it's in the Cranbrook Triangle, the region bordering the A12 between Ipswich and Lowestoft that is free of all major supermarkets) and retains quirky little shops along its delightful curving street, **The Thoroughfare.** Historic shop fronts are unspoiled by modern fixtures but marked with interesting historical plaques, and benches and hanging baskets create a pleasant ambience on this pedestrianised street.

The volunteer-run museum is in the railway station where moveable platforms were installed in 1888 and restored (for looks only, not for use) a few years ago. Halesworth is surrounded by marvellous countryside dotted with village bed and breakfasts and farm cottages for self-caterers; visit www.halesworth. ws/where-tostay/index.php for useful maps and links. The cycling in this area is unrivalled in East Anglia. You can follow the National Cycling Route 1 marked with red signs south from Beccles to Halesworth and beyond or carve out your own route along barely used minor roads, using Ordnance Survey map sheet 156.

Wet weather

Transport seems to be a popular theme among the museums of Lowestoft and the Broads – with land, sea and air represented, possibly because they are stuck out on their own, en route to nowhere (except by sea). In fact it was at Somerleyton that the engineer Christopher Cockerell invented the hovercraft in the 1950s, using the expertise of cabin cruiser operators on the Broads.

Recent modernisation of the seafront as a boost to tourism saddens some old-timers who remember Lowestoft when it was a vibrant commercial fishing port. This part of its heritage is celebrated in the excellent **Lowestoft and East Suffolk Maritime Museum** located under the lighthouse in Sparrow's Nest Park, where some of the attendants are ex-seamen who know the history of the fishing fleet backwards, from early sail, through steam and diesel. A Heritage lottery grant has allowed the museum to double in size for 2008.

MARITIME MUSEUM, Whapload Road, Lowestoft, NR32 1XG; ☎ 01502 561963; adults £2, children £0.50; open May to Oct 10am–5pm.

A typically English nostalgia for old transport is celebrated in the **Transport Museum** in Carlton Colville. Not only have local enthusiasts rescued derelict old trams, trolleybuses, etc. (initially an old Lowestoft tram was found in use as a garden house), but they have restored them to working order so that visitors can ride along a street kitted out as it would have been in the early 20th century.

EAST ANGLIA TRANSPORT MUSEUM, Chapel Road, Carlton Colville, Near Lowestoft NR33 8BL; ☎ 01502 518459; Adults £7, children £5; open varying times from Apr to Sept.

Twenty miles inland, aviation is celebrated at the **Norfolk & Suffolk Aviation Museum** in Flixton (www.aviationmuseum.net) which is especially strong on Second World War aircraft (admission is free).

Bungay's Chicken Roundabout

Unlikely as it may seem, a major roundabout on a busy A road outside Bungay on the way to Great Yarmouth is populated by a flock of feral chickens. They have been there for up to five decades, living in the trees and undergrowth and are a much-loved fixture of the locals. They seem to have adapted to their environment and very few defy death to cross the road to get to the other side. However the colony has been embattled for several years. Mutterings from the council rumble on complaining that they present a hazard to drivers who may be so distracted by the bizarre sight that they will fail to negotiate the traffic safely. Then it seemed there had been hen rustlers around because suddenly there were scores of cocks and only one hen. The most serious threat has come from bird flu. The roundabout isn't far from the Bernard Matthews turkey farm where the H5N1 strain of the avian flu virus was confirmed in February 2007. To avoid instant culling, the birds were quickly deemed to be 'wild' so were not subject to the regulation that flocks of poultry had to be housed indoors.

Steamed-up locals, including an elderly man who regularly fed them, raised a petition to save the chickens, claiming that this was the most famous visitor attraction. The roundabout's finest hour came in 2005 when a local musician, Andy Barber, composed an ode entitled 'The Bungay Chicken Protest Song' and was interviewed on Radio 4's programme *Home Truths*. The song had been written for a protest meeting held on the roundabout and subsequently sold as a CD at the Ditchingham Post Office and Green Dragon Pub in Bungay.

The flock is still in danger of eradication. Visitors who want to investigate should head for Ditchingham, and the roundabout on the A143. Even if the chickens don't survive, the name Chicken Roundabout certainly will, since it has entered the language of Bungayites.

What to do with children

All kids love mazes, so don't miss the challenging one at Somerleyton. But the star attractions for children in the region are **Africa Alive** at Kessingland and **Pleasurewood Hills**, East Anglia's largest theme park. Africa Alive is a large wildlife attraction set amidst pleasant woodlands allowing children to encounter giraffes, lions, rhinos, monkeys, flamingoes, etc. Kessingland, south of Lowestoft, has lovely unspoiled sand and shingle beaches.

AFRICA ALIVE, White's Lane, Kessingland NR33 7SL; ☎ 01502 740291; www.africa-alive.co.uk Entry: high/low season: adults £14.95/£10.95, children over 3 £10.95/£7.95; open daily all year except Christmas day and Boxing Day from 9.30am.

Pleasurewood Hills just north of Lowestoft has the usual range of death-defying rides, with the Wipeout recently added to several other roller-coasters, plus a log flume and a selection of gentler rides for younger children.

Look for fossils at **Pakefield Beach** (Pakefield is a suburb south of Lowestoft) where Jurassic fossils are often revealed after rain or high tides. The beach is reached by steep steps down the cliff but keep your eye on the tide. Just inland in an industrial unit, **Adventure Island Play Park** on Pinbush Road features climbing frames, slides and ball-pools (www.adventureislandplay park.co.uk).

Out in the middle of nowhere between Beccles and Halesworth is a charming attraction for young children. The **Moo Play Farm** has soft play for toddlers, climbing equipment and slides for children up to 12, and farm animals that don't mind being petted and groomed.

PLEASUREWOOD HILLS THEME PARK, Leisure Way, Corton, Near Lowestoft NR32 5DZ ; www.pleasurewoodhills.com; adults £15.50, children 3–11 £13.50; open daily July/Aug, weekends and half terms mid-March to June and Sept/Oct.

MOO PLAY FARM, Low Farm, Locks Road, Brampton NR34 8DX; ☎ 01502 575841; www.mooplayfarm.co.uk; adults £1, children £3.75 (more in half-term); open daily.

 ## Entertainment

Theatre

The Cut in Halesworth is a flourishing arts centre (www.newcut.org) created out of an abandoned maltings building, that is very impressive for a town with a population of less than 6,000. It draws audiences from a wide hinterland who come to the exhibitions, plays and concerts that it puts on. Radio 4 came in 2008 to record some lovely readings of specially commissioned short stories called 'Portraits of East Anglia'.

One of the candidates for the BBC's *Restoration* series was the small Georgian theatre in the centre of Bungay. A group of volunteers rescued it from dereliction (it hadn't been used as a theatre since 1844) and have opened it as the **Fisher Theatre** for small theatre and music events and with a wine bar (www.fishertheatre.org).

Special events

The oldest powerboat racing circuit in the country is on Oulton Broad. Races are on Thursday evenings from April, attracting large crowds of spectators to the waterfront at Nicholas Everitt Park. Since speeds reach 70mph, the tight turns make it exciting to watch and some drivers do capsize, which can be

Pakefield Beach

dangerous. Fixtures are posted by the Lowestoft and Oulton Broad Motor Boat Club site (www.lobmbc.co.uk); spectators pay a fee in July and August.

The lively market towns of Beccles, Bungay and Halesworth all have special events, such as the **Beccles Music Festival** in the third week of September (www.becclesfestival.co.uk), the **Bungay Festival** set in the ruined castle in July or the punning **Halesworth Thoroughfair** at the end of June, when food, drink and craft stalls are set up along The Thoroughfare.

Shopping

Niche shops fill the centres of Halesworth, Bungay and Beccles, and all three towns are especially lively on market day (Wed/Thurs/Fri, respectively). Shops worth browsing in Beccles include **The Marmalade Tree** (handmade wooden furniture) and **Coriander** (imported Asian handicrafts). Further afield, the **Henstead Arts Centre** in Toad Row (www.hensteadartsandcrafts.co.uk), inland from Kessingland, has filled a converted farm with studios for local craftspeople and artists, who welcome callers.

The second-hand bookshop in Halesworth (20 The Thoroughfare IP19 8AH; ☎ 01986 874447) is a treasure trove with many local-interest titles. The proprietor, James Hayward, has written a lexicon of gypsy language after developing an interest as a young boy from his Romany grandmother.

The best... PLACES TO STAY

HOTEL

Ivy House Country Hotel

Ivy Lane, Oulton Broad, Lowestoft NR33 8HY. ☎ 01502 501353
www.ivyhousecountryhotel.co.uk

Occupying a converted farmhouse on Oulton Broad, this hotel has a first-rate restaurant. The Crooked Barn restaurant is named for the 18th-century thatched building in which it is housed and aims to serve mainly locally sourced food. The hotel's summerhouse overlooks a lily pond and the hotel has direct access to Oulton Broad walking path through a gate in the rear fence.

Price: £89.95 for a double or twin in courtyard or farmhouse rooms; pets £15.

ORGANIC

The Old Hall & Cow Shed

2 Old Hall, Barsham NR34 8HB (2 miles west of Beccles)
☎ 01502 714661
www.bikeways.org.uk

This 3-acre organic smallholding in the Waveney marshes offers a variety of reasonably priced accommodation, including informal B&B, camping or self-catering. The Cow Shed has a wood-burning stove and two bedrooms with two sets of bunk beds. Seasonal produce and home-baked sourdough bread are normally available, and dinner may be requested at £5. The owners are enthusiastic cyclists and can advise on routes, etc.

Price: £100 for a night for Cow Shed that sleeps eight; £310 for a week; B&B £20 per person; tents cost £1 per person, £5 per car.

B&B

Duke House B&B

Beccles Road, Upper Holton, Halesworth IP19 8NN ☎ 01986 873259
www.halesworth.ws/dukehouse

Just east of Halesworth in the Blyth Valley, this one-time coaching inn is set back from a quiet road. The welcoming owners not only serve a good local breakfast in the conservatory overlooking the garden but also offer a babysitting and petsitting service on request.

Price: from £30 per person per night; £10 supplement for one-night weekend bookings in high season; pets £5; dinner by arrangement.

The Sandcastle

35 Marine Parade, Lowestoft NR33 0QN
☎ 01502 511799
www.thesandcastle.co.uk

This seafront B&B has an excellent position on Marine Parade between the attractive tourist office and Claremont Pier. The hearty Aga-cooked breakfasts comprise food from local markets rather than supermarkets.

Price: from £40 for a single; £64 for a double, children 10–15 £12, under 10 £6.

SELF-CATERING

Waveney River Centre

Staith Road, Burgh St Peter, near Beccles NR34 0BT. ☎ 01502 677343
www.waveneyrivercentre.co.uk

This riverside activity centre offers visitors a choice of three cottages (sleeping 4–8) and an apartment (up to 6). Guests are invited to make use of many leisure facilities from pool room to Canadian canoes.

Price: from £115 for a week; £75 for a short break; tent pitches and serviced campsites also available from £8 to £18.

FARM

Rumburgh Farm

Rumburgh, near Halesworth IP19 0RU
☎ 01986 781351
www.rumburghfarm.co.uk

This farm is famed for its free-range Bronze and Norfolk black turkeys, singled out by Rick Stein on his Food Heroes tour of the country. Top-notch breakfasts are served in the Old Dairy using eggs from the farm and local bacon and sausages (but no turkeys).

Price: £25–30 per person in a twin or double; self-catering lodges for four are also available overlooking a trout lake (£270–£515 a week).

The best... FOOD AND DRINK

Staying in

From the fishmongers of Lowestoft to the delis of Bungay, this is no desert for good-quality food. Lowestoft's family-run **World of Fish** (6 Cooke Road, South Lowestoft Industrial Estate, Lowestoft NR33 7NA; ☎ 01502 517171) is open to individual members of the public who come to ogle the huge range of wet fish and shell fish. Next door is a traditional smokehouse so smoked fish is also available.

One of the best delis in the region is **Baileys of Beccles** at 2 Hungate which has the rare distinction of specialising in Spanish cheeses, hams and wines since the proprietor is Spanish. The shop also carries a good stock of international cheese, Italian pasta and sauces and homemade pastries.

John Groom in Bungay is more than a first-class butcher. The shop in Wingfield Street also sells cheeses, fresh fruit and speciality beers. A few streets away the **Little Green Wholefood Shop** in Earsham Street is an outlet for local farms and carries some of the most famous food products from East Anglia from Metfield Bakery cakes to Booja Booja chocolates.

Farmers' markets take place at Beccles Heliport twice a month (first and third Saturdays) and in Bungay in the Earsham Hall Courtyard on the alternate Saturdays. For some of the most satisfying old-fashioned food shopping, the weekly country markets (formerly the Women's Institute markets) should not be missed. Home-made cakes and chutneys, and home-grown fruit and vegetables are sold between 9.30am and 11am at the Quaker Hall in Beccles on Friday mornings and the Honeypot Centre in Bungay on Thursdays.

Drinking

This northeast corner of Suffolk has a long tradition of brewing and malting, so it makes sense that there are some good microbreweries making beer to supplement the ubiquitous Adnams. For example the **Green Jack Brewing Company** based at the **Triangle Tavern** in Lowestoft uses local malted wheat but adds exotic hops that create hints of citrus in their prize-winning Orange Wheat. The brewster here likes to make unusual Belgian fruit beers from time to time; his very strong barley wine called Ripper (8.5%) was voted one of three Champion Beers of Britain in 2007. The Triangle Tavern also serves real ciders including the excellent Banham ciders from Norfolk. The Green Jack brewery split off from the **Oulton Brewery** a few years ago and is located a short walk from Oulton Broad North railway station.

EATING OUT

FINE DINING

Swan House Wine Bar & Restaurant
**by the Clock Tower, New Market, Beccles
NR34 9HE**
☎ **01502 713474**
www.swan-house.com

This quirky restaurant in a mainstream position is run by partners, one of whom is an escapee from the London art world; the other is besotted with south-east Asia (and runs the shop Coriander mentioned above). The cooking is more influenced by Italy than Asia, but is mainly contemporary English and very good. A one-course lunch for £8 might consist of a steak and stilton pudding or Italian meat balls with linguine.

GASTROPUB

The Castle Inn
36 Earsham Street, Bungay NR35 1AF
☎ **01986 892283**
www.thecastleinn.net

This Bungay pub has just re-opened with a new Londonish gastro-look and with an enticing menu at reasonable prices. For example char-grilled artichoke heart and root vegetable pastry parcels with Suffolk Gold cheese served on mash costs £8.50, and Coddenham rabbit stew with butternut squash £10.50. The portions are generous. An attractive courtyard is available for al fresco dining in summer.

The Duke's Head
Slugs Lane, Somerleyton NR32 5QR
☎ **01502 730281**
www.dukesheadsomerleyton.co.uk

This stone building on the Somerleyton Estate offers country views from the outdoor tables and good walks down to the River Waveney. The menu changes monthly and depends to a large extent on fresh food from the locality, as well as local Oulton ales.

CAFÉS

Earsham Street Café
11–13 Earsham Street, Bungay NR35 1AE
☎ **01986 893103**

This marvellous, friendly café serving excellent food is especially welcoming to children. The menu will suit all pockets with sandwiches for about £3.50 to a full-on meal such as parmesan and pea risotto, and calf's liver with bubble and squeak. In the summer they open a lovely courtyard.

Flying Fifteens
19a The Esplanade, Lowestoft NR33 0QG
☎ **01502 581188**

Famed for its huge array of teas (33 at last count) and for its garden overlooking the beach, this popular tearoom on the Seafront regularly wins the Tea Guild's Award of Excellence. The name comes from a 1940s design of sailing boat, 15ft long. Locally smoked salmon, Cromer crab and lots of cakes are on the menu.

Bateman's Barn Café
South Elmham Hall, St Cross South Elmham, Near Harleston IP20 0PZ
☎ **01986 782526**
www.batemansbarn.co.uk

Part of medieval South Elmham Hall (which can be toured on selected days), the historic architecture continues into the flint barn where good quality coffee, cakes and light lunches are served on Thursdays, Fridays and Sundays in the summer months, Sundays only otherwise. Excellent walking tracks fan out from this remote spot in 'The Saints'.

Another brew-pub worth seeking out is the **Green Dragon** on Broad Street in Bungay, where the beers they brew make the ideal accompaniment for Wednesday night curry(early arrival advised to get a seat). Fortunately they have dropped a couple of their strongest ales which were called Alzheimers and Slackbladder

The amazing gem of a discovery for beer lovers is **St Peter's Brewery** – an ancient hall that resembles a moated stately home at the end of a long drive off an obscure country road in 'The Saints' (see Further afield). An attractive collection of outbuildings houses the brewing equipment that produces an amazing range of beers, all chalked up on a blackboard. The cosy historic surroundings and intriguing choice of beers, like zesty grapefruit beer or dark and potent Winter Ale, make you wish that you didn't have to drive on. Tastings and an informative talk are given in the visitors' centre, and the shop carries the full range of beers bottled in the brewery's distinctive green bottles.

> **ST. PETER'S BREWERY**, St. Peter's Hall, St. Peter South Elmham, Near Bungay NR35 1NQ; ☎ 01986 782322; www.stpeters brewery.co.uk; price: tutored tastings £2.50; pub open daily; tastings hourly 12–4pm at weekends.

> **WISSETT WINES**, Valley Farm Vineyards, Wissett, IP19 0JJ; ☎ 01986 785535; www.wisset twines.com; open 10am–6pm; also interesting self-catering and B&B accommodation.

Grapes also grow well in this relatively warm dry part of England. **Wissett Vineyards** are tucked away in a wonderfully scenic valley corner of Suffolk near Halesworth, and are open daily for wine tastings and sales. They specialise in off-dry sparkling wines but grow several grape varieties.

Pubs

The **Locks Inn** at Geldeston (www.geldestonlocks.co.uk) just across the River Waveney between Beccles and Bungay is a classic riverside pub. It can get packed at weekends when bands play (Saturday night and Sunday afternoons) or when they host one of their occasional beer festivals. From Beccles, it is possible to travel 45 minutes to the Locks via the Big Dog Ferry. Departures are from the Old Iron Bridge four times a day; bookings are required (☎ 01502 717256/07866 279859).

This region invites a combination of boat trip and inn, and the same can be done from Oulton Broad to **The Swan** at Barnby. You can study the menu of this excellent fish restaurant-cum-pub while idling along the river, and the boat people will ring through to the pub with your choices. Or you can just stay put at Oulton Broad and quench your thirst at **The Commodore**, preferably sitting outside watching the sun set behind the sailboats.

Visitor information

Tourist Information Centres:
Lowestoft Tourist Information
Centre, East Point Pavilion, Royal
Plain, Lowestoft NR33 0AP, (☎
01502 533600,
touristinfo@waveney.gov.uk;
www.visit-lowestoft.co.uk, open 7
days a week year round, covers the
whole Sunrise Coast; Beccles
Broads Information Centre, The
Quay, Beccles NR34 9BH. ☎ 01502
713196, open 9am–5pm 7 days a
week Easter to the end of Oct.
Hospitals: A&E facilities available
at James Paget Hospital, Lowestoft
Road, Gorleston, Great Yarmouth
NR31 6LA (8 miles north of Lowest-
oft), ☎ 01493 452452.
Websites: www.halesworth.ws
www.beccles.info; www.bungay-
suffolk.co.uk.
Supermarkets: Tesco , Leisure Way,
Lowestoft NR32 4TZ, ☎ 0845 677
9440; Tesco , Station Road, Beccles
NR34 9QH, ☎ 0845 677 9870; Mor-
rison , George Westwood Way,
Beccles NR34 9EJ (junction of the
A145 and A146).
Radio stations: The Beach 103.4
FM and 97.4 FM
(www.thebeach.co.uk).
Bike rental: Waveney River Centre,
Staithe Road, Burgh St Peter, Near
Beccles NR34 0BT, ☎ 01502
677343, www.waveneyrivercentre
.co.uk, bicycle hire costs £7 a half
day, £11 a full day; Outney Meadow
Caravan Park, Bungay NR35 1HG,
☎ 01986 892338, www.out
neymeadow.co.uk, £12 a day.
Taxis: P J Taxis, Beccles, ☎ 01502
719718; Atlas Radio Cars. Lowest-
oft, ☎ 01502 500000; Richard's
Taxis, Lowestoft, ☎ 07074 585588;
Roy's Taxis, Carlton Colville,
☎ 01502 502111.

FURTHER AFIELD

The Saints

Suffolk is littered with overlooked pockets of interest and beauty. The Saints refers to a group of 13 villages south of the River Waveney, all with a saint in their names plus 'Ilkeshall' or 'South Elmham', where anyone entering is guaranteed to get lost. Without an OS map you might never emerge again. Some have more letters in their names than they have inhabitants; none has a pub or a shop. Two key attractions are mentioned above: **Bateman's Barn** (named after William Bateman who was Bishop of Norwich from 1344 to 1355) in St Cross South Elmham, and **St Peter's Hall** in South Elmham St Peter. Long before 1991 when it was turned into a brewery, South Elmham Hall was described by the great architectural historian Nikolaus Pevsner as a 'baffling building'. While is it basically a domestic building, it has Gothic windows and other features that were added by the owners in the 15th century, probably pilfered from the ruined church and priory in nearby villages.

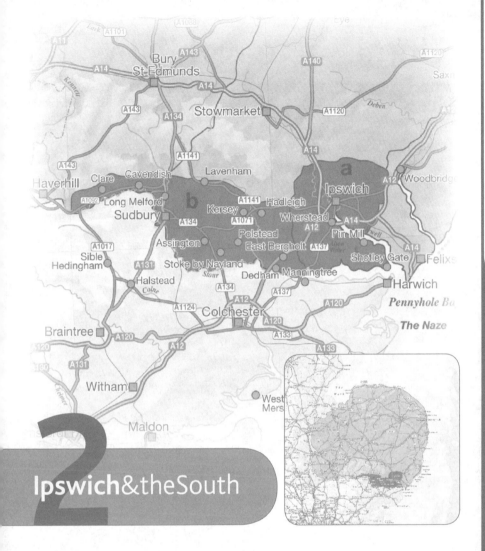

2

Ipswich&theSouth

a. Ipswich and the Shotley Peninsula

b. Constable Country and the Stour Valley

Unmissable highlights

01 Dine in a trendy bistro overlooking the smart regenerated marina in Ipswich
p.126

02 Attend a cutting-edge photographic exhibition at the non-profit Exposure Gallery in the centre of Ipswich
p.123

03 Stroll in the magnificent urban park, Christchurch Park, in Ipswich
p.120

04 Shop for the best regional produce at the newly opened Suffolk Food Hall overlooking the mighty Orwell Bridge
p.125

05 Hire a bicycle at Alton Water to pedal round the maze of surrounding lanes (where the comedian Griff Rhys Jones owns a house)
p.128

06 Visit the cottage at Flatford Mill immortalised in Constable's painting The Hay Wain
p.131

07 Impersonate a Tudor at one of the spectacular historical re-enactment days at Kentwell Hall in Long Melford
p.137

08 Drink organic cider made by the landlord of a country pub near Sudbury
p.143

09 Row a boat on the River Stour or take a foot ferry from Shotley Point
p.131

10 Marvel at the number of half-timbered buildings in astonishing Lavenham
p.133

IPSWICH AND THE SOUTH

Although Ipswich is the biggest urban centre in Suffolk today, it still has the status of a town rather than a city and is sometimes praised as a 'big little city'. It has always been a place of burghers rather than bishops and brigadiers, and has never had a cathedral or castle. You have to look harder to find its architectural gems than you do in Cambridge, Norwich, Ely or Bury St Edmunds, since often they are buried behind car parks and office blocks. But there are more than 600 listed buildings in town – Fore Street has the most – which are always rewarding to browse.

Beyond Ipswich are the lost lands between the Rivers Stour, Orwell and Deben, an unfailingly agreeable landscape punctuated with church spires, ancient trees, country houses and glimpses of the complex tidal waterways dotted with sails and ships. The walking in these parts is superb, and footpaths stretch virtually the whole way round the Shotley Peninsula, while the Suffolk Coast & Heaths Path links Ipswich with Felixstowe via Trimley Marshes.

The part of this region that is most familiar to tourists is the valley of the River Stour which forms the boundary between Suffolk and Essex, where two of England's preeminent artists, Constable and Gainsborough, were born and perfected their art. John Constable's meticulous yet worshipful paintings of the rural landscapes of his childhood are enough to inspire anyone to travel to Constable Country for the pleasure of seeing how little has changed. The area is awash with brilliant pubs and tea rooms, parish churches and local legends.

IPSWICH AND THE SHOTLEY PENINSULA

With the regeneration of its historic waterfront and with celebrated buildings peeking out from various corners of the city, Ipswich deserves more time than many visitors allow. From the sites associated with Cardinal Thomas Wolsey, Henry VIII's most powerful confidant, to the impressive 19th-century brewery buildings overlooking the River Orwell, the past glories of Ipswich slowly reveal themselves. A short drive or cycle ride over the Orwell Bridge brings you to pretty villages on the river estuary and wonderful country-side.

Ancient House with pargetting, Buttermarket, Ipswich

If approaching the centre of Ipswich from one of the exits off the busy A12 or from the railway station, it is easy to understand why this city has been overlooked and underrated as a destination for visitors. It will not be immediately apparent that Ipswich was once a great and prosperous trading city. Over the past hundred years – or even over the past decade – the city fathers have not been as assiduous as they might in safeguarding their historic town, although the present council is working hard to reverse that.

Founded as a Saxon settlement called Gipeswic, Ipswich depended on the sea for its livelihood, trading pottery and later wool with ports on the Baltic and the Rhine. Before AD1000 Ipswich was as important as York or even London, thanks to its natural harbour rivalling the Thames and The Wash. Originally all roads would have led to the waterfront. But post-war planners have ignored this pattern by imposing ring roads and roundabouts. Re-discovering the medieval town pattern requires exploration on foot. As the process of civic rejuvenation continues, exploring Ipswich will be rewarded not only with glimpses into its past but an appreciation of the vibrant present and ambitions for the future.

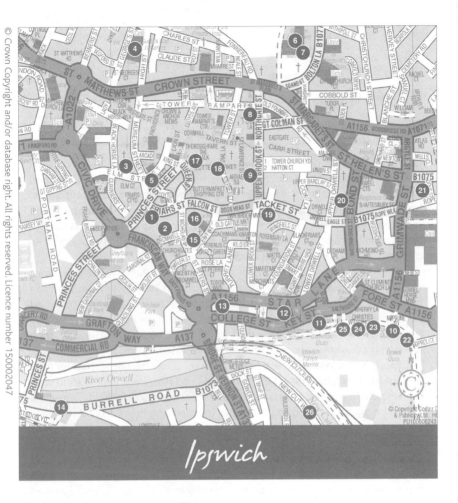

Ipswich

1. Willis Building
2. Unitarian Meeting House
3. St Mary at the Elms
4. Ipswich Museum
5. Basement Gallery
6. Wolsey Art Gallery
7. Christchurch Mansion
8. Pykenham Gate
9. Ancient House
10. Neptune Quay
11. Old Custom House
12. Key Arts
13. Wolsey's Gate
14. Leo's Deli
15. Gallery Restaurant
16. Trongs
17. Mizu Noodle Bar
18. Memorable Cheeses Deli
19. Zing Wine Bar
20. Baipo Thai
21. Dove Street Inn
22. Colours Continental Café
23. Salthouse Harbour Hotel
24. Il Punto
25. Bistro on the Quay
26. Steamboat Tavern

WHAT TO SEE AND DO

 Fair weather

Ipswich is perfectly walkable, and it makes for a pleasant stroll to set off from gracious Christchurch Park towards the pedestrianised **Butter Market** and **Cornhill** in the centre of town and on to the waterfront. In recent years, boarded-up warehouses and barracks from the Napoleonic era have been reclaimed for modern purposes, and one or two of Ipswich's six redundant medieval churches that were sliding into dereliction have found new uses. The most striking renewal has taken place along the historic waterfront.

Just to the north of the city centre, **Christchurch Park** provides acres of sloping green space and a picturesque backdrop to Christchurch Mansion (described below). This splendid urban park encompasses hills and varied habitats with many ancient trees, particularly chestnuts and oaks. It also has a great playground for children, a duck pond, tennis courts and a natural spring welling up out of the ground if you are lucky enough to find it.

Ipswich is well endowed with otherpleasant parks including **Chantry Park** west of town with the first-rate Stables Café and **Holywells Park**, a short walk from the old docks at Cliff Quay and good for children (see below). This whole area is being regenerated as part of the Transforming Ipswich project.

Waterfront

Ipswich has a fine maritime history which had been eclipsed somewhat by the rise of the container port at Felixstowe. The remarkable regeneration of the marina and wet dock from what was a grubby industrial port is ongoing, and huge investment is being poured into the town. The spanking new Neptune Quay backs onto Coprolite Street, named for the unglamorous processing of fossilised dung into fertilisers. Access to the waterfront is available at many points, though one of the most picturesque is via tiny **Wherry Lane** (named after a kind of riverboat for bearing cargo). **Fore Street** behind has been radically altered over the past few years, with the conservation of some timbered buildings including the pompously columned **Old Custom House** built in 1845, which did its best to stand out against the smuggling that was so rife in these parts. It still serves as the offices of the Ipswich Port Authority.

The docklands' renaissance includes the fine but crumbling shell of **St Mary at Quay Church** being turned into an airy exhibition space called Key Arts. If it's open, you can admire its hammerbeam roof. The newly created **University Campus Suffolk** is nearby, and will eventually be joined by a state-of-the-art dance theatre called **Jerwood Dance House** (www.danceeast.co.uk). Among the signs of much welcome gentrification are two waterfront café-restaurants,

Colours Continental Café and Coffee Link Espresso Bar; the latter has an upstairs reading room overlooking Neptune Quay.

Historic buildings

One of the oldest buildings is aptly called the **Ancient House** in Buttermarket, now occupied by the kitchenware chain Lakeland. The exterior of the timber-framed building built, in 1670, is decorated all over with pargetting, raised ornamental plasterwork, depicting among other things the four continents of the world (Australasia had yet to be recognised as the fifth continent).

Other interesting points on a walking tour of the town include two gates: **Wolsey's Gate** from 1528 (not well preserved) and **Pykenham's Gateway** from 1471. This latter building (located on Northgate Street) has characteristic crow-stepped gables, and is open mornings only on the first Saturday of the month from May to October.

The **Unitarian Meeting House** on Friars Street was built in 1700 for the flourishing dissenting community of Ipswich which is half a century earlier than a comparable building in Norwich, the **Octagon Unitarian Chapel**. It is open to the public on Saturday mornings, and features a carved pulpit, a door with a spyhole, and numbered box pews still with their hooks for hats. The Norman Foster building next door, the **Willis Building**, provides a stark architectural contrast with its curved smoked glass exterior and roof garden.

River cruises

Two cruises on the *Lady Orwell* leave from the Ipswich Marina. The choice is between a trip lasting two and a half hours to Pin Mill and another lasting three and a half hours to Harwich at the mouth of the River Orwell. These take place on summer weekends and on some other days in high season (see www.orwellrivercruises.co.uk for current timetable). **Freston Tower** (one of the landmarks on the banks of the Orwell, mentioned below as a place to stay) is a six-storey folly which was built for the education of Lord de Freston's daughter in the 16th century. Young Ellen is reputed to have used a different storey for different days and different subjects, e.g. tapestry on Tuesdays on the second floor and astronomy on Saturdays on the top floor. One version even has her on the roof canoodling with the tower's builder though it isn't known which day was reserved for that lesson.

 ## Wet weather

If the weather discourages you from tracing the Anglo-Saxon street pattern by foot, then several indoor retreats may be sought. The tourist information centre is housed in lovely **St Stephen's Church**, redundant as a parish church

Christchurch mansion

since 1975. Entry is still through the west door into a tastefully whitewashed interior which retains its font, 16th-century roof and wall tombs. If you like old churches, another gem which is always open is **St Mary at the Elms**, a short walk away.

Christchurch Mansion

At the base of Christchurch Park is the Tudor mansion which served as home to several prominent Ipswich families before the ubiquitous Cobbolds gave it to the borough council on condition that the park be acquired as well. In earlier times Cardinal Wolsey, probably the most powerful figure to have come from Ipswich, stayed here many times and is now remembered in a splendid portrait. The mansion with its amazing painted room dates from 1540 and now houses an important collection of East Anglian art, furniture and crockery. The gallery boasts the largest collection outside London of works by the two great Suffolk painters, John Constable and Thomas Gainsborough. Nearby is the most attractive church in Ipswich, St Margaret, with its double hammerbeam roof.

CHRISTCHURCH MANSION, Soane Street, Ipswich IP4 2BE; ☎ 01473 433554; free; open daily 10am–5pm; courtyard café serves good food.

Ipswich Museum

About half a kilometre to the west is the fascinating town museum of Ipswich, which is especially strong on local natural history. It retains its old-fashioned Victorian displays of fossils and mounted birds, and has a woolly mammoth as well as other full-size animals. One gallery tells the story of Ipswich's development since Roman times.

IPSWICH MUSEUM, High Street, Ipswich IP1 3QH; ☎ 01473 433550; free: open Tues to Sat 10am–5pm.

Galleries

Local arts organisations are active and many are well-funded. The **Town Hall Galleries** have a vibrant changing programme of visual arts exhibitions. The **Exposure Gallery** is a not-for-profit photography gallery in the town centre. Often exhibitions of photographs and digital art are based around an East Anglian theme.

- **Visual Arts Ipswich** The Town Hall Galleries, Cornhill, Ipswich IP1 1BH; (☎ 01473 432863; www.visualarts-ipswich.org.uk); entry: free; open Tues to Sat.
- **Exposure Gallery** 12–14 Princes Street, Ipswich IP1 1QT; ☎ 01473 214300; www.basementgallery.co.uk); entry: free; open Tues to Sat.

What to do with children

Sports and activities

Any offspring who happen to be football-mad might want to make a pilgrimage to **Portman Road**, home to Ipswich Town, the only professional football club in Suffolk. The *Tractor Boys*' stadium is just a five-minute walk from the railway station and is graced by two nearby statues, one of Sir Alf

Ipswich town sign now in Isaac Lord wine bar

Ramsay, who led England to victory in the 1966 World Cup, and the other of Bobby Robson, one of the team's most successful managers.

As part of the restoration of 67-acre **Holywells Park**, an ambitious play area has just been opened which will eventually incorporate a large galleon supporting two climbing nets, a bird's nest swing, a tug boat and water play.

The **Suffolk Leisure Park**, just south of Ipswich, is a great day out for older children with its three dry ski/snowboard slopes (lessons compulsory for beginners), tobogganing course, climbing wall and high ropes course. The pleasant café bar and restaurant in the lodge serves homemade food.

> **SUFFOLK LEISURE PARK**,
> Bourne Hill, Wherstead, IP2 8NQ;
> ☎ 01473 602347; www.suffolkski centre.co.uk; tobogganing £5 an hour for under-16s.

Crown Pools on Crown Street near Christchurch Park has a beach area, wave machine and water fountains; admission is £3.30 for adults, £2.20 for children. Local parents wanting to amuse the kids often repair to **Jan's Madhouse** (Cavendish Street IP3 8AX; www.jansmadhouse.co.uk) outside town, a play facility catering for all ages from infants to teenagers. Adults can

The best... PLACES TO STAY

BOUTIQUE

Salthouse Harbour Hotel

1 Neptune Quay, Ipswich IP4 1AX
☎ **01473 226789**
www.salthouseharbour.co.uk

This showpiece hotel with brasserie on the regenerated waterfront has fantastic views, especially at night when the boats are lit up. The contemporary style exploits original features of the converted Victorian warehouse, with huge modern bathrooms and DVD players (the hotel has a free DVD library). The hotel's sister hotel is the Angel in Bury St Edmunds.

Prices: B&B from £95/£130 to £170 for a double.

HOTEL

Gatehouse Hotel

799 Old Norwich Road, Ipswich IP1 6LH
☎ **01473 741897**
www.gatehousehotel.com

This elegant small hotel with extensive gardens is on the northern outskirts of Ipswich, easily accessible from the A14. Despite being part of the Best Western group, the Gatehouse aspires to be a country house hotel.

Price: from £90/£110 for a twin room including breakfast.

INN

Sorrel Horse Inn

Old Norwich Road, Barham, Ipswich IP6 0PG (5 miles north of Ipswich)
☎ **01473 830327**
www.sorrelhorse.co.uk

This comfortable 17th-century country pub has original beams, rustic fittings and open log fireplace. An adjacent barn has been converted into eight rooms. A large garden is equipped with children's play equipment, including a bouncy castle in summer.

Price: B&B £55 for a double.

FARMSTAY

College Farm

Hintlesham, Ipswich IP8 3NT (6 miles west of Ipswich)
☎ **01473 652253**
www.collegefarm.net

A stable conversion and listed building, 600-acre College Farm has historical connections with Cardinal Wolsey and Eton College (hence the name). Farmhouse breakfasts are cooked on an Aga.

Prices: from £42 for a single; £65 for a double; three-bedded family room on application.

B & B

Cranmoor House

20 Hatfield Road, Ipswich IP3 9AF
☎ **01473 721572**
www.cranmoorhouse.com

This two-roomed B&B behind the railway station is unusual for serving dinner. The catering is of a very high standard since the friendly owners are trained chefs and wine buffs. Prices for a three-course dinner start at £10.

Prices: B&B £50 single occupancy; £60 for a double; £10 surcharge on Fridays and Saturdays.

SELF-CATERING

Freston Tower

Freston, Shotley Peninsula (4 miles south of Ipswich)
☎ **01628 825925 (Landmark Trust booking)**
www.landmarktrust.org.uk

This many-windowed Elizabethan folly on the south shore of the Orford Estuary (see p.92) has recently been restored by the Landmark Trust for holiday lets. Despite having six storeys, it sleeps four (one double, one twin room), with the sitting room on the top floor for views over the estuary.

Price: three-night stay from £459 out of season and £740 in the summer.

spend time in the healthy food café or on the free computers while children amuse themselves. Entry is free for adults and babies. For the rest the fee is £5 at weekends, £3.50 off-peak.

Just outside town, a wholesome family destination (for non-vegetarians) is **Jimmy's Farm** in Wherstead, which has an adventure playground, nature trail and yummy sausages in a bun made from rare-breed, free-range pigs from their own farm. The farm is owned by Jimmy Doherty who gave up a PhD to raise pigs and talk about it on his BBC television series, *Jimmy's Farm Diaries*.

> **JIMMY'S FARM**, Essex Pig Company, Pannington Hall Farm, Wherstead, IP9 2AR; ☎ 0870 950 0210; www.jimmysfarm.com: farm free, nature trail adults £4, children £3; open daily all year round.

The best... FOOD AND DRINK

 ### Staying in

> **SUFFOLK FOOD HALL**, Wherstead Hall, Peppers Lane, Wherstead, Ipswich, Suffolk IP9 2AB; ☎ 01473 786616; www.suffolkfoodhall.co.uk; open daily 9am–6pm with shorter hours (10.30am–4.30pm) on Sun.

The newly opened **Suffolk Food Hall** near the western end of the Orwell Bridge makes holiday food shopping a downright pleasure. The converted barns contain a food hall which aims to sell the best regional produce, a café, deli, restaurant (described below) and plant nursery. There is a specialist butcher (which specialises in free range Red Poll beef from a local herd of this Suffolk breed), fishmonger and baker. The Suffolk Food Hall is very close to **Jimmy's Farm,** mentioned above, which hosts a farmers' market on the first Saturday morning of the month. Other farm shops within reach of Ipswich include **Hillside Nurseries** in Hintlesham (☎ 01473 652 682) and **Goslings Farm** near Felixstowe (☎ 01394 273361; www.goslingsfarm.co.uk) which has a coffee shop too. Goslings is famed for its PYO berries and also sells juices, cheeses, cakes, etc.

Good food shops in town include **Memorable Cheeses** (which sells far more than just cheeses, including farm produce) and **Procter's Speciality Sausages**, both on The Walk (just off the Butter Market). If you are in a car, you could make a trip to **Irene's** award-winning patisserie at 408 Foxhall Road.

Freston Tower

EATING OUT

FINE DINING
Mariners
Neptune Quay, Ipswich IP4 1AX
☎ **01473 289748**
www.marinersipswich.co.uk

No more romantic setting could be found for an intimate dinner than this boat moored at Ipswich Marina. Traditional French dishes aren't over-fussy and the prices aren't over-inflated, especially the £5 dishes from the snack menu such as Toulouse sausages and cod and spinach lasagne.

RESTAURANT
The Galley Restaurant
25 St. Nicholas Street, Ipswich IP1 1TW
☎ **01473 281131**
www.galley.uk.com

Flamboyant restaurateur Ugur Vata not only serves dishes from his native Turkey, such as spiced lamb with chickpeas and apricots, but also British cuisine including Ipswich almond pudding made from an old traditional recipe. Pleasant ambience with outdoor eating under umbrellas. Fixed price lunch menu costs from £13 for two courses, but a blow-out dinner with wine (they specialise in Chilean wines) will average £35.

Baipo Thai
63 Upper Orwell St, Ipswich IP4 1HP
☎ **01473 218402**
www.baipo.co.uk

Authentic Thai dishes are served at this restaurant recommended by the hard-to-please *Harden's Restaurant Guide*. Generous set menus will cost about £20 a head.

Mizu Noodle Bar
10 The Cornhill, Ipswich IP1 1DB
☎ **01473 288839**
www.mizunoodlebar.com

Housed on the ground floor of 16th-century Golden Lion Hotel in the historic heart of the city (where martyrs and witches were once burned), this trendy noodle restaurant serves a wide range of noodle dishes and soup, fresh and fast at affordable prices (mostly £5–7).

Trongs
23 St Nicholas Street, Ipswich IP1 1TW
☎ **01473 256833**

Considered to be the best Chinese restaurant in Ipswich, this small restaurant is often full so bookings are recommended. It's family-run with a friendly atmosphere and serves some spicy dishes plus delicious crispy duck. Set menus cost from £15.

BISTRO
Bistro on the Quay
3 Wherry Quay, Ipswich IP4 1AS
☎ **01473 286677**
www.bistroonthequay.co.uk

Part of the uptarted docklands area, the bistro is in a former salt warehouse. The informal restaurant has an eclectic menu with a choice of innovative fish, meat and vegetarian dishes. A lunch menu is available for £12 for two; dinner costs about £25.

GASTROPUB
The Ship Launch Inn
Cliff Road, Ipswich IP3 0AX
☎ **01473 287608**

This has a constantly changing blackboard menu prepared by a chef who likes to ring the changes. The menu might include double chilli cheese burger (at the insistence of the chef's father, who lives in Denver) with butcher-made burgers dressed with homemade chilli sauce made with bitter chocolate and coriander. Coffee and rum cake is made by the chef's mother. Mains cost from £12.

CAFÉ
Samford Restaurant Café
(Located in Suffolk Food Hall)
Wherstead Hall, Peppers Lane,
Wherstead, Ipswich, Suffolk IP9 2AB
☎ **07767 372151**
www.suffolkfoodhall.co.uk

Daytime venue for good quality wholesome lunches and teas. A sample dish of duck, hazelnut and orange salad with oriental dressing costs £5.25. Excellent views from the mezzanine café overlooking the Orwell.

Leo's Deli in Ipswich Railway Station (Burrell Road, Ipswich, IP2 8AL; ☎ 01473 687068), alongside its sister deli in Framlingham was the runner-up in the Suffolk Food and Drink Awards 2007 where all the entrants were of a very high standard. It sells an impressive range of specialist foods including baked goods, cheeses, home-cooked dishes and cold meats including Suffolk Salami from a Mid Suffolk farm in Brundish.

🍷 Drinking

Ipswich has a long history of brewing which all but ended in 2002 when the Tolly Cobbold Brewery on Cliff Quay was closed by the brewery that had bought it. However, a energetic new brewery stepped into the vacuum in 2006 with a tiny operation in a centrally located 18th-century coach house on Cardigan Street. **St Jude's Brewery** (apparently named after the patron saint of lost causes) is a two-person operation with a young woman as brewster (2 Cardigan Street, Ipswich, Suffolk IP1 3PF; ☎ 01473 413334; www.stjudes brewery .co.uk). It distributes its interesting range of ales such as Wolsey's Winter Warmer through a couple of local pubs, primarily **The Rose and Crown** on Norwich Road, **The Fat Cat** on Spring Road (described below) and the **Red Lion** on Caudwell Hall Road, while its bottled beer is sold at farm shops, delis and supermarkets in Ipswich. This modern brewery recycles its left-over grain to local allotments and invites customers to return their bottles.

The **Dove Street Inn** (76 St Helens Rd; ☎ 01473 211270; www.dove streetinn .co.uk) near Rope Walk and the Fat Cat (288 Spring Road; ☎ 01473 726524; www.fatcatipswich.co.uk) further to the east of the centre are both real ale lovers' pubs, each offering more than a dozen choices of bitter, ale and mild straight from the barrel. Both are popular and therefore crowded.

The Steamboat Tavern(78 New Cut West; ☎ 01473 601902) overlooking Ipswich Marina is a lively venue for music with a fortnightly folk session (every other Thurs) and regular jazz and other musical sessions. It is also the focal point for the **Ipswich Riverside Folk Weekend** held every June. While most of the pubs listed on CAMRA's national inventory of historic pubs are thatched or timbered or twee, the **Margaret Catchpole** on Cliff Lane (☎ 01473 252450) in south Ipswich is included because it is unreconstructed 1930s, with a spacious bow-windowed public bar and a verandah overlooking a bowling green.

For something more contemporary, visit **The Zing Wine Bar** (10 Tacket Street, Ipswich, IP4 1AY; ☎ 01473 280000; www.zingwinebar.com) which has a cocktail bar at the back (reputedly the best mojitos), a courtyard garden, an unusual selection of drinks, and music nights playing jazz, funk and soul. Wine drinkers aren't neglected. **Wines of Interest** at 46 Burlington Street (☎ 01473 215752; www.winesofinterest.co.uk) is rated one of the top (and least intimidating) wine merchants in the country, and their shop on the edge of the city centre features wines from many small producers especially in Spain and Argentina.

Visitor information

Tourist Information Centres: Ipswich Tourist Information Centre, St Stephen's Church, St Stephen's Lane, IP1 1DP, ☎ 01473 258070, tourist@ipswich.gov.uk; www.visit-ipswich.com, open Mon to Sat. The Suffolk Coast & Heaths Unit (www.suffolkcoastandheaths.org) distributes lots of information about exploring and conserving the coast. One of its publications is *Cycling around the Shotley Peninsula* which details 58 miles of cycle routes along quiet country lanes (£1.50).
Hospitals: A&E Department, Ipswich Hospital, Heath Road, Ipswich, IP4 5PD (situated 2 miles east of town centre on the A1189).
Supermarkets: Sainsbury's, 38–40 Upper Brook Street, Ipswich IP4 1DR, branches also on Hadleigh Road and in Warren Heath; Tesco Extra, Copdock Interchange, Ipswich IP8 3TS (near the junction of the A14 and A 12).
Bike rental: Bicycle Doctor & Hire Service, 18 Bartholomew Street, Ipswich, IP4 2RP, ☎ 01473 259853, www.bicycledoctor.gbr.fm); Alton Cycle Hire, Holbrook Road, Stutton, Suffolk IP9 2RY, ☎ 01473 328873, located near Alton Water on the Shotley peninsula.
Taxis: Anglia Taxis, ☎ 0800 666666 or ☎ 01473 255555 from a mobile; Avenue Taxis, ☎ 01473 407070; Hawk Express Cabs, ☎ 01473 222222; the journey from the railway station to the city centre will be about £4 during the day.

FURTHER AFIELD

Shotley Peninsula

The Orwell Bridge was an impressive engineering feat even in 1982, since its supports had to be sunk 40m into the tidal mud of the river. It is best viewed from afar, because when you drive over it on the A14, the sides come up too high to permit a view. Instead of taking the main road to Felixstowe, consider wending your way along a B road towards Shotley Gate at the end of the penin-sula between the rivers Stour and Orwell. Eventually you run out of land as the tip of the peninsula is squeezed between the mighty container port of Felixstowe and the busy Essex harbour of Harwich. From a car you may catch tantalising glimpses of scudding sails on the water, but it is far more satisfying to leave the car in a convenient layby, take the Ordnance Survey map and go for a walk.

Orwell estuary walk

One possible starting point is **Woolverstone** where you can park your car beside the B road and walk towards the bustling marina to join the long distance footpath along the shore. You may catch a glimpse of **Cat House**, so named because it is said that smugglers placed a painting of a cat in the window to indicate to their partners in crime that the revenue men were not about.

A short walk east brings you to the beauty spot **Pin Mill** where picturesque barges with dark coloured sails are still built and repaired. Just beyond Pin Mill is a fascinating community of barges and houseboats moored along this National Trust foreshore in an Area of Outstanding Natural Beauty. No road access, but a separate world of ricketty jetties, wooden gangways, painted gates and tubs of flowers right out of a children's book. In fact Arthur Ransome (author of *Swallows and Amazons*) lived and sailed in Pin Mill in the 1930s. You might want to turn inland at Chelmondiston where you gain some height and head back to the starting point via an alternative path over the fields which gives sweeping views over the estuary.

This half-day walk is just one possibility. Footpaths hug the shores and marshes all around the edge of the peninsula and good walks can also be enjoyed along the less frequented southern shore of the peninsula overlooking the Stour.

> **HARWICH HARBOUR FOOT FERRY**, Shotley Marina; ☎ 0791 991 1440; www.harwich harbourferry.com; 10-minute journey Shotley to Harwich £3; 15 minutes on to Felixstowe £6 in total.

There is one mode of escape apart from backtracking to Ipswich and that is to take the foot ferry from Shotley Marina to Harwich or Felixstowe.

Food and accommodation

The charming **Butt and Oyster** pub in Pin Mill (Suffolk IP9 1JW; ☎ 01473 780764; www.debeninns.co.uk/buttandoyster) has been discovered by a multitude of metropolitan daytrippers but all the same is a great place, especially on a bright day when you can sip your Adnams at a picnic table feet from the river. The chef sources his meat from Suffolk and Essex farms, and vegetables from Holbrook less than 3 miles away. Other good pubs that serve food in the area include **The Queens Head** in Erwarton, **Compasses** in Holbrook and the **Venture** or **Forester's Arms**, both in Chelmondiston.

Findley Cottage (Post Office Farm, Church Road, Stutton, Suffolk, IP9 2SJ (1473 327558; www.findleycottage.co.uk) is a period cottage in the village of Stutton near Alton Water, an area excellent for cycling (see Alton Cycle Hire above) and for walking, since Stutton sits astride the Stour Valley Path. There is the self-catering four-bedroom holiday cottage available from £300 to £580 depending on the season.

Water meadows, Sudbury

CONSTABLE COUNTRY AND THE STOUR VALLEY

The sinuous River Stour not only marks the southern boundary of the county of Suffolk, it epitomises the English landscape. We are culturally attuned to recognise the willow-fringed meadows, sunken green lanes and flowering thickets along the River Stour as an idealised rural England, even if the only Constable painting that can be reliably summoned up is the oft-reproduced *The Hay Wain*. The amazing discovery – and the reason to visit – is that so little has changed since Constable was painting in and around the place of his birth in 1776. Thatched cottages still nestle in folds of hills, tributary brooks still rustle and glorious church towers still toll bells for Sunday services. It is difficult not to fall under the romantic spell of chocolate-box-perfect villages such as Kersey and Stoke by Nayland.

Walkers and cyclists can hardly go wrong in this designated Area of Out-standing Natural Beauty. Classic circuits can be made not only along the river valley but along disused railways and through peaceful woods. On a summer's day, nothing can rival a stroll from East Bergholt to Flatford Mill on the River Stour. The outrageously picturesque water meadows at Sudbury are the perfect place to put some distance between you and your busy life, a place to have a picnic or read a paper or watch children messing about with toy boats.

The wealth of medieval wool towns like Lavenham and Long Melford resulted in grand flint churches, half-timbered guildhalls and lavish manors. It may sometimes resemble a film set but, like Constable's landscapes, these thatched and timbered villages and market towns are populated. Both locals and passionate converts to the Suffolk country way of life are often happy to strike up a conversation with visitors in any Bull, Cock or Eight Bells pub.

WHAT TO SEE AND DO

 ## Fair weather

East Bergholt and Dedham Vale

Straddling the border with Essex, the tranquil Dedham Vale lies between the well preserved village of Dedham on the Essex side of the Stour and East Bergholt in Suffolk. Walking between the two will take no more than an hour, since famous **Flatford Mill** which John Constable's father owned is a field studies centre and not open to casual callers. Just next to the mill, you can easily identify one of Constable's favourite subjects as featured in *The Hay Wain*, the cottage belonging to a tenant farmer, Willy Lott. The only attraction that you can enter is **Bridge Cottage**, where the National Trust has a free exhibition about Constable plus a teashop (☎ 01206 298260). Guided walks costing £2.50 are available in season, and boats can be hired. You can also hire rowing boats in Dedham, but expect to wait in a long queue on a fine day for one of the 26 wooden boats. More energetic walkers can extend the walk to Stratford St Mary, which Constable also painted.

The house in **East Bergholt** where Constable was born was demolished 170 years ago (because a neighbour grumbled that it was blocking his view) and the painter's studio is now part of the village garage. The idyllically positioned church is most famous for its bells which are the heaviest in the world and are at eye level because the tower was never completed. The parishioners built a wooden slatted structure in the churchyard in 1531 to protect the bells from the elements, and they are still there, and still rung. Instead of pulling on ropes, the bell ringers stand inside the 'cage' and push the bells using brute strength. The bells are rung every Sunday at 9.30am and in summer at 6pm and Thursdays at 8pm as well (www.eastbergholt-bells.org.uk).

> **THE BOATHOUSE**, Mill Lane, Dedham CO7 6DH; ☎ 01206 323153; http://dedhamboat house.com/boat-hire; £6 for 30 minutes, £12 for 1 hour, for a group of 4–5; open Apr to Oct; 1½ miles upriver from Flatford Mill.

Stoke by Nayland

Anyone who thinks that East Anglia is completely flat should jump on a bicycle and make haste for Stoke-by-Nayland. Set on a ridge between the River Stour and its tributary the Box, it is another of those villages depicted on up-market table mats, with oak beamed pubs and 16th-century timber-framed buildings in **School Street**. The church of **St Mary's** ornate tiered tower can be seen from all around, though it is also fascinating to see the church up close. Its medieval carved doors are rare and an elaborate black floor memorial commemorating

The Red Barn murder

The tragic tale of Maria Marten is synonymous with Polstead for it was here that she lived and died a violent death. The case was to become one of the most famous murders of the 19th century. It is the archetypal story of the squire's son having his way with a humble local girl and then discarding her when she gets pregnant and becomes too clamorous. In May 1827, Maria Marten had an assignation with her lover William Corder at the Red Barn on his property. Her plan was to elope with him in disguise to Ipswich. His plan was quite otherwise, and she was never seen again, though letters arrived from Corder on the Isle of Wight claiming all was well with them both. These were superstitious times and Maria's stepmother (not wicked in this case) dreamed repeatedly of a murder in the Red Barn. Sure enough the young woman's remains were found, with evidence that she had been shot in the head and stabbed. Corder was located living in wedded bliss near London, tried for murder, convicted (after which he confessed his guilt) and executed at Bury St Edmunds in the summer of 1828. The hanging was attended by a huge and frenzied crowd of onlookers who all wanted a souvenir, such as a scrap of the noose. A room in Moyse's Hall Museum in Bury is devoted to the case (see chapter on Bury St Edmunds).

Between the green and the pond in Polstead today, you pass a distinguished timbered farmhouse called Corder's House, now a posh residence. On a parallel lane (Marten's Lane) you come to Maria Marten's cottage where she was born and lived with her mole-catcher father. The current resident is a maker of fine furniture (see Shopping). The Red Barn disappeared in a red blaze of fire in 1842 but there is still a walking track called the Red Barn Path that passes the spot of the murder. The rolling countryside round about is criss-crossed with many delightful paths.

four children of Lady Anne Windsor, whom all of died at less than 15 months, is moving.

In a strange case of life imitating art, a local conservation group is creating a new woodland near the church from a once neglected cherry orchard. This labour of love by volunteers is being done carefully so as to retain the view painted by Constable in his giant canvas of 1835, *Stoke by Nayland*, a copy of which is due to be mounted in the church in the near future.

St Mary's Church, Stoke by Nayland

Polstead and Kersey

These villages, among others in the region, have been spared the ugly incursions of modern development, traffic and overhead power cables, so it is all the easier to appreciate their wonderful architecture. **Kersey** is usually described as the most picturesque village in Suffolk, helped enormously by the fact that its main road climbs up to the village from a stream-filled valley. The 'Splash' must be forded at a snail's pace and crossed by pedestrians on a bridge.

True to its name which means place of pools, **Polstead**'s main feature is its large pond (once used in the egregious practice of dunking women accused of witchcraft with their thumbs tied behind their backs). Further up the village, the pleasant village green can often be seen swarming with cyclists who have paused to refuel at **The Cock Inn**.

Lavenham

Whereas many of the once wool-rich merchant towns of Norfolk are a little down-at-heel, Lavenham exudes huge prosperity, and has a range of hotels, restaurants and shops to prove it. Not to mention Lavenham's 340 medieval buildings. With a tiny population, that equates to one listed building to less than six inhabitants. How did they do it? Incredibly, one of the most photogenic collections of buildings is along **Water Street**, another name for the A1141 linking Bury St Edmunds and Hadleigh. The absence of straight lines is

Lavenham Lady St

CELEBRITY CONNECTIONS

Ruth Rendell, famed for her crime novels and psychological thrillers, lived in a farmhouse near Polstead from 1977 until her husband's death in 1999.

Perhaps she felt at home in a place where the notorious murder of Maria Marten took place. She also had a beach house in Aldeburgh. As Baroness Rendell of Babergh, she sits in the House of Lords on the Labour side, while her friend and fellow crime writer P D James (who has also lived in Suffolk) sits as a Conservative peer.

Rendell, who also writes under the name Barbara Vine, has used Suffolk as a setting in many of her books including *A Dark Adapted Eye* which was dramatised by the BBC to great acclaim in 1994. Most of the filming took place at the Georgian mansion of Sotterley Estate set in an extensive park south of Beccles. Other settings have not been so successful. She has described the adaptation of her novel *A Judgement in Stone*, which was filmed in Toronto rather than Suffolk, as 'perhaps the worst film I've ever seen'.

Her books often evoke a vivid sense of place that complements the psychological tension in her plots and characterisation. She was sufficiently enamoured of Suffolk to decide to write her first non-fiction book, *Ruth Rendell's Suffolk*, about her favourite landscapes in the county, illustrated with photographs. She and her husband involved themselves in local affairs, for example Donald Rendell joined the organising committee for the Suffolk Music Festival one year. Ruth Rendell and another Polstead resident published a short booklet at the end of Mrs Thatcher's period as Prime Minister, arguing that political power was becoming too centralised. They used examples from Polstead, e.g. that the village school had been closed despite local protests and that housing was becoming more unaffordable for young people.

Now aged 78, her main home is in London but she still owns a small house in Suffolk and continues to write to a strict timetable.

aesthetically satisfying, as is the abundance of pargetting, patterns applied to the plaster exterior of timber-framed buildings. Another architectural term to acquire in Lavenham is 'jettied' where the upper storey overhangs the ground floor. Other useful words are 'crooked' and 'bulge' to describe the extraordinary buildings, creating streetscapes as they might have appeared before the time of Henry VIII.

St Peter and St Paul Church, Lavenham

The splendid church of **St Peter and St Paul** in Lavenham is considered by some experts to be the most beautiful in the county. The interior is so perfectly intact because the materials used in the 15th century were of such high quality that they haven't perished. The cloth merchants whose money built the church must have been delighted with its hillside position allowing them to flaunt their generosity and taste even more flamboyantly. Their successors today still predominate in Lavenham, which inevitably has become a des res for privileged Londoners and other urbanites. Many of the 2,000 residents are incomers who have renovated their dream cottages, opened galleries, and done all the other things that help Lavenham to remain the showpiece that it is.

Sudbury

Sudbury is a more down-to-earth market town where traffic rushes through the town centre and where the statue of the town's most famous son, Thomas Gainsborough, is marooned between parking bays and a redundant church used as an occasional sale showroom. His home is now a museum (see *Wet weather options*). Across the road is the fantastic timbered **Salters Hall** probably built in the reign of Henry VI.

Carry on a short distance along **Gainsborough Street** and you arrive at Sudbury's treasure. Soul-healing meadows embraced by a gentle curve of the River Stour stretch before you under a Constable-esque sky (but with few Gainsborough gentlefolk attired in frock coats and silk gowns). Highland cattle browse and wade through the River Stour. These meadows are said to be the oldest continuously grazed land in England. Weeping willows and alders sway in the breeze, a row of pastel cottages is visible, all with different roofs, and with a bit of luck you will see a kingfisher hover or swoop.

A short stroll away, the great church of **St Gregory's** has plenty of interesting detail, like the medieval font cover, typical of East Anglia, that is fashioned like an elaborate gothic tower suspended from the ceiling. When the font is needed for a baptism, the construction telescopes up into itself. If by any chance the vestry is open, ask the friendly parishioners to show you the skull of Simon of Sudbury who was Archbishop of Canterbury in the 1370s and was executed at the Tower of London by Wat Tyler during the Peasants' Revolt after he introduced the poll tax. His body was buried in Canterbury Cathedral, but his toothless skull was smuggled to his hometown. It is said that a later churchwarden made a tidy sum by selling more than 130 of what purported to be Simon's teeth.

Long Melford

A few miles north of Sudbury along the River Stour you reach another fine and prosperous town. Long Melford has not just one but two massive country houses, **Melford Hall** and **Kentwell Hall**, that are more or less contemporary (described below). There is no cosy centre to the village but rather a ribbon of (interesting) development along the main road, the A131. Long Melford is renowned for its range of lifestyle shops, as well as for its late 15th-century church. It is on a grand scale disproportionate to the size that Long Melford ever reached. The many windows allow the interior to be bathed in light, some of which is filtered through medieval stained glass along the north aisle.

Melford Hall

If the traffic wears you down, head off on one of the footpaths which head off from the village in all directions of the compass and one to spare. The 4 mile walk back to Sudbury passes, a riverside picnic site at Rodbridge, a mill at Borley and (with a slight detour) a church with a fine Tudor brick tower at Liston.

The Upper Stour

Cavendish, Clare and Stoke-by-Clare are tranquil, attractive villages on the upper stretches of the river which defines the Essex border. With the usual adornments of a village green, half-timbered cottages, leafy churchyards and long-redundant railway stations, they are always enjoyable to explore by car, bike or on foot. A lovely circular walk connects Clare and Cavendish; from whichever village you begin at, pleasant hostelries await you in the other.

Cavendish is the most immediately engaging. It is widely associated with the Sue Ryder Foundation whose headquarters are here. Until last year there was a small museum celebrating the founder's heroic achievements, first among the survivors of concentration camps in Poland and then in setting up a worldwide network of residential homes for people in distress. The museum has now closed though the shop is still open.

Clare boasts a castle begun in 1100 but it is really just a mound with a path spiralling up from the country park laid out around the former railway station. The pleasures it affords may be low-key but it is ideal for a picnic or for children who want space to run around.

Wet weather

MELFORD HALL, Long Melford, CO10 9AA; ☎ 01787 376395; melford@nationaltrust.org.uk, www.nationaltrust.org.uk; adults £6.60, children £3.30, families £16.50; open Apr to Sept, Wed to Sun afternoons; beg of Apr and Oct weekends only.

Long Melford makes a good destination for a rainy day. You might get a little wet on its very long high street (which stretches a mile and a half) if you want to browse in the dozens of appealing shops. But you will be warm and dry for hours inside one or both of its Tudor mansions. Whereas Kentwell Hall is privately run on an aggressively commercial basis (described below as a child-friendly attraction), Melford Hall is tastefully run by the National Trust.

The intriguing roofline of **Melford Hall** with its pepperpot turrets indicates straightaway that this is an Elizabethan house. In fact the good queen visited a decade or so after it was built in the 1560s. The Hyde Parker family acquired it in 1786 and their descendants still live there as tenants of the National Trust. The current baronet's grandmother's cousin was Beatrix Potter, who used to visit accompanied by a small menagerie of animals and the house has a small collection of her drawings associated with Melford.

What to do with children...

Kentwell Hall

Adults are perfectly capable of enjoying processing up the avenue of limes to visit Kentwell Hall and its many surprises. On an ordinary open day, visitors are permitted to ramble all over the Phillips' family home and note their various experiments in rescuing a great house that had been allowed to decay until

KENTWELL HALL, Long Melford, CO10 9BA; ☎ 01787 310207; www.kentwell.co.uk; adults £9.95, children £6.50, recreation days £14.95/ £10.80 (third off for late entry); check calendar on website for opening times; special events between Feb and Nov.

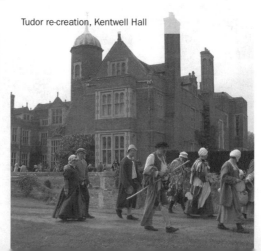
Tudor re-creation, Kentwell Hall

they bought it in 1970. But it's best known for its quite astonishingly ambitious historical re-creations that populate the house and huge gardens with literally hundreds of costumed characters (all volunteers) who play the part of Tudors, or on other special event days of characters from the Second World War, when Kentwell really was requisitioned. The main Tudor 'living history events' take place in late June and early July for school groups on weekdays and the general public at weekends. The Tudor skills demonstrated are fascinating, from the apothecary to the archers, and children are invited to participate in many demonstrations.

Other events at other times may appeal to children, such as lambing in February, since the owners have set up a rare breed farm over the past two decades.

Farm trail

About 2 miles north of Kersey, **The Hollow Trees Farm** has a farm trail (sometimes muddy) and a farm shop. Young children will enjoy Chicken City, Goat Mountain, Bunny Town and Guineas Stable, especially if their parents have splashed out 25p on a bag of food.

> **HOLLOW TREES FARM SHOP,** Semer, Near Hadleigh IP7 6HX; ☎ 01449 741247; www. hollowtrees.co.uk. Open year round.

 ## ... and how to avoid children

Gainsborough's House

Some children might enjoy looking at drawings and etchings of an 18th century portrait painter but there can't be many. To be sure of your escape, consider joining one of the printmaking workshops open to novices and people with experience.

> **GAINSBOROUGH'S HOUSE**, 46 Gainsborough Street, Sudbury CO10 2EU; ☎ 01787 372958; www.gainsborough.org; £4 except Tues free; open Mon to Sat 10am–5pm.

Pursuing the theme of short courses, **Flatford Mills Field Studies Centre**

Gainsborough's House

offers a varied programme of weekend and five-day courses with expert tutors on topics such as watercolour painting and garden birdwatching. Prices for a residential weekend are about £175 (www.field-studies-council. org/flatford mill/leisurelearning.aspx).

One-day courses on lots of rural arts and crafts such as bee-keeping, basket-weaving, apple juice-making and water-dowsing are offered at Assington Mill, between Sudbury and Stoke by Nayland (CO10 5LW; ☎ 01787 229955; www.assingtonmill.com).

Entertainment

Theatre
The lively little **Sudbury Quay Theatre** puts on a programme of comedy, drama, music, film and art exhibitions. It occupies an attractive riverside location (Quay Lane, Sudbury CO10 2AN; ☎ 01787 374745; www.quaytheatre. org.uk) with a bar and offers pre-theatre suppers in conjunction with **The Olde Bull Bistro** around the corner on Church Street.

Lavenham has its own concert promoters who each year put on occasional Sunday concerts performed by high-quality classical musicians (www.laven ham-sinfonia.co.uk).

Shopping

Long Melford's array of high-end independent shops has already been mentioned. It is especially well known for its antiques. Specialist shops can be found selling everything from organic baby clothes and accessories (at **Green Berry's**) to Italian shoes, Persian carpets and contemporary glass. The website www.longmelford.co.uk/shops1.html provides a guide to many of them.

Sudbury has been a silk-weaving centre for centuries, ever since the bottom began to fall out of the wool trade in 1600. Amazingly, two designer silk factories continue in Sudbury. **Stephen Walters & Sons** on Cornard Road and **Vanners** on Weavers Lane (which backs onto the garden of Gainsborough's house); both have shops where you can buy exclusive fabrics.

In almost every village, you will find craftspeople at work in studios. **Kersey Pottery** produces stoneware with unusual glazes (www.kerseypottery.com) and **Dylan Pym** in Polstead hand-makes lovely pieces of furniture in a storied house where Maria Marten was born.

OAKYARD WORKSHOPS,
Maria Marten's cottage, Marten's Lane, Polstead CO6 5AG;
☎ 01206 262380;
www.dylanpym.co.uk;
visitors by appointment.

The best... **PLACES TO STAY**

BOUTIQUE

Black Lion Hotel

The Green (10 minute brisk walk from town), Long Melford CO10 9DN
☎ **01787 312356**
www.blacklionhotel.net

Positioned between the church and the green, the cosy and delightful hotel has a top-rated restaurant (voted best in Suffolk in 2006) as well as informal bar dining area with an open fire. The rooms are as different as the fine wines they are named after, for example the Yquem room has a four-poster bed.

Prices: B&B £150, £165 or £195 for a double depending on room.

HOTEL

The George

The Green, Cavendish CO10 8BA
☎ **01787 280248**
www.thecavendishgeorge.co.uk

This welcoming 16th-century hotel with four rooms has exposed wood beams and brickwork. Since the chef-proprietor is an escapee from Conran, the food is several cuts above gastropub. It has a heated dining courtyard and provides Sunday papers.

Prices: From £55 a double.

INN

The Sun Inn

High Street, Dedham CO7 6DF
☎ **01206 323351**
www.thesuninndedham.com

This characterful Tudor inn has been recently revamped to a luxurious standard while retaining its friendliness as a local pub serving well-kept Adnams, Earl Soham and other ales. The Italian-influenced food has also gone upmarket and includes recherché dishes such as pasta stuffed with pigeon, juniper and nutmeg.

Prices: Sun to Thurs £85/£95, £120/£130 Fri/Sat for a double.

FARMSTAY/ORGANIC

The Hall, Milden

Milden, Near Lavenham CO10 9NY
☎ **01787 247235**
www.thehall-milden.co.uk

This huge 16th-century farmhouse is run by keen conservationists and historians who are full of imaginative ideas for getting back to nature and amusing the children. The large hall is heated by a huge wood-burning stove. Bicycles are lent free and breakfasts use produce from the farm.

Prices: from £60 for a double; self-catering sleeping 2–22 also available.

B&B

Lavenham Priory 10+

Water Street, Lavenham CO10 9RW
☎ **01787 247404**
www.lavenhampriory.co.uk

This rambling Grade I-listed mediaeval house has been turned into a luxury B&B which has won multiple prizes (including the AA's nationwide 'Guest Accommodation of the Year'). The rooms are individually decorated, most with four-poster beds. Interesting features include Elizabethan wall paintings, three acres of grounds and an honesty bar.

Prices: from £98 to £138 for a double, plus weekend supplement of £22.

SELF-CATERING

The Pump House

Scotland Place, Scotland Street, Stoke by Nayland CO6 4QG
☎ **01787 211115**
mark@grove-cottages.co.uk
www.grove-cottages.co.uk

With an idyllic riverside setting in the Box River valley, this small architect-designed cottage has a meadow for a garden. In addition to a double bedroom, it has a loft where two more can sleep. It comes equipped with a powerful telescope and bicycles, including one with a child's seat.

Prices: £344 per week in low season, £696 in high season with last-minute 15% discount.

The best... FOOD AND DRINK

Staying in

The market town of **Sudbury** hosts a bustling market on Thursdays and Saturdays. The last Friday of the month sees local food producers gathering from a 30-mile radius in **St Peter's Hall** on Market Hill. Here you can find savoury handraised pies from local business **Gilbert's Galloping Chef, Granny Straughan's Country Cakes**, honey from Bildeston, and so on. A smaller farmers' market is held in Long Melford village hall on the third Saturday of each month (☎ 01787 280031).

Farm gate sales of free-range meat aren't uncommon in the region, for example from Scotland Place Farm in Stoke by Nayland. One of the best farm shops in the East of England is **Hollow Trees Farm Shop** in Semer about 2 miles north of Kersey (address above). Its 10 acres in vegetable production mean that is has a wonderfully fresh range of seasonal crops and also sells bread and jam, milk and honey. Just before you reach Cavendish you come to another farm shop at **Willow Tree Farm** (Lower Road, Glemsford CO10 7QU; ☎ 01787 280341) which also sells superb quality produce (including asparagus in season) plus cheeses, chickens and ready meals.

Considering their clientele, it isn't surprising that places such as Lavenham and Long Melford have plenty of tempting food shops, like **Matthews' Fine Foods** in Long Melford (1 Dudley House, Hall Street CO10 9JR; ☎ 01787 881361), which has an amazing collection of specialist foods from the region and around the world including rillettes and cassoulet from the Dordogne. It's open every day in summer.

Dedham is another well favoured town, and the **Dedham Gourmet** on the High Street should not be missed for cheese, charcuterie, olives and wines (CO7 6HA; ☎ 01206 323623).

EATING OUT

FINE DINING

Case Restaurant with Rooms

Further Street, Assington, Near Sudbury CO10 5LD, ☎ 01787 210483
www.thecaserestaurantwithrooms.co.uk

There is no mistaking that this is a family-run business where the owners really care about food and service. Memorable meals might include Tuscan soup, shredded duck in filo and white and dark chocolate cheesecake. This place is also recommended as a boutique place to stay, where the good value prestige rooms come with corner jacuzzis.

The Great House Restaurant and Hotel

Market Place, Lavenham CO10 9QZ
☎ 01787 247431
www.greathouse.co.uk

Authentic French cuisine is served here without the Michelin restaurant fussiness of France. Both classic and less familiar dishes appear on the set menu, priced at a reasonable £27 for three courses, but not available Saturday when only the à la carte menu is available (mains £19–24).

Scutchers of Long Melford

Westgate Street, Long Melford CO10 9DP, ☎ 01787 310200
www.scutchers.com

Scutchers used to call itself a bistro but has higher aspirations. Stylish British cooking might include slow roast breast of local duckling with orange sauce served with a rosti. Two-course deals are priced at £15, three courses at £20.

GASTROPUB

Henny Swan

Henny Street, Great Henny, near Sudbury CO10 7LS, ☎ 01787 269238
www.thehennyswan.co.uk

This converted barge house is located right on the River Stour. Take away the picnic tables from the garden and the scene might make a suitable subject for Constable. The contemporary menu might include grilled halloumi cheese with roasted peppers (£5) and aubergine gratin with pine nuts (£9.50).

Angel

Polstead Street,
Stoke by Nayland CO6 4SA
☎ 01206 263245

This delightful relaxed old inn has comfortable armchairs and a modern menu that might feature whole grilled plaice or stilton and artichoke tart. The same menu is served in the bar as in the more formal bookable restaurant.

CAFÉS

Essex Rose Tea House

High Street, Dedham CO7 6DE
☎ 01206 323101
www.trooms.com/essexrose_tearoom.php

This heavily timbered tearoom is owned by the massive Tiptree Fruit farm near Colchester so the cream tea features 'Tiptree strawberry conserve with Tiptree scones, butter and fresh cream, served with the Tiptree tea of your choice'. Waitress service.

The Guildhall of Corpus Christi

Market Place, Lavenham CO10 9QZ
☎ 01787 247646

A superlative building in a town full of them, this early 16th-century hall is managed by the National Trust (£3.75 admission) which of course has a tearoom. After a cream tea, you can visit the walled garden planted and an exhibition of 100-year-old photos of the town.

Tickled Pink Tea Room

17 High Street, Lavenham CO10 9PT
☎ 01787 248438

Freshly baked scones and light snacks, including decent ploughmans, are served daily on both floors of a crooked, half-timbered cottage. Food is served on Portmerion china and even the loos are twee.

Drinking

The **Nethergate Brewery** in Pentlow, less than a mile from Cavendish, brews several luscious brews such as Old Growler porter and the unusual Umbel ales flavoured with toasted coriander seeds, a custom that goes back many centuries. The newest addition is a stronger bitter called Essex Border. Brewery tours are available to pre-booked groups or you should look for their ales in local pubs that include **The Bull** in Cavendish, **The Cock** in Clare and **The Angel** in Lavenham, all first-rate pubs. Sudbury also has a microbrewery, **Mauldons Brewery** from which you can buy bottle-conditioned bitters, stouts and porters, the most famous being the award winning Black Adder stout.

MAULDONS BREWERY,
13 Churchfield Road, Sudbury,
CO10 2YA; ☎ 01787 311055;
www.mauldons.co.uk

In the village of Edwardstone lost amongst the tiny lanes between Sudbury and Hadleigh, the proprietors of the **White Horse Inn** (Mill Green, CO10 5PX; ☎ 01787 211211; email: john.norton@nortonorganic.co.uk) are in the process of building an eco-friendly microbrewery. The pub (which mounts three beer festivals a year) also serves the organic cider the landlord makes at his home, **Castling Heath Cottage**, which gives its name to the cider. (Castling Heath Cottage Cider, Castling Heath Cottage, Groton, near Sudbury CO10 5ES; ☎ 01787 210899)

On the B road between Hadleigh and Stowmarket, you pass a brew pub called **The King's Head** (132 High Street, Bildeston IP7 7ED; ☎ 01449 741434; www.bildestonkingshead.co.uk) which for a one-pub brewery brews a good choice of interesting beers such as NSB 2.8% (which stands for Not Strong Beer) and Crowdie's Strong Oatmeal Stout (nearly twice as strong).

The whole area is peppered with good pubs. To pick out just four, try the friendly **Globe** in Clare which serves tasty pies, the 14th-century **Bell Inn** in Kersey, popular for Sunday lunch, the dog-friendly (and people-friendly) **King's Head** near the beginning of Flatford Lane in East Bergholt, and the foodie **Anchor** in Nayland which as well as featuring guest ales also serves wine from its own vineyard near Colchester, Carter's Vineyard (www.cartersvineyards.co.uk).

Visitor information

Tourist Information Centres: East Bergholt/Flatford Tourist Information Centre, Flatford Lane, Flatford, East Bergholt CO7 6UL, ☎ 01206 299460, flatfordvic@babergh.gov.uk, open daily until end October and then weekends only until Easter; Sudbury Tourist Information, Town Hall, Gaol Lane/Market Hill, Sudbury CO10 1TL, ☎ 01787 881320, sudburytic@babergh.gov.uk, open all year, Mon to Sat 9am–5pm, with shorter opening hours on Sat, especially in winter; Lavenham Tourist Information Centre, Lady Street, Lavenham CO10 9RA ☎ 01787 248207, lavenhamtic@babergh.gov.uk; East of England Tourist Board, Dettingen House, Dettingen Way, Bury St Edmunds IP33 3TU ☎ 01284 727470]; www.visiteastofengland.com, distributes Cycling Discovery Maps for the East of England (£1.50).

Hospitals: The nearest hospital with 24-hour A&E department is Ipswich; Heath road, Ipswich IP4 5PD (01473 702905), 2 miles east of Ipswich town centre on the A1189 (Heath Road)

Websites: www.lavenham.co.uk; www.foxearth.org.uk/StourFrom SourceToSea.html – useful (although old) description in detail of the River Stour.

Supermarkets: Waitrose, Station Road, Sudbury CO10 2SS (☎ 01787 880373); Somerfield, 100 East Street, Sudbury CO10 2TP (☎ 01787 375915).

Bike rental: Street Life Cycles, Hamilton Road, Sudbury CO10 2UU, ☎ 01787 310940, www.streetlifecycles.co.uk, £10 per day. Hire may also be available for three-day periods at a discounted rate; The Hall, Milden, Near Lavenham CO10 9NY, ☎ 01787 247235, www.thehall-milden.co.uk, approx. £12.50 per day. Approximately 20 bikes for hire with priority for guests who are staying at The Hall. No bikes suitable for children but two come fixed with child seats.

Local Taxis: Elite Taxis, Sudbury, ☎ 08458324556 (local rate) or ☎ 01787 881212; Manor Cars, Sudbury, ☎ 01787 880880; Felix Taxis, Long Melford, ☎ 01787 310574.

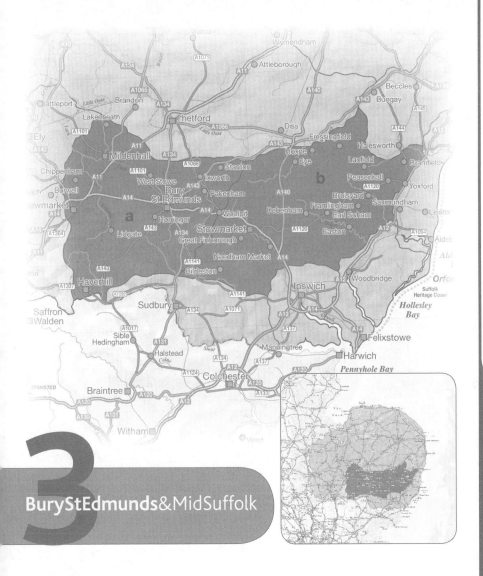

3

BuryStEdmunds&MidSuffolk

a. Bury St Edmunds

b. Heart of Suffolk

Unmissable highlights

01 Have a picnic inside the ruined abbey of Bury St Edmunds,
p.150

02 Follow a new nature trail from the open-air Museum of East Anglian Life to the River Rat,
p.166

03 See a play at the Theatre Royal in Bury, newly restored to its former Georgian glory,
p.152

04 Be revolted at Moyse's Museum by the book bound in the human skin of a legendary hanged criminal,
p.151

05 Stroll round the Italianate gardens overlooking the magnificent park landscaped by Capability Brown at Ickworth House,
p.158

06 Enjoy lunch at the prize-winning Leaping Hare Restaurant at the Wyken Vineyard after attending its Saturday farmers' market,
p.156

07 Take the children to a rare breeds farm in the lambing season,
p.166

08 Get up early to watch the thoroughbreds being walked to the gallops at Newmarket racecourse,
p.162

09 Sample organic Aspall cider which has travelled along a new pipeline direct to the local pub,
p.173

10 Stride along the ramparts of Framlingham Castle,
p.165

BURY ST EDMUNDS & MID-SUFFOLK

This chapter encompasses a vast swathe of Suffolk from the north-west corner of the county marked by the River Little Ouse to the scenic west–east routes through Mid-Suffolk along the A1120 and the B1078. With the honourable exceptions of Bury St Edmunds, considered one of the finest small towns in England, and Framlingham Castle, no must-see sights dictate a route. The pleasure (not the devil) is in the detail, and exploring the ancient rural landscape of the Heart of Suffolk overlaid with a network of lanes and byroads will reveal lots of unexpected delights: isolated churches at the bottom of farm tracks (Gipping), granaries and cartsheds turned into holiday cottages (Fressingfield), picnic sites where wild orchids bloom (Barham), farmers passionately devoted to raising rare breeds (Baylham) and farmers' wives who make and sell mulberry vodka from their own mulberry tree (Haughley New Street).

The rich history of Bury St Edmunds is tangible on almost every street corner. At its heart are the ruins of the original abbey church of St Edmund, king and martyr, now incorporated into Bury's most attractive municipal gardens. Elegant townhouses surround Angel Hill and charming streets such as Guildhall Street are lined with flower-adorned houses and shops that bespeak a prosperous and proud place.

The environs of Bury St Edmunds encompass plenty of interest, even if the far northwest corner of Suffolk isn't one of the county's most glorious landscapes. Originally it was breckland as described in the chapter on the Norfolk Brecks but so much of the land has been ploughed or planted by the Forestry Commission that little of the hedged pastures and lonely droving routes survive. And yet pleasant strolls can be taken along the banks of the Rivers Lark, Linnett and Kennett, especially during the bluebell season in spring, and the 100 mile Icknield Way, an ancient trading route between the Thames and South Norfolk, provides some lovely walking possibilities.

BURY ST EDMUNDS

Bury is a delightful town for sauntering and window shopping. Despite its ancient foundations, the buildings you see are mainly Georgian, such as the elegant town hall designed by Robert Adam, the pre-eminent neo-classical architect of the 18th century who also did the interiors of the Athenaeum in Bury. The ruined abbey is astounding in its scale and its role in history. And yet it is tamed by the town gardens which provide its setting, complete with tennis courts, rose garden and aviary, all completely free of charge and right in the middle of town.

Best of all, Bury St Edmunds is anything but a clone town. It is bursting with civic pride, and even the casual visitor will agree that that pride is justified. Streets are mainly lined with independent shops rather than national franchises. The twice-weekly outdoor provisions market was awarded Highly Commended status, along with just two others nationwide, in a 2008 Market of the Year contest. With one of East Anglia's two foremost breweries, Greene King, its worthy brewing tradition manifests itself in good pubs including one that nearly qualifies as the smallest in the country.

WHAT TO SEE AND DO

 Fair weather

Setting off from the **Abbey Gate** across the wide space of **Angel Hill**, the grand-looking 18th-century **Athenaeum** and other Georgian buildings proclaim the town's long prosperity. When Charles Dickens came to Bury in 1859 and 1861 to give public readings in the Athenaeum, he stayed at the Angel Hotel. Until recently the Queen Anne townhouse called Manor House at 5 Honey Hill, originally built for the Bristol family of Ickworth House, was a museum of clocks but it has been sold to a private buyer as a family dwelling and part of the clock collection has gone to the town museum.

Market Cross in the centre includes a Robert Adam building, now **Bury St Edmunds Art Gallery,** a council-run contemporary space with shop and café (www.burystedmundsartgallery.org) and gives onto Cornhill with the museum and the Traverse and a lovely building called the Cupola built in 1693, now a La Strada restaurant with a grand staircase to the upper level. The view from the roof is reputed to be the best in Bury but isn't generally available. Cornhill turns into Guildhall Street where the **Old Guildhall** has a 13th-century dogtooth doorway inside a 15th-century porch. Churchgate and Abbeygate Streets lead downhill back to the abbey and are lined with shops and restaurants.

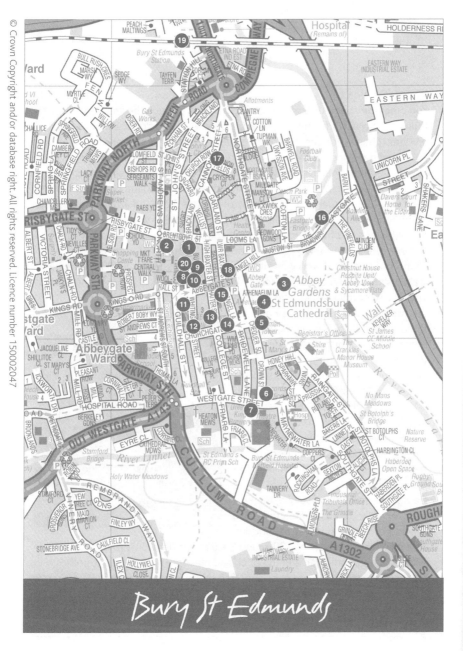

Bury St Edmunds

1 Moyse's Hall Museum	**8** Harriets Café	**15** Barwells Food
2 Art Gallery	**9** La Strada	**16** The Fox
3 Abbey Ruins	**10** Nutshell	**17** Old Cannon Brewery
4 St Edmundsbury Cathedral	**11** Baileys 2	**18** Tourist Information Centre
5 Athenaeum	**12** Hide Bar	**19** Station
6 Green King Brewery	**13** So Bar	**20** Market
7 Theatre Royal	**14** Maison Bleue	

Abbey Gardens

You enter the spacious and welcoming gardens through the imposing Norman foursquare gatehouse near the centre of town. On a sunny day you will find children chasing ducks, a wedding party being photographed in the rose garden and perhaps a musician or juggler practising for a busking gig.

The impressive ruins make it easy to imagine defiant English barons gathering here in 1214 to hatch a plan to limit King John's absolute power by making him ratify Magna Carta. In its heyday of the late 12th and 13th centuries, the Benedictine **Abbey of St Edmund** (01284 764667, www.english-heritage. org.uk) was one of the largest Romanesque churches in the land, if not in all Europe. The structure would have been nearly a tenth of a mile long, a lavish shrine to St Edmund who was killed by Danish invaders in AD869 as he heroically tried to defend his province. He is patron saint of Suffolk and also of wolves. According to legend, a wolf guarded Edmund's severed head for three days before his men located it; the legend is depicted in a carving on the bishop's throne in the cathedral next door to the ruins and also on the exterior of Moyse's Hall.

Elisabeth Frink's statue of King Edmund, St Edmundsbury Cathedral gardens

When the diocese of Edmundsbury and Ipswich was created less than a hundred years ago, the church of St James was chosen to be upgraded to become the **Cathedral**. Unlike that other unfinished cathedral, the Sagrada Familia of Barcelona, this one has recently been completed. You would not spot the tower as modern, though it was built between 2000 and 2005 as a millennium project. The design is Suffolk perpendicular, and the brick and masonry spire is held together with lime mortar rather than steel or concrete. Note Elisabeth Frink's 1976 bronze sculpture of a boyish and vulnerable- looking King Edmund.

 ## Wet weather

Moyse's Hall Museum

Not many Norman domestic buildings survive and the building in which the fascinating local museum is housed is one of them. Moyse's Hall dates from 1180 and although restored still has some mediaeval doorways, window seats and undercroft. The museum collections cover all the usual topics expected of

MOYSE'S HALL MUSEUM,
Bury St Edmunds, IP33 1DX; ☎
01284 706183; www.stedmunds
bury.gov.uk/sebc/visit/moyses-hall.
cfm; adults £5, children and
concessions £3; open daily
10am–5pm.

Moyse's Hall Museum

a local museum, from prehistoric archaeological finds to evidence of superstitions about witches.

Greene King Brewery

Brewing has been an important industry in Bury for centuries and Greene King has been around since 1799 and making beer on the same premises since 1806. The visitor centre on the corner of Westgate and Crown Streets incorporates a museum of brewing and is the place to book a

GREENE KING BREWERY,
Bury St Edmunds, IP33 1QT;
☎ 01284 714297 or 714382;
www.greeneking.co.uk; tours: Mon
to Sat 10am–5pm; evening tours
available (£10.50) but must be
pre-booked.

tour of the brewery. Tastings are available at the end of the tour which costs £8.50. The brewery logo is of an Abbot, specifically Abbot Samson who was in charge of the abbey in the late 12th century when it was at its most powerful. Ironically he was not a big drinker himself. According to a young monk who was there at the time, Samson was a very upright man who planted beans where once casks of wine had been stored and who ordered the smashing of a building in the graveyard because it had been used for 'frequent drinking bouts and certain things which can't be mentioned'.

 ## What to do with children

The **Abbey Gardens** are an ideal destination for children. Long before they reach the playground by the river they will be distracted by the aviary and by the climbing possibilities afforded by the abbey ruins.

Moyse's Hall Museum has a large exhibit devoted to the true tale of the Red Barn murder. The trial of the accused, William Corder, took place at Bury St Edmunds Assizes in 1828. He pleaded not guilty to the murder of his lover Maria Marten in Polstead but was nevertheless found guilty and hanged soon afterwards. A local surgeon dissected the cadaver, removing the skeleton, which ended up in London, the scalp and skin. The preserved scalp still with one ear visible is on display as is a book retelling the story of William and Maria which is bound in 'leather' made from the murderer's skin. The features on the death mask are distorted, with veins visibly bulging, since the cast was taken after the hanging. A story not suitable for small children prone to nightmares.

Entertainment

Theatre Royal

Incredibly for a town with a population of 35,000 Bury St Edmunds has its own theatre, and a jewel of a theatre at that. It is the last remaining Regency theatre in the country, re-opened in September 2007. It has undergone sensitive restoration, applauded by Judi Dench, Stephen Fry and

> **THEATRE ROYAL**, Westgate Street, Bury St Edmunds, IP33 1QR; ☎ 01284 769505 Box Office; www.theatreroyal.org; tours: £6; Tues/Thurs afternoons plus weekends at 11am.

Timothy West. Regular tours are held, though the best way to experience the intimate little theatre and to have the leisure to admire its friezes and *trompe l'oeil* painting, is to attend a performance.

Special events

The summer festival is a colourful affair with a carnival queen, floats, fairground rides in the Abbey Gardens and fireworks. A series of six summer concerts takes place in an unusual setting of a thatched 16th-century barn at Blackthorpe, 3 miles from Bury (www.blackthorpebarn.com). Tickets for professional concerts as various as a percussion quartet and an up-and-coming Russian pianist can be bought through the Theatre Royal box office as above; prices from £15. Arts and crafts fairs are also hosted here.

Shopping

When Daniel Defoe visited Bury in the 1720s, he noted a lack of manufacturing and decided that the town depended on the local gentry spending money in the town. There still isn't much manufacturing and still plenty of well-heeled people come to enjoy Bury's up-market shopping opportunities. The controversial new Arc Shopping development is being built on the site of the old Cattle Market a few minutes walk from the historic centre. When it opens in February 2009 it will include more than 30 shops plus a music venue, restaurants and cafés.

In the meanwhile shoppers can luxuriate in the independent shops on streets such as Abbeygate, Hatter, Guildhall and St John's. Gift shops, boutiques and high fashion abound, tending to the conservative (e.g. Jaeger on St John's

The Visitors' Book

A family day trip to Bury St Edmunds

'Turning off the A14 by the white plumes rising from the chimneys of the sugar beet factory, we quickly escaped from the 21st-century to the 18th-century townscape of Angel Hill, the broad market square fronted by coaching inns and assembly hall, outside the imposing gates of what was once one of the largest and richest abbeys of medieval England. A farmers' market was serving spit-roast pork on the Sunday we visited, along with other local produce.'

'Our twin boys enjoyed the playground and aviary set amidst the evocative ruins which once housed the shrine of the local saint, the Saxon King Edmund martyred by the Danes, and where the barons met to force King John to accept Magna Carta. We strolled through the delightful Georgian townscape on the grid of a miniature medieval Manhattan laid out by the medieval abbots, before visiting the small museum in Moyse's Hall, a rare survival of a 12th-century house.'

'We rounded off the day with a visit to the National Trust's Ickworth House, 3 miles outside the town, a vast rotunda of a country house built by the eccentric Earl Bishop of Bristol, with beautiful landscaped gardens, an intriguing collection of eighteenth-century fans, and a deer park for the children. The food served at the Beehive in Horringer near the entrance to the park was first-rate, especially when accompanied by the excellent beer from the local Greene King brewery.'

Philip Hardie, Cambridge

The best... PLACES TO STAY

BOUTIQUE

Ickworth Hotel and Apartments

Horringer, Bury St Edmunds IP29 5QE
☎ **01284 735350**
www.ickworthhotel.co.uk

Set in an idyllic location surrounded by 1,800 acres of English parkland, this National Trust stately home belonged to the Hervey family for over 200 years. Now part of the exclusive Von Essen group of luxury family hotels, the hotel offers a range of facilities including bikes that are free to borrow, babysitting service and crèche.

Prices: B&B from £165 to £285 for standard double; from £215 per night for a one-bedroom apartment.

INN

Old Cannon

The Old Cannon Brewery, 86 Cannon Street, Bury St Edmunds IP33 1JR
☎ **01284 768769**
www.oldcannonbrewery.co.uk/stay.html

Described by the *Good Beer Guide* as *the* place to go in Bury for real ale, the Old Cannon also offers comfortable double rooms and one twin, all with large en-suite shower rooms. Breakfast ingredients are sourced from Suffolk and the attached restaurant offers a smart menu.

Prices: B&B £55 for a single; £69 for a double.

B & B

The Manorhouse

The Green, Beyton IP30 9AF
☎ **01359 270960**
www.beyton.com

A 15th-century Suffolk longhouse, the Manorhouse overlooks the village green to the front and a lovely garden behind. Period features have been retained in the four individually furnished rooms. One room, the Dairy, is situated in the cheerfully decorated barn conversion next to the house.

Prices: from £50 to £60 for a single; from £32 to £38 per person in a suite.

CAMPSITE

Brighthouse Farm Campsite

Brighthouse Farm, Melford Road, Lawshall IP29 4PX (nearly 10 miles south of Bury) ☎ **01284 830385**
www.brighthousefarm.co.uk

This flat and grassy 6-acre site with mature and newly planted trees is run by a family who take pride in offering non-regimented pitches. Several private walks are described in the site's welcome sheet, several of which lead to the village of Lawshall with its wishing well and Elizabethan hall.

Prices: from £11 per night for caravans with electric hook-up; £8–11 for tents.

SELF-CATERING

The Grange Farm Bothy

Woolpit, Bury St Edmunds IP30 9RG
☎ **01359 241143/** ☎ **07740 780460**
www.farmstayanglia.co.uk/grangefarm

A self-contained cottage that lies adjacent to the listed Grange Farm building. The Bothy was originally an apple and corn store. The cottage is set in attractive countryside a short walk from the village, just off the A14. Accommodation for two includes a landing area with internal balcony.

Price: from £270 for a week.

UNUSUAL

Badwell Ash Holiday Lodges

Hunston Road, Badwell Ash IP31 3DJ (12 miles east of Bury) ☎ **01359 258444**
www.badwellashlodges.co.uk

This adult-only retreat built on the edge of a lake offers self-catering log cabins, sleeping four, for a minimum of three nights. Spaced out around two fishing lakes, each has a hot tub on a decked terrace which gives good views of the wildlife and surrounding countryside. Complimentary champagne and chocolates greet new arrivals, and bicycles and DVDs can be borrowed.

Price: from £420 per lodge for three nights up to £895 for one week.

Street and nearby a pearl jewellery boutique called Lilyo). Good quality English-made shoes for men can be found at **Alfred Sargent Shoes** in Risbygate Street, while shoe-loving women might like the selection at **Chica** on Hatter Street. Stylish women's clothes can be found at **Anna's** in Guildhall Street and **Sampa** on Hatter Street. Good-quality regional crafts are available from the shop in the Market Cross Art Gallery.

The best... FOOD AND DRINK

▶ Staying in

Bury has been a market town for centuries, and market traders have fought for the right to carry on setting up their stalls twice a week. On Wednesdays and Saturdays, cars are banished from Butter Market and Cornmarket, and a produce market continues to flourish. Stalls vary but you can usually find a good selection of olives, cheese, bread and fruit.

On Abbeygate Street, **Barwells** is a long-established delicatessen selling gourmet foods, game pies, seasonal goodies, cakes and wine. Among their range of renowned pies is a picnic pie made of chicken and thyme. On Saturday market day they set up a cart outside the shop selling excellent hotdogs and the shop has free tastings to entice you to buy. For a treat visit the **Bury Chocolate Shop** at 77a St John's Street.

Further afield, the exceptional weekly **farmers' market** at Wyken Vineyards (see *Eating Out*) takes place every Saturday from 9am to 1pm. Another superb destination is **La Hogue Farm Shop and Delicatessen** in Chippenham just north of Newmarket (technically in Cambridge on the edge of the Fens, CB7 5PZ; ☎ 01638 751128; www.lahogue.co.uk). The young couple who run it tirelessly extend their range of wonderful food from Suffolk venison to Italian salamis, plus a deli counter with more than 80 mainly British cheeses, and a separate wine shop. Opening times are Tuesdays to Fridays 10am–7pm (6pm in winter), and Saturdays 10am–5.30pm and Sundays 10am–4pm.

EATING OUT

FINE DINING
Maison Bleue
**31 Churchgate St, Bury St Edmunds IP33 1RG, ☎ 01284 760623
www.maisonbleue.co.uk.**

The signature dish in this upmarket eatery which calls itself an 'unconventional fish restaurant' is a platter of crab, langoustines, oysters, whelks, tiger prawns and mussels for £22 per person. The restaurant is closed on Sundays and Mondays.

COUNTRY RESTAURANT
Leaping Hare Vineyard Restaurant
**Wyken Vineyards, Stanton IP31 2DW
☎ 01359 250287
www.wykenvineyards.co.uk.**

This is an unexpectedly perfect country destination for lunch, tea or dinner. It is open daily for lunches and dinners are available on Friday and Saturday only. Booking is often necessary. The immaculate conversion of the 16th-century barn into a restaurant and café at either end creates an airy light atmosphere which is matched by the cooking. All ingredients are seasonal and many are produced in the immediate vicinity. The menu might include for instance Wyken Estate lambshank and Wyken pigeon and wild mushrooms. The appealing Vintner's menu at lunchtime costs £17 for two courses plus a choice of wine made from grapes grown on the doorstep. Once you have got this far off the beaten path, it is tempting to spend extra hours exploring the grounds of the Elizabethan manor house. The country store here stocks Wyken wines of course and many unusual items.

GASTROPUB
The Beehive
The Street, Horringer, Bury St Edmunds IP29 5SN, ☎ 01284 735260

Near Ickworth House, this village pub has a warren of cosy low-ceilinged rooms and a compact terrace garden. The extensive menu offers appealing unfussy dishes at a range of prices such as salt beef sandwiches with horseradish and salad for £5.95. If you haven't booked, get there early. The pub doesn't serve food on Sunday evenings.

The Fox
**1 Eastgate St, Bury St Edmunds IP33 1XX
☎ 01284 705562
www.thefoxinnbury.co.uk**

The Fox takes great care with its cooking. Their freshly prepared chips are recommended, as is their cheese board, tortilla wraps (e.g. brie and caramelised onion) and great range of puddings.

The Star Inn
**The Street, Lidgate CB8 9PP
☎ 01638 500275**

Although this isn't the only pink-washed thatched country pub in Suffolk to serve great food, it is one of the few to specialise in Spanish cuisine. Renowned for its superior cooking, this pub is so popular that tables should be booked in advance. Two-course lunches will cost about £12.50.

The Red Lion
214 The Street, Kirtling Green, near Newmarket CB8 9PD, ☎ 01638 731976

The landlord of this traditional village local is from Galicia and has boundless enthusiasm, sometimes cooking authentic tapas dishes and serving behind the bar simultaneously. If you don't get carried away ordering, you can eat very cheaply here.

CAFÉ
Bailey's 2 Restaurants and Tearooms
5 Whiting Street, Bury St Edmunds IP33 1NX, ☎ 01284 706198

A Bury institution with a blackboard menu including sandwiches, toasties made with Suffolk ham, and homemade cakes.

Harriets Café Tearooms Ltd
**57 Cornhill, Bury St Edmunds IP33 1BT
☎ 01284 756256
www.harrietscafetearooms.co.uk**

This 1940s tearoom (complete with piano music of the era) opened in 2001. Waitresses wear retro white caps and aprons. Its open daily till 5.30pm, and on Thursday to Saturday until 9pm.

🍺 Drinking

Greene King owns most of the pubs in Bury though lots serve guest beers as well as the ubiquitous IPA and Abbot. Compared with the giant Greene King, the **Old Cannon Brewery** in Bury and **Bartrams Brewery** in Rougham just outside town are Lilliputian in scale. Both microbreweries make delicious brews available only locally. Old Cannon uses East Anglian grown and malted pearl barley in its stylish stainless steel brewing equipment, housed in the pub and

THE OLD CANNON, 86 Cannon Street, Bury St Edmunds, IP30 0QN; ☎ 01284 768769; www.oldcannonbrewery.co.uk; brewery, pub, restaurant and B&B located a short walk north of the town centre.
Bartrams Brewery, Rougham Estate, Ipswich Rd, Rougham, Bury St Edmunds, IP30 9LZ; www.bartramsbrewery.co.uk.

used to make Old Cannon Best Bitter, Gunner's Daughter, Blonde Bombshell and seasonal ales. Punning names for the beers from Bartram's like Rougham Ready and Coal Porter are sold through a handful of welcoming, country free houses including the Fox and Hounds in Bradfield St George and the Blue Boar in Walsham le Willows.

The Nutshell (17 The Traverse) in the middle of town is an astonishingly minute pub, though it has been bumped from the position of Smallest Pub in Britain by the Signal Box Inn in Cleethorpes and the Rake in London's Borough Market (both opened August 2006). Its dimensions are 15 x 7ft with a wall bench along both ends and a single table. On a busy night they have about 30 customers, some of whom spill out onto the pavement, have hosted wedding receptions and discos and once squashed in 102 people, each with at least

The tiny Nutshell pub

one foot on the floor, in a bid for a place in the *Guinness Book of Records*. A human leg bone and desiccated cat hang from the ceiling; the latter was found behind the panelled fireplace in 1952, and is left over from a time when it was believed that an animal skeleton in the fabric would guard against witches' spells. The pub keeps its Greene King beer well, and should not be missed.

Pleasant real ale pubs abound in the town and surrounding villages. Other good town choices include **The Mason's Arms** (Whiting Street), **The ancient Bushe** (St John's Street), and **The Tollgate** (142 Fornham Road)

Visitor information

Tourist Information Centres:
6 Angel Hill, Bury St Edmunds IP33
1UZ, ☎ 01284 764667/ 757083,
tic@stedsbc.gov.uk, www.stedmunds
bury.gov.uk/sebc/visit/links.cfm,
open Mon to Sat 9.30–5pm,
Good Friday to end Oct, Sun 10am–
3pm (closed Sun in winter) with
slightly shorter opening hours on
other days. Housed in a fine building
inhabited in the early 18th century by
Edward Crisp, the intended victim of
a grisly murder.
Hospitals: West Suffolk Hospital,
Hardwick Lane, Bury St Edmunds
IP33 2QZ (☎ 01284 713000; A&E ☎
01284 713333). A&E has been
threatened with closure.

Websites: www.moreheart.info
(online guide to promote Bury St
Edmunds in association with the
Borough Council: links from the site
of the local newspaper might also be
useful, (www.buryfreepress.co.uk).
Supermarkets: Sainsbury's, Bed-
ingfeld Way, Bury St Edmunds IP32
7BT (near Junction 44 of the A14);
Tesco, Stamford Court, Horringer
Road, Bury St Edmunds IP33 2DF;
Waitrose, Robert Boby Way, Bury St
Edmunds IP33 3DH (centrally
located, near the new Arc shopping
development).
Taxis: A1 Cars, ☎ 01284 766 777;
ABC Cabs, ☎ 01284 717141.

north of the A14. Just off the A143 northeast of Bury, the Elizabethan **Pykkerel
Inn** (☎ 01359 230398) dominates the high street of Ixworth, offering good
food plus B&B. Ixworth is a good starting point for walks to Pakenham with its
watermill and windmill.

But it isn't all real ale and open fires. Busy **SoBar** (1 Langton Place) aims to
please a stylish clientele with its arty retro fittings and range of cocktails
whereas **Hide Bar and Kitchen** (74 Whiting Street) is more of a wine bar.

FURTHER AFIELD

Ickworth House and Park

This stately home has bizarre architecture and a chequered history. The wife
of the Earl-Bishop whose grandiose architectural ambitions were responsible
for the house called it a 'stupendous monument of folly' when it was built in the
1790s.

The park and gardens incorporate 1,800 acres of woodland walks under a
magnificent canopy of mature trees, deer park, 300-year-old summer house, a

ICKWORTH HOUSE, Park and Gardens, The Rotunda, Horringer, Bury St Edmunds, IP29 5QE; ☎ 01284 735270; www.national trust.org.uk/ickworth; adults/children/families £9.50/ £3.75/£22.50; park and garden only: £4/£1/£8; park/gardens open year round (gardens closed Wed/Thurs); house open Mar to Nov; adventure playground next to car park is free.

Ickworth House

lake full of lily pads, an ornamental canal and isolated church. The history of the Hervey family, whose ancestral estate this was from 1467 ended ignominiously in 1998 when the seventh Marquess (half-brother of the socialite celebrity Lady Victoria Hervey) died aged 44; typical newspaper headlines read 'Junkie Marquess died penniless after spending millions on drugs.' The National Trust is now in charge and the wing where decadent parties lit by black candles took place is now leased by the Trust to an up-market hotel chain (see The best... *places to stay*).

WEST STOW ANGLO-SAXON VILLAGE, Icklingham Road, West Stow, Bury St Edmunds IP28 6HG; ☎ 01284 728718; www.sted mundsbury.gov.uk/sebc/play/wests tow-asv.cfm; adults/children £5, family £15, special event days £6/£5/£17.50; open daily 10am–5pm.

West Stow Anglo-Saxon village

Seven miles north of Bury is the fascinating reconstructed village at West Stow. The village and adjacent museum shed light on the dark ages when Angles,

West Stow Anglo Saxon Village

Local legends: Woolpit's green children

In the mists of the 12th century, reapers came across two mysterious creatures near the old wolf pits. They resembled a human girl and boy but their skin was green and they would eat none of the food the villages offered them unless it was green. The boy malingered and died but the girl gained strength, her skin turned pink and she was eventually able to explain that her people lived in a sunless land beyond a wide river. She and her brother had followed the delightful sound of bells into a cavern and eventually emerged at the wolf pits from which there was no way back. More prosaically the girl is said to have married a man from King's Lynn.

Jutes and Saxons would have been swarming into and settling this area. In the 1840s, an Anglo-Saxon cemetery was found on the site but it wasn't fully excavated until the 1960s. Since then imaginative archaeologists have had a field day speculating on materials and methods of construction, and have reconstructed buildings according to different theories. Crops are grown, pigs and hens are reared and costumed re-enactments take place in summer and some school holidays. From the free car park you can follow trails into West Stow Country Park and take longer walks along the River Lark and on the fringes of Breckland.

Woolpit

Although many Suffolk towns derived their wealth from wool, the name Woolpit comes from earlier Saxon times when wolves roamed the forests and were trapped in deep ditches. Holes in the ground play an important part in the legend that makes Woolpit famous, as depicted on the village sign.

The frilly buttressed church spire of **St Mary's Church** is easy to see from the A14, less than 10 miles east of Bury St Edmunds, and this thriving pretty village justifies a detour. The church is one of the best in the county with a profusion of angels adorning the hammerbeam roof, a magnificently decorated porch and carved bench ends. The village has some attractive cottages, a half-timbered **Weaver's Hall** and a tiny museum run by volunteers, open on summer weekends. A popular carboot sale takes place at Bridge Farm every Sunday from 8am.

Bradfield Woods

In his *History of the English Countryside* Oliver Rackham calls Bradfield Woods a 'treasure' and describes them as a 'place of colour and song, of gnarled tree stools and mysterious ponds, and of rare and difficult fungi'. These woods (Felsham Road, Bradfield St George, near Bury St Edmunds IP30 0AQ; www.suffolkwildlife.co.uk/nr/sites/brad.htm) are little changed since they belonged to the Abbey of Bury St Edmunds in 1252 and have been managed and coppiced in the same way through the centuries. Almost no alien trees have been planted, and native trees such as ash, maple, hazel, lime, elm, birch, alder and oak all flourish.

Newmarket

By rights the town devoted to the sport of kings should be in Cambridgeshire. By a fluke of historical boundaries, it is joined to Suffolk by a narrow isthmus of land, though is easily accessible via the A14 from Cambridge or Bury St Edmunds. The town is remarkable for one thing, its association with horse racing and breeding. Surrounded by stud farms and training stables, Newmarket is where approximately 2,500 thoroughbreds are being trained at any one time. It is a marvellous sight to see a string of sleek racehorses being led through the early morning mist to the gallops on Newmarket Heath. The Devil's Dyke ridge footpath passes close to the Rowley Mile course on one side and the July Course on the other. On race days (most Saturdays in summer,

NATIONAL HORSERACING MUSEUM, 99 High Street, Newmarket; ☎ 01638 667333; www.nhrm.co.uk; adults £6.50, children £3.50, families £15; open daily Mar to Dec 10am–5pm.

CELEBRITY CONNECTIONS
You might not have predicted that one of the Rolling Stones would become a pillar of the community in a Suffolk village. But bass player **Bill Wyman** has fallen for the charms of North Suffolk. He bought Gedding Hall, in a village near Bradfield Woods, in 1968 and spends much of his time here pursuing his new passion, metal detecting. This rock 'n' roller, who suffered from anxiety attacks in the 1960s, is now described as being the Rolling Stone most at peace with himself. Perhaps it's because of his long association with rural Suffolk.

Wyman's country retreat isn't many miles away from the Elizabethan mansion, Coldham Hall in Stanningfield, owned by **Claudia Schiffer** who was married in the 14th century parish church of St George's in the village of Shimpling in 2002.

among other dates), you can get an excellent free view of the action including sometimes the rich and famous arriving by private plane. To see the race from the inside you should book a ticket in advance: prices range from £5 in the garden enclosure to £22 in the posh enclosure (www.newmarketracecourses.co.uk). The annual

NATIONAL STUD, Newmarket CB8 0XE; ☎ 01638 663464; www.nationalstud.co.uk; tours: adults £6.50, children £5, families £20; at 11.15am and 2pm from 1 March; pre-book if possible.

Town Plate amateur race at the end of August commemorates the first race run in Newmarket in 1664. The prize is a box of Powters Newmarket sausages and a voucher to a Newmarket tailor.

Even if your visit doesn't coincide with a race, the **National Horseracing Museum** will be of interest to anyone who has followed racing, with its display about famous jockeys and horses such as Frankie Dettori and Red Rum.

Newmarket is home to the **National Stud** which can be toured. The guides are often ex-jockeys and will tell you how King James I of England preferred the sporting life of Newmarket to the serious affairs of state, and how his frivolous and decadent grandson Charles II turned Newmarket into a centre for gambling and whoring.

Mildenhall and Lakenheath

Mildenhall and Lakenheath are primarily associated with the US Air Force. The base at Mildenhall is one of the most important American installations in the country and Lakenheath is just 3 miles away.

MILDENHALL MUSEUM, King Street, Mildenhall, IP28 7EX; ☎ 01638 716970; www.mildenhallmuseum.co.uk; entry: free; open Mar to Dec Wed–Sat afternoons.

But it isn't all a case of concrete and barbed wire, for both towns, as the centres of huge parishes, have among the largest and best churches in East Anglia, founded on the wealth accruing from the mediaeval wool trade. If you are lucky enough to find the church in Mildenhall open, you must admire the wooden roof with its beautifully carved figures and winged angels on the beams. Lakenheath

Inside Mildenhall Museum

also has splendid features such as a Norman tower and wall paintings along the north aisle.

Mildenhall's museum will introduce you to the famous Mildenhall Treasure, a hoard of priceless Roman silver, famously found by a ploughman during the Second World War. Not realising the magnitude of what he had found, he showed his blackened finds to his boss who took them home. By chance a few years ago, a visitor recognised their value and they became 'treasure trove' and therefore the property of the state. They now reside in all their splendour in the British Museum, but the museum in Mildenhall has convincing replicas.

Three Churches Walk

This superb half-day walk (6.5 miles long or just over 9 miles with the Denham loop; see www.dalham.com) could equally be called 'The Three Pubs Walk'. You can start at any of three delightful villages east of Newmarket: Gazeley, Dalham or Moulton. From Moulton, go to the 15th-century arched **Packhorse Bridge** and set off along the riverside lane to the church. The waymarked route continues through woods, over bridges and along fields to **Dalham**, a village full of thatched buildings, including the pub. **The Affleck Arms** is a freehouse serving good country food, with outdoor tables overlooking a brook. On the outskirts of Dalham you come to a strange beehive-shaped brick structure that looks like a Mycenaean tomb but is an early Victorian malt kiln. This was once prime brewing country.

Instead of following the road here, take the straight footpath through an avenue of fine chestnuts trees up an incline to the strong Perpendicular church of St Mary the Virgin made of flint and stone. The raised position allows wonderful views over the valley of the River Kennett. Nearby is **Dalham Hall**, the manor house constructed in the early 1700s by the Bishop of Ely, who longed to see his old home 12 miles away in his retirement. The top storey has since been lost to a fire, but it is still a fine Queen Anne building, once owned by Cecil Rhodes.

The walk continues along the edge of **Brick Kiln Woods**, which is carpeted with bluebells in April. Shortly after passing the woods, you can either turn west along the Icknield Way towards Gazeley or add an extra loop to Denham Castle. Remains of a 12th-century motte and bailey castle can be seen on the Denham estate whose owners subscribe to the Countryside Stewardship Scheme, and have allowed the arable land next to the castle to revert to grazing for rare breeds such as Soay sheep. The long-term plan is to restore the castle and clear the moat, with the help of English Heritage. The walk resumes to **Gazeley Church**, where **The Chequers** is another welcoming pub, and back to the starting point in Moulton. If you have resisted the other pubs (or even if you haven't), you can finish your walk at the excellent **King's Arms** in Moulton, where a plate of battered cod, chips and mushy peas costs £5.50.

HEART OF SUFFOLK

In 1086 Eye was the only town in this large section of Suffolk, although Stow-market and Hoxne had recognisable town plans by then. Country estates are rare in this area that has always been composed of small individual landhold-ings and irregularly shaped fields that retain their hedgerows and pollarded oaks. Isolated, sometimes moated timber-framed farmhouses, set in peaceful little-known valleys of the rivers Deben, Dove and Gipping, make for a gentle landscape that seems to be less spoiled by modern development and industry than most other parts of the country. At one time there was more industry than there is now but it tended to be along the lines of the Suffolk Seed Drill Company which was the mainstay of now-sleepy Peasenhall.

You won't find celebrity enclaves or night clubs, but you might find a plough-ing competition with Suffolk punch horses or a group practising the arcane arts of Morris dancing or bell ringing in tiny country churches. Small local museums are run by committed volunteers who enjoy talking to visitors. For this is a region full of enthusiasts for traditional arts, whether renovating steam trains as at Brockwood Station, making quilts (at **Quilter's Haven** in **Needham Market**) or making wine as at Wissett. No one much has heard of any of these places but all you need is an Ordnance Survey map (Landranger 156) and a car or a bicycle to discover some of these surprises for yourself.

WHAT TO SEE AND DO

 Fair weather

Like most places, the Heart of Suffolk is at its best on a spring day when meadows are filled with cowslips. Cyclists can freewheel down surprisingly steep hills and head for landmark church spires such as the 19th-century one at **St Andrew's** in Great Finborough, which is said to have been built at the request of the local squire who was worried that his wife might otherwise lose her way when out riding.

For a great drive, head out along the A1120 scenic route from Stowmarket to Yoxford, and stop at Framlingham Castle or one of the pretty villages with their interesting church interiors (such as **Dennington**), their amazing food shops (**Earl Soham, Peasenhall**) and good second-hand bookshops (**Yoxford**).

Framlingham

Framlingham is a fetching town. Picturesque, colour-washed cottages on streets such as Castle Street and Queen's Head Alley cut through timbered

Curtain wall, Framlingham Castle

buildings. The main street links the spacious market square with the biggest castle in the county. Built in about 1190 by the earl named after an expletive (Bigod), **Framlingham Castle** is surrounded by a majestic stone wall known as a curtain wall that connects no less than 13 turreted towers. Walking round the top of the curtain wall (which anyone without a head for heights may find tricky) affords wonderful views over the artificial lake, Framlingham Mere.

FRAMLINGHAM CASTLE,
Framlingham IP13 9BP; ☎ 01728 724189; www.english-heritage.org.uk; adults £6.60; children £3.80; families £16.40; open daily Apr to Sep 10am–5pm, Jul to Aug 10am–6pm, Oct to Mar 10am–4pm, closed Tues/Wed; free audio guide.

If you have waterproof footwear, you can walk to the other side of the mere and get an equally magnificent view looking back at the castle. Mary 'Bloody' Tudor made her base here in 1553 after her brother Edward died, while she waited for court machinations to determine whether she could legally succeed to the throne against the wishes of Edward's will. When the call to the throne came, she and many of her followers who had camped at Framlingham set off in a grand procession to London. When the castle was no longer needed its interior buildings were substantially demolished to make way for a workhouse for the poor. Now this is a visitor centre with an exhibition detailing the castle's history.

Stowmarket

The chief attraction for visitors to Stowmarket is the **Museum of East Anglian Life**. This isn't a museum in the conventional sense, but more an open-air village, so a visit on a fine day is recommended. Occupying 70 acres right in the middle of town, the museum has a number of historic buildings and reconstructions such as a working water mill, blacksmith's shop, Victorian classroom, displays of gypsy life in painted caravans, and demonstrations of rural crafts.

MUSEUM OF EAST ANGLIAN LIFE, Stowmarket, IP14 1DL; ☎ 01449 612229; www.eastanglianlife.org.uk; adults £6.50, children £3.50, families £17.50, winter all £2; open daily Mar to Oct, Mon to Sat 10am–5pm, Sun 11am–5pm; plus Jun to Aug until 8pm on Thurs; only grounds open in the winter.

The museum has an innovative eco-emphasis, and maintains some Suffolk sheep, Red Poll cattle and Large Black pigs (who in due course find their way onto the menu of the on-site deli; see Café below). There are several nature trails, including access to the new **River Rattlesden Nature Reserve** equipped with footbridges, boardwalks and carefully chosen picnic spots along the River Rat, a tributary of the Gipping. Heading downriver along the Gipping, the old towpath can be followed all the way to Ipswich, a distance of about 20 miles by foot.

The **Mid-Suffolk Light Railway** based at a former station now in the corner of a large field, is an object of affection for steam train buffs. Optimistically a line was opened in 1904 between tiny Haughley, near Stowmarket, and Laxfield. The line was doomed to economic failure, though it limped on until 1952. Keen volunteers are involved in its ongoing restoration.

MID SUFFOLK LIGHT RAILWAY, Brockford Station, Wetheringsett, Stowmarket, IP14 5PW; ☎ 01449 766899; www.mslr.org.uk; steam days adults £5, children £2.50, families £12.50, non-steam days half-price all; open Easter to Sept, Sun/bank holidays.

 ## Wet weather

Thornham Parva is an atmospheric thatched and galleried parish church without a village, 2 miles west of Eye, with a rare medieval altarpiece and well-preserved wall paintings depicting the martyrdom of Suffolk's saint, Edmund. Although the **Laxfield Museum** is located in a 500-year-old guildhall, its contents are about the modest lives of ordinary farming families in the 19th and 20th centuries.

More objects from bygone days are at the **Mechanical Music Museum and Bygones** 6 miles north of Stowmarket. The collection includes miniature music boxes and huge organs from old funfairs and cinemas.

LAXFIELD AND DISTRICT MUSEUM, The Guildhall, Laxfield IP13 8DU; ☎ 01986 798461; free; open weekends 2–5pm in summer.

MECHANICAL MUSIC MUSEUM AND BYGONES, Blacksmith Road, Cotton, Near Stowmarket IP14 4QN; ☎ 01449 613876; adults £5, children £1; open June to Sept, Sun afternoons.

 ## What to do with children

Baylham House Rare Breeds Farm is a wholesome destination, geared up for children to maximise contact with the rare breeds of sheep, cows, goats, pigs and poultry, most of whom have names like Prudence the Pig. Seasonal activities include lambing and shearing. The farm is situated right on the River Gipping not far from Needham Market and encompasses two Romano-British

Easton Farm Park

BAYLHAM HOUSE RARE BREEDS FARM, Mill Lane, Baylham IP6 8LG; ☎ 01473 830264; www.baylham-house-farm.co.uk; adults £6, children 4–16 £3 (includes a bag of animal feed); open daily Feb to Oct 11am–5pm or later.

EASTON FARM PARK, Easton, IP13 0EQ; ☎ 01728 746475; www.eastonfarmpark.co.uk; adults £7.95, children £6.75, families £28; open Mar to Sept plus half-term holidays 10.30am–6pm (or 4pm).

SUFFOLK OWL SANCTUARY, Stonham Barns, Pettaugh Road, Stonham Aspal, IP14 6AT; ☎ 08456 807897; www.the-owl-barn.com; adults £6.50, children £4, families £20 (reduced rates in winter) open daily 10am to late afternoon; donations are encouraged.

forts which might catch the interest of older children too.

Easton Farm Park on the River Deben a couple of miles north of Wickham Market is another winner with children. Little ones may 'pat a pet', ride a pony, operate an electric digger in a sandpit, and play on indoor and outdoor playgrounds. The farm has three cottages available for holiday lets sleeping six or 10 people.

Stonham Barns, a retail complex in the straggling village of Stonham Aspal on the A1120, also houses **The Suffolk Owl Sanctuary**, with owls raised in captivity who are unafraid of humans and will approach very close to visitors. The keepers do shows with commentary between March and September. The site includes a hospital for injured raptors, a bird hide and a children's maze.

CELEBRITY CONNECTIONS

One of Britain's best-loved DJs and broadcasters John Peel made his home in Suffolk, which he loved passionately. He and his wife Sheila moved there in the 1970s at a time when mid-Suffolk was, in John's words, 'red neck country but in a nice way', where if two cars met on a narrow road, the oncoming one would pull over and the drivers probably wind down their windows for a chat.

Although born in the Wirral and a devoted fan of Liverpool FC, John put down deep roots in Suffolk. His wife Sheila supported Ipswich Town as well as Liverpool. He referred to his home as 'Peel Acres', a thatched cottage with an eight acre garden and tennis court, located in the picturesque village of Great Finborough near Stowmarket. He would regularly grumble on his Radio 1 programme about having to leave his country bolthole for the miserable commute to London. Eventually he had a home studio built from where he presented his influential two-hour show on Radio 1 three times a week up until his death from a heart attack in Peru in 2004. He had to build an extension to house his record collection after he had filled up the barns and outbuildings on his property. Fortunately for the Great Finborough postman/woman, most of the sackfuls of demo tapes and homemade singles he received every week were sent to him c/o the BBC. Among the ground-breaking trance and German punk, he also played unsigned local bands such as the Vaults from Stowmarket.

More of John's personal life and times in Suffolk crept in to his Radio 4 programme *Home Truths* when he would share with his interviewees the small triumphs and upsets of life at Peel Acres. It was a cosy family-oriented home furnished in country pine, with an Aga and dogs. When asked to support a building for the BBC programme *Restoration*, he threw his considerable weight and charm behind an East Anglian building-in-need, Greyfriars Tower in King's Lynn which didn't win but has since been restored with Heritage Lottery money. In 2008, his gravestone was installed in St Andrew's Church in Great Finborough bearing the epitaph 'Teenage dreams so hard to beat' from his all-time favourite record, *Teenage Kicks* by the Undertones.

Entertainment

Special events

Framlingham hosts a fortnight-long arts festival from the last week in June. As well as putting on a few headline acts in the theatre of the local boarding school (most recently the Ukelele Orchestra of Great Britain), **Framlingham Arts** fills the town with art, music and workshops, and also organises history walks.

The privately owned **Heveningham Hall**, a fine Georgian mansion, opens to the public for a lavish fair on the first or second Sunday of July. Originally just a small fundraiser for the local churches, the Heveningham Hall Country Fair (www.countryfair.co.uk) now attracts up to 10,000 visitors, who come to admire the wonderful landscaped gardens, browse among all the craft and food stalls, and watch the fireworks.

Celebrating trees, wood and people who work with wood, the two-day **Weird and Wonderful Wood** festival on the third weekend of May features tree climbing over suspended nets (for adults too), whittling, furniture-making and chainsaw carving. Visitors can have a go at various activities like pole-lathe-turning (www.haughleyparkbarn.co.uk/wierd&wonderfulwood.htm). Beautiful Haughley Park Gardens and Woods where the festival takes place (just off the A14 a few miles north of Stowmarket) are massed with bluebells in the spring.

Shopping

Among the many quirky arts and crafts practised in Mid-Suffolk, there is one that stands out is making teapots. At **Carter's Teapot Pottery** in lovely Debenham (Lav Road, IP14 6QU; ☎ 01728 860475; www.cartersteapots.com), Tony Carter and his wife have been creating unusual and collectable teapots for nearly 30 years. In the Ceramic Café you can customise your own teapot by painting your own design. The pottery is open seven days a week.

The best... FOOD AND DRINK

Staying in

Dozens of local producers raise, make or grow marvellous foods in this agricultural heartland of Suffolk. **The Alder Carr Farm Shop** near Needham Market is among the best outlets (Alder Carr Farm Shop and PYO, Creeting St Mary IP6 8LX; ☎ 01449 720820; www.aldercarrfarm.co.uk; open daily in summer;

The best... PLACES TO STAY

HOTEL

Crown Hotel 🔌 🍴

Market Hill, Framlingham IP13 9AN
☎ **01728 723521**
www.framlinghamcrown.co.uk

This heritage coaching hotel sitting squarely in the marketplace is Framlingham's premier hotel. The adjoining Reubens Bar & Grill (opened 2007) makes a change from the usual hotel dining room (try the Italian meatballs and pasta). The exuberantly planted courtyard garden is a secluded retreat in summer.

Prices: B&B £115 on weekdays/£150 Sat/special rate £75 Sundays for a double.

INN

Crown Hotel 🏠 🥾 🔌 🍴

High Street, Bildeston IP7 7EB (8 miles south of Stowmarket)
☎ **01449 740510**
www.thebildestoncrown.com

Having just been deemed worthy of inclusion in the *Good Food Guide*, this country pub is also full of character with a flagstone floor bar, inglenook fires, architectural features from the 1500s and 10 rooms recently renovated in 10 different styles. An unusual modern addition is a personal jukebox in every bedroom.

Prices: B&B from £70 to £90 for a single; from £120 to £180 for a double or twin; pets £10.

ORGANIC/FARM

Brights Farm 🏠 🥾

Bramfield IP19 9AG (between Yoxford and Halesworth)
☎ **01986 784212**
www.brightsfarm.co.uk

Spacious, comfortable B&B accommodation is provided in this old Suffolk farmhouse on a 250-acre working organic farm in north-east Suffolk. Lovely views over a pond, meadows and woodlands sometimes include a glimpse of wildlife such as hares, red deer and dragonflies. Breakfasts often use produce from the farm, e.g. eggs and damson jam.

Prices: £40 for a single; £70 for a double or £65 if stay is two nights or longer.

B&B

Verandah House 🥾 🍴 ♿

29 Ipswich Road, Stowmarket IP14 1BD
☎ **01449 676104**
www.verandahhouse.co.uk

Once a gentleman's townhouse, this listed building has a conservatory, pond and walled garden, and is close to the town centre.

Prices: B&B from £49.50–£55 for a single, £65–£68 for a double.

SELF-CATERING

Oak Hill Granary

Willow House Vineyard, Fressingfield, Near Eye IP21 5PE
☎ **01379 586868**
www.oak-hill.co.uk/granary.htm

This flint-walled former granary with one double room and a pull-out sofa has been restored by the owner (who is also a style consultant). A complimentary bottle of the local vintage is included in the welcome pack of groceries. Guests are invited to make use of the 7 acres of grounds and even to volunteer to help with the grape harvest in autumn.

Prices: £395 for a week in high season, £345 in mid-season and £290 in low season (or £150 for three-night weekend stay in winter).

New Inn

Peasenhall IP17 2JE
☎ **01628 825925**
c/o www.landmarktrust.org.uk

This attractive range of buildings on the A1120 consists of sleeping chambers leading off a late mediaeval hall built before 1478. Each of the end cottages sleeps four, with one especially grand room in the high end with a crown-post timbered roof. Groups that rent all three of the cottages may be permitted to use the hall, though it is unheated in winter.

closed Mon in winter). It is most famous for its home-made pure ice creams which have been praised variously by Nigel and Nigella (Slater and Lawson), with irresistible flavours such as rhubarb and ginger, gooseberry and elderflower or tayberry. It also sells free-range meats including Highland beef raised on the farm, cakes and ready-made vegetable quiches, all baked on-site, from their well-stocked deli counter. The large farmers' market is held on the third Saturday of the month (9am–1pm).

Other farmers' markets take place at the Stowmarket Museum of East Anglian Life (first Friday), at Eastern Farm Park mentioned above (fourth Saturday) and in Stradbroke near Eye (first Saturday).

You would think that one high-calibre ice cream-maker would suffice, but members of the family at the **Marybelle Dairy** in Rendham sell their Suffolk Meadow ice cream, sorbets and Greek style yogurt through local shops and farmers' markets.

Suffolk has traditionally been under-supplied with cheese, but in 2004, an energetic couple set up a cheese-making operation from scratch at Coddenham near Needham Market. Look for **Suffolk Farmhouse Cheeses** such as Suffolk Blue and Golden Lady (www.suffolkcheese.co.uk).

The family-run **Palmers Bakery** (established 1752) has five shops in Suffolk including Haughley (near the bakery) and Stowmarket. It claims that its bread and cakes are superior because they use the original brick ovens (www.palmersbakery.co.uk). They supply 600 different kinds of cake and a range of bread.

Good family butcher's can also be tracked down. **Neave & Son Butchers and Delicatessen** at 21 Cross Green in Debenham specialises in Suffolk hams and bacon, sausages and smoked chipolatas (☎ 01728 860240; www.feneave.co.uk). Alternatively call in on **Revett and Sons** in Needham Market where you can indulge yourself in good sausages as well as bread and wine.

Delis

One of the most appealing aspects of food culture in Suffolk is that enterprising village stores such as the Mace in Fressingfield and even garages carry local produce, so you don't always have to go to a fancy deli. The village stores in Yoxford and more famously in Peasenhall carry day-to-day items as well as high-quality local food. **Emmett's Stores** of Peasenhall cure their own hams and bacon using Guinness. Also on the A1120, Earl Soham boasts another prize-winning general store called **Eat Anglia** (☎ 01728 685557; www.eatanglia.co.uk; open every day in summer), which describes itself as a new style of delicatessen/café. It stocks a dazzling array of local produce, for example the fruit from High House Fruit Farm elsewhere in Suffolk. There are

EATING OUT

FINE DINING
The Fox and Goose Inn
Fressingfield IP21 5PB
☎ 01379 586247
www.foxandgoose.net

This is only a pub in name since the cuisine here is very haute, a highlight being in the multi-course Taster Menu for a whole table costing £38 per head. The inn first came to national attention in the 1990s when it was run by Ruth Watson, of Channel 5's *Hotel Inspector*, one of the early pioneers of the gastropub.

GASTROPUB
The Queen's Head
The Street, Bramfield IP19 9HT
☎ 01986 784214
www.queensheadbramfield.co.uk

Applauded by reviewers, its menus depend largely on local organic produce. A choice of vegetarian mains starts at £10 and organic beef dishes cost £15. This dining pub is as close to the Heritage Coast as it is to Mid-Suffolk. Before rushing off, pause in Bramfield to see the unusual stand-alone round tower of the church and the charming pargetting on the other pub, the Bell Inn.

CAFÉ
Gilbert's at Stowmarket
The Museum of East Anglian Life, Crowe Street, Stowmarket IP14 1DL
☎ 01449 775239
www.gallopingchef.com/bistro.php

This bistro-café, open to non-museum customers, serves a Stowmarket breakfast with local bacon, sausages and the works as well as homemade soups, sandwiches, prize-winning pies and pasties, and cakes throughout the day. The menu also features a proper Suffolk Cheese Ploughman's with local chutney.

The Dancing Goat
33 Market Hill, Framlingham IP13 9BA
☎ 01728 621434

If you go at a less busy time, you might snag a window seat and do some people-watching while sipping proper coffee and munching on a dainty French fruit tart. This welcoming café provides newspapers and a cosy ambience.

Weaver's Tea Room
2 The Knoll, Peasenhall IP17 2JE
☎ 01728 660548

A good traditional place to stop for tea and scones.

free tastings of local produce on the first Saturday of the month, and they also offer a picnic and home-prepared supper for people arriving at holiday cottages.

Fressingfield Stores is another shop that offers a visitor service allowing holidaymakers to ring through an order ahead so it will be boxed for collection on their arrival in the area. The always enterprising proprietors here bake pizzas on Friday evenings and croissants on Sunday mornings.

Framlingham has not one but two excellent delis on Market Hill: **Leo's Deli** at number 17 (☎ 01728 724059) was runner up in the last Suffolk Food & Drink Awards, and **Carley & Webb Purveyors of Fine Food** at number 29 is also superb.

◧ Drinking

SHAWSGATE VINEYARD,
Badingham Road, Framlingham, IP13 9HZ; ☎ 01728 724060; open daily Apr to Oct with evening tours.

BRUISYARD VINEYARD,
Church Road, Bruisyard, IP17 2EF; ☎ 01728 638281; tearoom and restaurant which serves their wines made from Muller Thurgau grapes.

OAK HILL WINES,
Willow House Vineyard, Fressingfield, IP21 5PE; ☎ 01379 586868; www.oak-hill.co.uk.

ASPALL CYDER, The Cyder House, Aspall Hall, Debenham, 1P14 6PD; ☎ 01728 860510; www.aspall.co.uk.

ANGEL INN, 5 High Street, Debenham, IP14 6QL; ☎ 01728 860954.

BUSHES BREW LIMITED,
Haughley Bushes, Haughley New Street, Near Stowmarket, IP14 3JL; ☎ 01359 242681.

Pageant Wines in Framlingham (www.pageant wines.com) is an exceptional wine merchant's. It carefully chooses the best organic and biodynamic wines from around the world, and can also be found at farmers' markets.

As it is one of the driest areas of Britain, grapes grow well in Suffolk and there are several wine-producing vineyards. **Shawsgate Vineyard** about a mile past Framlingham Castle and **Bruisyard Vineyard** (between Framlingham and Yoxford) are both long-established Suffolk wineries and welcome visitors. Shawsgate grows five varieties of white grape and one red which is made into wines that can be tasted at the vineyard and the vines explored on your own (both free of charge). **Oak Hill Wines** in Fressingfield (see Self-catering accommodation above) makes medium, dry and oaked fumé-style wines, which have all won prizes including 'best wine in East Anglia'.

Apple orchards are commoner than vineyards, so inevitably apple juice and cider are produced here. One familiar name in premium cider and (especially) cider vinegar, **Aspall's**, is located at moated Aspall Hall just north of Debenham, where cider presses have been operating since the 1720s, still by the same family. It went organic in the 1940s, making it one of the oldest organic companies in Britain. The best place to sample Aspall cider is at the Angel pub in Debenham, which recently became the recipient of a pipeline direct from the cider maker.

Country liqueurs involving the infusion of mulberries, sloes and other fruits with vodka and gin are made at **Bushes Brew Limited** in the village of Haughley New Street. The mulberries and greengages are from their own tree and the sloes are collected from local hedgerows.

Breweries
Barley also grows brilliantly in the country and the **Earl Soham Brewery** in the village of the same name has been brewing since 1984 (The Old Forge,

ⓘ Visitor information

Tourist Information Centre:
Heart of Suffolk Tourism Association, Tourist Information Centre, Wilkes Way, Stowmarket IP14 1DE, ☎ 01449 676800; www.southand heartofsuffolk.org.uk; closed Sun.
Hospitals: The nearest hospitals with 24-hour A&E departments are Ipswich Hospital; Heath Road, Ipswich IP4 5PD; 2 miles east of Ipswich town centre on the A1189 (Heath Road) and West Suffolk Hospital in Hardwick Lane, Bury St Edmunds IP33 2QZ (☎ 01284 713000). A&E has been threatened with closure.
Websites: www.stowman.plus.com – covers Stowmarket's history and heritage in interesting detail.
Supermarkets: Tesco, Cedars Link Road, Stowmarket IP14 5BE (☎ 0845 677 9661), with in-store pharmacy and weekday closing time of midnight; Asda/Aldi, in Stowmarket town centre; Lidl on 36 Bury Road.
Bike rental: Barton's Bicycles; 5 Marriotts Walk, Stowmarket IP14 1AF ☎ 01449677195 have a small stock of bicycles for hire at pprox. £12 per day with discounted rates available for groups. Notice is appreciated.
Taxis: Stowmarket Cabs Co, Stowmarket, ☎ 01449 677777; Goldstar Taxis, Stowmarket, ☎ 01449 676767; Debenham Taxi Service, Debenham, ☎ 07985 636552; Framlingham Taxi Service, Framlingham, ☎ 01728 724799.

The Street, Earl Soham, IP13 7RT; ☎ 01728 684097; www.earlsoham brewery.co.uk). To keep beer-miles to a minimum, sample their tasty beers like Victoria bitter (named for the original pub, now owned by the brewery), as well as pale ale and porter. Bildeston is blessed with a brew-pub, **The Kings Head**, which produces a heady dark ale called Dark Vader and a quaffable best bitter (132 High Street, Bildeston, IP7 7ED, ☎ 01449 741434; www.bildestonkingshead.co.uk/brewery.html).

Pubs
Swilling in Swilland is an absolute delight at **The Moon and Mushroom** (☎ 01473 785320) where a range of local beers and excellent food is served in front of a log fire. The director of Adnams' Brewery, Simon Loftus, rates the **King's Head** (☎ 01986 798395) in Laxfield as one of the most unspoiled pubs, with a snug for the locals, a fire for the winter and a large beer garden for the summer – and yes it serves Adnams, alongside tasty dishes such as steak and ale pie.

  The Gardener's Arms (☎ 01449 673483)in the hard-to-locate village Moats Tye south of Stowmarket is another classic pub with the winning combination of friendly landlords (including to children), a range of ales, and well-priced posh food.

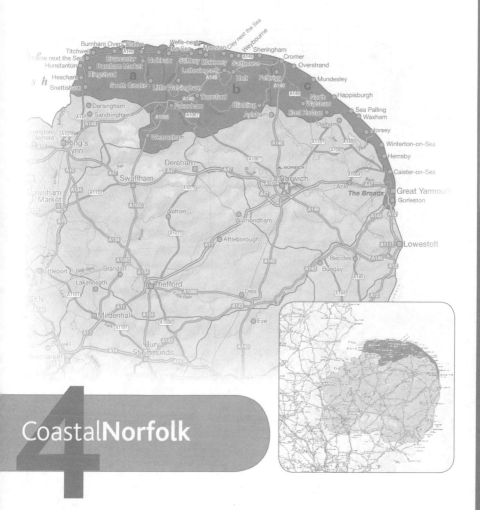

Coastal**Norfolk**

4

a. Hunstanton to Holkham

b. Wells to Sheringham

b. Cromer to Great Yarmouth

Unmissable highlights

01 Board an open ferry at Morston Quay to see the hundreds of seals that make their home at Blakeney Point, p.197

02 Eat a lobster salad at Cookie's Crab Shop at Salthouse at a bargain price, p.208

03 Walk through the blinding azaleas and rhododendrons in elegant Sheringham Park and catch a Poppy Line steam train back to Sheringham from Weybourne, p.200

04 Stay at the self-styled 'posh' Byfords B&B in the upmarket Georgian town of Holt, p.205

05 Dodge the incoming tide on Stiffkey Marshes, p.194

06 Listen to the music of the breeze in the rigging of moored yachts at Burnham Overy Staithe, p.180

07 Poke around in tidal pools on beautiful sandy Hunstanton Beach, p.178

08 Watch for the winter spectacle of a huge flock of Brent or pink-footed geese twisting and turning en masse overhead, p.179

09 Learn about the remarkable number of daring sea rescues carried out by Cromer lifeboatman Henry Blogg during his 53-year career, p.217

10 Catch the view over the Broads and the sea from the top of five-storey Horsey Windpump, p.215

The best of... SUFFOLK

COUNTRY LANES LEAD TO VILLAGE GREENS LINED WITH PINK-WASHED
COTTAGES. MULTIPLE ESTUARIES, WITH INDIVIDUAL CHARMS, MEANDER
INDECISIVELY TOWARDS THE SEA. COASTAL AND RIVERSIDE MARSHES HAVE
KEPT INTRUSIVE ROADS AND DEVELOPMENT AT BAY, PRESERVING LOVELY OLD-
FASHIONED SEASIDE AND FARMING COMMUNITIES. MEANWHILE IN THE SOUTH,
THE MEADOW-LINED RIVER STOUR EPITOMISES THE ENGLISH RURAL LANDSCAPE.

Top: Marram grass-covered sand dunes behind Southwold Beach;
Middle: Oulton Broad at sunset; Bottom: Beach huts and lighthouse, Southwold

Top: Old half-timbered cottages, Lavenham high street;
Middle: Fields near Blythburgh; Bottom: Hen Reedbeds Nature Reserve

Top: Lowestoft South Beach; Bottom: Metfield Church

The best of... NORFOLK

ALONG THE NORFOLK COAST THE MEETING PLACE OF LAND, SEA AND
SKY ENDLESSLY FLUCTUATES, AS THE PALETTE OF COLOURS SHIFTS
FROM STEELY GREY TO AZURE, DELICATE YELLOW TO BLOWSY SUNSET-
SCARLET. THE LOWLAND COASTAL WILDERNESS COMPRISES PERFECT
BEACHES AND MUDFLATS, DUNES AND CRUMBLING CLIFFS, SALTMARSH
AND REEDBEDS, ALL BELOVED OF SEA BIRDS AND WINDMILL BUILDERS.

Holkham Beach, Holkham Hall Estate

Top: Thurne Dyke Wind Pump, Norfolk Broads;
Middle: Norwich city centre Christmas lights; Bottom: Brancaster Beach

Top: Blakeney harbour; Middle: Market Square, Norwich;
Bottom: Boats moored outside a pub, Norfolk Broads

The best of... CAMBRIDGESHIRE

THE MAJORITY OF VISITORS NEVER GETS PAST THE UNRIVALLED ARCHITECTURE OF CAMBRIDGE. THEY MISS OUT ON THE SECRETIVE FLATLANDS OF THE FENS, AT TIMES SHROUDED IN MIST AND AT OTHER TIMES BRINGING THE VAST DOMED SKY INTO SHARP FOCUS. TRAMPLED BY GHOSTS, THE ANCIENT FENLAND OFFERS A RAW AND UNCONVENTIONAL BEAUTY.

Top: Reed-lined drove footpath, Wicken Fen; Middle: Christ's College, Cambridge;
Bottom: Cottage in Little Wilbraham, Cambridgeshire

Top: The nave and ceiling of Ely Cathedral; Bottom: Ely at sunset

COASTAL NORFOLK

Chelsea, Islington, Putney – all have been identified as the main source of visitors to the North Norfolk coast. Rubbish. There may be pockets of excessive wealth and privilege, and celebrities from Les Dennis to John Major have taken over architect-converted barns along this coast. Yet its miles of magnificent empty beach and its atmospheric tidal sand and mudflats are democratically available for everyone to enjoy.

The A149 follows the 90 miles of coast between King's Lynn and Great Yarmouth, but to really experience the marshes and reedbeds, mudflats and dunes, you should leave the car behind. The walking is wonderful, with the Norfolk Coast Path leading you on your intricate way along lonely stretches of saltmarsh, around inlets and tidal incursions, with evocatively named wildflowers and grasses growing in profusion. You can walk for miles in one direction and then catch the Coast Hopper bus back to your starting place.

In the quiet of the off-season you can appreciate the call of the curlew, the slap of the waves and the tinkling of masts on boats sitting lop-sided on the mud of a boatyard. Vast skies arch over the glittering (or leaden) North Sea. Local fishermen busy themselves repairing boats and gutting fish, and there is always a reviving drink round an open fire to be enjoyed in one of the many snug pubs.

In summer, attractive flint-and-brick villages and towns are a-buzz with activity of the boating and holiday-making kind. It is an endlessly entertaining spectacle to watch the urgent scramble as small dinghies struggle to catch the tide to navigate out of tricky little harbours and then muscling homeward on a strong tide and brisk breeze.

Visitors buy fresh crabs in brown paper bags from little huts. Families pack picnics and climb aboard small shabby ferries to be taken to remote points, islands and sandbanks to see birds and seals. Or for nostalgia's sake, they board narrow-gauge steam trains to visit a market or pilgrimage centre. Friendly proprietors of bed and breakfasts offer not only tea in the garden but a lesson in bird identification. If the crowds and queues are more than you were expecting, penetrate the maze of leafy lanes heading inland to discover ancient Norfolk where superb churches, ruined abbeys and splendid gardens can be visited.

HUNSTANTON TO HOLKHAM

The westerly third of the Norfolk coast from The Wash to the amazing beach at Holkham encompasses all that is magnificent about this coast, from jolly seaside attractions to lonely marshes filled with seabirds. On a clear day, you can look west across the evocative stretch of water north of King's Lynn to see the Boston Stump, the highest parish church tower in England. But even when you focus on your immediate surroundings, you will stumble across natural wonders like a dew-encrusted spider's web in the sun or sculpted driftwood. On a grey and misty day, coastal walks acquire a mysterious beauty and are guaranteed to make you feel as though you are much more than a few hours away from London or Birmingham.

WHAT TO SEE AND DO

 Fair weather

Hunstanton

Along with Great Yarmouth and Cromer, **Hunstanton**, or 'Hunston' as the locals call it, is a byword for mass-market Norfolk resort. Some are fond of it for being a safe, friendly, nightclub-free traditional family resort, which retains elements of Victorian sedateness. Others condemn it as tacky and chavvy. One thing that isn't in dispute is that the sandy beaches are exceptionally pleasant. Acres of sand separate the noisy funfair, nautical-themed pubs and soft ice cream vendors from the surf, and on a bright warm day, strolling along the sand and dipping into tidal pools to look for crabs is delightful. The beach in summer has lifeguards and a dog ban, and the water is shallow and clear (though with some recent concerns over cleanliness). People, famously, swim on Christmas Day, an eccentric tradition that has just celebrated its 50th anniversary, to raise money for charity.

Those who are rude at the expense of Hunstanton are probably unaware that **Old Hunstanton**, north of the resort, is a pretty town also with buildings made of local flintstone flecked with orange. A pleasant walk between the two either takes you over the cliffs (rare for Norfolk) or under them, in which case you should check in winter that it is low tide. Between the two you come to an atmospheric ruined 13th-century church and a disused lighthouse. The sedimentary cliffs are remarkably colourful, with a sharp contrast between the red limestone on the bottom layer and the white chalk above. You may find among the frequent cliff falls fossils of fish, sea urchins or shells.

The focal point of the town is the **Promenade** and the **Green**, a large sloping centrepiece near the shopping area. Watch the sunset sipping a drink from **The Golden Lion Hotel** on the Green, Hunstanton's oldest building. Because Hunstanton looks west over the Wash, it's the only place in East Anglia where you can see a sunset over water.

St Mary's Church in Old Hunstanton has elaborate tombs of the le Strange family who originally came to the area with the Norman conquest. But the more memorable tombs are of two local men who were murdered within a day of each other in 1784. Webb was shot from his horse and the next day one imagines his enraged friend Green decided to tackle the brigands but without success. His epitaph reads, 'Here lie the mangled remains of poor William Green, an honest officer of the Government, who in the faithful discharge of his duty was inhumanely murdered by a gang of smugglers in this Parish.' You can't miss the graves because of the two ugly white signs that mark them.

Snettisham

Those who want something more active, might be tempted by the 8 mile walk south from Hunstanton to **Snettisham**. Good views of **The Wash**, often dotted with windsurfers and powerboats as well as avocets and bar-tailed godwits, can be enjoyed along the route which follows the coast on sand and shingle beaches and along a concrete sea wall between Heacham and Hunstanton. You can take a bus back to your starting point. Snettisham is well known for its bird life, especially in winter, when at dawn you may see thousands of pink-footed geese flying in from The Wash. The RSPB reserve at Snettisham can advise on tidal conditions that will optimise viewing (☎ 01485 542689; www.rspb.org.uk/reserves/guide/s/snettisham).

Titchwell

At **Holme next the Sea**, the North Sea meets The Wash, and a dunes nature reserve can be visited. You might spot the rare natterjack toad with a yellow stripe down its back. From here, all the way to Holkham and beyond is an interconnected series of nature reserves, protected and maintained by the National Trust, the RSPB, Natural England and the Norfolk Naturalists' Trust.

> **TITCHWELL MARSH RESERVE**, Titchwell, PE31 8BB; ☎ 01485 210779; titchwell@rspb.org.uk; parking charge; open all year daily 9.30am–5pm in summer, 9:30am–4pm in winter; refreshments and picnic area.

Titchwell is pre-eminent among bird reserves. Dubbed 'Twitchwell' by some, dedicated birdwatchers (known as 'twitchers') congregate whenever a rarity has been sighted, and even when one hasn't. The shallow reedy lagoons are

Walking up to Barrow Common from Burnham Deepdale

managed specifically for birds and attract little egrets, grey plovers and many other migratory birds. The mile-long walk from the Visitor Centre to the bay takes you past three hides overlooking reed beds, freshwater marsh, brackish lagoon and foreshore dunes.

Brancaster

Brancaster is the next stop along the coastal road and is about two miles from Brancaster Staithe (staithe is the Norfolk term for landing place or quay). Famed for its mussels, your walk to the sea will have you crunching over discarded shells past whelk, cockle and mussel fishermen's sheds. Reeds are still cut in the vicinity for thatching roofs. The bird life here is superb too, with 4 miles of salt marsh and intertidal mudflats so beloved of sea birds. Brancaster Beach was recently voted the top destination for picnickers. Funding bodies have recently agreed to invest in building a new fishing quay at Brancaster, while repairing the current quay (built in 1750) for the benefit of visitors.

The Burnhams

If your destination is 'Burnham', you should make sure you know which one. Originally there were seven. Today the dominant one is the ultra-chic shopping town of Burnham Market, which has very little in common with Burnham Overy Staithe, the little harbour for pleasure boats, or with Burnham Thorpe, further inland. All are charming, even if, on a summer weekend, they can seem overrun with holiday-makers. To avoid the summer traffic, lovely walks connect the villages and take you past the picturesque restored mill buildings and windmill on the River Burn.

Everything in **Burnham Overy Staithe** revolves around the tide, since it is a challenge to manoeuvre a little boat out of the channel at the best of times. You often see walkers who have misjudged the tide wading back. The Rolls Royce (or perhaps the MG) of sailboats is the sharpie, a long, narrow, flat-bottomed boat with an extremely shallow draft, suited to the silted-up harbours of this coast. If you pass a field with a sign 'Sharpies only', stop to admire these beautiful wooden vessels.

Burnham Deepdale is closer to Brancaster Staithe than to the other Burnhams and is best known for its enterprising 1,700 acre farm, Deepdale Farm which has been in the Borthwick family for several generations. Alongside the arable farming activities, they have opened a backpackers' hostel, campsite (see *The best... places to stay* below) and information centre, as well as hosting jazz festivals and food fairs. It has also become a popular film location. The one-storey Marsh Barn and surrounding fields (currently on the market for more than a million pounds) played a role in the James Bond film *Die Another Day*, doubling as a paddyfield in the scene when a Ferrari and Lamborghini are jettisoned from a plane.

The largest of the Burnhams is **Burnham Market**, which can seem like Hampstead High Street transplanted to a glorious Norfolk setting. The boutiques and tempting foodie shops (see *Buying in* and *Shopping*) are as far removed from a tacky seaside resort as you can imagine.

The most secretive of the Burnhams is two miles further inland. **Burnham Thorpe** is worth visiting even if you aren't a Nelson anorak. His father was Rector of several of the Burnhams but it was in the parsonage here (pulled down long ago) that Horatio was born, and the nearby waters are where he learned to sail, although he couldn't have logged many hours in Brancaster Bay because he joined the Navy when he was 12. Before sailing off on the 64-gun *Agamemnon* in February 1793, Nelson treated the village to a meal in the pub then called the Plough but renamed the Lord Nelson two years after his death in 1805 (see *Drinking*). To locate the white house with a plaque in front which shows where he was born, carry on south from the village for a quarter of a mile.

About a mile further inland along a country road, not only do you come to the photogenic ruins of **Creake Abbey** beside the River Burn but you also feel as if you have crossed a border into the real Norfolk. These 14th-century

Tide filling at Burnham Overy Staithe

Scolts Head National Nature Reserve

remains are of an Augustinian priory abandoned a little over a century after it was built when the monks all fell victim to the plague.

Scolt Head

This nature reserve just offshore is usually cut off by rivulets of sea water but is accessible by the small private ferry that operates from Burnham Overy Staithe, weather and tides permitting. The uninhabited sand dune that makes up **Scolt Head** is veined with creeks and is a favoured breeding ground for terns, ringed plovers and oystercatchers. It is a splendid destination for a picnic. Although it's possible to walk out to the island at low tide, this is dangerous and, if you have to be rescued by the local coastguard, you will have to pay for the privilege. Once you are on the 'island' there is a one km nature trail.

SCOLT HEAD NATIONAL NATURE RESERVE, Scolt Head Warden; ☎ 01328 711866; www.naturalengland.org.uk; reached by ferry from Burnham Overy Staithe Apr to Sept.

Holkham Beach

By any international measure, Holkham Beach is a gem. The scale of it is quite out of keeping with what you expect to find in Britain, because it extends for 5 miles and beyond. If the tide is out and you want to get to the water's edge, you have to walk over sand and dunes for what seems like ages. Typically you will approach the beach from Lady Anne's Drive (opposite the Victoria Hotel on the main road), pay your parking fee and set off with rising anticipation through the belt of pine woods. When you emerge, the staggering vastness can protect everyone's privacy including film crews, naturists and the Royal

Courtyard Organic Farm

The Labour lord and landowner, Peter Melchett, has held high office over the years in the Ramblers' Association, Greenpeace and now the Soil Association. This hero of the organic movement owns the 890-acre Courtyard Farm near Ringstead, a few miles inland from Hunstanton. Courtyard Farm is the only fully organic farm in the whole of East Anglia to welcome visitors, who come to walk on the 10 miles of public footpaths, to see the humanely raised farm animals, to spot butterflies and skylarks, which have increased dramatically in number since the farm went

family, who sometimes come to ride or walk their dogs here when they are in residence at Sandringham (less than 20 miles away).

Wet weather

Across the coastal road from the beach is the mansion and park with the same owner as Holkham Beach. **The Holkham Estate** is one of the great agricultural estates of England, founded more than 300 years ago by an ancestor of the present owner Viscount Tom Coke, and extending nowadays an unbelievable 15km along this coast. The great mansion of Holkham Hall was built over the decades following 1728 in the then popular Palladian style. Currently 12 state rooms are open to the public, some with sumptuous velvet-lined walls full of statuary, paintings (some by Old Masters) and original furnishings).

HOLKHAM HALL, Holkham, Wells-next-the-Sea, NR23 1AB; ☎ (01328) 710227; www.holkham.co.uk; adults £11, children £5.50, families £28; includes entry to Bygones Museum with a collection of working steam engines; open Apr to Oct, Bygones Museum open daily, Holkham Hall open Sun, Mon and Thu afternoons.

A 15km long wall encloses the magnificent landscaped park which contains much of interest, including a deer park, grouse woods, obelisk, a folly temple and miles of freely accessible walking paths. There is even a large lake on which a small boat makes pleasure trips (£3). Some of the businesses run by the estate of possible interest to visitors are a pottery and an environmentally friendly paint shop.

What to do with children...

To learn more about the sea you have two options. Amphibious vehicles trundle out from the promenade in Hunstanton, over the sands and shallows and into the sea on seal-spotting **sea tours**. If your holiday in Norfolk will take

organic, and to enjoy art installations. The farm shop sells pork, bacon, sausages and Red Poll beef raised on the farm, but is open only on Wednesday afternoons (3–5.30pm). There is basic bunkhouse accommodation in a converted barn, mainly for long-distance walkers on the Peddars Way which passes through Ringstead and joins the Norfolk Coast Path not far away in Old Hunstanton. The bunkhouse sleeps 12 and costs £7 per person per night (Courtyard Farm, Ringstead, Norfolk PE36 5LQ; ☎ 01485 525251).

you around the coast to Morston and Blakeney, it might be better to wait to take the seal trip there.

Alternatively, the **Sea Life Centre** in Hunstanton is now also a seal sanctuary where rescued seals and seal pups from the offshore 'Stubborn Sands' or 'Sunk Sand' are coaxed back to health. The rest of the centre is underwhelming with a mild-mannered shark, tropical fish and a couple of homesick-looking penguins, though children may enjoy the touch-pools. The centre also has a small colony of otters; apparently otters' spraint (excrement) is bright green.

Amazing Maize Maze

Near South Creake on the B road inland from Burnham Market, stop at a maze covering more than seven acres, located at a working farm where corn grows to heights of nine ft. Every year, the maze designers pick a theme and, like a giant 'art attack', pull out the plants in a pattern to confound.

Sports and activities

Older children might be attracted to a one-day taster course in kite-surfing (but it takes at least a week of tuition before you get to experience the sensation of being pulled through the surf by the wind). Contact Kite Kit (www.kite-kit.co.uk) or Oceanside (www.oceanside.co.uk) for information about riding the shallows at low tide. At Brancaster Staithe, you can hire canoes and other small boats for pottering around. Dinghy sailing, windsurfing and water-skiing lessons are also available in high season (see panel).

SEARLE'S SEA TOURS HUNSTANTON, ☎ 07831 321799; www.seatours.co.uk; also runs other coastal tours and hires out bikes.

HUNSTANTON SEA LIFE SANCTUARY, Southern Promenade, Hunstanton, PE36 5BH; ☎ 01485 533576; www.seal sanctuary.co.uk/hunt1.html; adults £10.25, children £8.25, families £32.25; open daily from 10am–4pm.

AMAZING MAIZE MAZE, Compton Hall, South Creake, NR21 9JD; ☎ 01328 823224; www.amazingmaizemaze.co.uk; adults £5, children £4, family £15; open daily mid-July to early Sept.

SAIL CRAFT SEA SCHOOL, The Boatyard, Brancaster Staithe, PE31 8BP; ☎ 01485 210236; www.sailcraft.co.uk; RYA sailing courses for children 8–11 and 12–15; sample two-hour course £105, and four-hour course £195

... and how to avoid children

Any of the bird reserves such as Snettisham, Titchwell or Cley should take you away from children. You can leave the children behind, sticky with candy floss, at the Hunstanton amusement park, and walk by the cliffs into more refined Old Hunstanton. No matter how many families have congregated on Holkham Beach, you can easily move out of view of any buckets and spades by walking west. **Deepdale Farm** puts on various short courses usually on weekdays out of season such as on conservation and a Local Norfolk Produce Cookery Course (for £15).

Entertainment

The lively **Princess Theatre** on the Green in Hunstanton hosts a variety of shows around the year, and usually sends a celebrity from its pantomime to switch on the Christmas lights in Burnham Market. The **Hunstanton Carnival** takes place on the first Sunday in July and the annual **Kite Festival** is in mid-August; check dates and other events on www.hunstanton-on-line.co.uk/calendar.htm. Various arts events take place in the summer, such as the classical concerts every August held in several of the Burnham churches.

BURNHAM MARKET CONCERTS, The Stud House, Stratford St. Andrew, Suffolk IP17 1LW; www.burnhammarketconcerts.org.uk; tickets from early July, from the White House bookshop in Market Place.

 Shopping

Designer fashion and contemporary jewellery shops flourish in Burnham Market, for example **Anna's Boutique** which started here but now has branches in London and elsewhere, and are patronised by stars such as Kate Winslett. Some shops like **Ruby and Tallulah** are exclusively high-end (fashion leather boots for about £500) but others have items across the range of prices, for example **Treasure Island** on North Street, a gift shop with a highly original selection, said to have been visited by members of the Royal family when Christmas shopping. The website www.burnhammarket.co.uk/Index.asp links to all shops in Burnham Market.

Try **The Saltwater Gallery** run by leading British landscape photographer Harry Cory Wright who may well be on hand to show you around. The newest **Burnham Grapevine Gallery** (sibling of Grapevine Arts in Norwich) often exhibits paintings of the North Norfolk coast.

Naturally local crafts and books old and new are sold in Burnham. **The Brazen Head Bookshop** (☎ 01328 730700) and **White House Bookshop** (☎ 01328 730270) are both full of character with an excellent stock.

For non-lifestyle shopping, travel a few miles along the A149 to the new retail site **Dalegate Market** in Burnham Deepdale .

A mecca for shoppers in Hunstanton is **Le Strange Old Barns** which takes its name from the gloriously named Henry Styleman Le Strange, the entrepreneur who created the seaside resort of Hunstanton in the 1840s (much as Glencairn Ogilvie invented Thorpeness on the Suffolk coast 55 years later). As well as an antiques showroom, a number of workshops are open to the public where a jeweller, potter, wood-

LE STRANGE OLD BARNS, Antiques Arts and Crafts Centre, Golf Course Road, Old Hunstanton, PE36 6JG; ☎ 01485 533402; open daily 10am-5pm.

Caley Mill, Norfolk Lavender, Heacham

turner and other crafts-people practise their arts. If you are in the market for a bridal tiara or a wooden duck, this is the place to go.

Norfolk Lavender (Caley Mill, Heacham, near Hunstanton, PE31 7JE; ☎ 01485 570384; www.norfolk-lavender.co.uk) is a well-known visitor destination near Hunstanton, especially popular with the older generation. About a hundred different lavenders are grown in the grounds and sold in the shop. The shop opens daily, 9am to 5pm (closes 4pm Nov to Feb).

The best... PLACES TO STAY

BOUTIQUE

Titchwell Manor Hotel 🏠 🌊 ♿ 🍴 ♿

Titchwell, Near Brancaster, Norfolk PE31 8BB. ☎ 01485 210221
www.titchwellmanor.com

Overlooking the sea and the RSBP bird reserve, this family-run hotel has won many accolades such as 'Small Hotel of the Year for East Anglia'. Flawless cooking (the proprietor's son is the chef) makes the breakfasts special, and the all-day tapas and gourmet dinners a great treat. Local fishermen bring their catch to the kitchen door, and herbs are grown in the walled garden.

Prices: B&B from £110 to £190 for a double; special off-season deals for two-night stays Sun to Thurs from £150 per person.

Hoste Arms 🏠 🌊 ♿ 🍴

The Green, Burnham Market PE31 8HD ☎ 01328 738777
www.hostearms.co.uk

In this 17th-century coaching inn, rooms at the rear are more spacious than the older rooms overlooking the Green. The décor isn't typically village twee especially in the Zulu wing. The 21-day dry-aged New York rib steak is one of the dishes that made it winner of the 'Restaurant of the Year' in the *Eastern Daily Press* food awards.

Prices: B&B from £231 weekdays for two nights and £305 weekends for two nights.

HOTEL

Caley Hall Hotel

Old Hunstanton Rd, Old Hunstanton PE36 6HH ☎ 01485 533486
www.caleyhallhotel.co.uk

Set around a 17th-century manor house and converted farm buildings, this hotel is a 10-minute walk from the beach.

Prices: From £40 per person in low season, £55 in high season.

INN

The White Horse 🌊 🏠 @ £10 ♿ 🍴

Main Rd, Brancaster Staithe PE31 8BY ☎ 01485 210262
www.whitehorsebrancaster.co.uk

This multi-award-winning country pub has been assigned Condé Nast's 'Most Excellent Coastal Hotel' award. In the superb 'Room at the Top', a telescope is provided to enhance the sea views over the salt marshes, though the view over the hotel's sundeck is also good. The Norfolk Coast Path crosses the bottom of the garden.

Prices: B&B £50–£74 per person in a double; low season offer of £68 per person for dinner, bed and breakfast for two-night stay.

Gin Trap Inn ♿ 🍴

6 High Street, Ringstead PE36 5JU ☎ 01485 525264. www.gintrapinn.co.uk

This rustic and charming country inn has an excellent reputation for food. With just two double and one twin room, all with wrought iron beds, advance booking is recommended. The restaurant menu extends from fish and chips to tagliatelle with caviare.

Prices: B&B from £35 to £60 per person in a double; a two-course dinner from the à la carte menu will be £16–£25.

B&B

Twitchers Retreat 🌊 ♿

9 Beach Road, Snettisham PE31 7RA ☎ 01485 543581
www.twitchers-retreat.co.uk

This simple accommodation is perfectly located for birdwatchers who visit Snettisham Reserve; you also see birds in the garden of the Twitchers Retreat. The garden also has a fish pond and aviary.

Price: B&B from £75 per night based on two people sharing.

The best... PLACES TO STAY

CAMPING

Deepdale Backpackers' Hostel

Deepdale Farm, Burnham Deepdale PE31 8DD
☎ **01485 210256**
www.deepdalefarm.co.uk

Eco-friendly (and people-friendly) hostel and campsite where you can stay in a Sioux-style tipi with its own pot-bellied stove and lantern. Summer barbecues are held in the courtyard.

Prices: dorm beds from £10.50; tipis from £40 for two though they can sleep six.

SELF-CATERING

Creek Farm

Brancaster, c/o Sowerbys Cottages
☎ **01328 730880**
www.sowerbysholidaycottages.co.uk

This isolated mid-18th-century rambling farmhouse has excellent views over the marshes at Brancaster. With seven bedrooms and seven bathrooms, it easily accommodates 13 and has a large garden for summer and open fire for winter. Note that Sowerbys Holiday Cottages based in Burnham Market specialises in coastal properties in North Norfolk.

Prices: from £1,700 to £3,500 for a week according to season.

Nelson's Loft

Burnham Thorpe
☎ **01328 738311/** ☎ **07774 996634**
www.nelsonslocal.co.uk/stay/nelsons loft.htm

This tasteful barn conversion is situated almost exactly where Nelson was born. It sleeps four in two bedrooms, and is cosy in winter. In summer guests enjoy the sun terrace and garden. Next door is Nelson's Barn which sleeps 10.

Prices: £300 – £670 per week.

Headmaster's Study

The Old Schoolhouse, South Creake NR21 9JE
☎ **01328 823778**
CreakeOldSchool@aol.com

This cosy cottage for two is a glorified bedsit with a large light bedroom equipped with a fridge containing food for breakfast.

Prices: B&B from £60.

Cranmer Country Cottages

Home Farm, Cranmer, near Fakenham NR21 9HY (located 2m south of South Creake on the B1355)
☎ **01328 823135**
www.norfolk-luxury-cottages.co.uk

With a heated swimming pool in a converted barn and an attractive play area, this complex of five cottages (sleeping 4-6) is an exceedingly child-friendly place. Victorian farm buildings have been given a spare contemporary look, mixing the traditional (e.g. wood-burning stoves or Rayburns in some) with the modern (wireless access).

Prices: £390 for a week in low season for smaller cottage to £1,140 in summer holidays for cottage that sleeps six.

UNUSUAL

The Triumphal Arch

Holkham Estate NR23 1RG
☎ **01328 711008**
www.holkham.co.uk/victoria/ triumphal.html

One of the gatehouses on the southern border of the Holkham Estate has been made into two luxurious holiday flats, both with one double bedroom. This grand entrance was designed by the great 18th-century English architect William Kent, who designed the Hall.

Prices: from £440 to £560 for two-night stays at weekends; from £120 to £170 for a one-night midweek stay.

The best... FOOD AND DRINK

🔊 Staying in

This coast is a food paradise. The clear waters between Hunstanton and Burnham make this an ideal place to harvest Pacific oysters, mussels and cockles. In Brancaster Staithe the inappropriately named **Olive House** (close to the Jolly Sailors pub) is the place to head for fresh shellfish including lobsters and crabs, supplied by the Large family who have fished these waters for generations. The lobster and crab season lasts from April to October while plump Brancaster mussels are best between September and April.

The **Humble Pie Delicatessen** in Market Place (☎ 01328 738581; www.humble-pie.com) has an imaginative selection of foods, including ready meals for people who are self-catering. **Groom's Bakery** nearby sells both local breads (such as the rustic Norfolk blob which they have revived) and continental breads (e.g. sea salt focaccia). **Gurney's Fish Shop** with its famous potted shrimp, **Plumbe & Maufe Farming** with its 30 varieties of plums and other locally picked fruit, and **Satchell's Wine Shop** with a good selection of organic wines, all these complete the range of necessities for a first-class meal eaten on a beach or round a cottage table.

The Marsh Larder in Holkham (see Café below) will make up wonderful picnic hampers full of local cheeses and chutneys, pork pies and shell-on prawns.

The **Old Hunstanton Post Office** doubles as a deli selling good local cheeses, sausages, fresh bread and croissants. Around the corner of the coast between Holme and Thornham is **Drove Orchard** (PE36 6LS; ☎ 01485 525652) where you can pick your own fruit (more than 20 varieties of apple) and shop at a mobile deli called **Moveable Feasts** that sell a range of cheeses, patés and condiments in the car park every day. The Burnham Market/North Creake Farmers' Market takes place on the first Saturday and third Friday of the month at Burnham Market Village Hall (confirm times on ☎ 01953 681715).

EATING OUT

FINE DINING
The Mulberry
Heacham Manor Hotel, Hunstanton Road, Heacham, PE31 7JX
☎ **01485 536030**
www.heacham-manor.co.uk/mulberry-restaurant/restaurant-hunstanton.php

The dinner menu at Heacham Manor draws from Norfolk's long history of using ingredients of exceptional quality. The menu includes lamb and beef sourced from the Queen's Sandringham Estate, as well as local seafood and organic vegetables. The restaurant serves breakfast, lunch, dinner and even afternoon tea (although you need to book for this). Sustainably produced food isn't cheap anywhere and certainly not here where three-courses are roughly £35 but head chef Neil Rutland argues it's worth it for the quality of locally-sourced food.

Neptune Inn and Restaurant
85 Old Hunstanton Road, Old Hunstanton PE36 6HZ
☎ **01485 532122**
www.theneptune.co.uk

When the plastic and neon of Hunstanton begin to overwhelm and the ubiquitous fish and chips and kebabs lose their appeal, the Neptune provides a welcome contrast. The flash menu includes starters from £11.95, mains from £23.95 and puddings for £9.50. The Neptune was recently voted on to Condé Naste's list of 'Inns of Excellence' (double rooms from £120).

GASTROPUB
Rose and Crown
Old Church Road, Snettisham PE31 7LX
☎ **01485 541382**
www.roseandcrownsnettisham.co.uk

One of the most highly praised gastropubs in Norfolk has just been voted Family Friendly Pub of the Year, while one of its

chefs won the accolade of Young Pub Chef of the Year. The innovative menu identifies the origins of local ingredients, for example 'Game in season is supplied by the gentleman in wellies in the back bar!'.

The Victoria at Holkham
Park Road, Holkham NR23 1RG
☎ **01328 711008**
www.holkham.co.uk

This perennially praised pub has occasionally been accused of resting on its laurels though with the recent appointment of a new chef, this may change. But it can be superb on a good night and even if it isn't ,the Rajasthani décor is interesting. Any game dishes such as lightly roasted partridge, rabbit pie and woodcock are made from game raised on the estate.

CAFÉ
Marsh Larder at Holkham
The Ancient House, Main Road, Holkham NR23 1AD
☎ **01328 711285**
www.themarshlarder.co.uk

This deli has a lovely tearoom which is a perfect place to repair for hot chocolate after a bracing walk on the beach and serves traditional cakes such as Nelson's slice full of currants and spices and gingerbread. Open daily in summer, closed Mondays in winter.

🍷 Drinking

Breweries

Until recently West Norfolk was a desert for real ale and cider makers. Five years ago, the new landlords of **The Fox and Hounds** pub, a roadside pub in Heacham, decided to fill the gap. The **Fox Brewery** (22 Station Road, Heacham, Norfolk PE31 7EX; ☎ 01485 570345; www.foxbrewery.co.uk) now produces nine beers of varying strengths which can be bought in bottles too. The most famous is Nelson's Blood Bitter which uses a rum liqueur distilled by the Lord Nelson pub in the village of the hero's birth, and tastes faintly medicinal. Brewery tours with a meal in the pub cost £13.50 (only for groups of 10 or more).

The welcoming **Jolly Sailors** pub (☎ 01485 210314; www.jollysailors.co.uk) in Brancaster Staithe has a brewery next door where they brew the dangerously strong Old Les, named after a beloved local pictured on the label, as well as the more sensible IPA.

Pubs

Spoilt for choice along this coast, it is difficult to go wrong in choosing a pub at random in any of these coastal villages or indeed the ones a few miles inland too. While locals are unlikely to patronise the most glamorous places such as **The Hoste Arms** and **The Victoria**, quite a few pubs manage to maintain their credentials as friendly locals with upmarket food, such as the **Rose and Crown** in Snettisham described below, **The Jolly Sailors** in Brancaster Staithe and **The Lifeboat Inn** in Thornham (☎ 01485 512236; www.maypolehotels. com/lifeboatinn/index.html), which often feature the famous local oysters on their menu.

It is worth braving the tourist hordes at the historic Lord Nelson in Burnham Thorpe (☎ 01328 738241; www.nelsonslocal.co.uk) to try a drop of Nelson's Revenge, fortified Nelson's Blood or Lady Hamilton's Nip, made to a secret recipe known only to the landlord.

If the renowned coastal pubs seem too crowded, the less well known pubs in inland villages are all gems, such as the **Railway Inn** in Docking, the **Crown** in Stanhoe and the **Ostrich Inn** in South Creake. The pubs in Hunstanton are more hit-and-miss, though the cliffside setting of the large garden of the **Ancient Mariner** in the Le Strange Arms Hotel in Old Hunstanton, popular with families, can't be improved on.

ⓘ Visitor information

Tourist Information Centres: Hunstanton Tourist Office, Town Hall, The Green, Hunstanton PE36 6BQ, (☎ 01485 53261, hunstanton.tic@west-norfolk.gov.uk, open daily Apr to Sept 10am–5pm and Oct to Mar 10.30am–4pm; Deepdale Farm Visitor Information Centre, Burnham Deepdale PE31 8DD, ☎ 01485 210256, www.deep dalefarm.co.uk, open daily 10am–4pm (roughly) as a private information service. Publishes useful information on its website and in leaflet form on cycling and walking routes in the area, and on travelling around without a car. Good selection of maps and guidebooks, plus internet access available.

Hospitals: The Queen Elizabeth Hospital in King's Lynn has the nearest 24-hour A & E department, Gayton Road, King's Lynn PE30 4ET ☎ 01553 613613.

Supermarkets: Tesco, Southend Road, Hunstanton PE36 5AW, ☎ 0845 6779370, open until 10pm; Leftley's Costcutter Supermarket, Dalegate Market, Burnham Deepdale PE31 8DD, ☎ 01485 210350.

Public transport: Norfolk Green, King's Lynn, ☎ 01553 776980, www.norfolkgreen.co.uk. The excellent CoastHopper Bus operates daily between Hunstanton and Sheringham, hourly in summer (with some services connecting to King's Lynn) and less frequently in winter (Nov to Apr). One-day Rover ticket for adults is £5, children £3 and family £11. A combined ticket with the Bittern rail line (Norwich to Sheringham via Cromer) adds only £1 to the adult fare and £3 for a family. Other useful bus services operated by Norfolk Green include the X8 Fakenham to King's Lynn service every two hours and the X6 hourly service Fakenham to Cromer.

Bike rental: A E Wallis, 34–40 High Street, Heacham PE31 7EP, ☎ 01485 571683, www.aewallis.co.uk, adult cycles cost £5 per half day, £9 per day or £7 if more than one day booked, and £30 for a week, discounts for children's bikes; Fat Birds Don't Fly, 12 King's Lynn Road, Hunstanton PE36 6AN, ☎ 01485 535875, www.fatbirds.co.uk, the hire centre is beside an off-road cycle route leading to the Peddars Way, and the shop can provide information on reaching Heacham and Ringstead off-road.

Taxis: Note that evening taxis should be pre-booked; Cars 2 Go, Docking and Hunstanton, ☎ 01485 518588; Thaxters, Hunstanton, ☎ 01485 532196; Estate Cars, Holkham Estate, ☎ 01328 711307.

WELLS TO SHERINGHAM

Whereas in some parts of the country, you would expect to find Wells- or Cley-*on*-Sea, here even the description 'next-the-Sea' is wishful thinking. At least a mile of beach, saltmarsh and mudflat separates the towns and villages from the water. At one time prosperous Wells and Blakeney were bustling ports of some significance in European trade and warfare. But land reclamation and the subsequent silting-up brought this era to an end, although Wells was a functioning port as recently as the 1980s. Nowadays small harbours for small boats are marooned a long way from the open sea, leaving fast stretches of rare features to be explored on foot. At high tide, the distance you will have to walk will be much smaller, something to bear in mind if you are with small children or carrying lots of clobber. But even if you never make it down to the shoreline, you can potter happily in the dunes and sun-warmed pools left by the retreating tide.

Plenty of man-made pleasures have been lovingly retained from an earlier era such as the historic Dutch *Albatros* charter ketch normally moored at Wells, the wonderful North Norfolk Steam Railway and the iconic windmill at Cley, which was owned by the family of the singer James Blunt for almost three generations. And the wide selection of superb eateries in Blakeney and Cley is as inviting as anywhere on the East Anglian coast.

WHAT TO SEE AND DO

 Fair weather

Wells-next-the-Sea

As a family resort, Wells is best enjoyed on a sunny day when buckets and spades can provide hours of fun on one of the best beaches in the country, with a backdrop provided by Corsican pines and the ramshackle painted beach huts on stilts, some more than a century old. The town's long history as a trading port accounts for its attractive cobbled streets, redundant warehouses and historic buildings, especially around the elongated village green known as **The Buttlands** set well away from the sea and lined with Georgian houses and trees. It's here that the town's two best pubs are situated.

The main street, The **Quay**, isn't so genteel with the usual resort paraphernalia of amusement arcade, fish and chip shops, gift shops and ice cream parlours. In fact it's sometimes a slightly schizophrenic place with many

Wells harbour, Blakeney

aspects of an old-fashioned seaside resort intermingled with up-market delis and shops.

The friendly little narrow-gauge **Harbour Railway** follows the sea wall to the lifeboat station on the beach if you don't fancy the walk (see *What to do with children*, which also describes the four mile-light-railway journey to Little Walsingham).

Stiffkey

Following the coastal trail from Wells about 5 miles further east that marks the line between marsh and dry land brings you to Stiffkey, making a lovely walk of at least two hours. Some maintain that the village name should be pronounced 'Stewkey', which is certainly the correct way of referring to the famous local cockles. Stewkey blues – alas no longer collected commercially – are so-called because of the bluish tinge they acquire in their muddy habitat. In former times, cockling was done by women with true grit who would venture out onto the treacherous flats and fill their sacks as much as they dared before the tide turned and began cutting off their escape route. Naturally tales are told of those who didn't make it, like Nancy who ignored the warnings and lost her way on a foggy night, only to have her body washed ashore the next day and her spirit left roaming the mud bank. If you venture out on the raised paths over the marshes you should keep a sharp eye behind to see whether the silent waters are filling up the channels and muddy creeks between you and the village.

The village houses are mainly stretched along the main road and are very attractive with their knapped flint walls, painted woodwork and pantile roofs. Both **The Red Lion** pub (see *Drinking*) and the untarted-up campsite occupying a historic Second World War military base are heartily recommended.

Just a couple of miles inland takes you to a remote-feeling rural Norfolk and the extremely pretty village of **Binham**, easily reached by foot or bicycle along quiet lanes. Along with an attractive green and **The Chequers** pub, it has a ruined Priory (sacked by Henry VIII) adjacent to a disproportionately grand parish church with wonderful arcades, a carved font and painted screen.

Blakeney and Morston

Blakeney is one of those enchanting 'honey pot' villages which is full of second homes you can't help coveting, plus all the infrastructure that goes with it, great pubs, delis and so on. But visitors can still enjoy the fantastic scenic harbour and walk onto the mudflats to enjoy the prolific birdlife and the dramatic skies. In addition to all the colourful small yachts a-tilt in the mud if the tide is out, look for the large black sailing barge, the *Juno* which looks too big to launch in the shallow waters. The flat-bottomed design of the locally made boat is based on the Thames cargo barges that would have been common along this coast before they fell out of use in the early 20th century. *Juno* can be chartered from **Charlie Ward Boats**.

CHARLIE WARD TRADITIONAL BOATS LTD, Tide's Reach, Morston, NR25 7AA; ☎ 01263 740377; www.charlie ward.co.uk; half-day charter of Juno for £685, full day £985.

Strolling past the flint-built fishermen's cottages along the **High Street**, and glimpsing secret courtyards and a pleasing mixture of architectural styles, is a real pleasure, not to mention popping into the deli selling organic chocolates and estate-bottled olive oil. The double-towered church of **St Nicholas** up the hill from the harbour has a touch of Victorian self-importance and is also visitor-friendly, with informative labels near the font.

No finer trip exists in East Anglia than to take a ferry to **Blakeney Point** to see the seals, have a picnic and then walk back along the beach (one and a half hours) and along the dyke over the marshes to Cley. Morston is the best

Blakeney harbour at low tide

The Rector of Stiffkey

In the 1930s the Rector of Stiffkey was the diminutive Harold Davidson, who became notorious for befriending prostitutes and other social outcasts. He frequently disappeared up to London where he led a double life. One day he arrived back late for a special service, which made the Bishop of Norwich suspicious so he had him followed by a private detective. Although the detective could find almost no hard evidence of wrongdoing, Harold was charged with several counts of immoral behaviour, one of which was embracing a girl in a Chinese restaurant. Consequently he was defrocked, which he always claimed was a miscarriage of justice.

As part of his campaign to rescue his reputation, Harold paraded the Golden Mile at Blackpool in a barrel, protesting his innocence. Later he ran away to join the circus in Skegness where he came to a nasty end. Within minutes of impersonating Daniel in the Lion's Den, an elderly lion called Freddie mauled him and he died two days later. Some wag has written a limerick about the case:

"A notorious Rector named Harold
Showed his Stiffkey to girls unapparelled
They rated it so-so
And went back to Soho
But he was defrocked, shamed and barreled."

You can read Harold's epitaph in the churchyard – 'He was loved by the villagers, who recognised his humanity and forgave him his transgressions. Rest in peace.' His granddaughter is still working to clear his name and has uncovered some new evidence that casts real doubt on the testimony that convicted him. Surprisingly, Harold Davidson was nominated alongside Nelson for the title of Norfolk's greatest son at the launch of the *Dictionary of National Biography*.

starting point. You can't fail to see scores of seals; on average there are about 200. The best time is at low tide (though the boats prefer high tide). Usually you can be put down at Blakeney Point and when the tide is out you can get quite close to the seals.

Two Norfolk families, the **Beans** and the **Temples**, operate similar trips from Morston; the Beans will sell you a big bag of mussels for £4, though they need a good clean. From Blakeney Quay you can take a similar trip with Bishop's Boats. All companies charge £7.50 or £8 for adults, £4 for children. This is a very exposed coast so you might think twice before making the trip on a freezing January day, since all the boats are open to the elements. In the high season, it is wise to book ahead. Departure times change daily to follow the

Cley Mill at sunset

tides. If you need to get back to your car, you can take the CoastHopper bus if you have checked the timings.

- **Bishop's Boats, Blakeney Quay** (☎ 01263 740753; www.norfolksealtrips.co.uk); trips last one to two hours departing from Blakeney.
- **Bean's Boat Trips**, 69 Morston Road, Blakeney, NR25 7BD (☎ 01263 740505; www.beansboattrips.co.uk); departure from Morston Quay.
- **Temple Ferries**, The Anchor Pub, The Street, Morston, NR25 7AA (☎ 01263 740791; www.sealtrips.co.uk).

Cley-next-the-Sea

Cley Marshes Reserve is one of the oldest nature reserves in the country, having been set up in 1926. Recently a new eco-visitor centre opened, blending unobtrusively into a low ridge, and powered by wind and sun. Here you can learn to recognise curlews, gannets and red-throated divers, marsh harriers and black-tailed godwits. You can also buy tasty local food in the café and eat it while gazing out of the picture windows over the marshes.

In the tidal surge of late 2007 the north Norfolk coast took a hammering, although not as seriously as the Suffolk coast. The saddest loss was Arkwright's Café, usually referred to simply as the Cley Beach Café, beloved of walkers and birdwatchers for generations. The waves crashed over sea defences dumping four ft of shingle on top of this flimsy wooden structure by the sea, and bits of the outbuildings and contents turned up a mile inland. It looks as though the owner, the Norfolk Wildlife Trust, won't be rebuilding it.

Cley has a fine church, with incredible figures in the niches of musicians, a huge lion with a bone as big as a pillar and George outfacing the dragon, some with traces of original paint. In the south aisle look up to see a carving of a man mooning, and among the interesting wooden bench ends there is a mermaid sticking her tongue out. Richard Greve is buried here – second in command to

Admiral Cloudesley Shovel, also from Cley made it into the history books by returning victorious from wars with Spain, only to sail his fleet literally into the Scilly Islands and sink them, with the loss of 1,400 men.

Holt and Letheringsett

Even if you aren't particularly attracted to the retail charms of **Holt** (see *'Shopping'*), the engaging, flower-covered town centre with its rows of Georgian houses deserves a visit and there are excellent places to stop for refreshments.

Just a mile or so along the main road in the lovely valley of the River Glaven is the last working watermill in Norfolk at **Letheringsett**. The admirably industrious owner has rescued these fine red brick buildings from oblivion over many years and has just opened the top two storeys. The mill produces 17 different kinds of organic flour and delicious cakes and bread, which are sold in its prize-winning café.

Just down stream on the river Glaven, **Bayfield Hall** (near Glandford, NR25 7JN; ☎ 01263 711091; www.birdventures.co.uk) is a country house in private ownership, where film crews are made welcome from time to time but not the general public. But inside the 200-acre park and estate you can visit an eco-garden centre and shop called **Natural Surroundings** and the adjacent **Wildlife Gardens** (gardens and meadow nature reserve: adults £3, children £2, families £8.50). Special conservation walks and events are sometimes organised. An unusual shell museum can be visited a half mile away at Glandford.

> **LETHERINGSETT WATERMILL**, Riverside Road, Letheringsett, NR25 7YD; ☎ 01263 713153; www.lether ingsettwatermill.co.uk; adults £2, children £1.50; open year round, closed Sun.

> **GLANDFORD SHELL MUSEUM**, Church House, Glandford, NR25 7JR; ☎ 01263 740081. Entry: adults £2, children 50p; open Easter to end Oct, Tues to Sat 10am–12.30pm and 2–4.30pm.

Sheringham

For anyone afflicted with a nostalgic wish to go back in time, Sheringham is the perfect old-fashioned family resort. Its attractive sandy beach and gentle attractions give it a reassuringly genteel atmosphere. It is the kind of place which might produce a singing postman.

Sheringham is lucky to be connected to the rest of the country by rail. The Bittern line (www.bitternline.com) passes some lovely scenery between Norwich and the coast. Rail enthusiasts will also want to experience the private steam train to Holt. But most come for the beach. Sheringham enjoys a relatively dry climate compared with the rest of the country, though the heavy rains of 2007 washed debris into the sea, which put a Blue Flag for beach quality just out of reach.

Local knowledge

Mike Fenwick's family has owned a house in Cley since the 1960s. An avid sailor, he keeps his boat moored at Blakeney and sails the coastal waters of North Norfolk whenever he can.

Favourite pub: We have always favoured the Three Swallows in Cley, with cosy open fires and a good garden, that serves cheerful traditional food like steak and kidney pie at keen prices.

Best view: Upstairs at the Blakeney Hotel is an enchanting place to enjoy a sunset. This lounge is mainly for residents but if you ask politely they might be happy for you to take your drink upstairs at the sundowner hour to gaze out over the marshes to the setting sun.

Best kept secret: If you can get out from Stiffkey to the vast remote tidal sandflats between Wells and Blakeney Point you will have them to yourselves since access is very tricky, if not dangerous. Timing the tides is crucial and it may be necessary to wade across the channels. Do not be tempted to swim.

Best local takeaway: The seafood caravan in Blakeney car park sells fresh-from-the-sea prawns by the pint and oysters by the dozen. The prices are amazingly cheap.

Favourite shop: The shop on the High Street now occupied by Cley Pottery used to be the old general store. The old-fashioned wooden shop fittings and tiny drawers are still there, making a lovely space to display the hand-thrown pottery, jewellery and other crafts.

Fun things to do with children: Crabbing at Blakeney Quay guarantees a catch of at least 50 crabs which are all allowed to scuttle back into the water.

Favourite restaurant: Just along the coast you come to Cookie's Crab Shop at Salthouse which sells impeccably fresh shellfish year round accompanied by bread and salad but you bring your own wine or beer.

The singing postman

Allan Smethurst (1927–2000) was a Sheringham postman who used to hum to himself on his rounds and eventually wrote and recorded songs. Despite his goofy looks, his music found a wide audience and, incredibly, in 1966 one of his hits replaced a Beatles song on the East Anglian hit parade; its title tries to reproduce a broad Norfolk accent: *Hev Yew Gotta Loight, Boi?* Another of his immortal song titles was *I Miss My Miss from Diss*. His songs seemed to express a longing for a Norfolk that was even then disappearing.

Most of the attractions of Sheringham revolve around the sea. The working lifeboat station on West Promenade is open for special events, while the **Sheringham Museum** on Station Road and the **Fishermen's Heritage Centre** in restored fishing sheds on West Cliff both tell aspects of the town's story of fishing and boat building.

A couple of miles inland, the superb landscaped **Sheringham Park** offers delightful walks with good views from specially constructed towers. One walk goes all the way to the Poppy Line halt near Weybourne. The best time of year to visit is mid-May to the end of June when masses of rhododendrons and azaleas bloom. Nearby Beacon Hill is the highest point in all of Norfolk (at only 26m of elevation).

> **SHERINGHAM PARK VISITOR CENTRE**, Wood Farm, Upper Sheringham, NR26 8TL; ☎ 01263 820550; www.nationaltrust.org; free entry but pay and display car park £4.50 for non-members of the National Trust.

 ## Wet weather

In the winter months the weather on this north coast can be bracing (to use a euphemism), and windy and wet at any time. Most people simply come prepared with boots and waterproofs, and carry on regardless. Holt holds plenty of indoor charms of the retail and culinary kind. Or you can make a pilgrimage of a less tangible kind.

Little Walsingham

Not many people know that England's answer to Lourdes is tucked away in rural Norfolk at the end of the light railway from Wells. In 1061 Lady Richeldis de Faverches had a vision of the Virgin Mary, and built a replica of the humble house in Nazareth where the angel told Mary what was in

> **WALSINGHAM ABBEY GROUNDS AND SHIREHALL MUSEUM**, Common Place, Little Walsingham, NR22 6BP; ☎ 01328 820510; www.walsinghamabbey.com; entry £3.50; open daily Feb to Oct, entrance to Abbey grounds available through Walsingham Estate Office Nov to Feb (office hours Mon to Fri 9am–5pm)

store for her. An Augustinian priory was built on the spot and it established itself as one of the great pilgrimage places in Christendom. Today as many as half a million pilgrims come by the coachload to visit the Roman Catholic or Anglican shrines. Some come hoping to throw away their crutches, while others like to browse in the half-timbered shrine shops for devotional souvenirs. It is a tradition for devout Catholics to walk barefoot along the 'Holy Mile' between the Friday market place and the tiny **Slipper Chapel** south of the village. Even Henry VIII walked barefoot here in 1511 before he turned rampantly Protestant many years later. Those who want to go for a walk in normal footwear can spend £1 on the 'Walsingham Walks' brochure which details five walks.

Thursford Collection

The North Norfolk countryside holds lots of surprises and this is one of the bigger ones. This massive tourist village is housed in a collection of barns and farm buildings, encompassing several restaurants. The old-fashioned fairground

> **THURSFORD COLLECTION**, Thursford, Near Fakenham, NR21 0AS; ☎ 01328 878477; www.thursford.com; adults £8; children £4; open Apr to Sept (closed Sat).

rides are charming, especially the three that are in working order and rideable. The highlight is the daily shows at 1.30pm and 3pm on a huge 1930s Wurlitzer organ, reviving the era of silent cinema. For information about their season of Christmas musical spectaculars, see *Entertainment*.

What to do with children

The pristine beaches at Wells are ideal for small children since the tide laps in gently and the water is shallow. **Gillying** means fishing for crabs from the shore in the time-honoured way of dangling bits of raw bacon into the water. Wells Quay is perfect, and crab lines can be bought from Walsingham's Hardware at 78 Staithe Street.

> **ABRAHAM'S BOSOM**, Beach Road, Wells-next-the-Sea; ☎ 01328 710872; www.norfolk beachleisure.co.uk; open Easter to Oct at weekends, July/Aug daily (weather permitting).

The boating lake in Wells rejoices in the name **Abraham's Bosom**, said to be because many of the early mariners were Jewish and were always grateful to come into the welcoming harbour at Wells. The lake is near the sea and past Pinewoods Campsite. Their go-karts and trampolines are both popular, and there is even a qualified instructor on hand. Canoes and kayaks can be hired at the harbour, and water-skiing, windsurfing and sailing also take place.

The high-ropes adventure course, **Extreeme Adventure,** located in Weasenham Woods 8 miles south of Fakenham is for children over 10 (and adults).

Zipwire at Extreeme Adventure

Various obstacles must be overcome high in the tree tops, some as high as 40ft above the ground, including rope bridges and a giant drop swing.

EXTREEME ADVENTURE LTD, High House, Weasenham, Norfolk PE32 2SP; ☎ 01328 838720; www.extreemeadventure.co.uk; adults £29, young people 10–18 £25; some features incur an extra charge, e.g. a 1,000ft zip wire for £6.

Light railways

In addition to the Harbour railway at Wells, there are two narrow-gauge railways which operate some steam and some diesel services. The 4-mile **Wells Walsingham Railway** owes its existence to retired Lieutenant Commander Roy Francis who built the 10¼-inch gauge railway on the trackbed that had been abandoned at the time of the Beeching railway closures.

The **Poppy Line** links Sheringham with Holt on the North Norfolk Railway, with halts at Kelling Heath Park (for campers) and Weybourne's country station charmingly preserved from 1900. The very scenic trip covers more than 10 miles altogether and takes about half an hour.

WELLS WALSINGHAM RAILWAY AND HARBOUR RAILWAY, The Station, Stiffkey Road, Wells-next-the-Sea NR23 1QB; ☎ 01328 711630; www.well swalsinghamrailway.co.uk; adult return £8, children £6.50; operates daily Apr to Oct half-term; each trip takes half an hour.

NORTH NORFOLK RAILWAY, Sheringham Station, Station Approach, Sheringham, NR26 8RA; ☎ 01263 820800 or Talking Timetable: ☎ 01263 820808; www.nnrailway.co.uk; adults £10.50 for the whole route, £6 for one leg; children £7/£4.

North Norfolk Railway

The Visitors' Book

Camping in North Norfolk

'The highlight of our camping stay in north Norfolk was a ride on the steam railway right from our campsite at Kelling Heath to Sheringham. The enthusiasm of all the volunteers working on the line was contagious, and we half expected to see Jenny Agutter and the other railway children waving at us from the bank. We found Sheringham a delightfully old-fashioned seaside resort and loved buying local crabs from the wet fish shop on Church Street, which tasted fantastic back at the campsite.'

'We aren't regular campers (to put it mildly) but our 10-year-old daughter Caitlin persuaded us to drive up from Hampshire to spend a few nights under canvas at the Kelling Heath Holiday Park with her friend Natalia and family. We found it a touch more suburban than we were expecting (complete with spa and leisure centre), but enjoyed the nature trails, the evening bat walk and especially enjoyed an impromptu game of hide and seek in the woods. Families staying longer than us had brought bicycles so that their children went off exploring the vast heathland adjacent to the campsite, reminding us of our own less restricted childhood. We wished we had brought torches so that the children could have played capture-the-flag after dark.'

'We happened to have superb weather in early August, so didn't need all the site facilities, though these would have been welcome in wet weather. There was absolutely no light pollution so we marvelled at the night sky.'

Anne Hogan, Peter Lloyd, Caitlin Lloyd, August, 2007

Entertainment

The largest Christmas show in England takes place in a tiny hamlet in rural Norfolk. **The Thursford Collection** mentioned above has built a reputation for such musical glitz and glamour that coaches congregate from all over the country to attend one of the twice-daily spectaculars put on between 10 November and Christmas Eve. Tickets range from £24 to £30.

Sheringham has a **Little Theatre** that puts on an eclectic programme for locals and tourists (www.northnorfolk.org/littletheatre).

Special events

Traditional seaside carnivals take place for a 10-day period from the end of July. These are colourful and hilarious free events with competitions in old seaside skills such as sail-hoisting as well as the usual panto-horse racing and tug of war. Visiting children can participate in the sandcastle and crabbing competitions. Carnivals take place at Blakeney, Wells (www.wells carnival.co.uk) and Sheringham (www.sheringham carnival.co.uk).

The impressive ruined priory at Binham mentioned earlier is the venue for a series of classical music concerts in July. International soloists and ensembles come to perform in about 10 different concerts.

> **BINHAM PRIORY CONCERTS**, Warham Road, Binham, NR21 0DW; ☎ 01328 830362; www.binhampriory.org; tickets: from £10 to £14.

 Shopping

Parting with your money will be a sore temptation when exploring Holt. **Art-e-Fax** at One Fish Hill displays limited edition prints and original paintings (www.art-e-fax.com). But the most wonderful emporium is **Bakers & Larners**, a remarkable department store founded in 1770 which manages to remain unpretentious but has a superb food hall stocking 700 products (see *Staying in*; 8–12 Market Place, Holt, NR25 6BW; ☎ 01263 712323; www.bakersand larners.com).

In Cley, the **Made in Cley** pottery and workshops were set up by four artists in 1984, all of whom are still there along with four other potters (High Street, Cley-next-the-Sea, NR25 7RF; ☎ 01263 740134; www.madeincley.co.uk). The pottery is open daily year round, 10am–5pm (Sun 11am–4pm).

The main shopping street in Wells-next-the-Sea is Staithe Street where some lovely old-fashioned shops can be found selling everything from shoes to iron-mongery, organic meat to vintage clothing. An unusual shop nearby is the

The best... **PLACES TO STAY**

BOUTIQUE

Byfords Posh B&B

1–3 Shirehall Plain, Holt NR25 6BG
☎ 01263 711400
www.byfords.org.uk

Actually only six of the very individual nine rooms have been deemed 'posh' by the owners. This place really feels youthful and original, even a bit quirky with breakfast pizza on the morning menu. The centrally located flint building is full of nooks, crannies and character, but the rooms are modern with Bang & Olufsen entertainment centres and luxuriously large beds. Fridays are £25 more and Saturdays must be included in a two-night stay.

Prices: from £145 for a double Sun to Thurs including a 'posh' breakfast; dinner bed and breakfast costs £180.

INN

The Globe Inn, Wells

The Buttlands, Wells-next-the-Sea NR23 1EU, ☎ 01328 710206
www.holkham.co.uk/globe

As a satellite of the Holkham Estate, the Globe has recently been spruced up by the people who run the famous Victoria Hotel and Restaurant at Holkham. Now a smart contemporary seaside hotel, the beds are wonderfully comfortable. The front rooms with a view are especially cheerful. Even the locals are impressed with the good-value steak nights on Wednesdays: rump, sirloin or rib-eye cuts from cows reared at Holkham cost £10.

Prices: B&B from £100 for a low-season mid-week double to £130 for a weekend night; weekend bookings must be for two nights.

CAMPSITE

Pinewoods

Beach Road, Wells-next-the-Sea NR23 1DR. ☎ 01328 710439
www.pinewoods.co.uk

This huge campsite down between the lifeboat Station and the boating lake in Wells is divided from the beach only by some pine trees and sand dunes. You can have your very own beach hut for a day, equipped with an elevated deck and steps down to your two deckchairs and windbreak. For the night you can hire one of the many static caravans or pitch a tent in the horse paddock in summer.

Prices: tent pitches from £10–£17; beach huts cost from £10 in low season to £25 in high season for a day.

Kelling Heath Holiday Park

Kelling Heath, Near Weybourne NR25 7HW (5 minute drive from Sheringham).
☎ 01263 588181
www.kellingheath.co.uk

In some ways resembling Center Parcs, this campsite is massive. Its 250 acres of woodland and gorse are criss-crossed with bike paths, though eventually all paths converge on the leisure centre complete with pool, gym and restaurants. Regular organised activities include pond dipping and bat spotting. People in need of more comfort can stay in wooden lodges with verandahs.

Price: touring pitches from £16.50 per night low season, £29.50 in high summer; two-bedroom Scandinavian redwood lodge costs £239 for three nights.

The best... PLACES TO STAY

SELF-CATERING

The choice of attractive holiday accommodation, especially for self-caterers, in this area is astounding. Try the Blakeney Cottage Company in Blakeney (☎ 01263 741773; www.blakeneycottagecompany.co.uk) and Countryside Cottages in Holt (☎ 01263 713 133; www.holiday-cottage-norfolk.co.uk).

Pollywiggle Cottage 🗹

West Raynham, Near Fakenham NR21 7EX. ☎ 01603 471990 (in Norwich)
marilyn@pollywigglecottage.co.uk
www.pollywigglecottage.co.uk

Situated in a good location for cyclists and walkers (but not public transport users), this pretty cottage features an unfenced pond (with tadpoles or 'pollywiggles') and a lovely big garden. It not only sleeps eight (in five bedrooms) but also has parking facilities for eight bicycles.

Price: from £310 to £890 for a week.

UNUSUAL

Cley Mill 🗹 🛏 with honesty bar 🍴

Cley-next-the-Sea NR25 7RP
☎ 01263 740209
www.cleymill.co.uk

In a magical isolated location right on Cley Marshes, this familiar landmark operates as a bed and breakfast, and is also open for dinner including to non-residents who book ahead. Despite the mill's brush with celebrity – James Blunt's parents owned and ran it for many years until 2004 – it retains its down-to-earth character, even though some rooms are up-in-the-sky. Its restored sails, cap and wooden galleries are all well maintained, and the viewing gallery at the top is accessible by a ladder from the bedroom below.

Price: B&B from £92 to £145 for a double (minimum two-night stay sometimes required); rooms across the courtyard are cheaper; three-course dinner costs £32.50.

1950s Shop, which carries everything from retro telephones to old signs with 1950s typography (14 Shop Lane, ☎ 01328 711362). For more down-to-earth shopping, there is a Saturday car boot sale in the car park of the Ark Royal pub in Wells, and the market town of Fakenham has a good Thursday market thronged by people from the North Norfolk hinterland.

Book lovers are in for a treat. Some of the most perfect second-hand bookshops can be found in places such as Holt where **Simon Finch Books** (www.simonfinchnorfolk.com) has creaking old winding staircases connecting rooms of well-organised stock including a whole room of art books. Other shops to check out in the area are the **Old Station Pottery and Bookshop** in Wells (☎ 01328 710847) and **Crabpot Books** in Cley (☎ 01263 740218).

Cley Mill

The best... FOOD AND DRINK

 ## Staying in

Residents and visitors along this coast rarely feel the need to drive to Fakenham or Hunstanton to find a supermarket (in fact it would be criminal to do so) and the good people of Sheringham have been successfully campaigning against a Tesco for many years. How much more satisfying it is to stock up at **Bakers & Larners**, which is frequently compared to Harrod's Food Hall. Its cheese counter is one of the best in the south of England and they also sell an intriguing array of delicacies such as stuffed figs.

In Cley, the **Cley Smokehouse** (☎ 01263 740282; www.cleysmokehouse.com) uses traditional methods to smoke its cod, prawns, mackerel, etc. and is located alongside the long-established prize-winning deli **Picnic Fayre** in the village's Old Forge (☎ 01263 740587; www. picnic-fayre.co.uk). With luck, they will be offering free samples of an interesting local product such as lavender bread or fig and orange-blossom chutney. The **Wells Deli** is another glorious purveyor of local foods from venison to honey, ice cream to Gloucester Old Spot pork pies. One of the best traditional butchers is **Arthur Howell** at 53 Staithe Street in Wells, selling specialist sausages and burgers (e.g. lamb and mint) ideal for a holiday barbecue.

The supremacy of the innovative **Farm Shop** in Little Walsingham (Guild Street, Little Walsingham, NR22 6BU; ☎ 01328 821877; www.walsingham farmsshop.co.uk) was acknowledged last year when it won prizes for the 'Best of Norfolk' and the 'Food Retailer of the Year' (open Mon to Sat 9am–6pm; Sun 10am–4pm). An attractively converted barn in the centre of the village has an ambitious collection of food outlets, where the emphasis is always on local products. You can buy delicious pies, soups and ready meals here. And the 40-seat fish and chip restaurant nearby at 2 Wells Road, **The Norfolk Riddle**, takes the quality of its potatoes just as seriously as its fish.

As you would expect in an area where more than a dozen fishing boats remain active and travel offshore as far as 35 miles to catch lobster and crabs, shrimp and skate, fishmongers such as **Richard's Wet Fish Shop** on Church Street in Sheringham are fantastic.

Chocoholics should look out for the shop **Tiramisu** in **The Courtyard** off Station Road. It sells the full range of products made by Intensely Chocolate (www.intenselychocolate.co.uk). A traditional farmers' market takes place on the last Saturday morning of the month in Fakenham (www.fakenhamfarmers market.co.uk).

Local cheeses

In a radical career switch, a former pharmacy lecturer married into a North Norfolk farming family and set about making artisan cheeses. **Mrs Temple's Cheeses** are distributed throughout the area from her farm in Wighton, which is one of the halts on the Wells to Walsingham Railway. Of the three main types, Binham Blue, is the most famous and can be found on the menus of top Norfolk restaurants.

The other name to remember is **Ferndale Farm** in North Norfolk, where another female cheese-maker has established Norfolk Dapple as a superb cheddar and Norfolk Tawny with beer-infused rind. Ferndale Farm is located in the village of Little Barningham 6 miles south-east of Holt.

Even in the small community of Stiffkey the local shop is a marvel. **Stiffkey Stores and Post Office** is run by a twenty-something couple who stock lots of locally grown groceries and frozen meat.

Takeaway

Cookie's Crab Shop in Salthouse just east of Cley is an institution. It's located just beside the main road but easily missed (The Green, Salthouse, NR25 7AJ; ☎ 01263 740352; www.cookies.shopkeepers.co.uk). Out of a humble wooden hut emerges the freshest, tastiest seafood salads you can imagine. Bring your own wine and have a feast for £8 (open daily, 9am–7pm in summer, 11am–5pm in winter with earlier closing times on wet days).

Willie Weston's **Seafood Caravan** parked in Blakeney or Morston Quay in summer sells dressed crab, mussels and whatever else is in season. In Wells, **Frary's Crab Stall** on the Quay has been doing a brisk trade in crabs and lobsters bought that morning for more than half a century.

For superior fish and chips, you might have to queue, for example at **French's** on the Quay in Wells (☎ 01328 710396; www.frenchs.co.uk) before getting to choose haddock, cod, plaice or rock salmon, and whether you want to eat in or take away. **Dave's Fish and Chips** in Sheringham is another excellent place to order a nostalgic meal of fried fish (in huge quantities) plus chips, mushy peas and milky tea for a set price.

EATING OUT

FINE DINING
Morston Hall
Morston, near Holt NR25 7AA
☎ **01263 741041**
www.morstonhall.com

The top-rated Morston Hall country house hotel has at the helm of its kitchen celebrity chef and cookery writer Galton Blackiston. Galton and his wife have run the hotel since 1992 and he was recently quoted as describing north Norfolk as 'an area stuck in the past in many ways, but I wouldn't live anywhere else'. With gushing reviews for his restaurant in many of the broadsheets and a Michelin star, you may decide that the £60 price tag on dinner is justified.

GASTROPUB
Crown Hotel, Wells
The Buttlands, Wells-next-the-Sea NR23 1EX. ☎ **01328 710209**
www.thecrownhotelwells.co.uk

This Michelin-listed restaurant has an ambitious menu with Pacific Rim (i.e. Sydney) leanings. The local mussels, pigeon and duck all come highly recommended. Meals served in the bar rather than the restaurant are cheaper and still excellent, for example the Seafood Slate for £12 or £15.

Wiveton Bell
Blakeney Road, Wiveton NR25 7TL
☎ **01263 740101**
www.wivetonbell.co.uk

Winning the most recent Best Pub Food for Norfolk prize was an impressive achievement for landlords who had only just taken over and refurbished the pub. Standard bistro dishes are served with care and flair, such as a mushroom starter stuffed with local Binham Blue, celery, shallots, walnuts and Parmesan (£5.45).

Red Lion, Stiffkey
Wells Road, Stiffkey NR23 1AJ
☎ **01328 830552**
www.stiffkey.com

The splendid homely, welcoming and dog-friendly Red Lion pub on the main road through the village serves first-class unfussy food such as rabbit pie and Blakeney white-bait, as well as a nice drop of Norfolk Woodforde ales. Fish pie, chips and salad cost £9.

CAFÉ
Morston Hall
Morston, near Holt NR25 7AA
☎ **01263 741041**
www.morstonhall.com

Even if you can't stretch to a meal at Morston Hall, you can at least experience the grandeur of the place by taking tea on the terrace or by the log fire in winter. Cream teas cost £10 and must usually be booked ahead for between 3.30pm and 5.30pm.

The Moorings
High Street, Blakeney NR25 7NA
☎ **01263 740054**
www.blakeney-moorings.co.uk

Just at the bottom of the high street, this cheerful café-restaurant serves cappuccinos, espressos and homemade cakes and pastries all day, as well as an appetising blackboard lunch menu including chowders, salads and filled ciabattas.

Bean 2 the Coast Coffee House
20 Staithe Street, Wells-next-the-Sea NR23 1AF
☎ **01328 711 842**

Notwithstanding the name, this is a lovely new spot to pause for a cup of decent coffee (from a list of half a dozen choices) and cake.

DELI
Byfords
1–3 Shirehall Plain, Holt NR25 6BG
☎ **01263 711400**
www.byfords.org.uk

This marvellous institution in the centre of up-market Holt has all the culinary bases covered. The varying menus for breakfast, elevenses, lunch, tea and dinner will have you drooling. The atmosphere is informal but the food is impeccable. Next door is the equally splendid Byfords Deli which crams an astonishing range of food items into a small space.

🍺 Drinking

The Three Horseshoes in Warham between Wells and Stiffkey is a classic pub with real fires and stone floors, and sausages and old-fashioned puddings on the menu. A similarly welcoming hostelry is **The Chequers** in Binham which is full of character and serves good food as well. **The King's Head** in Letheringsett is especially recommended for families. Their huge garden comes with a miniature castle and toys for toddlers, plus they have an indoor playroom and an inexpensive children's menu which features jam sandwiches. Locals congregate here at the regular gig evenings too.

Even the most popular pubs such as **The George** in Cley and **The King's Head** pub next to Blakeney's chandlery shop are brilliant for beer and atmosphere as well as food. Non-residents are usually welcome to have a drink at the bar of the genteel old hotels such as the **Blakeney Hotel**. If you ask nicely, you might be able to take your drink upstairs to the residents' loungw with its huge windows to enjoy the magnificent views over the marshes. In Upper Sheringham, the flint-built **Red Lion** free house (☎ 01263 825408) serves good ale and food from a blackboard menu.

Anyone who has ever enjoyed a good pint should try to stop at the **Real Ale Shop** located at the end of a farm track off the B1105 south of Wells. The energetic barley farmer of 1,000-acre Branthill Farm, Teddy Maufe, opened his farm shop in order to promote Norfolk-brewed beers and to sell an amazingly varied range of bottle-conditioned beers.

THE REAL ALE SHOP, Branthill Farm, Nr Wells-next-the-Sea, NR23 1SB; ☎ 01328 710810; www.therealaleshop.co.uk; open Tues to Sat 10am-am–6pm and Sun 10am-am–4pm.

WHIN HILL CIDER, The Stables, Stearman's Yard, Wells-next-the-Sea, NR23 1BW; ☎ 01328 711033/711821; www.whinhillcider.co.uk; open Tues-Sun in summer holidays, weekends only Easter-June and Sept-Oct.

An enticing range of locally grown cider and apple juice is sold from cider works in a converted 18th-century barn in the middle of the main car park in Wells. **Whin Hill Cider's** orchards at Stanhoe (ten miles inland) grow eight varieties of cider, perry pears and some old Norfolk varieties 'just for fun'. You can sample the delicious products in their courtyard in Wells before making your choice.

ⓘ Visitor information

Tourist Information Centre:
Official tourist offices in Sheringham, Holt and Wells-next-the-Sea, all
open Mar to Oct 10am–5pm (Sun
close 4pm with longer hours in
July/Aug): Sheringham Tourist Information, Station Approach, Station
Road, Sheringham NR26 8RA, ☎
01263 824329/0871 200 3071, sher-
inghamtic@north-norfolk.gov.uk/ww
w.northnorfolk.org; Wells Tourist
Information, Staithe Street, Wells-
next-the-Sea NR23 1AN, ☎ 01328
710885, wellstic@north-
norfolk.gov.uk; Holt Tourist
Information, 3 Pound House, Market
Place, Holt NR25 6BE, holttic@north
norfolk.gov.uk; Walsingham Tourist
Information Centre, Shirehall
Museum, Common Place, Little
Walsingham, ☎ 01328 820510, seasonal opening.
Hospitals: The nearest hospitals
with 24-hour A&E departments are
either the Norfolk and Norwich University Hospital, Colney Lane,
Norwich NR4 7UY, ☎ 01603 286 286
or the Queen Elizabeth Hospital in
King's Lynn – Gayton Road, King's
Lynn PE30 4ET ☎ 01553 613613.
Cromer and District Hospital also
has a Minor Injuries Unit, open 8–
7.30, ☎ 01263 513571.
Websites: www.wells-guide.co.uk;

www.glavenvalley.co.uk – links to a
wealth of information for visitors to
North Norfolk.
Supermarkets: Tesco, Oak Street,
Fakenham NR21 9DX, ☎ 01328
757400; Morrisons, Clipbush Lane,
Fakenham NR21 8SW, ☎ 01328
855295.
CoastHopper bus service:
Bike rental: Walsinghams, 78
Staithe Street, Wells-next-the-Sea
NR23 1AQ, ☎ 01328 710438, open
all year, mountain bikes for hire; The
Bikeshed, 28 Beeston Road, Sheringham NR26 8EH, ☎ 01263 822255,
www.thebikeshed.biz, £9 a day, £30
a week; Huff and Puff Cycle Hire,
Kelling Heath NR25 7HW, ☎ 07788
132909, www.cyclenorfolk.co.uk, £9
per day, £6 children; On Yer Bike
Cycle Hire, The Laurels, Nutwood
Farm, Wighton NR23 1NX, ☎ 01328
820719, www.norfolkcyclehire.co.uk,
£12 per day (£6 for under-11s) or
£60 for one week – will deliver bikes
to local accommodation and also
have self-catering accommodation
at the farm.
Taxis: Elite Travel, Wighton, ☎
01328 821812; Steve's Taxis, Wells,
☎ 01328 712066;
Coastal Cabs, ☎ 01328 711114/
(mobile)07919 020917.

Cromer Pier looking towards town

CROMER TO GREAT YARMOUTH

The eastern section of the Norfolk coast down to the Suffolk border is more proletarian than the north coast, with many small coastal towns that retain the traditional charms of seaside resorts of 'yesteryear'. The top right-hand corner of East Anglia was historically a remote and impoverished part of the country, though the arrival of the railway in 1877 made access easier. By the 1890s, Cromer was a fashionable destination for people wanting to take the sea air and in 1901 seaside piers were opened in both Cromer and Great Yarmouth. Despite intervening fires and disasters, both are still flourishing and feature end-of-the-pier shows beloved by generations of regular holidaymakers. Garish hoardings advertise Elvis impersonators and old style stand-up comics.

But caravan parks, amusement arcades, and pensioners' discounts aren't the whole story. Stretches of this huge coast are adorned with modest fishing stations, Blue Flag sandy beaches, and small art galleries.

Turning to face inland, visitors find that the Broads are on their doorstep. Inland from Yarmouth is a marshy area between the Rivers Yare and Waveny with few people and no roads. The long distance footpath christened the Weavers Way navigates gingerly through this watery landscape. In fact the Weavers Way covers the entire 56 miles between Cromer and Great Yarmouth, not by following the coast but along a picturesque inland route through the Broadland towns of Stalham and Potter Heigham.

The coastal walking is also very rewarding, with a mixture of cliffs and sandy beaches between Cromer and Mundesley. This coast can suffer bleak and cutting winds and be buffeted by rampaging storms. But on a sunny day, you will find it hard to believe that this is one of Black Shuck's favoured patches.

Tales of the devil hound flourished here, probably encouraged by smugglers who wanted to frighten off snoopers. If Edward Lear is to be believed, reading the classics might also present a risk:

"There was an old person from Cromer
Who stood on one leg to read Homer
When he found he grew stiff
He jumped over the cliff
Which concluded that Person from Cromer."

WHAT TO SEE AND DO

 ### Fair weather

Cromer

Cromer is an archetypal English seaside resort, even though donkey rides have long disappeared. It hasn't been allowed to decline too much into shabbiness, partly thanks to European Union investment, but retains its Victorian and Edwardian red brick ambience. The pier has been revived and the promenade made more welcoming to pedestrians with illuminations and paving slabs bearing quotations such as Oscar Wilde's 'I find Cromer excellent for writing, Golf better still' , as well as Winston Churchill's 'I am not enjoying myself very much,' written when a young lad. Just as pasties go with Cornwall, crabs are synonymous with Cromer, although the advertising slogan, 'Come to Cromer and catch crabs' was an unfortunate choice. The sweet plump little beasties boiled and dressed can be bought everywhere and on a fine day should be consumed on the beach.

Cromer has good reason to be proud of its lifeboat heritage celebrated in the brand new RNLI Museum (see *Wet Weather*).

Overstrand to Mundesley

As well as simple promenades in Cromer, clifftop walks west to Sheringham (6 miles) or south to Overstrand (4 miles) afford good views to the North Sea. The area was christened Poppyland in the 1880s, a name that survives in the steam railway from Sheringham. When travel journalist, Clement Scott, visited he was soon smitten by the sight of massed poppies on the walk to the villages of Sidestrand and Overstrand (and the poppy is still the county flower of Norfolk).

Seven miles east of Cromer, **Mundesley** is an old-fashioned little resort with a superb beach for

MUNDESLEY MARITIME MUSEUM, Beach Road, Mundesley NR11 8BG;
☎ 01263 720879; adults 50p; open summer only.

families, lined with colourful beach huts, the tiny **Maritime Museum** housed in a coastguard lookout tower and pre-Victorian Stow Mill which still operates.

Less than 2 miles south of Mundesley is **Paston**. Amateur students of medieval history will be familiar with the name because of the Paston Letters, a remarkable collection of family letters that survive from the decades following the Black Death. The Pastons were a nouveau riche family who went in for showy building projects, namely a huge thatched tithe barn built next to the church in 1581, now closed to the public because it houses a colony of rare bats, and an elaborate tomb in the church for Katherine Paston, who was struck down aged 24.

Happisburgh

The stretch of coast on either side of Happisburgh (pronounced 'Haze-br'h) is one of the most seriously eroded areas in East Anglia. The ruins of past sea defences and slipway are there for all to see. But the erosion has revealed evidence of very early human occupation in Britain that pushes back previous estimates, for example charcoal flakes and, more recently, remnants of a hand-axe estimated to be 700,000 years old. The coast here is of immense interest to geologists. But most come to see the jolly candy-cane striped lighthouse and the mighty bell tower of **St Mary's Church** almost as tall as Cromer's, which also served as a beacon for sailors. If you happen to be there on a clear day when the tower is open, you should climb the 133 steps to see how many of the North Norfolk features you can see from the list promised by the church: 30 churches, two lighthouses, seven water towers, five corn mills, five drainage mills, two wind farms, Trimingham radar installation, Bacton gas terminal, reefs at Sea Palling and the Cathedral spire in Norwich.

> **ST MARY'S CHURCH**, Happisburgh tower open 11am–4pm on alternate Saturdays year round plus Wed from Apr to Oct (subject to weather and services); minimum height restriction is 4ft 7in; admission adults £2, children £1.

Horsey

At Horsey the Norfolk Broads almost meet the sea with only a line of steep dunes keeping the salt sea out. The whole area is fringed with unspoilt

Happisburgh lighthouse

Horsey

HORSEY WINDPUMP, Horsey, NR29 4EF; ☎ 01263 740241; adults £2.50, children £1; open daily 10am–4.30pm Apr to Oct, Weekends only in Mar.

beaches and one of the best is at Horsey Gap where grey seals can often be seen cavorting near the shore. The calving season is in December when people congregate to observe dozens of seal families on the beach.

The National Trust runs the five-storey **Horsey Windpump**. Even if you aren't particularly interested in drainage mechanisms, it is worth paying the entry fee for the views over the reed-filled mere (like a broad but enclosed by banks). Walking paths along both sides of the dyke allow access to the marshes and a range of wildlife including wintering wildfowl.

Great Yarmouth

Snobs such as Henry James have always enjoyed being rude about Yarmouth and its 'Cockneyfied sea-front', while the hard-to-please Paul Theroux described it as a 'raucous and profane town' on his walking tour round the coast of Britain in the early 1980s. But this brash and blowsy resort has weathered better than might have been expected and much nostalgic fun can be

The Norfolk Giant

In the first half of the 19th century a family of giants lived in the village of West Somerton just a mile from the sea between Happisburgh and Winterton-on-Sea. **Robert Hales** was born in 1813, grew to over 7ft 6 in and weighed 32 stone. One of his sisters was 7ft 2in and the others were all over 6 ft. Robert lived in a caravan for a time, where it is rumoured he chased his wife around with a knife, before realising that he could make money by parading himself at fairs such as the Tombland Fair in Norwich and even a precursor of Barnum & Bailey's circus in the USA. He returned to his home village where he died aged 50 and was buried in a tombchest (of average size) in the churchyard. His wife must have been a forgiving woman since the inscription indicates that his tomb 'was erected by an affectionate widow'.

had by strolling along the seafront, visiting a rock candy shop and attending a show on the pier. Miles of **safe sandy beaches** make for enjoyable bucket-and-spade activities in good weather, although the town also has decades of experience of amusing the throngs of holidaymakers in the rain with plenty of indoor family attractions. Recent investment (and the promise of more) is trying to address ongoing problems of boarded-up shops on the approach road from Norwich (the Acle Straight) and of litter, graffiti and groups of bored youths.

History isn't Great Yarmouth's strong suit. Most of what Dickens liked about the town, when he made it the home of David Copperfield's faithful friend Peggotty, was destroyed by the Second World War bombs. Originally the three main streets running in a long line parallel to the sea were cross-hatched with hundreds of narrow alleys known as 'rows' where specially invented 'troll-carts' delivered goods around the town. Virtually none of these rows remains, though the word troll cart is preserved in the name of a pub on Regent Street.

Very little is left from the time when Great Yarmouth was a prosperous member port in the Hanseatic League, nor even from less than 100 years ago when the town supported an enormous herring fleet. Remnants of an early mediaeval tower stand watch at North Quay, but mostly the town's history will have to be imagined from its museum displays, for example English Heritage has restored Row 111 as it would have been in 1942 before it was bombed.

National Trust country houses

Two of the finest landscaped houses in East Anglia can be visited in this far corner of Norfolk. Less than 3 miles inland from Cromer, **Felbrigg Hall** might be familiar to film-goers, having been the location for much of *The Cock and Bull Story* with Steve Coogan and Rob Bryden. One highlight of the house is the collection of paintings of the 18th-century Grand Tour. The lovely grounds with a walled garden, lake, church and paths, are a delight to explore, and even nicer if you arrange to stay for a night in one of the holiday cottages on the estate.

Blickling Hall is older and grander, and is considered one of the great Jacobean houses of the land. Anne Boleyn's family lived here at one point and she may even have been born here; her headless ghost is meant to appear on the anniversary of her execution for adultery and incest, so if you visit on 19 May listen for the rumble of carriage

FELBRIGG HALL, Garden and Park, Felbrigg, Near Cromer, NR11 8PR; ☎ 01263 837444, www.nationaltrust.org.uk; adults £9.15, children £4.30, families £22.60; open Mar to Oct 1pm–5pm, closed Thu/Fri, open daily Jul to Sept; gardens open until Christmas 11–5pm; walks/cycle rides on the estate are free all year round.

BLICKLING HALL AND GARDEN, Blickling, NR11 6NF, 10 miles south of Cromer; ☎ 01263 738030; adults £10.75, children £5.25, families £29 (less for garden only); house open Mar to Oct 1–5pm (closed Tues and also Mon outside high summer); garden open year round 10.15am–5.15pm but closed Mon to Wed in Nov to Feb; walks/cycle rides on the estate are free all year round

Felbrigg Hall

wheels pulled by four headless horses. The house has the usual fine furniture, decorated plasterwork and a long gallery now a library. But it is the park and gardens that are particularly spectacular with topiary, sunken gardens, a temple and a lake.

Wet weather

RNLI HENRY BLOGG MUSEUM, The Rocket House, The Gangway, Cromer, NR27 9ET; ☎ 01263 511294; www.rnli.org.uk/who_we_are/the_heritage_trust/henry-blogg; free; open Feb to Nov 10am–5pm (4pm in off-season); closed Mon; donations welcome.

CROMER MUSEUM, East Cottages, Tucker Street, Cromer, NR27 9HB; ☎ 01263 513543; www.museums.norfolk.gov.uk; adults £3.40, children £1.90; open all year Mon to Sat 10am–5pm (4pm in winter), Mar to Oct, also open Sun.

The **RNLI Henry Blogg Museum** at the end of Cromer's promenade is dedicated to telling the story of local heroes who made dramatic sea rescues, most notably Henry Blogg who worked as a lifeboatman for 53 years until his death in 1954. The waters of Cromer Bay are treacherous for seafarers and in centuries past were dubbed the Devil's Throat, claiming up to 1,000 lives on a single night in 1692. But things were different once the Lifeboat Institution had been created, and Henry Blogg is credited with having rescued nearly as many over the course of his career. Hands-on activities should interest children.

The **Cromer Museum** tells the fascinating story of the West Runton Elephant. As the cliffs at West

Runton near Cromer are progressively eroded, more fossil deposits are being revealed including in 1990 the massive pelvis of an elephant pegged at 600,000 years old. Because of the size and fragility of the bones, only a few are on display.

The new **Time and Tide Museum of Great Yarmouth Life** is situated in a rare survival from the town's herring heyday, a well-preserved Victorian curing shed. This splendid small museum is like a lament for the lost fishing industry (partly due to European policies) but also covers the entirety of Yarmouth's history, including a 'Seaside Holidays' gallery as a nostalgic celebration of holidays as they used to be.

Since Norfolk is Nelson's county, a visit to the lively Norfolk Nelson Museum is in order if only because of the Grade II listed merchant's house it occupies on South Quay. It doesn't suppress the more sensational aspects of the Admiral's love life and the discomforts of life aboard a naval warship.

TIME AND TIDE MUSEUM, Blackfriars Road, Great Yarmouth, NR30 3BX; ☎ 01493 743930; adults £6, children £4.15; open all year Mon to Fri 10am–5pm, Sat/Sun 12–5pm, winter closing time 4pm.

NELSON MUSEUM, 26 South Quay, Great Yarmouth, NR30 2RG; ☎ 01493 850698; www.nelson-museum.co.uk; adults £3.20, children £1.90, family £8.50; open Mon to Fri 10am–4/5pm, Sun 1–4pm.

 ## What to do with children...

GREAT YARMOUTH PLEASURE BEACH, South Beach Parade, Great Yarmouth, NR30 3EH; ☎ 01493 844585; www.pleasure-beach.co.uk; free with pay-as-you-go rides (£1 or £2 each) or £14/£16 wristband for unlimited rides; open daily May to Sept and Easter, Whit and Oct half-term holidays, plus weekends in Mar to May and Sept/Oct 11am–5.30pm (late closure of 9pm/10pm in summer).

JOYLAND CHILDREN'S FUN PARK, Marine Parade, Great Yarmouth, NR30 2EH; ☎ 01493 844094; www.joyland.org.uk; tokens £1 per ride, 12 tokens for £10.

Parents will be reassured by the high rating given to beaches along this coast. Mundesley, Sea Palling and Gorleston are all Blue Flag beaches. The 3km-long sandy beach at Gorleston at the southern extension of Great Yarmouth also has lifeguard cover.

Attractions in Great Yarmouth
If adults are tempted to be deprecating about Great Yarmouth, kids love it. Its **Pleasure Beach** isn't just a beach but a seafront amusement park with 20 rides including a wooden roller coaster built in 1928, plus crazy golf and water slides.

Clamouring signs along the Golden Mile promise thrills around every corner. In fact the thrills are quite mild at the small-scale **Joyland Fun Park** (about a mile north of the Pleasure Beach), where the Snails – their version of a roller coaster – depend mainly on gravity to meander along a pleasant route. This ride, among others, has been around since the park opened in 1949.

Nearby is the **Sea Life Centre** with its shark tanks, breeding seahorses, sea turtles and jellyfish. One remarkable sight is the open-topped tank with turbots and rays which respond to attention and come up to have their tummies tickled by aquarium staff.

For a more cultural outing, the **Elizabethan House** on Great Yarmouth's South Quay reveals how families lived in different periods of Yarmouth's history. There are Tudor costumes to try on, a room of toys and games from the past, and activities that bring to life what it was like to work in the scullery.

Boat trips to **Scroby Sands** 3km offshore set off from Yarmouth beach. Until recently, the seals had these sandbanks to themselves but, controversially, now have to share with one of the five most important offshore wind farms in Britain, clearly visible from the shore. The short boat trip costs £6 for adults, £4 for children.

Sports and activities

Although not usually associated with **surfing**, the beach at Cromer can pick up good North Sea swells. Short right and longer left rides can be achieved near Cromer Pier and also a little to the west at East Runton. Several local surf shops that offer board hire also run lessons, and the condition of the waves can be checked on www.eastcoastsurf.co.uk.

- **G-Side Surf School**, Cromer (☎ 07887 605789); Geoff can organise instruction between May and September.
- **The Glide Surf School**, Cromer (☎ 07966 392 227; benjaminkewell@hotmail.com); instruction given by Benjamin Kewell in the spring half-term holiday. Novices must be over 10 and able to swim 50m. Wet suits are compulsory.

The network of back lanes in north-east Norfolk is ideally suited to cycling and many families undertake a section of the 43 miles of **Norfolk Coast Cycleway** between Cromer and Great Yarmouth along Regional Route 30 (signposts show a white 30 on a blue square) with a couple of offroad sections for mountain bikers.

... and how to avoid children

A few miles inland from Happisburgh brings you to a remarkable and surprising garden, one that has been created out of nothing. The microclimate in this part of Norfolk, otherwise rather bleak, allows exotic plants to flourish at **East Ruston Old Vicarage**. The 30 acres contain 30 'rooms' or areas of gardens on different themes from a walled courtyard full of succulent plants to a vivid, exotic garden filled with banana trees, canna lilies and many other unlikely plants. You can book on one of the regular owner-guided tours followed by lunch in the tearoom at a cost of £35.

> **EAST RUSTON OLD VICARAGE**, East Ruston, NR12 9HN; ☎ 01692 650432; www.e-ruston-oldvicaragegardens.co.uk; adults £7; open from Mar to Oct, Wed/Fri/Sat/Sun/bank holidays 2–5.30pm.

Entertainment

Theatre
With the end-of-the-pier summer show still going, the **Pavilion Theatre** on Cromer Pier (Cromer NR27 9HE; ☎ 01263 512495; boxoffice@thecromer pier.com; www.cromer-pier.com/Pavilion-theatre.html) is a treat of a destination. The theatre has recently been renovated and seats more than 500 people, and also has a bar and restaurant with fabulous views. The summer special family show opens in late June and ticket prices are £15.50 for adults.

Cromer also has a small four-screen cinema, the **Regal Cinema** (Hans Place NR27 3EQ; ☎ 01263 510151/01263 513311; www.regalfilmcentre.co.uk), so offers a decent choice of films on a rainy day.

Special events
Cromer is always mobbed for a week in summer during the annual **Carnival** which features exuberant parades, firework displays, music and dancing. The main day is always the third Wednesday in August (www.cromer carnival.co.uk).

Shopping

Cromer has some small independent shops, some of which seem to be caught in a time warp – they still observe half-day closing at 1pm on Wednesdays.

In Great Yarmouth, the pedestrianised Regent Road, leading from the waterfront to the town centre, is lined with touristy shops. One favourite is **Docwra's Rock Shop**, the largest rock candy factory in the world (13 Regent Road NR30 2AF; ☎ 01493 844676) where the famous seaside confection has been made for three generations.

The best... **PLACES TO STAY**

BOUTIQUE

Incleborough House

Lower Common, East Runton, near Cromer NR27 9PG (300m from the beach) ☎ 01263 515939 www.incleboroughhouse.com

This small country house B&B occupies a listed building dating from 1687, recently restored using traditional materials and workmanship. It retains traditional charms in its drawing room with a log fire while being fully modernised throughout, and serves complimentary wine, fruit, chocolates and cream tea.

Prices: B&B from £165 for a double.

HOTEL

No. 78 Hotel

78 Marine Parade, Great Yarmouth NR30 2DH. ☎ 01493 850001. www.no78.co.uk

This Victorian townhouse hotel at the north end of the Golden Mile benefitted in 2007 from a visit from Ruth Watson, of Channel 5's *Hotel Inspector* and is now quite unlike the usual bedraggled seaside guest house. The enthusiastic owners maintain their new property beautifully and could not try harder to give visitors a relaxing stay.

Prices: from £35 for a single, £50–70 for a double.

FARMSTAY

Shrublands Farm

Northrepps, near Cromer NR27 0AA (2 miles southeast of Cromer) ☎ 01263 579297, youngman@farming.co.uk; www.shrublandsfarm.com

Ann and Peter Youngman offer self-catering bungalow and cottage, B&B and camping accommodation on their arable farm. The eggs served at breakfast are from the farm, and other food is locally produced. Children must be over 12 for the B&B.

Prices: from £30 to £32 per person; from £320 to £625 for a bungalow.

B&B

The Eiders Bed and Breakfast

Holt Road, Aylmerton, Near Cromer NR11 8QA. (2 mile pleasant walk to the coast at West Runton). ☎ 01263 837280 www.eiders.co.uk

With a duck pond in the grounds, the friendly proprietors will lend binoculars for surveying the birdlife from the room balconies and the conservatory dining room. The choice of breakfast menu – all are generous – includes orange pancakes and smoked salmon.

Prices: from £90 for a double, £125 for a family room sleeping four.

CAMPSITE

Deer's Glade Campsite

White Post Road, Hanworth NR11 7HN ☎ 01263 768633 www.deersglade.co.uk

This recently opened campsite is open all year round and has many attractive features including a fishing lake, shuttle service to local restaurants and pubs and easy access on foot to a deer park at Gunton Hall.

Prices: from £5 to £7.50 per adult depending on season, from £1.75 to £2.75 per child.

UNUSUAL

The Hermanus Holiday Centre

The Holway, Winterton-on-Sea NR29 4BP (8 miles north of Great Yarmouth) ☎ 01493 393216 www.hermanusholidays.com

This eccentric collection of round beach houses with thatched roofs is modelled on a bayside resort in South Africa. The family-run nature of Hermanus means that it avoids a mass market holiday camp atmosphere, while still providing family entertainment.

Price: from £360 to £497 for a double round-house (sleeps six) in the high season.

The best... FOOD AND DRINK

Staying in

Fishing has been taking place along this coast for millennia and is still going strong. You can watch the Cromer crab fleet land their catch after winching their boats over the beach with old tractors. The season lasts from April to November.

For dressed crab in Cromer head for **Richard and Julie Davies'** shop at 7 Garden Street which has its own crab boat. Davies is a famous name in Cromer since there have been four generations of Davies active in the lifeboat crews. The shop also sells lobsters, cockles, whelks, wet fish and (in season) mussels and samphire, and provides ice so that you can get it back to your holiday accommodation as fresh as possible.

Of Great Yarmouth's important fish smoking industry, the only smokery left is **H S Fishing 2000 Ltd** (Sutton Road, Great Yarmouth, NR30 3NA; ☎ 01493 858118) that smokes and cures fish in the traditional way. It sells kippers and other cured fish directly to the walk-in public.

One of the most dedicated farm shop operations in Norfolk is located on the Blickling estate. Samphire trades only in meat (including award-winning pork pies), bread and produce from local small-scale producers.

The nearest farmers' market is in the handsome market town of Aylsham, 10 miles south of Cromer, 12 miles west of Mundesley, on the first Saturday of the month in the morning (☎ 01263 734580). Another possibility is the Acle farmers' market on the second Saturday.

SAMPHIRE, The Estate Barn, Blickling Hall, Nr Aylsham, NR11 6NF; ☎ 01263 734464; www.samphireshop.co.uk; open daily 9.30pm–5pm.

Takeaways

Peggotty's at 6 Hamilton Road and **Mary Jane's** at 27 Garden Street are renowned for their fish and chips. The latter even fries up skate wings. In the busy season queues out the door indicate the quality and freshness of the fish they serve.

Predictably there will be no problem locating fish and chips along the Golden Mile in Great Yarmouth. And in Gorleston-on-Sea at the southern end of Yarmouth, **Tony's Fish Bar** is famous for its quality frying. It is located a couple of minutes from the seafront on the corner of Lower Cliff Road and Bells Road (☎ 01493 603757).

EATING OUT

FINE DINING
The Courtyard Restaurant
New Street, Cromer NR27 9HP
☎ **01263 515419**

Tucked away behind the Wellington Hotel near the Esplanade, interesting vegetarian, fish and meat dishes such as seafood chowder and Moroccan spiced steak are prepared by an enthusiastic young chef.

Old Vicarage Hotel and Restaurant
The Street, Hemsby, Near Great Yarmouth NR29 4EU
☎ **01493 731557**

The three-course table d'hôte menu at £27 is suitable for special occasions. The building is Victorian but the décor is modern. Dishes try to use local produce such as guinea fowl, sea bass or scallops for the main course, or cranachan for dessert.

RESTAURANT
Moments Restaurant
Beach Road, Scratby, Near Great Yarmouth NR29 3NW
☎ **01493 732126**

This charming family restaurant is unexpected but welcome. It serves delicious skewered king prawns in garlic butter, and peppered beef.

GASTROPUB
The Crown
Front Street, Trunch, near North Walsham NR28 0AH
☎ **01263 722341**
www.trunchcrown.co.uk

Unpretentious home-cooked food in a proper local pub with a small but cheerful dining room. Sample dishes include parsnip soup, steak and onion pudding and lemon meringue pie, all at reasonable prices.

Fisherman's Return
The Lane, Winterton-on-Sea NR29 4BN
☎ **01493 393305**
www.fishermans-return.com

Located near the sandy beach and extensive dunes at Winterton, this brick and flint hostelry has a cosy atmosphere and welcoming landlords. A specials board menu might include hot Winterton-smoked salmon (£5.75), boozy beef pie (£8.50) and ginger sponge and custard (£3.50).

CAFÉ
The Clifftop Café at Overstrand
22 Cliff Road, Overstrand NR27 0PP
☎ **01263 579319**

This unpretentious café with a superb view of the sea serves breakfast sausages of great renown and a good Sunday lunch on formica tables with plastic table cloths. In winter, it's a favourite haunt of local fishermen.

 Drinking

The pubs in this part of Norfolk have to contend with fewer second-home owners and tourists and therefore find it easier to extend a genuine welcome. Most village locals will serve a decent drop of bitter and will knock up a wholesome meal to warm you after a bracing walk on the coast or in the countryside. Try for example the unpretentious **Nelson Head** in Horsey (Beach Road, Horsey,

NR29 4AD; ☎ 01493 393378) which serves Nelson's Revenge (naturally) which you can sip in front of a roaring fire or in the garden.

Another old-style gem is **The Buckinghamshire Arms** (Blickling, NR11 6NF; ☎ 01263 732133) located at the gates of Blickling Hall and in the safekeeping of the National Trust, so you will not come across any fruit machines. The range of drinks includes Adnams and Woodfordes ales as well as local cider, while the upmarket food can be eaten in the bar, restaurant or garden.

The nearest brewery in East Norfolk is the relatively new **Tipples Brewery** in Acle (see the chapter on the Norfolk Broads). More than a century ago, Arthur Conan Doyle stayed at the **Hill House** hotel in Happisburgh Beside the village church (NR12 0PW; ☎ 01692 650004), now an amiable pub with beams and a woodburning stove, which takes its beer seriously enough to mount a beer festival every June. The pub has plenty of Sherlock Holmes memorabilia.

 ## Visitor information

Tourist Information Centre: Cromer Tourist Information, Bus Station, Prince of Wales Road, Cromer NR27 9HS, ☎ 01263 512497, cromertic@north norfolk.gov.uk, open year round 10am–5pm (longer hours in summer), ☎ 0871 200 3071; Greater Yarmouth Tourist Information, Maritime House, 25 Marine Parade, Great Yarmouth NR30 2EN, [tel]01493 846346, tourism@great-yarmouth.gov.uk/www.great-yarmouth.co.uk; Ramblers Association (Sales), 2nd floor, 87–90 Albert Embankment, London SE1 7TW, 020 7339 8500, www.ramblers.org.uk/info/publica tions/pubsbooks.html, guidebooks to long distance footpaths in Norfolk.

Hospitals: A&E facilities available at James Paget Hospital, Lowestoft Road, Gorleston, Great Yarmouth NR31 6LA, ☎ 01493 452452.

Supermarkets: Morrisons, Beech Station Road, Cromer NR27 9SW, ☎ 01263 515275, open until 8pm; *Sainsbury*, St Nicholas Road, Great Yarmouth NR30 1NN, ☎ 01493 330313; *Sainsbury*, Bacton Road, North Walsham NR28 9DS (8 miles from Cromer), ☎ 01692 500498.

Bike rental: Pedal Revolution, West Street, Cromer NR27 9HZ, ☎ 01263 510039, hire charges are £10 per day, £50 for a week plus delivery can be made anywhere between King's Lynn and Yarmouth for £25.

Taxis: A1 Cabs, Cromer, ☎ 01263 513371; Anglia Taxis, Great Yarmouth Railway Station, ☎ 01493 855855; Swift Taxis, Great Yarmouth, ☎ 01493 300300.

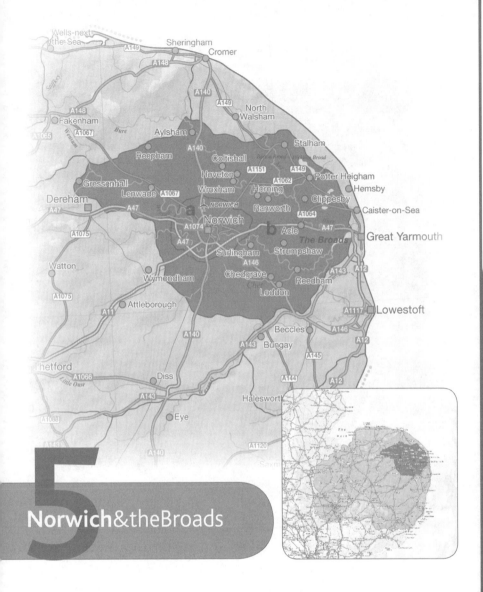

5 Norwich&theBroads

a. Norwich

b. Norfolk Broads

Unmissable highlights

01 Linger over a cappuccino on the overgrown roof terrace of the Briton's Arms Coffee House, p.246

02 Compare images of George and the Dragon on mediaeval wall paintings and roof carvings in the church and cathedral, p.231

03 Stroll along the River Wensum through Norwich or take a riverbus downstream to Whitlingham Country Park, p.237

04 Attend the prize-winning farmers' market in the 'Golden Triangle' area of Norwich, p.244

05 Find your way to the back street Fat Cat brew pub where every day is a beer festival, p.247

06 Treat the children to a day at Dinosaur Adventure Park, p.238

07 Attend a performance of the famous Norwich Puppet Theatre company in a medieval church-turned-theatre, p.239

08 Dine at Delia Smith's smart restaurant at her beloved Norwich City Football ground, p.245

09 Visit the eclectic art collection at the Sainsbury Centre for the Visual Arts, p.236

10 Race on the zipwires or down the wide slide at BeWILDerwood in the Broads, p.257

11 Stroll along Fleet Dike to see the ruined abbey in the Marshes, p.255

12 Hire a cruiser for a day and let the children steer, p.253

13 Watch the sun set from the Ferry Inn (at least three good Broadland pubs bear that name), p.261

NORWICH AND THE BROADS

Partly due to its geographical isolation off the main north–south axis, Norwich and its environs have gone their own way. Refreshingly, the city does not automatically look to London for a lead and never has done. The Norwich Mercury, founded in 1727, was the first regional newspaper in the country. Its history of radical dissent percolates down to the present day, so for example the council has more Green Party councillors than any other in England (10 seats on Norwich City Council). The University of East Anglia's motto is 'Do Different', an admirable sentiment, if not very grammatically expressed. In many ways, Norwich is independent and idiosyncratic, and a delight to visit at any time of year. Most people are bowled over by the sophistication of its artistic and gastronomic life.

The pleasures to be found on the Broads aren't really of the modern hectic era. Most people come to pootle about on the lazy stretches of water, but those who come to cycle or walk along dingly-dell footpaths through meadows and woodlands, past bird hides, cottages with their own landing stages and thatched churches will also experience the tranquillity. Discovering quiet beauty calls for quietness, and this is an area where relaxation is the chief point. Pulses will race not at speed – for the speed limit for boats on the Broads is normally no more than 5mph, to conserve the banks and reedbeds – but at the sight of herons, dragonflies and water lilies or, if you are lucky, a marsh harrier or the rare swallowtail butterfly, the biggest in Britain and found only in the Broads.

NORWICH

Norwich is often under-rated and is seldom swamped with visitors. Which is a mystery since its many delights, left over from the Middle Ages when the city was the largest walled city in Europe, stand comparison with those of Bruges or Siena. In some ways it has a European atmosphere with narrow lanes leading to light courtyards softened with baskets and pots of greenery. As the second city of England when Elizabeth I visited in 1578, it has a rich heritage. Norwich has a long and proud tradition as a capital of culture, even if its bid to become official European Capital of Culture for 2008 didn't succeed (some say partly because of the negative impression given by the spoof Norwich radio presenter Alan Partridge).

Remarkably, nearly three dozen medieval churches survive, not all as places of worship but as creches, art galleries and hands-on science centres. The city's remarkable ability to value its past while looking to the future results in historic buildings put to new purposes, such as the brand new art house cinema in an Elizabethan merchant's house, the hip Norwich Arts Centre and Café in the redundant St Swithin's Church and the King of Hearts Centre in a Tudor house.

WHAT TO SEE AND DO

In the Middle Ages, the wool merchants' fabulous wealth financed magnificent churches and domestic buildings, sometimes on adjacent street corners. The characteristic flint work, 'knapped' or sliced to shine like obsidian, can be enjoyed on a random walking tour of the city's picturesque cobbled byways. Even the names of the streets and passageways stir the imagination – Maddermarket where cloth dyes were traded (named for the plant roots used for red dyes); Fishergate where the valuable cargoes of salty herrings from the North Sea were unloaded, Pottergate where archaeologists found remains of an 11th-century kiln.

 Fair weather

The leafy **Riverside Walk** alongside the River Wensum offers rewarding views of the 14th-century defensive **Cow Tower** (☎ 01603 213434, www.english-heritage.org.uk), the three-arched mediaeval **Bishop's Bridge** (best viewed from the car park of the Red Lion pub) and a watergate and ferry house called **Pull's Ferry**, named after John Pull who worked here as a ferryman for nearly 50 years. The cathedral spire (second highest in the land after Salisbury) is best seen from Pull's Ferry, where the honey-coloured stone used in the construction of the cathedral arrived from Normandy on river barges.

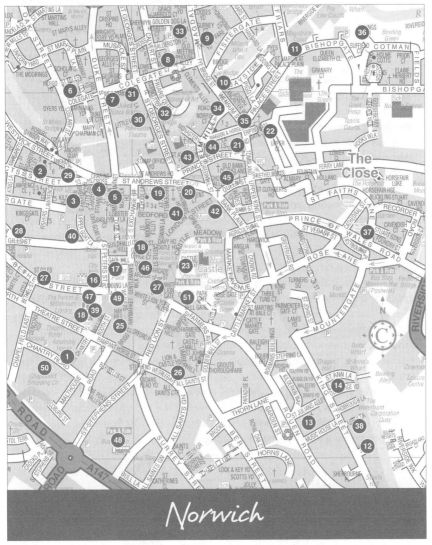

Norwich

1	Assembly House	18	Jarrold's Store	35	Maid's Head Hotel
2	Norwich Arts Centre	19	Bridewell Museum	36	Adam & Eve
3	St Gregory Pottergate	20	Cinema City	37	Rocco's
4	Strangers' Hall	21	Erpingham Gate	38	The Waterfront
5	Maddermarket Theatre	22	Norwich Cathedral	39	Café Bar Marzano
6	Inspire Discovery Centre	23	Norwich Castle	40	Belgian Monk
7	Playhouse	24	Coleman's Mustard Shop	41	Wild Man
8	Octagon Chapel	25	St Peter Mancoft	42	FizzBuzz Brasserie
9	Gurney Court	26	Mustard Lounge	43	Elm Hill Brasserie
10	King of Hearts	27	The Greenhouse	44	Briton's Arms
11	Puppet Theatre	28	St Giles House Hotel	45	Shiki
12	Wensum Lodge/Music House	29	St Benedict's Restaurant	46	Walnut Tree Shades
13	Dame Julian's Cell	30	Last Wine Bar	47	Tourist Information
14	Dragon Hall	31	Golden Star	48	Bus Station
15	Forum	32	By Appointment	49	Market
16	City Hall	33	Gothic House	50	Chapelfield Shopping Centre
17	Guildhall	34	Ribs of Beef	51	Castle Mall

Cow Tower

The city's rickety byways, secret courtyards, flint houses with sagging lintels and Gothic overhangs are worth exploring. **Elm Hill**, now lined with antique shops, is film-set perfect. It came within a whisker of being demolished in the 1920s, as the council was equally divided between the developers and the conservers, and it was only the mayor's casting vote that saved it. This impulse persisted through the 1950s and 1960s, when so many other British city councils were voting to have the hearts torn out of their city centres, accounting for the survival of the architectural magnificence in Norwich today. Not much is visible from main arterial routes so it's a city made for walking.

At some point you will end up in **Tombland**, which means 'unoccupied ground' although it does contain a graveyard of sorts. Victims of the Great Plague were buried in the plague pits beneath where **Samson and Hercules House** now stands. Tombland is buzzing with pavement cafés, restaurants, a good second-hand bookshop and the historic **Maid's Head Hotel**.

The southern extension of Tombland is **King Street** which is a busy road for cars and the subject of current regeneration plans, with several architectural gems. **Wensum Lodge** at number 169, now an adult education centre, encompasses the **Music House** built in 1175, which is the oldest domestic residence in Norwich and, like the ancient Moyse's Hall in Bury St Edmunds, was originally owned by a wealthy Jewish merchant.

Norwich in the Second World War

Norwich and East Anglia generally suffered more during the war than many other areas of the country because of their proximity to the continent. In retaliation for the Allies' bombing of the Hanseatic city of Lübeck, the Germans decided to bomb cities awarded three stars in the Baedeker guidebook. After Bath and Exeter and before York came Norwich – the target of bombing raids on 27 and 29 April 1942, which killed nearly 350 citizens and destroyed 2,000 homes. Surprisingly few great buildings were destroyed, with the notable exception of St Julian's, one of the city's oldest churches (mentioned below).

Many shops were flattened in the Baedeker blitz on Norwich, among them Bond's department store (now John Lewis). The proprietor Ernest Bond showed true British grit by scrambling to get back in business three days after the raid, selling whatever stock his staff had salvaged, from a number of out-of-service buses parked near the bomb site.

From the ashes of the great fire of 1994 that tragically destroyed the Norwich Public Library and Archive has risen a spangling new glass, metal and concrete horseshoe-shaped building called the **Forum**, behind one of the city's finest churches (St Peter Mancroft) and overlooking the market. The striking chequerboard pattern of flint with ashlar on the early 15th-century **Guildhall** stands out in marked contrast to the 1930s **City Hall**.

In the unexpectedly interesting **Norwich-over-the-water**, where a 'wrong side of the tracks' atmosphere is absent, further historic streets deserve a wander, including Colegate lined with houses once occupied by merchants and weavers; you can tell the latter because of the dormer windows that let in plenty of light onto the looms located on the upper storey. Colegate leads to Magdalen Street which extends up from the city's oldest river crossing at Fye Bridge. Elizabeth Fry (née Gurney – a banking family who eventually sold out to Barclays) was born at Gurney Court, which you can peek into from Magdalen Street. She was a Quaker prison reformer deemed important enough to have her picture included on the £5 note.

Norwich Cathedral

The most glorious of Norwich buildings is the great romanesque cathedral with its soaring 315ft spire, built of Norman Caen stone, and its magnificent medieval cloisters, the largest in England. Don't miss the carved misericords under the choristers' seats which include several exuberant green men, also to be found among the roof bosses, most easily viewed in the cloisters. Bosses are carved images at points where vaults intersect, and there are more than one thousand in Norwich Cathedral. Some people go so far as to bring

Hitler may have been eager to punish the British by obliterating some of Norwich's treasures but he didn't want to destroy the City Hall, at that time brand new. He greatly admired this monolithic red brick building with its 200ft clock tower and porticoed entrance. In fact he even entertained the idea of using it for his government if he managed to conquer England.

Plane-spotters and war buffs will enjoy the City of Norwich Aviation Museum which celebrates the key role Norfolk played in the Second World War (see *What to do with children*). This is on the site of Station 123 (now Norwich International Airport), the closest US airbase to Norwich, where the Eighth US Airforce was stationed. In the Broads, the small museum at Neatishead devoted to the history of air defence radar has just won a prize for best small tourist attraction (see chapter on the Broads).

binoculars to get a better look at the animals in Noah's ark, the creation of Eve, George slaying a red-eyed fire-breathing dragon and so on. The juxtaposition of pagan green men with stories from the Bible is fascinating. It's worth joining one of the daily free guided tours that will point you towards all the treasures, including the late 14th-century painting of the Crucifixion that survived the Reformation only because it was in use face down as a table when the iconoclasts came to call.

> **NORWICH CATHEDRAL,**
> 12 The Close, BR1 4EH;
> ☎ 01603 218440; www.cathedral.org.uk; open 7.30am–6pm daily (7pm in summer); choral evensong services take place every weekday at 5.30pm; free hour-long tours take place daily Mon to Sat (last tour 3pm)

The plucky secular tendencies of Norwich can be seen in one of the two magnificent gates leading to the cathedral. On **St Ethelbert's Gate** (built 1272), it seems to be a daring peasant rather than a knight or saint who confronts a fierce dragon. The gates separate the busy urban streets and the serene cathedral precinct full of sacred and secular buildings including **Norwich School**, founded in 1096. You will also come across the **Jubilee Labyrinth**.

Norwich Castle

The splendid Norman castle presides over the city centre, and houses a regional museum and distinguished art gallery. The moat and ditch have been turned into pleasant civic gardens. Robert Kett, local insurgent and now hero, was hung up outside the castle walls in 1549 where he slowly starved to death, as punishment for leading a rebellion against the government's policy of land enclosures and high prices. The castle served as a prison from the 14th to the 19th centuries with increasingly intolerable conditions for prisoners. Exciting tours can be taken of the dungeons where the guide may plunge everyone into total darkness. On display in the dungeon is a scold's bridle (or brank), a barbaric device that would be clamped round a gossiping woman's head and fitted with a tongue depressor. The museum also tells the story of ducking chairs which were used on 'strumpets' (prostitutes) who were dunked in the River Wensum. You can see a plaque on Fye Bridge which marks the site of where the dunkable stool was fixed in the 16th century. Brutal practices continued right up until 1867 when the last public execution took place at the castle. The castle contains various hands-on exhibits, for example children are allowed to clamber aboard a recreated chariot as Boudicca might have ridden in battle against the Romans.

> **NORWICH CASTLE MUSEUM AND ART GALLERY**, Castle Meadow, NR1 3JU; ☎ 01603 493625; www.museums.norfolk.gov.uk; adults £4.75, children £3.25, including the Castle Art Gallery £6.50/£4.75; open Mon to Fri 10am–4.30pm, Sat 10am–5pm, Sun 1–5pm; extra £1.90 for tours of the battlements (for excellent views over Norwich) and dungeon.

Local knowledge

Martin and Lyn Ayres are both involved in the buzzy artistic life of Norwich. Martin works for Screeneast, which is devoted to developing, supporting and promoting film and media activity in the area. One of their projects is to allocate funding for archives of moving images about the heritage of the East of England. Lyn Ayres is an arts teacher with a special interest in textiles.

Favourite local pub: It's hard to choose from the excellent selection, but the Golden Star at 57 Colegate is a small old-fashioned pub with a great atmosphere. The Playhouse bar and Garden is good if you like an arty crowd.

Favourite restaurant: St Benedict's Restaurant is a small bistro-style restaurant in St Benedict's Street near the city centre with sensational food.

Secret tip for lunch: Shiki Japanese restaurant at 5–6 Tombland by the Cathedral does great sushi.

Favourite shop: Thorns Ironmongers in Lobster Lane near the Market is DIY heaven. Two related fabric shops in Magdalen Street are a magnet for people who love materials. The one at number 40 sells furnishing fabric and the other at number 29 stocks dress fabrics.

Favourite activity: The Norwich Puppet Theatre is absolutely great for both children and adults.

Best view: Driving to Great Yarmouth along the Acle Straight (the A47) is like steeping back in time. Even if they make it dual carriageway, it will still take a long time to feel like modern Britain.

Best walk: The riverside walk along the Wensum in the centre of Norwich from Anchor Quay to Prince of Wales Road.

Quirkiest attraction: The Bridewell Museum was once the town gaol but is now a gem displaying Norwich's historic trades from mustard and textiles to shoes, chocolate and beer.

Best kept secret: The Exotic Garden off Cotman Road with tea and cakes and a tree house.

Favourite haunt: Cinema City recently reopened with three screens inside a medieval merchant's house.

Favourite treat: A trip with the family on the Holt to Sheringham railway as seen in *Dad's Army* or Apple day at Gressenhall Museum of Rural Life.

The **Castle Museum** has a fine collection of Norwich School paintings, archaeological remains from the region and natural history galleries. The Norwich School paintings aren't as well known as they should be, but they are remarkable for being by self-taught painters from the working classes, Cotman, Crome and Stannard. While their contemporaries from elsewhere in East Anglia, Constable and Gainsborough, moved to London to make their names, the Norwich painters formed the first school of art to thrive in the provinces. It was not until 2001, nearly 200 years after the school was founded, that a major exhibition was shown in London, at the Tate. Many of the paintings depict scenes of everyday life in Norwich and its environs.

Parks and gardens

With luck balmy weather will entice you to discover some of the city's many secret gardens and other green spaces. If you wander along Colegate, pause at the non-conformist **Octagon Unitarian Chapel** built in 1756 whose past adherents include the Victorian feminist and writer Harriet Martineau. The unpretentious quiet garden alongside has a footpath composed of memorial tablets, all to long-lived citizens so it isn't a sad place.

The delightful **Plantation Garden** with Gothic fountain and Italianate terraces has been restored by volunteers to its Victorian splendour. Although only a third of a mile from the city centre, along the Earlham Road, these 3 acres of tranquillity are relatively undiscovered and tricky to find; the entrance is next to the Beeches Hotel and the only available parking across the road in the car park of the Black Horse pub.

PLANTATION GARDENS, 4 Earlham Road, Norwich NR2 3DB; ☎ 01603 621868; www.planta tiongarden.co.uk; £2; open all year 9am–6pm; Sun: teas served on summer afternoons (£1.50 tea and cake).

The **Exotic Garden** off Cotman Road is even less well known. An adventurous garden designer called Will Giles has succeeded in nurturing many tropical plants on a south-facing slope without the benefit of a hothouse. Several varieties of banana and ginger plant are grown, though these aren't necessarily on the afternoon tea menu. A solidly built tree house affords very good views.

THE EXOTIC GARDEN, 6 Cotman Road, Thorpe, Norwich NR1 4AF (less than a mile behind the station); ☎ 01603 623167; www.exoticgarden.com; £4.50; open late June to late Oct, Sun 1–5pm.

Further out is **Mousehold Heath** incorporating nearly 200 acres of woodlands and hills from where you get great views looking down at the cathedral and the city. The highest point is St James' Hill, with nature trails and picnic areas. It was here that Kett and his rebel army camped in preparation for fighting the nobles and where, after the rebellion was defeated, nine of his chief allies were hanged on the so-called Oak of Reformation.

Wet weather

It's easy to find a museum or indoor attraction of interest in Norwich besides the majestic cathedral. **Dragon's Hall** is a timber-framed merchant's building, saved from dereliction and magnificently restored thanks to a recent Heritage Lottery grant. In the 15th century, a great trading hall-cum-showroom was built for the wealthy Toppes family of wool traders who owned it, and the story of this important mediaeval warehouse is told through the exhibits. The name derives from the carving of the orange-winged dragon, rediscovered in a damaged form less than three decades ago.

DRAGON'S HALL, 115–123 King Street, NR1 1QE; ☎ 01603 663922; www.dragonhall.org; adults £5, children £3, family £12.50; open Apr to Nov, Mon to Fri 10am–4pm, Sun and bank holidays 12pm–4pm.

Strangers' Hall is another splendid and even older house dating from 1320, which evokes not only mediaeval Norwich but Elizabethan, Georgian and Victorian Norwich in successive rooms furnished in period.

STRANGERS' HALL, 4 Charing Cross, NR2 4AL; ☎ 01603 667229; adults £3.50, children £1.90; open Wed/Sat 10.30am–4pm.

Norwich's mercantile and social history has waxed and waned over the centuries, a story that is well told in the **Bridewell Museum**. Posters display Norwich products from Colman's mustard to bicycles and there is a captivating reconstruction of a chemist shop as it would have been in living memory and of a pub counter from the 1950s when you could buy a nip bottle of Norvic ale for 11½d. The beguiling collection of prototype handmade shoes from slippers made of sealskin to exotic knitted mules are from a time when Norwich was the Milan of shoe fashion. After the Bridewell ceased to be a women's and paupers' prison in the 19th century, it became a shoe factory itself, until a local footwear magnate gave it to the City in 1925 as a museum of local industries. The venerable history of shoe- and boot-making in Norwich – eight million pairs were made here as recently as 1965 – came to an end about four years ago when Start-rite moved its manufacturing operations to Asia. The museum hosts lots of activities for children (see *What to do with children*).

BRIDEWELL MUSEUM, Bridewell Alley, NR2 1AQ (short walk along London Street from the market); ☎ 01603 629127; adults £3.10, children £1.70, family £8.50; open Apr to Oct, Tues to Fri 10am–4.30pm; Sat 10am–5pm.

Churches

The Diocese of Norwich has 31 medieval parish churches, apparently more than London, York and Bristol combined. Some have marvellous wall paintings. For example at **St Gregory Pottergate** near Strangers' Hall you can see a superb St George and his noble steed outfacing the dragon, while the damsel-in-distress looks on appreciatively. This church was opened to the public for the first time in the summer of 2007 (Tues mornings only).

Stained glass is the attraction of other churches, principally **St Peter Mancroft** towering over the market. Its massive east window incorporates more than 40 panes, many of them original 15th-century glass, depicting donors to the church, scenes from the New Testament and the lives of the saints. **St Julian's Church** on King Street near the Dragon Hall contains **Dame Julian's cell** (Julian as a variant of Gillian) where the saintly woman withdrew from the world to lead a life of mystical contemplation (mainly contemplating Christ's decaying body) and wrote *The Revelations of Divine Love* in about 1393, reputed to be the first book written by a woman in the English language. The restored 'cell' is more like a chapel shrine but atmospheric all the same.

Visit www.norwichchurches.co.uk/visits.html for information about opening times and visiting arrangements for all Norwich churches.

Sainsbury Centre for the Visual Arts

This interesting and eclectic art collection is housed in a superb gallery filled with light on the campus of the University of East Anglia. The building was one of Norman Foster's first commissions (built in the 1970s) and has lasted well. The core of the collection was donated by Robert Sainsbury, grandson of the founder of the grocery empire. Over a period of six decades, he and his wife Lisa collected art from around the world and from periods stretching from the Baby-

SAINSBURY CENTRE FOR THE VISUAL ARTS, University of East Anglia, Earlham Road NR4 7TJ; about 3 miles from the city centre on bus routes 22 and 25–27; ☎ 01603 593199; www.scva.ac.uk; free except special exhibitions; open Tues to Sun 10am–5pm.

Sainsbury Centre for the Visual Arts, University of East Anglia

lonians to their contemporaries. They counted Henry Moore, Alberto Giacometti and Francis Bacon among their friends, so their works are well represented. The small café serves tasty fresh salads which can be taken out onto the terrace on a fine day.

What to do with children ...

Children and adults are guaranteed to be riveted by any show from the world-class puppet theatre, described in the section on entertainment. The **Inspire Discovery Centre** across the river near Colegate is a delightful hands-on science centre, recently refurbished, housed in an elegant 16th-century church. Its permanent exhibits are on the themes of force, light, perception and medieval engineering as relevant to the building of the church in which the centre is located. Favourites are usually the beach ball hovering due to the Bernoulli effect and the chance to enter a tornado.

For an extra charge at the **City of Norwich Aviation Museum**, children can enter the cockpit (under supervision) of an Avro Vulcan bomber as used in the Falklands War.

> **INSPIRE DISCOVERY CENTRE**, St Michael's Church, Oak Street, NR3 3AE; ☎ 01603 612612; http://inspirediscovery centre.com; adult £4.50, children £4, family £13, open Mon to Fri 10am–4pm (term time), Sat/Sun 11am–5pm.

> **CITY OF NORWICH AVIATION MUSEUM**, Old Norwich Road, Horsham St Faith, Norwich, NR10 3JF; ☎ 01603 893080; www.cnam.co.uk; adults £4.25, children £2, families £20; open year round; Apr to Oct, Tues to Sat 10am–5pm, Sun 12am–5pm; Nov to Mar, Wed/Fri/Sat 10am–4pm, Sun 11am–3pm.

Play areas

The most centrally located play area for toddlers is in Chapelfield Gardens; for older children, there is a giant chess/draughts game (in summer). Waterloo Park (between Aylsham and Angel Roads) in the north of the city has a bigger play area and paddling pool. Any horsey offspring who have a fondness for *Black Beauty* might like to be driven past the house where Anna Sewell wrote her children's classic (White House, 125 Spixworth Road, Old Catton; privately owned).

Even some of the smarter cafés and restaurants are very child-friendly including Marzano's in the Forum with a small play area, and Rocco's (86 Prince of Wales) which lets children eat at their unexpectedly excellent Sunday afternoon carvery for £5, half the adult charge.

Boat trips

City Boats operates a riverbus and cruise boat along the River Wensum until it merges with the River Yare, leading to Whitlingham Country Park where there are woodland walks and a new Water Sports Centre to sample sailing, canoeing or windsurfing. Departures are from a quay across the Prince of Wales Bridge from the railway station and are accompanied by an imaginative commentary. You can also hire a day cruiser for the day.

CITY BOATS, Highcraft Marina, Griffin Lane, Thorpe St Andrew, Norwich, NR7 0SL; ☎ 01603 701701; www.cityboats.co.uk; daily scheduled river cruises last from quarter of an hour to half day. Bookings not usually necessary.

Dinosaur Adventure Park

This dinosaur park is 10 miles north-west of Norwich near the A1067. Typical Norfolk woodland is a good place to encounter pterodactyls and stegosauruses, and the many other attractions make this equivalent to a major family theme park. Children can cuddle rabbits or handle creepy-crawlies in the fun barn, explore the adventure playground, and count T-rexes lurking in the 100 acre park.

DINOSAUR ADVENTURE PARK, Weston Park, Lenwade, Norfolk NR9 5JW; ☎ 01603 876310; www.dinosauradventure.co.uk; summer/winter: adults £9.95/£6.95, children over 3 £10.95/£7.95; open daily 9.30am–4pm Oct to Mar, 9.30am–5pm mid Mar to Jul, 9.30am–6pm Jul to Sept.

 ## ... and how to avoid children

Any of the hip and alternative arty venues are usually child-free zones. **The Norwich Arts Centre** in St Swithin's Church on St Benedict's Street (☎ 01603 660352; www.norwichartscentre.co.uk) is a venue for installations, performances, indie music and a grown-up bar-café. Similarly the **King of Hearts** centre near Fye Bridge (*see Café listings*) is a miraculously welcoming space where you can savour a carefully chosen exhibition, choose a CD from the shelf to play while you read an art magazine or have a coffee in the courtyard.

The 'Golden Triangle' area of the city is populated by students and well-heeled locals. And there are plenty of smart bars, cosmopolitan caf[eacute]s and trendy shops between the city and University of East Anglia, principally between Earlham Road and Unthank Road.

The **Assembly House** (Theatre Street, NR2 1RQ; ☎ 01603 626402; www.assemblyhousenorwich.co.uk) has a Georgian music room with lunchtime string concerts or evening classical performances in a period setting. The elegant in-house **Ivory's Café Bar and Restaurant** features changing art exhibitions as well as good food. It is a daytime venue though serves pre-theatre suppers until 7pm if you have tickets to see the resident Great Hall Players perform in the adjacent chandeliered ballroom.

Entertainment

With such a large student population and vibrant arts culture, a huge choice of affordable music and performance is guaranteed in Norwich.

Theatre

You can tell how unique the **Norwich Puppet Theatre** is from its generic web address: www.puppettheatre.co.uk. The professional company's home near the river is at St James Church recognisable by its unusual polygonal

tower set atop a square tower. Yet again, visitors will admire how a church space has been re-imagined as a theatre seating 300. Often choosing classic myths and stories to depict, the shows are always inventive, making use of physical theatre, live music, digital projection, shadow puppetry and the theatre of animation. Ticket prices are very reasonable both for performances and for the puppet-making workshops held on selected Saturdays.

The unusual **Maddermarket Theatre** (St John's Alley NR2 1DR; ☎ 01603 620917; www.maddermarket.co.uk) with its excellent amateur company is a great Norwich institution that puts on 12 productions a year. Long before Sam Wannamaker thought of his Globe project, a man glorying in the name of Nugent Monck in the 1920s decided to build a mock-Elizabethan theatre. Besides enjoying the good acoustics made possible by its barrel roof, you might just see the friendly monk (not Monck) who is said to haunt the theatre.

The open-air **Whiffler Theatre** in the castle grounds hosts occasional comedy or theatre-in-the-park events during the summer months; Norwich City Council publishes summer theatre programmes in a leaflet called 'Open Stages'.

Cinema

In the fine tradition that Norwich has established for combining ancient architecture with the best in modern design, the three-screen **Cinema City** (St Andrew's Street, NR2 4AD; ☎ 0871 704 2053; cinemacity@ picture houses.co.uk) opened to great acclaim at the end of 2007. The architects made elegant use of ceiling vaults in the new dining space, arched doorways and 17th-century panelling and installed huge sheets of glass so as not to cloak the building's glories and to create an interior terrace. The medieval hall with timbered roof has been re-invented as the bar. Fittingly, Geoffrey Rush was on hand for the grand opening, since in the film *Elizabeth: The Golden Age*, he plays Sir Francis Walsingham who accompanied the Virgin Queen when she visited Robert Suckling, mayor of Norwich in the 1570s and whose grand merchant's house, Suckling Hall, is now incorporated into the fabric of the cinema. The cinema shows a range of independent films.

Nightlife

Most of Norwich's nightclubs are along none-too-beautiful Prince of Wales Road near the station, plus more are springing up in the nearby Riverside development among the chain stores, a bowling alley and a 14-screen cinema. **Optic** at 50 Prince of Wales Road is smaller and classier than most. **The Mustard Lounge** (2–8 All Saints Green NR1 3NA) is an up-and-coming dance venue popular with musicos rather than hardcore clubbers, playing garage, R'n'B, Hip Hop and Urban. The **Waterfront** on King Street (on the west side of the river across a footbridge), an alternative music venue partly run by the student union at the University of East Anglia, features top DJs and some all-nighters. Close by, the historic and sedate **Music House** features a series of short drop-in acoustic acts every Friday night (www.blackcatmusic.org.uk).

Of the many Norwich pubs that have live music, one of the best is right in the heart of the city. **The Walnut Tree Shades**, down a narrow alley (Old Post Office Court, NR1 3NA), has excellent service, a wonderful Deep South menu including catfish, a superb bar and fun evenings of jazz and blues.

Special events

As has been hinted, Norwich punches well above its artistic weight, which becomes especially apparent during the first two weeks of May when the city hosts an international arts festival. Many dance, comedy and other events take place outside the Forum and are free of charge, and in a range of venues. Programme details can be found at www.nnfestival.org.uk.

The Royal Norfolk Show is the biggest two-day agricultural show in the country and takes place at the Norfolk Showground in late June (www.royal norfolkshow.co.uk). Another highlight of the Norwich calendar is Heritage Open Days in early September when more than 200 properties are opened to the public.

 # Shopping

The photogenic striped awnings of England's biggest **open-air market** are cheerful and inviting year-round. It's open six days a week, with a venerable history in its location, gently sloping down from St Peter Mancroft to Gentleman's Walk. There are nearly 200 stalls selling everything from garden tools to discount greeting cards, handmade leather belts to novelty baseball caps, alongside fruit and fish, organic produce and sweets. Many of the traders have been in the family business for generations and most seem to have adjusted to the recent revamp which opened up the layout to more space and light. The

CELEBRITY CONNECTIONS

The singer-songwriter **Beth Orton** was born on a pig farm in East Dereham and then lived in Norwich until she was 13. She attended the Hewett School on the south side of the city (which is also the school that the Radio 1 DJ Tim Westwood attended).

Before she chose music, she dabbled in theatre and joined a struggling theatre company that toured the seaside villages of Norfolk, free camping in parks and football pitches, which she loved. Although she now calls London her home, she has said in interviews that she is sometimes tempted to live in the country, and that she still has friends in Norfolk.

When an American asked her what Norwich was like, she described it in poetic terms, 'It's an hour's drive to beaches that look like muted over-exposed photographs, and countryside every shade of green you ever saw all at once. And the trees and bushes would have a kind of light for a bit like skunk weed, and the trees seemed to glisten.' She went on to paint more pictures of her Norfolk past, 'Kissing in a wheat field as the sun begins to set on a summer's evening, with the haze of that light. The sky is high there, and there's an arc in some parts. There were lots of characters there. It's surrounded by coast and there were pirates of all sorts running around. Norfolk is not on the way to anywhere, you don't stop off on the way somewhere else – it's an end in itself. You have to want to go there.'

Origins Gift Shop (www.originsgiftshop.co.uk) in the Forum has an unusual selection of gift ideas, toys, etc. Interesting shopping arcades radiate off the market on the other side of Gentleman's Walk where you can find second-hand clothes, records, crafts and books. For mainstream shopping, head for either of the two covered shopping malls, **Chapelfield** and **Castle**, but the heritage department store you should visit is **Jarrolds**, which occupies five grand floors on London Street and also has a decent café.

For funkier, offbeat specialist and charity shops head for Magdalen Street, or the Pottergate area of town where you will find niche shops such as the **Laundry Room** for men's wear, Cigs and Papers for Honduran cigars and many others (www.norwichlanes.co.uk). Good independent music shops staffed by experts include **Soundclash Records** at 28 St Benedict's Street for underground/indie genres (ska, funk, etc.) and Prelude Records at 25b St Giles Street for classical, opera and jazz. Both act as ticket agents for local events.

There are also numerous car boot sales on Sunday morning in the towns and villages of Norfolk, for example Stalham and North Walsham Lazybones (so-called because it doesn't start until noon).

The best... **PLACES TO STAY**

BOUTIQUE

St Giles House

41–45 St Giles Street, Norwich NR2 1JR
☎ **01603 275180/2**
www.stgileshousehotel.com

Behind the grand pillared frontage, the rooms of this relatively new luxury hotel are decorated in differing styles while retaining an art deco unity. The central location is an attraction, as is the helpful service, in-house spa and Dimitri's Restaurant with a Russian menu.

Prices: B&B off-season special rates start at £120 for a double for a minimum stay of two days.

By Appointment

25–29 St George's Street, Norwich NR3 1AB

☎ **01603 630730**
www.byappointmentnorwich.co.uk

Primarily known for its exclusive restaurant with an ambitious and pricey menu, By Appointment also offers five bedrooms distributed over three 15th-century merchants' houses. Character and atmosphere are guaranteed if not downright eccentricity, since the clutter of antique furnishings includes things such as hatboxes and coal fires. Children must be over 12 to stay, but there are no family rooms.

Price: B&B from £120 for a double.

HOTEL

Georgian House Hotel

30–34 Unthank Road NR2 2RB (5-minute walk from Norwich City Hall)
☎ **01603 615655**
www.georgian-hotel.co.uk

A Holstein cowhide-covered three-piece suite is a trifle unexpected in the lobby of a hotel bearing the name 'Georgian House Hotel' but the décor in the rooms is less aggressively styled. Rooms in the new 'executive' wing are spacious, contemporary and colour-harmonised, with some giving straight on to the attractive garden. The RARE Bar and Grill aspires to become a destination restaurant with a well-judged menu skewed towards beef lovers.

Prices: B&B from £110 for a double or family room; £150 with dinner.

The Old Rectory

103 Yarmouth Road, Thorpe St. Andrew, Norwich NR7 0HF (2 miles east of city centre)
☎ **01603 700772/**☎ **0845 365 2614**
www.oldrectorynorwich.com

This grand ivy-coloured Georgian building set in extensive gardens overlooking the River Yare and Whitlingham Country Park is full of character. The service is personal and they have a heated outdoor pool. The proprietors won a Green Tourism Business Scheme Award for 2007.

Prices: from £125–£155 for a double.

Catton Old Hall

Lodge Lane, Old Catton, Norwich NR6 7HG (2½ miles northeast of city)
☎ **01603 419379**
www.catton-hall.co.uk

This former mayor's house dating from the 17th century is near historic parkland. Some rooms have antique beds (one with a four-poster) made up with Egyptian cotton linen. On certain occasions, a family-style dinner is available using produce from the garden. The house has a small honesty bar. Children must be over 10 to stay.

Prices: from £75 for a double.

The best... PLACES TO STAY

FARM

Salamanca Farm

116–118 Norwich Road, Stoke Holy Cross, Norwich NR14 8QJ (5 miles south of Norwich). ☎ 01508 492322

This comfortable farmhouse located near the Tas Valley is pleasant for cycling or riding horses. The mill where Jeremiah Colman first set up mustard production, now a restaurant, is in the village, though the best place to eat is the Wildebeest Arms (www.thewildebeest.co.uk), recent finalist in the Norfolk Restaurant of the Year competition.

Prices: B&B from £20–£35 for a single; from £20–£70 for a double.

VEGETARIAN/ ORGANIC

West Lodge

**24 Fakenham Road, Drayton, Norwich NR8 6PR (4 miles northwest of Norwich, not far from the airport)
☎ 01603 861191
www.vegetarian-bedandbreakfast-norwich.co.uk**

This late Victorian village property with a well-tended garden takes pride in using organic, fair-trade food in its meat-free breakfasts. Proprietors dote on their Birman cats.

Prices: £75 or £95 for a double.

B & B

Wedgewood House

**42 St Stephen's Road, Norwich NR1 3RE
☎ 01603 625730
www.wedgewoodhouse.co.uk**

Edwardian Wedgwood House has 12 comfortable rooms and a good range of local produce on the breakfast menu. A short walk from the centre, Wedgwood House is located on the major approach road (A11).

Prices: B&B from £65 for a double; seasonal offers available.

Gothic House

**King's Head Yard, Magdalen Street, Norwich NR3 1JE
☎ 01603 631879
www.gothic-house-norwich.com**

This Regency townhouse on one of Norwich's oldest streets on the north side of the river has only two rooms, a double and a twin, both recently refurbished. The location in a leafy gated courtyard off the busy street is a plus. Children must be over 10 to stay.

Prices: £95 for a double; single occupancy is £65.

Beeches Lodge

**80 Unthank Road, Norwich NR2 2RW
☎ 01603 621105
www.mjbhotels.com/beecheslodge**

The clean and friendly Beeches Lodge has a sister guesthouse on Earlham Road next to the Plantation Gardens. Good value family rooms have two sets of bunkbeds.

Prices: from £70 for a family room; breakfast costs an extra £7.50 per person.

GUEST HOUSE

Wensum Guest House

**225 Dereham Road, Norwich NR2 3TF
☎ 01603 621069
www.wensumguesthouse.co.uk**

This attractive Victorian rectory with 18 rooms is within walking distance of the city centre and is also frequently served by buses along the Dereham Road. Four en suite rooms are suitable for families.

Prices: B&B from £60 for a double; four-bedded family room for £100. Prices include breakfast.

The best... FOOD AND DRINK

Staying in

Norwich Market has a full range of food stalls. **G Taylor and Son** has recently been voted Greengrocer of the Year 2008 so for a friendly chat with someone who knows exactly where all his produce comes from, seek out Mel Taylor. Norwich has three farmers' markets, covering three out of four weeks of the month, and purveying the wares of some outstanding Norfolk producers of baked goods, cheese, meat and other produce. The Forum in the centre of town hosts a market on the first and third Sunday of the month; the others are held at the Norfolk Showground (in the direction of the university) on the second Saturday (9am–1pm) and the **Golden Triangle Farmers' Market** is on the second Sunday of the month (10am–3pm). The latter was only set up in early 2007 and still won the Norfolk Food Award the same year. It is an offshoot of the nationally renowned ethical shop, **The Green Grocers** (Earlham House Shopping Centre, Earlham Road, NR2 3PD; 01603 250000; www.thegreen grocers.co.uk), where almost everything is organic and fairly traded. Despite the name, it carries a complete supermarket range of items, including organic meat from Courtyard Farms (see the box in the chapter above Hunstanton to Holkham) and pizzas and curries.

Harvey's Butchers & Game Dealers (63 Grove Road, NR1 3RL; 01603 621908; www.puremeat.org.uk) sells some of the best organic meat money can buy. The Christmas turkeys are legendary. And **Archers of Norwich** (179 Plumstead Road, NR1 4AB 01603 434253); is an established family butcher that regularly wins prizes for its sausages and also sells an inviting range of marinated BBQ meats. The delicatessen takeaway serves hot carved meats in baguettes.

Like hand and glove, sausages need mustard, and Norwich is the English capital of that condiment. Although now owned by the multinational Unilever, the Colman brand survives and has been associated with Norwich ever since Jeremiah Colman went into production nearly 200 years ago. You can buy from the Colman's range or just learn of the company's honourable history from the small museum at **Colman's Mustard Shop** in the art nouveau Royal Arcade behind Gentleman's Walk.

THE MUSTARD SHOP, 15 Royal Arcade, NR2 1NQ; 01603 627889; www.colmansmustard shop.com; free.

Several beers are brewed in Norwich, primarily in brewpubs (see *Drinking*). A regular stallholder at the monthly farmers' market at the Norwich Showground

EATING OUT

FINE DINING

Elm Hill Brasserie
2 Elm Hill, NR3 1HN
☎ **01603 624847**
www.elmhillbrasserie.co.uk

You might have expected a restaurant at this address to depend for custom on its postcard-perfect location, but the unpretentious French-influenced food is reliably first-class. A two-course evening menu consisting of for example duck leg confit and spicy pumpkin and haddock stew costs £15.95.

St Benedict's Restaurant
9 St Benedict's Street NR2 4PE
☎ **01603 765377**
http://stbenedictsrestaurant.co.uk

Along quirky St Benedict's Street, this cheerfully decorated bistro serves immaculately prepared dishes yet retains a relaxed atmosphere. Two of its signature dishes are slow-cooked crispy duck with braised chicory and double baked cheese soufflé. A complete dinner should cost less than £25.

The Dining Rooms
Cinema City, St Andrew's Street NR2 4AD, ☎ 07504 356378

Not often would a cinema restaurant and bar be recommended for fine dining. But in the case of the stylish yet historic Cinema City just opened, the restaurant is overseen by Prince Charles's former chef who is committed to making use of the full range of local ingredients. Classic Norfolk dishes such as Gressingham duck and Cromer crab are impeccably prepared.

Delia's Restaurant & Bar
Norwich City Football Club, Carrow Road NR1 1JE, ☎ 01603 218704
www.deliascanarycatering.co.uk

Modern British cuisine is served by the doyenne of television cookery. A set price of £32 applies across the menu to three courses plus coffee. Sample dishes are Fenland celery soup, braised steak with five kinds of mushroom and steamed Panettone pudding with hot punch sauce. The restaurant is open only Friday and Saturday evenings, so advance booking is essential.

Inside Delia's Restaurant and Bar

FizzBuzz Brasserie
8–10 St. Andrews Hill NR2 1AD
☎ **01603 767321**

FizzBuzz opts for modern cooking with an emphasis on the wine list and friendly service. You might be able to order lobster ravioli or avocado and crab tian as a starter, an interesting risotto for the main course and rum pannacotta with mango for pudding. Two courses will cost around £25.

RESTAURANT

Shiki Japanese Restaurant
6 Tombland NR3 1HE, ☎ 01603 619262
www.shikirestaurant.co.uk

Excellent service coupled with authentic Japanese cooking makes this a good choice. Even the weird-sounding dishes such as eel sushi (*unagi zushi*) are delicious. A summer visit gives you the choice of sitting at an outdoor table under the genial trees of Tombland. The sushi and sashimi here are outstandingly fresh. Two courses will cost about £25, and three courses £30.

The Last Wine Bar & Restaurant
76 St George's Street NR3 1AB
☎ **01603 626626**
www.lastwinebar.co.uk

The excellent value bar menu includes starters such as home-made soup or humous for £5.25 and good choice of main courses such as chicken in a tarragon sauce for less than £8.90. The double-height ceiling to floor windows on the bar side make for good daytime people-watching, and the Middle Eastern-style interior is no doubt influenced by the Lebanese chef.

EATING OUT

GASTROPUB
Up at the Mad Moose Arms
Warwick Street NR2 3LD
☎ **01603 627687**
www.themadmoose.co.uk

This restaurant is upstairs from a student pub buried in a quiet residential street off Unthank Road. Included in the *Michelin Eating out in Pubs* guide (the only Norwich pub to be included) the upstairs is less raucous pub than elegant ornate restaurant where you can order dishes such as grilled green figs with pomegranate and Parma ham, roast Norfolk pheasant or warm smoked duck. The *menu du jour* is good value at £22.50 for three courses.

Unthank Arms
149 Newmarket Street NR2 2DR
☎ **01603 631557**
www.theunthankarms.com

This pub in the Golden Triangle is especially popular on a sunny Sunday when beautiful people gather in its garden to eat crispy Stilton and walnut parcels or mussels in a cider and Saffron sauce.

CAFÉ
Briton's Arms
9 Elm Hill NR3 1HN
located at the bottom of Elm Hill,
☎ **01603 623367**

At this charming coffee house, you can climb the narrow stairway to a little over-grown garden to have a perfect piece of carrot cake and cappuccino, or stay indoors in front of an open fire with a traditional Norfolk pork pie.The building is bursting with atmosphere. This was spotted by the makers of the fantasy film *Stardust* who converted it into the Slaughtered Prince inn for a scene in the 2007 film.

The King of Hearts
7–15 Fye Bridge Street NR3 1LJ
corner of Fishergate Magdalen Street,
☎ **01603 620805**
www.kingofhearts.org.uk.

This hospitable daytime retreat located just across Fye Bridge is housed in two beautifully renovated Tudor houses, alongside a small free art gallery and shop selling only handmade East Anglian crafts. Hot dishes and baguettes change daily and a good range of cakes is served to accompany tea and coffee (open till 5pm).

Café Bar Marzano
The Forum, Millennium Plain, Norwich, Norfolk NR2 1TF
☎ **01603 665504**
www.theforumnorwich.co.uk/explore-the-forum/caf%C3%A9-bar-marzano

This is an excellent meeting place with a heated outdoor terrace overlooking the market. Marzano's welcomes children, participates in any event going at the Forum and has live music, jazz on Tuesdays and Thursdays, acoustic or DJ sets on Fridays.

Caley's Cocoa Café
The Guildhall, Gaol Hill NR2 1JP
☎ **01603 629364**
www.caleys.com/about-cocoacafe

Celebrating a product that was manufactured in Norwich for more than a century, this café is located in the 15th-century Norwich Guildhall on Market Square.

VEGETARIAN
Pulse Café Bar
The Old Fire Station Stables, Labour in Vain Yard, Guildhall Hill NR2 1JD
☎ **01603 765562**
http://pulsecafebar.co.uk

In an airy light-filled attic space with exposed brick above Rainbow Wholefoods, the Pulse Café serves organic beverages and snacks during the day, and an inventive vegetarian menu in the evenings. Meals cost £10–£14.

The Greenhouse
42–46 Bethel Street NR2 1NR
☎ **01603 631007**
www.greenhousetrust.co.uk

This vegetarian café is located in Norwich's environmental centre behind the Forum, where solar panels have been installed. You can grab a coffee and chocolate brownie for about £3 to eat in the courtyard garden before browsing for organic and Fairtrade items.

is **Buffy's Brewery** where bottle-conditioned beer made from East Anglian malted barley is sold.

For wines, **Peter Graham Wines** has vast holdings of carefully chosen wines from around the world. But you will have to drive out to the Norwich bypass to visit their new purpose-built premises (Martineau Lane, NR1 2EN; ☎ 01603 598910; www.petergrahamwines.com).

Drinking

Pubs

Mastering the nuanced differences between Norwich's hundreds of pubs would be the work of a lifetime. All tastes are catered for from raucous to cosy, stylish to unreconstructed boozer. Real ale aficionados may wish to venture out of the city centre to **The Fat Cat** (49 West End Street, NR2 4NA; ☎ 01603 624364; www.fatcatpub.co.uk) which simulates a beer festival every day. The pub brews several tipples on-site including Fat Cat bitter which retails for an unheard-of £1.90 a pint.

CELEBRITY CONNECTIONS

Delia Smith is almost as famous for being director, majority shareholder and diehard fan of Norwich City Football Club (NCFC) as she is for being a TV chef and cookery writer. As one of the richest women in the country and a season-ticket holder, she was invited to buy into NCFC when it was in the financial doldrums. She blotted her copybook with some but not all fans when she made a drunken half-time outburst in a game against Manchester City in front of the TV cameras at Carrow Road in 2005. Delia shouted 'A message for the best football supporters in the world: we need a 12th man here. Where are you? Where are you? Let's be 'aving you!' over the public address system after the Canaries had thrown away a two-goal lead before half-time. Some feel that she should stick to the cooking. Her restaurants at the football ground are highly regarded (see description of Delia's Restaurant and Bar and Yellows below).

Although she has been involved with Sainsbury's for years, she has also recently given her endorsement to the 'Shop Local' campaign promoted by the *East Anglian Daily Times*. In an interview with the paper in 2008, Delia advocated shopping at farm shops and delis, and even mentioned her favourites within range of her home near Stowmarket, Suffolk. She buys produce from the Alder Carr Farm Shop near Needham Market and smoked foods from Pinney's in Orford.

Local legends: Norwich ghosts

A phantom monk, murdered maiden, beheaded sheriff and many other ghosts inhabit Norwich. You have to exercise a lot of imagination to believe that 19 Magdalen Street is haunted. Apart from the punning name, the shopfront of Presence looks like a cheery gift shop, which is what it is. But in the 19th century it was an occasional house of ill-repute where a young girl called Sarah was murdered by one of her clients before he absconded. A mournful face is sometimes seen at an upstairs window and a whiff of lavender detected, which was used to perfume the rooms in the 1850s.

Cobbled Bedford Street in the Norwich Lanes is reputed to be haunted by quite a different kind of ghost. The Wild Man pub at 29 Bedford Street is named for a young lad (some say a gypsy, others a German) who was incarcerated here when it was a prison (or was it an asylum?). His friends decided to attempt a daring night-time rescue. When they couldn't batter the door down, they decided to burn it. But the fire took hold, and despite the desperate clawings at door and window,

Another microbrewery can be found at **The Coach and Horses** (82 Thorpe Road NR1 1BA; ☎ 01603 477077; www.thecoachthorperoad.co.uk) behind the station, which serves five ales from the Chalk Hill brewery next door, from the quaffable Brewery Tap to the potent Old Tackle. It also serves brilliant well-priced pub grub like the 'Beastless Burger', rated among the best veggie burgers ever, and great chunky partially skinned chips.

The Belgian Monk (7 Pottergate NR2 1DS; ☎ 01603 767222; www.thebelgianmonk.com)in the city centre offers an impressive range of Belgian beers – best drunk by the half – to accompany boar's sausage and mash for £9.95 for example, or many variations on the theme of mussels.

Walk past Tombland with its chain pubs like Yates towards the river and you come to one gem, **The Ribs of Beef** (24 Wensum Street NR3 1HY; (☎ 01603 619517), where you can join the throng at the bar to order ales or local ciders.

Most visitors stop at the ancient **Adam & Eve** (17 Bishopgate, NR3 1RZ (☎ 01603 667423) for a drink at some point to enjoy the marvellous Dutch-gabled building, even if it is on the tourist trail and overpriced. Apparently it is haunted by the Sheriff who was brought here after being wounded in battle by Robert Kett's men but expired on a pub table. Not far away is the more down-to-earth **Red Lion** (79 Bishopgate, NR1 4AA (☎ 01603 620154) with a garden right on the river, which is especially popular for its generous and affordable Sunday roast lunches.

the imprisoned inmate burned to death. The landlord of the pub reports that strange noises can sometimes be heard at night.

When the Great Plague visited Norwich in the 1570s, entire households were wiped out. The policy was not to bury the dead, but to shut the infectious corpses away inside their houses, which is what happened to Augustine Steward House, now an antique shop in Tombland. When the rates of infection subsided, the house was opened and the bodies removed. At first no one paid much attention to the bite marks on the bodies, assuming they were the work of the ubiquitous rats, but the tooth marks were much too big. A young girl dressed in grey was found to have human flesh in her throat. She had been immured when alive and in her extremity had resorted to cannibalism. The Lady in Grey is said to haunt the house and sometimes the street. A DJ investigating a possible intruder when the Sampson and Hercules building was Ritzy's nightclub claims to have come across a young woman in grey rags, seemingly floating along a corridor.

Bars

A cluster of chic bars and cafés as well as traditional pubs can be found in the Golden Triangle around Earlham Road and Unthank Road. The new **Mirror Bar** in the Georgian House Hotel (see *Accommodation*) is aiming at an air of hip urbanity but is stronger on upmarket lagers and wine than cocktails. In good weather, its French doors open onto the hotel's peaceful garden.

Theatre bars aren't usually worth seeking out except at intermission time, but the **Playhouse** (42–58 St George's Street NR3 1AB; ☎ 01603 598598; www.norwichplayhouse.co.uk) over the water has an intimate yet modern ambience. It is at its best in good weather when you can spill out onto the riverside terrace.

A late-night bar that might tempt you is **Indulge** (1 Queen Street NR2 4SG; ☎ 01603 666868; www.lovetoindulge.com) off Tombland, known for its good service, as well as for its tapas menu.

FURTHER AFIELD

Many picturesque villages with superb pubs, historic churches, nature reserves and other places of interest are located within a radius of 20 miles of Norwich, some of which are included in other Norfolk sections, especially the chapter on the Norfolk Broads.

Gressenhall Museum of Norfolk Life

This museum is 20 miles from central Norwich and less than a mile east of the village of Gressenhall. The central building is a restored 18th-century workhouse or 'house of industry' for destitute peasants. The extensive grounds contain the reconstructed workshops of a wheelwright and a blacksmith, a school, chapel and typical tied cottage, with plenty of authentic farm tools and machinery about. The stories of particular residents told through recordings, videos and information boards help you to picture the harsh conditions endured by the rural poor.

GRESSENHALL MUSEUM, Gressenhall, Dereham, Norfolk, NR20 4DR; ☎ 01362 860563; 24-hour info ☎ 01362 869263; adults £7.20, children £5.10; open daily Mar to Oct 10am–5pm.

Riverside walks, a working farm with rare breeds and an adventure playground in the surrounding 50 acres means that it is easy to make it a whole day's visit. Apple Day on the first Sunday of October half-term is the biggest apple day event in the Eastern region.

 Visitor information

Tourist Information Centres: Norwich Tourist Information Centre, The Forum, Millennium Plain, ☎ 01603 727927, tourism@norwich.gov.uk/www.norwich.gov.uk, open daily Apr to Oct, closes 6pm (Sun 4.30pm), Nov to Mar open Mon to Sat.

Hospitals: 24-hour facilities at Norfolk & Norwich University Hospital A&E Department, Level 2, East Block, Colney Lane NR4 7UY, ☎ 01603 287325, www.nnuh.nhs.uk, near the University of East Anglia, off the A47.

Websites: www.visitnorfolk.co.uk/norfolk/norfolk-norwich.aspx (Norfolk Tourism); Pocket Norwich – Norwich was the first UK city to launch an electronic guidebook in November 2007 which can be viewed and listened to on mobile phones (see www.pocket norwich.co.uk).

Supermarkets: Sainsbury's, Long-water Lane, William Frost Way, New Costessey NR5 0JS, (☎ 01603 741655); Sainsbury's Pound Lane, Thorpe St Andrew NR7 0SR, ☎ 01603 300023; Tesco, Harford Bridge, Ipswich Road NR4 6DZ, ☎ 0845 6779507; Waitrose Eaton Centre, Church Lane, Eaton, Norwich NR4 6NU, ☎ 01603 458114.

Taxis: Courtesy Taxis, ☎ 01603 633336; Canary Taxis, ☎ 01603 414243; Arrival Cars, ☎ 01603 408484 (more up-market).

NORFOLK BROADS

The Broads of Norfolk are unique and peculiar to one single region that covers about 300 square miles. Belatedly awarded National Park status in 1989, the Norfolk Broads are now recognised as a rare and precious wetland habitat, England's very own Everglades. Most remarkable about this vast area of flat expanses of water is that it's all the doing of Man. For about three centuries in the Middle Ages, our ancestors dug peat by hand for fuel, not knowing that the water from all the rivers that meander over this region would soon seep in to fill up the holes, forming great shallow lakes or 'broads'.

Soon you will see why villages such as Stokesby with Herringby have chosen as their tagline 'A little piece of heaven on the Broads'. A low-tech week on the Broads will tick most of the boxes for a green holiday, but without a hint of self-denial since the area is full of lovely waterside pubs and places to stay. On a spot on the River Bure you will need to give the ferryman a ring. He should show up within a few minutes, as happens in season at Horning Ferry if you have walked from Woodbastwick.

A cliché about the Broads is that they are unbearably crowded in summer, and that the waterways become clogged like the M25. This might be true of a handful of key places (namely the self-proclaimed capital of the Broads, Wroxham) but it's easy to leave the crowds behind, especially in the more languid northern Broads (between Ranworth and Stalham). This is always going to be a populated landscape rather than a wilderness, where physical geography and human history have got muddled up together, a key part of the charm.

WHAT TO SEE AND DO

 Fair weather

The activity which attracts most people is of course boating from a kayak to the luxury of a Riviera-style motor cruiser. For centuries, buildings have been built to face the water and not the roads, so the views are always better from the rivers and broads. If you aren't inclined to DIY boating, plenty of short boat trips are on offer. Anyone can enjoy half a day in a canoe or a rowboat.

Boat trips
The trips described in this section illustrate the variety available. Some may sound touristy but crass commercialism is rare, and visitors don't usually come away feeling exploited. The Mississippi paddle steamer, **Southern Comfort**,

makes trips from Horning along the River Bure to Ranworth Broad that last an hour and a half to two hours in the day or evening. The prices in the boat's bar are no higher than a pub.

Because of the undeniable pollution, efforts have been made to invent and promote electric boats. The Broads Authority has taken a lead by offering trips on these green vehicles with an emphasis on spotting wildlife, one from How Hill Nature Reserve near Ludham across marshes and through dykes, the other from Ranworth Staithe (staithe just means landing bank or quay):

Electric Eel Wildlife Water Trail, Toad Hole Cottage Museum, How Hill, near Ludham, ☎ 01692 678763; adults £5.50, children £4.50, family £14.50; 50-minute trip for six people; daily in summer, weekends in spring and autumn.

Helen of Ranworth ☎ 01603 270453; adults £4.50, children £3.50, hour-long guided tour of Malthouse Broad in an open boat seating eight; departures from Ranworth Staithe; ferry operates for £1 per person between Ranworth Staithe and the floating Broads Wildlife Centre.

Ra – a solar-powered boat trip on Barton Broad, departs from Gayes Staithe between Neatishead and Irstead; price: adults £5.50, children £4.50; four times a day Apr to Oct.

Traditional sailing boats are also available to non-sailors. From an old traditional boat yard in Ludham, Hunter's Yard, two-hour skippered sailing trips on the Broads are offered on one of the fleet of 1930s wooden yachts.

The Norfolk Wildlife Trust runs a two-hour Water Trail by electric boat that penetrates the quiet backwaters of lovely Hickling Broad. The destination is the 60ft Tree Tower, which can be climbed for a magnificent view over Broadland.

Hickling Broad

DIY boating

With 125 miles of navigable waterways, exploring on your own holds great appeal. The six main rivers, the Bure, Thurne and Ant in the northern Broads, and the Yare, Chet and Waveney in the south form a beautiful patchwork of serene waters, marshes and woods. Because the Broads are so flat, there are no locks. Day hire is probably better for the uninitiated, although some people go straight for a week-long hire.

The boat-hire industry in the Broads, like British resort tourism generally, has been in mild decline for a decade, and some of the hire fleets have been allowed to run down. But 2008 has seen an upturn and if you go on the waters you will see a high proportion of cruisers bearing the livery of the two main hiring agencies, **Blakes** ('B' on a flag) and **Hoseasons** (bluebird on the bow).

The range of choices in boat rivals the choice of holiday cottage, and you will need to do quite a bit of research comparing vessels, prices and routes. The website of the Norfolk Broads Authority has links to boat hire companies (www.broads-authority.gov.uk/visiting/boat-hire.html) or you can try EasyrouteHolidays.com, an online booking service for Norfolk Broads boating holidays.

Standards differ, so do try to obtain feedback on the boat yard before choosing. The Norfolk Broads Forum at www.the-norfolk-broads.co.uk is worth investigating.

Your average Broads cruiser has all the mod cons from microwaves to DVD players. Quarters will be a little cramped but basically this will be far more comfortable than camping – and a lot more expensive. To give just a sample of costs (from Martham Boats): a three-berth motor cruiser hired for a week in June might cost £350, seven berths for £725. Bigger boats in the school holidays will cost over £1,000. If you are a novice, the yard staff should take you out for a 15-minute demonstration. But if you feel confident enough you will be let loose straightaway. In general the smaller yards are in a better position to offer a more personal service. One small yard is **Whispering Reeds** on Hickling Broad which hires out six cruisers, a picnic boat and four houseboats, for an hour or a day in the off-season but for a minimum of a week between Easter and October.

HICKLING BROAD VISITOR CENTRE, Stubb Road, Hickling, NR12 0BW; ☎ 01692 598276; www.norfolkwildlifetrust.org.uk/big%205/hickling.htm; nature reserve – adults £4, children free; 2 hour water trail boat trip tickets £10 for adults, £6 for children, May to Sept three times a day.

BLAKES HOLIDAY BOATING, Lancashire; ☎ 0870 336 7788; www.blakes.co.uk; sailing boats and cruisers. Hoseasons Boating Holidays, Lowestoft, NR32 2LW; ☎ 0870 543 4434; www.hoseasons.co.uk; cruisers only.

WHISPERING REEDS, Staithe Road, Hickling, NR12 0YW; ☎ 01692 598314; www.whisperingreeds.net; half-day hire of the picnic boat *Bittern* costs £56–£79 depending on number of people/time of year.

Sailing on the Norfolk Broads

Sailors will turn their noses up at these luxury craft, preferring the silence of sail power on classic 5- mile stretches such as the one near Thurne where the River Thurne joins the Bure heading towards Acle. As a guide, traditional sailing boats might cost £330 for a week for two berths and £500 for four berths. If you can read the tide table, you can be helped on your journey by the turn of the tide. One hiring yard to try is **Easton Whelpton Ltd** based at Upton Yacht Station (Upton, Near Acle NR13 6BN; ☎ 01493 750430; www.eastwood-whelpton.co.uk) which has recently amalgamated with another long-established yacht hirer, Camelot Craft, formerly based in Hoveton.

Although boats on the Broads don't pick up much speed, manoeuvring them takes practice and skill. Sailing can be quite hairy. In the peak season there are around 100 boats for every kilometre of waterway. Potential embarrassments include getting stuck under the very low arches of Potter Heigham Bridge or reversing into a sailing boat while trying to avoid another one. In the most shallow broads like Martham, you must navigate along narrow marked channels to avoid a grounding. Most hire yards will lend or sell you a detailed map and guide. Although not up to date, **Pete's Cruising Guide to the Broads** is a useful online resource (www.broadsnet.co.uk).

You could always stick to a canoe though. Bank's Dayboats at Wayford Bridge on the River Ant near Stalham hires out canoes and can suggest a day trip to Barton Broad and Neatishead.

Exploring on foot

The long-distance **Weavers' Way** skirts the eastern edge of the Broads. The 13-mile stretch between Stalham and Thurne passes through Hickling Broad National Nature Reserve and gives panoramic views over broads and grazing marshes. A

River Thurne

brand new long-distance footpath has been carved through the southern Broads: the **Wherryman's Way** (www.wherrymansway.net) covers 35 miles between the railway stations in Norwich and Great Yarmouth, mainly following the River Yare and passing through open marshes, reedbeds, grazing marshes and riverside villages. The creators have kept families in mind, so that walking can be combined with pushchair, bicycle or public transport on water or rail. Life-size models, information panels and audio posts bring alive the history of the area along the way. Wherries are the sailing barges peculiar to Norfolk for negotiating the shallow Broads. They were cargo-carrying workhorses supplying coal, timber, grain and liquor to Norwich, Great Yarmouth and all the villages in between. The railways rendered them obsolete, and today only seven restored wherries remain in sailable condition.

> **BANK BOATS,** Staithe Cottage, Wayford Bridge, Stalham, NR12 9LN; ☎ 01692 582457; £50 per half day for all-weather day boats; £35 per day for two to three seater canoes.

Of the hundreds of lovely short walks that could be recommended, consider doing the one from **Coltishall Common to Belaugh.** The agreeable village of Belaugh is unusual for Norfolk because it is built on a hill. The church in this unspoiled village with its fine painted rood screen is apparently the building that first captured the attention of John Betjeman when he was only eight years old, and feeling cooped up on a boating holiday with his parents.

The crumbling ecclesiastical building left over from the Anglo-Saxons, **St Benet's Abbey**, stranded in the Ranworth Marshes and up against the ruin of an 18th-century brick windmill is a memorable landmark on the River Bure. Parking is possible in South Walsham at the southern end of Fleet Dike from which it is about a mile and a half to the river. Approaching from the north, a long farm track leads down to the ruin.

> **FAIRHAVEN GARDEN TRUST,** School Road, South Walsham, NR13 6DZ; ☎ 01603 270449; www.fairhavengarden.co.uk; adults £5.50, children £3; open daily all year 10am–5pm; evening openings on Wed/Thurs in summer; cruise on South Walsham Broad for 20 minutes, £3.50 for adults, £2.50 for children.

Gardens and bird reserves

At the heart of the Norfolk Broads, **Fairhaven Woodland and Water Garden** encompasses a private broad surrounded by acres of ancient woodland with a birdwatching hide and water gardens accessed by 15 bridges.

Strumpshaw Fen is an RSPB bird reserve near the River Yare which encompasses diverse habitats. Rarely seen birds like marsh harriers, bitterns and kingfishers frequent this reserve, but almost anyone visiting in the warm seasons will spot plenty of dragonflies and butterflies.

> **STRUMPSHAW FEN,** Low Road, Strumpshaw, NR13 4HS; ☎ 01603 715191; www.rspb.org.uk/reserves/guide/s/strumpshawfen/index.asp; adults £2.50, children 50p, family £5; open all year, dawn to dusk.

Wet weather

MUSEUM OF THE BROADS,
The Staithe, Stalham, NR12 9BZ;
☎ 01692 581681;
www.northnorfolk.org/museum
ofthebroads; adults £4, children
£1, family £10; open daily Easter
to Oct 10am– 4pm.

**RAF AIR DEFENCE RADAR
MUSEUM**, Royal Air Force
Neatishead, Near Horning, NR12
8YB; ☎ 01692 631485;
www.radarmuseum.co.uk; adults
£5, teenagers £3.50, children £1.50,
under 7s free; open Apr to Oct, Tues/
Thurs and on the second Sat of the
month year round.

The **Museum of the Broads** evokes the way people survived in the Broads in past times through displays of tools for thatching, sail and rope making, eel catching, reed cutting, boat building and mill wrighting. Fifty-minute boat trips on a steam launch take place on Barton Broad on Tuesdays and Wednesdays (add £3.50 for adults and £2.50 for children to the entry price in the box).

The **Air Defence Radar Museum** near Horning has radar equipment that is still operational and visitors may visit the re-created operations room as it would have been during the Battle of Britain. The museum's hands-on approach and lively tours won it an award last year for 'best small visitor attraction'.

The Bure Valley Railway, one of Norfolk's narrow-gauge railways follows the Bure River Valley and, at 9 miles, is the longest route in the county to feature steam services in summer. The starting points are Aylsham and Wroxham with several stops between. You could take the train in one direction and walk or cycle back, since a footpath extends the whole distance parallel to the railway.

A fascinating church is **St Helen** at Ranworth which is so famous that it has a visitor centre and coffee shop. The medieval rood screen is decorated with sophisticated paintings of saints and martyrs on 26 panels, including both St George

BURE VALLEY RAILWAY,
Aylsham Station, Norwich Road,
Aylsham, NR11 6BW; ☎ 01263
733858; www.bvrw.co.uk; one way –
adults £8, children £5; return
£12/£6.50.

and St Michael grinding the dragon and the devil under their heels. If the weather clears while you have been busy admiring these paintings and the illuminated manuscript with the music for the liturgy, you may be tempted to climb the 89 steps of the church tower for the fabulous view to the staithe below and over the broad.

 ## What to do with children...

Get out on the water and let them steer. Take lots of stale bread for the ducks, and spot herons. Sometimes the cheeky water birds join you, especially if you're eating something they fancy. The tourist industry is completely geared to families, so activities for children abound.

BeWILDerwood

BeWILDerwood is a whimsical 50-acre family attraction near Norwich (located on the A1062 between Wroxham and Horning, and poorly signposted), which opened in 2007. Aimed squarely at children aged six to eleven – though family members of all ages will enjoy themselves – this fantasy land of natural features is charmingly un-'Disneyfied'. Access is via BeWILDerboat (actually pensioned-off Broadland ferries). Aerial walkways, rope tunnels and 'broken' bridges connect painted treehouses. The middle of the 'Muddle Maze' is endlessly elusive but there is no doubt which way to go on the Slippery Slope, a three-abreast slide, installed alongside a near-vertical-drop 70ft slide. A popular feature is the two pairs of zip-wires on which impromptu races sometimes take place. This forest domain is peopled with swamp-dwelling Boggles and tree-loving Twiggles, who emerged from the fertile imagination of the site's owner, Tom Blofeld, who grew up here. Reverence for the environment is also obvious from the restaurant menu which consists of organic burgers and healthy options.

> **BEWILDERWOOD**, Horning Road, Hoveton, NR12 8JW; ☎ 01603 783900; www.bewilderwood.co.uk; 105–250cm £11.50, 92–105cm £8.50, under 92cm free; open daily Apr to Oct (closed on some Tue and Wed – check before visiting).

Activities

The Norfolk Schools Sailing Association (NSSA) based at Filby Broad runs a programme of subsidised short sailing courses for young people. They also run 'Come and Try It' days in May and July for newcomers to dinghy sailing which tend to get booked up in advance. The training courses take place on Optimists and Toppers. Contact info@nssa.co.uk for dates and information. NSSA membership costs £30 per year. Other sailing schools also put on courses, such as the Norfolk Broads School of Sailing, with its operation base at Upton Yacht Station (www.norfolksailingschool.co.uk). Try Sailing (☎ 01603 782897; www.trysailing.com) also offers taster half-days on

Twiggles' treehouses, BeWILDerwood

Barton Broad for £49 or £22 if several people book.

The largest collection of novelty candles can be found at the **Candlemaker Workshop** at Stokesby overlooking the River Bure. During school holidays, they organise candle-dipping activities for children over five, and candles can be coloured and decorated.

... and how to avoid children

Woodforde's Brewery in the heart of the Broads at Woodbastwick has established itself over the past quarter of a century as Norfolk's pre-eminent brewery, and its excellent Wherry bitter, citrusy Sundew, glugable Nelson's Revenge and powerful Norfolk Nog (with 'hints of chocolate, treacle and liquorice') should not be missed. Tours take place at 7pm on Tuesdays and Thursdays and last 90 minutes. This includes sampling the products at the end of the tour.

Entertainment

Special events

Long ago, regattas were referred to as 'water frolics'. Many water-based races and carnivals take place today. The most famous race is the punishing **Three Rivers Race** in early June which sees hardened sailors limping back to base in the wee small hours after covering 45 miles along the rivers Ant, Bure and Thurne. It's organised by the Horning Sailing Club (www.horningsc.co.uk). Gentler sailing regattas take place on Barton Broad on the August bank holiday weekend. A new Green Boat Show on Salhouse Broad aims to promote non-polluting electric boats and eco-boats that are being developed to run on biofuels.

The **Festival of the Broads** is a week-long celebration at various venues throughout the national park of what makes the Broads unique. Treasure hunts, adventure cycle rides, and cider tastings are standard. If you might be visiting in the third week of September, check out www.discoverthebroads.com.

One annual event takes place on the first Sunday of August when the Bishop of Norwich arrives by wherry to take a service at the ruins of St Benet's Abbey.

The best... **PLACES TO STAY**

BOUTIQUE

Broad House Country Estate Hotel

The Avenue, Wroxham NR12 8TS. ☎ 01603 783567
www.broadhousehotel.co.uk

The energetic owners of this Queen Anne mansion opened it as an exclusive hotel in October 2007. The 24 acres of grounds adjoin Wroxham Broad and the hotel has its own jetty. Plans for the future include installing a swimming pool in a disused greenhouse, solar panels and a flock of free-range chickens.

Price:s B&B from £106 for an attic double; £156–£190 for double suites.

INN

King's Head

26 Wroxham Road, Coltishall NR12 7EA ☎ 01603 737426
www.norfolkbroads.com

The owner of this inn is also the chef, and great store is set by the reasonably priced menus that usually include the Norfolk catch of the day. The lovely setting is on the banks of the River Bure, and fishing boats can be hired from the inn. The pub is a free-house serving a good range of beers.

Prices: B&B from £35 per person in a double, £58 for a single.

B & B

Broadland B&B

West End Lodge, Norwich Road, Ludham NR29 5PB, ☎ 01692 678420
www.bedbreakfast-norfolkbroads.co.uk

This friendly B&B with period features is situated between the old-fashioned riverside village of Ludham and tranquil How Hill with its restored drainage mill and marshman's cottage. An authentic 1930s sailing experience is available locally from Hunter's Yard (www.huntersyard.co.uk).

Prices: from £30 to £33 per person in a double; £48.50 in a single.

CAMPSITE

Clippesby Hall

Clippesby, Near Great Yarmouth NR29 3BL. ☎ 01493 367800
www.clippesby.com

This spacious leafy site with 100 pitches and jolly facilities such as an outdoor swimming pool and on-site pub occupies part of the family grounds of the owner who is active in the Broads Tourism Forum. Potter Heigham, 4 miles away, gives access to the water, and the Weavers' Way long distance footpath passes close by.

Prices: from £10 for a tent pitch mid-season to £23 in high season; lodges and cottages are available on the site year round.

SELF-CATERING

Barn Owl Holidays

Bryons Green, Big Back Lane, Chedgrave NR14 6BH, ☎ 01508 528786
www.barnowlholidays.co.uk

This easy-going conversion of an 18th-century barn has resulted in three oak-beamed cottages with courtyard gardens, all of which sleep six. The country house setting of these cottages is within walking distance of the valley of the River Chet in the southern Broads.

Prices: from £240 to £680 for a week; short breaks of three nights cost £220 Oct to Mar or as a last-minute booking.

UNUSUAL

The Boathouse

c/o Barnes Brinkcraft Holidays Afloat, Riverside Road, Hoveton NR12 8UD ☎ 01603 782625
www.barnesbrinkcraft.co.uk

Newly opened for 2008, this boathouse-style lodge has been built within a busy boatyard on the River Bure near Wroxham Broad. Rental of one of the three units, with a choice of two or four bedrooms, comes with free use of a motor launch.

Price: from £292 to £696 (sleeps 4) or from £566 to £1220 (sleeps 8) for a week.

Shopping

As on the Norfolk coast, individual artists and craftspeople have moved to these tranquil parts to practise their arts. For example Sutton Pottery (Church Road NR12 9SG; ☎ 01692 580595; www.suttonpottery.com) is a one-man open-plan studio workshop in rural East Norfolk, established in 1977 in the Broadland village of Sutton, near Stalham. The potter, malcolm Flatman, throws appealing every-day objects on his hand-made potter's wheel and welcomes visitors on most weekdays.

A collection of workshops can be found at the mainstream tourist attraction **Wroxham Barns** (Tunstead Road, Hoveton NR12 8QU; ☎ 01603 783911; www.wroxham-barns.co.uk). The complex of once-disused farm buildings includes a stained glass workshop, a shop selling designer children's clothes and of course plenty of gift ideas. There is also a Junior Farm that will appeal to children.

The best... FOOD AND DRINK

 ## Staying in

Norfolk-produced food is never far away in the Broads, since this is a traditional region. The best deli in the region is the Galley Deli in Horning (43 Lower Street NR12 8AA; ☎ 01692 630088) where you can find an impressive array of local cheeses and chutneys, pies and ice cream, beers and ciders.

Nearby Wroxham is dominated by the Roy trademark. **Roys of Wroxham** (www.roys.co.uk) advertises itself as the 'world's largest village store' and it certainly sells an impressive range, especially in the Food Hall where local organic produce is carried, for example Norfolk beef grazed on Halvergate Marshes.

Farmers' markets take place at the Church Hall in Acle on the second Saturday of the month and in the Hoveton Village Hall on the fourth Saturday with up to two dozen stalls selling everything from venison to honey. The Stalham farmers' market is on the first and third Saturdays of the month.

EATING OUT

RESTAURANT
Staithe 'n' Willow Restaurant
16 Lower Street, Horning NR12 8AA
☎ **01692 630915**
www.broads-norfolk.com

This pretty thatched cottage restaurant occupies a lovely location with a garden adjacent to the River Bure. Prices for its fresh but unflashy dishes are fair, for example Sunday roasts at £8, traditional dishes such as fish pie for £12 and bargain Winter Warmer Lunches for £5 including sausages and mash.

The Hermitage Restaurant
64 Old Road, Acle NR13 3QP
☎ **01493 750310**
**www.thehermitageseafood
restaurant.co.uk**

After acquiring a smart new conservatory, this pub is now more a restaurant concentrating on fish but also with a steak menu. The chef-proprietor chooses his own fish from Lowestoft market and chalks up specials on a daily board. Sample dishes include fresh soft roes on toast for £4.50 and pan-fried turbot with wild mushrooms for £15.50.

GASTROPUB
Recruiting Sergeant
Norwich Road, Horstead NR12 7EE
☎ **01603 737077**
www.recruitingsergeant.co.uk

On the north-western edge of the Broads near Coltishall, this pub uses mainly local produce including beef bought directly from Swannington Farm less than 10 miles away. Appetising dishes from the extensive menu include tempura prawns with a chilli dip (£5.50) and slow baked lamb shank with redcurrant (£11).

CAFÉ
Alfresco Tea Rooms
Norwich Road, Ludham NR29 5QA
☎ **01692 678384**

This cosy, thatched, family-run family-friendly tea shop is renowned for its fruit cakes which are sold online. Cream teas, home-made cakes and tasty simple lunches are also served. A courtyard is available in fine weather.

**Wroxham Barns Café Restaurant
Tunstead Road, Hoveton NR12 8QU**
☎ **01603 783762**
www.wroxham-barns.co.uk

Afternoon tea, cakes and light lunches are served in a converted 18th-century barn completely refurbished for 2008 at this well-known destination for tourists. The food is sourced locally and prepared fresh every day.

 ## Drinking

Boats that at one time plied the Broads carrying malt to brewers now convey visitors to excellent riverside hostelries which provide their own boat moorings. The theme is obvious when considering the name that so many pubs share: **The Ferry Inn at Horning** with its good-value carvery, the **Ferry Inn at Reedham** with a constantly changing menu; the **Ferry Inn** in Stokesby on the River Bure east of Acle; and **The Ferry House** in Surlingham. All these pubs are some distance from the villages and of course all have outdoor seating where you can watch boaters jockeying for a mooring, because these famous boating pubs can get very busy of a summer's evening. In the case of the first two, ferries still operate. The pub at Reedham Ferry is on the north side of the River Yare, so if you are approaching by car from the south, you might have a long wait for the ferry which can only carry three vehicles across the river at a time.

Other congenial pubs that attract the boating fraternity include **The White Horse** at Neatishead, adorned with cheerful pictures of the Broads and serving Adnams' and Tetley's along with traditional dishes like sausages and mash with onion gravy. Another classic Broadlands pub is **The Maltsters Inn** in Ranworth, where once again arrival by boat might involve queuing for a place, but which will be rewarded with a great steak and ale pie.

The splendid Woodforde's Brewery owns and runs the pub next door which it calls its 'taphouse', although the décor is modern and the food menu innovative without being pretentious. **The Fur & Feather Inn** (Slad Lane, Woodbastwick, NR13 6HQ; ☎ 01603 720003; www.thefurandfeatherinn.co.uk) looks like a thatched cottage, has a wonderful garden and serves an average of eight different ales in top condition.

The same brewery has recently acquired another thatched pub, **The Swan at Ingham** (☎ 01692 581099) on the northern edge of the Broads. Originally part of a mediaeval priory, its eccentric layout and untarted-up atmosphere should be in safe hands with Woodforde's.

Breweries

As well as **Woodforde's** mentioned earlier, the area boasts several other excellent breweries. **Tipples Brewery** in Acle (Unit 6 Damgate Lane Industrial Estate NR13 3DJ; (☎ 01493 741007; www.tipplesbrewery.com) was set up several years ago by a burned-out financier, Jason Tipple, who would have been wise in the first place to choose his calling based on his surname. Using Norfolk's excellent quality barley, the brewery has an ambitious programme of adding new artisan brews, such as a seasonal raspberry beer and a strong barley wine. The brewery is open to the public and there is also a brewery shop in Norwich at 32 Elm Hill and a regular stall at the Acle farmers' market on the second Saturday of every month.

The longer-established **Humpty Dumpty Brewery** is based in Reedham 6 miles to the south (Church Road, Reedham NR13 3TZ;☎ 01493 701818; www.humptydumptybrewery.co.uk), named for a locomotive that once chugged along the Norfolk coast. Its products, such as Norfolk Nectar and Reedcutters, appear regularly at regional beer festivals and local pubs such as the Lord Nelson in Reedham. The brewery shop sells a range of East Anglian beers, ciders, country wines and foods from local producers (open daily in summer 12–5pm, weekends in winter; occasional tastings and tours).

Cider

Wroxham Barns described earlier is the ideal location for a craft cider maker, and sure enough the Norfolk Cider Company (www.norfolkcider.co.uk) is located here. This is the oldest cider company in Norfolk. Anyone who calls by the shop, open seven days a week, can taste the range before choosing including the products of the sister company, Norfolk Apple Juice Ltd.

Burgh Castle

Visitor information

Tourist Information Centres: Broads Authority, 18 Colegate, Norwich NR3 1BQ, ☎ 01603 610734. broads@broads-authority.gov.uk/www.broads-authority.gov.uk/visiting/tourist-information-centres.html, free tourist newspaper called *Broadcaster* which carries useful articles and resources; Hoveton/Wroxham Information Centre, Station Road Hoveton NR12 8UR (☎ 01603 782281, hoveton.info@broads-authority.gov.uk, open summer only; seasonal National Park information centres also located in Ludham, Potter Heigham, Ranworth and Whitlingham

Hospitals: 24-hour A&E facilities available at Norfolk & Norwich University Hospital, Colney Lane, Norwich NR4 7UY, ☎ 01603 287325; www.nnuh.nhs.uk; Anglian Medical Care, ☎ 01603 424255; Norfolk-wide emergency health service run by the East Anglian Ambulance Trust; Hoveton & Wroxham Medical Centre, Stalham Road, Hoveton NR12 8DU, ☎ 01603 782155 or 488488; www.h-wmc.co.uk, daytime opening hours only.

Websites: www.discoverthebroads.com – ideas for10 days in the Broads, prepared by the Broads Tourism Forum, www.visitnorwich.co.uk/broads.aspx or www.adayinthebroads.co.uk – canvases lots of touring ideas.

Supermarkets: Tesco, Upper Staithe Road, Stalham NR12 9AE, ☎ 0845 6779773); Roy's of Wroxham, Wroxham, food hall is open 8am–8pm, shorter hours on Sun (Roy's Department Store also in Wroxham).

Bike rental: Broadland Cycle Hire, BeWILDerwood, Horning Road, Hoveton NR12 8JW, ☎ 07887 480331; www.norfolkbroadscycling.co.uk, open daily in school holidays and other times for pre-booked bicycles, hire charges are £14 a day, £50 a week for adults, £8/£35 for children, £25 a day for a tandem, discounts for multiple rentals; Broads Bike Hire has outlets at Clippesby Hall Campsite (☎ 01493 367800), Ludham Bridge Boat Services (☎ 01692 630486), Riverside Stores Stokesby (☎ 01493 750470) and Whitlingham Country Park (☎ 01603 632307).

Taxis: 24/7 Cars, Hoveton Railway Station, ☎ 01603 782247; Stalham Cabs, ☎ 01692 581666; Acle Cars, Reedham, ☎ 01493 752222

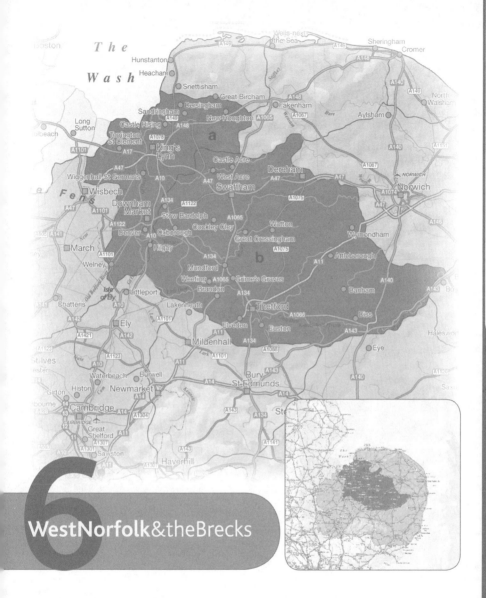

6

WestNorfolk&theBrecks

a. King's Lynn and around

b. The Brecks

Unmissable highlights

01 Explore the timbered buildings of King's Lynn left over from when it was one of the most important trading ports in Europe, p.268

02 Walk part of the gentle Peddars Way follows a Roman road north from Knettishall Heath in the heart of Breckland, p.287

03 Take a ferry to West Lynn to get a superb view of the King's Lynn skyline with its medieval churches and merchants' houses, p.275

04 Marvel at the sight of thousands of migrating swans and ducks at their stopover at Welney, p.286

05 Stay in an award-winning country house boutique hotel in Swaffham where the owners put their eco-principles into practice both in the hotel and their superb restaurant, p.295

06 Relax beside the land-scaped lake surrounded by shady plants at Sandringham House, when the Queen isn't in residence, p.283

07 Count the deadly sins carved on the church pews at Wiggenhall St Germans, a village alongside the River Great Ouse, p.282

08 Hold your breath while your kids climb trees, slide across high wires and cross rope bridges in Thetford Forest, p.293

09 Visit Seahenge, which predates Stonehenge, as it finally goes on display in King's Lynn Museum a decade after its discovery offshore, p.274

10 Find the tiny lane near Castle Acre that leads down to a bridge over the River Nar to the meadows behind the ruined priory, a perfect location for a picnic, p.288

WEST NORFOLK & THE BRECKS

Surprisingly few visitors make the straightforward journey by car or train to the end of the line at King's Lynn. West Norfolk is a radically under-visited part of the country. Considered by many to be an area of economic and social deprivation, the architectural treasures of King's Lynn, forgotten rural landscapes and beauties of the coastline are often overlooked.

The neglect adds to the historic atmosphere; the heritage is less processed here than in some places, though recent injections of regeneration money have made it possible to improve the infrastructure and enhance visitor facilities, to make visits to this part of the country comfortable as well as interesting. King's Lynn is a town with a splendid historic townscape for exploring on foot and in detail.

Past Cambridge, Ely and Downham Market you move into the primordial flatlands of the Fens. A large part of the region's appeal is this feeling of otherness, as though you have stepped outside the grasp of the metropolis. King's Lynn is a watery place stretching along the wide brown River Great Ouse to which the town owes its glorious history as one of the foremost ports in the land.

West of the A10 you enter a different landscape. Even some East Anglian locals are unfamiliar with the area known as the Brecks. They will know Thetford Forest (location of a Center Parcs) and be acquainted with the well-known tourist sites of Castle Acre, Oxburgh Hall and the market town of Swaffham, all included in this chapter. But they may recognise the name Breckland only from the District Council that stretches from Dereham to the Suffolk border. The term Brecks refers to a specific landscape of ancient grassy heathland, cultivated by our ancestors but later given over to the farming of rabbits whose foraging depleted the vegetation creating a unique sandy landscape. Breckland pines are gnarled and twisted specimens that grow in this sandy soil, and the area supports rare birds like the stone curlew and rare orchids with poetic names like Spiked Speedwell and Spanish Catchfly. The sparsely populated 370 square mile area that includes the River Little Ouse is great for walking and cycling.

KING'S LYNN AND AROUND

An idiosyncratic back street local pub in King's Lynn called the Live and Let Live features something on the wall that speaks volumes – a clock that runs backwards. Although the town of 35,000 is just over an hour and a half by direct train from London King's Cross, and about half that from Cambridge, gentrification is only just coming to King's Lynn (often shortened to Lynn). Where you might expect a Starbuck's, you find a Wimpys advertising cups of tea for 75p. From a stall in the Tuesday Market an old-fashioned haberdasher sells colourful ribbons and tapestry sewing boxes. The past, both remote and near, doesn't seem as foreign a country here as in other places, which makes King's Lynn a fascinating place to visit.

Strolling along the pleasant quays, past a restored warehouse, an environmental interpretation centre and a wine bar, you gaze out across an empty expanse of river that was once so crowded that it was said you could cross to the other side by stepping from boat to boat. You can take the humble commuter ferry across the river to West Lynn in order to get a distant view on the townscape dominated by the striking Custom House, and possibly to take a stroll along a grassy stretch of the Fen Rivers Way.

WHAT TO SEE AND DO

From about 1100, Lynn grew as a mighty port with ease of access to the Baltic Sea and Northern Europe. The town grew up around two market places which still serve as dual hubs. The poet John Betjeman described the walk between the two markets as 'probably the most beautiful walk in England'. Timbered buildings that once belonged to wealthy merchants, two mediaeval guildhalls and a college for priests dating from 1510 with an exquisite carved door set in a stone arch can all be admired along the way.

The Hanseatic League was the European Union of its day, facilitating trade among dozens of port cities in Northern Europe. The oversailing timbered upper storey of England's only surviving Hanseatic warehouse stretches along **St. Margaret's Lane**. By the 14th century, King's Lynn was home to some of England's leading shipping magnates. Most worked from home, since their grand houses extended out the back to warehouses adjoining their own jetties. The architectural treasures along **King, Queen** and **Nelson Streets** give a sense of how prosperous a port Lynn was. The charming frontages are mostly Georgian and you need to stray along the cobbled side lanes and alleys towards the river to catch glimpses of older structures, particularly recommended in the

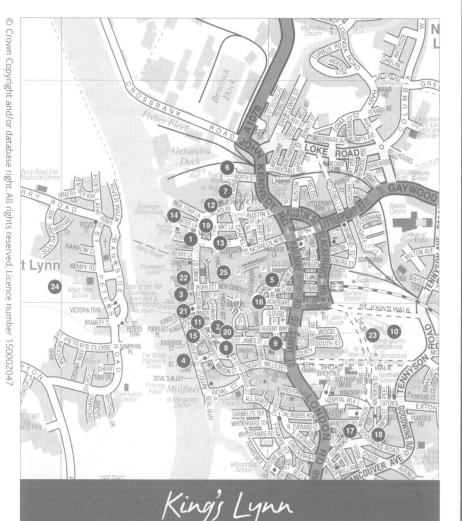

King's Lynn

1. St George's Guildhall/Riverside Restaurant
2. Trinity Guildhall/Tales of the Old Gaol House
3. Custom House/Tourist Information
4. Green Quay
5. Lynn Museum
6. True's Yard Museum
7. St Nicholas Chapel
8. St Margaret's Church
9. Greyfriars Tower
10. Red Mount
11. Clifton House
12. Tudor Rose Hotel
13. Duke's Head Hotel

14. Crown & Mitre
15. Bradley's Wine Bar
16. Antonio's
17. Live & Let Live
18. Stuart House Hotel
19. Tuesday Market
20. Saturday Market
21. King Staithe Square
22. Purfeet Quay
23. The Walks
24. West Lynn
25. Vancouver Centre

case of Clifton House at 17 Queen Street, whose Elizabethan watchtower is visible only from the back. Buildings of note are helpfully marked with green plaques.

Fair weather

Waterfront

Ambling along the pleasantly spruced up quayside promenade, it will be necessary to use your imagination to transform this quiet backwater, sometimes victim of stiff winds, into the third port of England, a hive of shipping activity with stevedores unloading wine and other goods from the watergates into warehouses. Turn away from the river at Purfleet Quay which reveals the elegantly proportioned, Dutch-influenced **Custom House** built in 1683 as a merchants' exchange. It now houses the tourist office plus a free exhibition about King's Lynn's maritime heritage including its smugglers. When the Purfleet was a navigable channel, it allowed ships into the heart of town but eventually became silted up. Massive anchors and chains plus a statue of explorer, sea captain and native of King's Lynn, George Vancouver, looking out to sea, all celebrate the town's illustrious maritime history.

Grand schemes are afoot for the southern end of the waterfront. Not only is a new marina to be built at Boal Quay, but a navigable channel between the Great Ouse and the River Nar is to be created, plus a sea lock that is intended to become a gateway between the inland Fen Waterways and the open sea of the Wash and the North Sea.

Tuesday Market

Tuesday Market is considered one of the finest squares in the country, though it isn't well known. Over the centuries it has also been the setting for nasty things too such as the execution of witches and impromptu high-speed chases by chav boy racers. However, mainly it epitomises Georgian grandeur with fine pedimented bank buildings and the pink and white stucco confection which is the **Duke's Head Hotel**.

One of the curiosities of Tuesday Market can be found above the blocked-in door of a dental office on its north side, the so-called **Witch's Brick** in the shape of a diamond enclosing a crudely carved heart. Various stories are told of Mary Smith who was denounced as a witch in 1616, probably when a neighbour fell ill after receiving a tongue-lashing from Mary. In any case, when she was hanged (or some say boiled alive) in Tuesday Market, her heart exploded from her chest and went splat against a nearby wall, said to belong to her accuser, the Reverend Alexander Roberts.

CELEBRITY CONNECTIONS

Stephen Fry has long put his money (and his time) where his heart is, which is in Norfolk. He grew up in the village of Booton near Reepham in a comfortable middle-class home which in the 1950s had a gardener, cook and housekeeper. In fact 40 years later, he is still in touch with Mrs Riseborough, the Norfolk housekeeper, who served treacle tart and apple jellies to the family. As soon as he made a substantial sum from a writing project – the script of *Me and My Girl* in the late 1980s – he bought a rambling Victorian farmhouse in the straggling village of West Bilney, on the A47 between King's Lynn and Swaffham, where he still lives when he isn't in London. For many years he has played his best friend Hugh Laurie and family here at Christmas time.

Stephen was one of the key patrons of the bid (unsuccessful) for Norwich to become city of culture in 2008, when he persuasively pointed to Norwich's 'café society, adventurism and an openness to the new'. He lends his weight to many initiatives in the arts, such as the lavish restoration of the Theatre Royals in Norwich and in Bury St Edmunds, and is patron of the remarkable summer theatre and non-profit-making River Studios at Westacre. On the death in 2005 of fellow Norfolk enthusiast John Timpson (former presenter of the *Today* programme), he became patron of the Norfolk-based literature group Centre Poets. He occasionally pops up at various Norfolk events such as the opening of the annual Sandringham Flower Show in late July or a fundraising performance of a Shakespeare play at Houghton Hall. Most of these are no more than 15 miles from his home.

One of his favourite haunts is the Norwich City Football Ground since he is an avid Canaries fan, and has sometimes been seen as a guest of Delia Smith in the Director's Box. His favourite place to eat out is Strattons, a superb restaurant and eco-friendly boutique hotel, in Swaffham (see chapter on Breckland). He spent a good part of 2007 filming in Swaffham for the ITV comedy drama series *Kingdom* in which he plays a kindly solicitor in the fictitious country town of Market Shipborough. Fry has confessed to an ambition to do for Norfolk what *All Creatures Great and Small* has done for the Yorkshire Dales, and claimed in an interview to relish the prospect of showing viewers the locations he loves, and the chance of 'an hour in front of the television that will wash them in colours, textures, landscapes and characters that delight'. As well as waxing rhapsodic, he also has an unsentimental understanding of Norfolk: 'You either get Norfolk, with its wild roughness and its uncultivated oddities, or you don't. It's not all soft and lovely. It doesn't ask to be loved. But there's something so fantastically beautiful about it; the skies are so big that they have an effect on the mind.'

Just off the Market on King Street is **St George's Guildhall**, the largest surviving medieval guildhall in the country, now the welcoming King's Lynn Arts Centre and café.

Saturday Market

Saturday Market is the older of the two squares, though less unified a space. The main church, St Margaret's, is massive and much Victorianised, with a most unusual clock on one of its three towers. Instead of showing the time, it shows the phases of the moon, and the high and low tides. When read (clockwise, naturally), the letters spell out 'Lynn High Tide'. Next to the west door of the church, note the high water marks from the floods of 1883, 1949, 1953, 1961 and 1978.

Along the bend from Saturday Market into Queen Street, four buildings form a delightful sequence. The striking chequered flint and stone frontage belongs to **Trinity Guildhall**, reminiscent of the Norwich Guildhall, and now the Town Hall.

Parks and gardens

In the **Walks Park** is an unusual octagonal buttressed red-brick building. The **Red Mount** was built in the time of Richard III as a wayside chapel for pilgrims en route to Walsingham Abbey. The rumoured tunnel all the way to Castle Rising (about 6 miles away), might have allowed the imprisoned Queen Isabella of France to worship without showing her face in public as commanded by her son Edward III. A more recent tale is told of a drunken fiddler and his dog who entered the tunnel never to re-emerge, though excavations have not uncovered a tunnel longer than about 5ft.

Not far away another octagonal and equally intriguing structure can be found, surrounded by newly landscaped **Tower Gardens**. Until recently **Greyfriars Tower** was leaning just as precariously as the tower of Pisa. Its predicament was considered serious enough to be considered as a competitor for the BBC2 programme *Restoration* where it was championed by the late John Peel. Although it didn't win, the publicity attracted funding and the unusual building has now been underpinned.

Once a bell tower, Greyfriars is one of the only Franciscan friaries from the 1230s that survives of the 60 that were built in England. It is thought that the tower was left because it served the useful purpose of acting as a landmark for sailors negotiating the treacherous waters of The Wash.

Wet weather

St Nicholas Chapel

Despite its grand proportions, this was never a parish church but rather a chapel of ease for the overspill of parishioners from St Margaret's. After collecting the key from True's Yard Museum or the Tudor Rose Hotel, you approach through a wrought iron gateway and peaceful churchyard and enter the light and airy interior with beam angels which escaped the reforming hackers, unusual tracery over windows and doors and mercantile memorials to traders, mayors and merchants. The name on a stone engraved in the floor commemorates Robinson Crusoe, who died age 10 in 1773. Since Defoe visited Lynn in 1724, five years after his book *The Life and Most Surprizing Adventures of Robinson Crusoe* was published, the name looks as though it must be a coincidence.

True's Yard

Just before the last remaining cottages belonging to the fisher folk of the North End of Lynn were to be pulled down, a campaign was mounted to save and restore them, and turn them into what has become a fascinating little museum.

TRUE'S YARD FISHING MUSEUM, North Street, PE30 1QW; ☎ 01533 770479; www.truesyard.co.uk; adults £3, children £1.50; open all year, Tues to Sat 10am–4pm; tearoom.

The hero of this rescue operation was an elderly resident, Patricia Midgley, whose two main interests are history and knitting, preferably in combination. When some slum demolitions were taking place, she spotted two original cottages, disguised by a roof of corrugated iron, which were saved and are the centrepiece of **True's Yard Fishing Heritage Museum**. Right into the 20th century, families of up to nine lived as they had for centuries in one up, one down cottages, in which up to five children shared a bed while the parents slept on the floor. The downstairs had bare floors so that they could be hosed down after the children had sorted the fish. Original 19th-century rag hearthrugs have the red eye of the devil woven into them; if the devil happened to peek down the chimney, he would see the eye and think he need not to bother. Chamber pots were emptied out the windows and in winter babies were covered with goose grease and sewed into their snug clothes, which sounds more like Tibet than East Anglia a hundred years ago.

The display of old photos and memorabilia is a valuable record of these hardy fishermen (one of whose surnames was Fysh) who were inshore fishermen catching only shellfish as they still do, though the industry is winding down.

LYNN MUSEUM, Market Street, PE30 1NL; ☎ 01553 775001; www.museums.norfolk.gov.uk/defau lt.asp?Document=200.31; free; open Tues to Sat 10am–5pm.

Lynn Museum

Recent investment in regeneration projects has benefitted the main museum which aims to tell the story of west Norfolk and make Lynn's history accessible through an audio guide and

Lynn Museum

animations. The ambitious redevelopment exploits the structure of the non-conformist chapel in which it is housed, in the heart of the shopping area. Like all good regional museums, it has a wonderfully eclectic collection.

A great coup for the museum is the imminent arrival of Seahenge. A special gallery is devoted to the mysterious Bronze Age timber circle found in 1998 just off the coast at Holme-next-the-Sea near Hunstanton. The decision to excavate the circle, which is older than Stonehenge and among the oldest man-made structures anywhere, was extremely controversial at the time, since some thought that removing them from their watery home would spell their doom. Not surprisingly, they have been painstakingly conserved and are now considered imperishable.

What to do with children

Tales of the Old Gaol House

Attached to the Trinity Guildhall is a building that served as King Lynn's police station in the 1930s. Now it is an interactive museum with audio guide that most children enjoy. Tiny cells where smugglers and drunks were impounded are at the back, along with stocks and other means of punishment. Stories are recounted of witch trials and executions, of highwaymen and murderers.

GAOL HOUSE, Saturday Market Place, PE30 5DQ; ☎ 01553 774297; www.west-norfolk.gov.uk/Default.aspx?page=2 1849; adults £2.80, children £2, family £8; open Apr to Oct, Mon to Sat 10am–5pm, Nov to Mar, Tues to Sat 10am–4pm.

The Green Quay

Green Quay

This environmental centre overlooking the Great
Ouse is primarily educational but also has an
aquarium in which freshwater creatures of The
Wash including some contented looking lizards
can be viewed. Interesting photographs from the
great flood of 1953 are on display. The centre has
a shop and pleasant licensed café.

GREEN QUAY, Marriott's Warehouse, South Quay PE30 5DT;
☎ 01553 818500; www.thegreen
quay.co.uk; free; open daily
9am–5pm.

Lynn Ferry

The old-fashioned cross-river ferry with its awning
runs frequently across to West Lynn between
7am and 6pm Monday to Saturday. The first ferry
service at Lynn was recorded in 1285, and Henry
V did the trip in 1421, presumably without queuing
along the quay, something that has become more common with a doubling in
passenger numbers over the past six years. There isn't much to see in West
Lynn apart from the magnificent view back to King's Lynn.

WEST LYNN FERRY, c/o S N
Kingston Marine Services, Ferry
Square, West Lynn, PE34 3JQ;
☎ 01553 766029; one-way 60p;
pedestrian ferry Mon to Sat 7am–
6pm, three times an hour (or more
frequently at rush hours).

If you have bicycles, there is a short circuit you can do past West Lynn's
cruciform St Peter's Church and along the footpath, over the Clenchwarton
Road bridge and back along the riverside cycleway through South Lynn. Once
a derelict area, **Hardings Pits** is now a nature reserve with a sculpture trail,
which includes some acrobats by woodcarver Ben Platts-Mills (see p.299)
based on children's drawings, and a giant whale to celebrate the whaling history
of the area.

Sports and activities

The **Norfolk Arena** has a superior speedway track
with a busy schedule of motorsport racing including stock cars and bangers, quad racing, drifting
(on motorbikes) and even caravan racing. Gordon
Ramsay and his film crew treated themselves to a
trip to the races when they were filming *Kitchen Nightmares* in King's Lynn.

**SPEEDWAY AT THE
NORFOLK ARENA**, Saddlebow
Road, PE34 3AG; ☎ 01553
771111; www.norfolkarena.co.uk;
adults £15, children aged 12–15 £5,
under 11s free.

Entertainment

There has been a long tradition of theatrical events in the town. The huge **Guildhall of St George** was used as a theatre in Elizabethan times and even earlier for nativity plays and medieval guild plays. The ancient building was brought back from the brink of dereliction some decades ago and now serves as a theatre venue in the **King's Lynn Arts Centre**. The audience can admire the 15th-century roof of trussed rafters while attending a play, concert, film, comedy night, jazz evening, etc.

> **KING'S LYNN ARTS CENTRE**, 27–29 King St, PE30 1HA; ☎ 01553 764864; www.kingslynnarts.co.uk; box office here also serves the sister venue at the Corn Exchange in Tuesday Market where popular and classical concerts, opera and ballet performances take place.

Special events

The Arts Centre is the headquarters of the annual **King's Lynn Festival**, though concerts and other performances take place in venues around the town and outside it. This first-class arts festival held in the last two weeks of July dates from when the Guildhall of St George was reopened in 1951. The chief mover was Princess Diana's maternal grandmother Lady Fermoy who had moved with her husband to King's Lynn two decades earlier and then given up her own ambitions of a career as a concert pianist. Because of her connections, the Queen Mother became patron and many distinguished musicians participated in the first festival, which set a precedent. Top musicians and ensembles come from around the world to participate, and many supplementary talks, events and guided walking tours take place during the festival. The programme is finalised by May each year and can be consulted online at www.kingslynnfestival.org.uk.

Tuesday Market is the venue for the annual **Festival Too,** held on the first two weekends in July, when free concerts, featuring famous artists from the 1960s to 1980s take place. It has now become one of Europe's biggest free festivals (www.festivaltoo.co.uk).

 Shopping

There is no chance of forgetting the time and place for Lynn's weekly markets. More than 80 stalls gather on Tuesdays in the Tuesday Market square, and almost half set up on Fridays. At first glance it may seem as though most stalls are selling cabbages and over-sized undergarments, but on closer inspection, the market's appeal grows: one stall sells 100% brand name wool jumpers for £3 and another peddles Spanish snacks and olives. The Saturday Market on Saturday Market Place is smaller, though cheerful all the same.

The best... PLACES TO STAY

BOUTIQUE

King's Head Hotel

**Great Bircham, King's Lynn PE31 6RJ
(14 miles north-east of King's Lynn)
☎ 01485 578 265
www.the-kings-head-bircham.co.uk**

The King's Head offers first-class hotel facilities while remaining a village local pub, voted West Norfolk Branch Pub of the Year for 2007. Contemporary design and daring colours serve as background to a friendly hotel. Fresh flowers and toiletries produced in the local area, homemade biscuits and a decanter of port are all nice touches. The prize-winning restaurant has an interesting menu at lunch and dinner, for example Parma ham ciabatta with marinated artichoke and pesto for £6.

Prices: from £125 to £175 for a double Sun to Thurs; £25 extra at weekends; £50 extra if dinner for two is included; single occupancy £75.

HOTEL

Stuart House Hotel

**35 Goodwins Road, King's Lynn PE30
5QX. ☎ 01553 772169
www.stuart-house-hotel.co.uk**

In a gracious secluded setting, this hotel is only 10 minutes on foot to the town centre. Its pub has earned inclusion in the *Good Beer Guide,* serving non-residents from 7pm and hosting live music.

Prices: £96 for a standard double, £125 for a family room.

Congham Hall Hotel

**Grimston, King's Lynn PE32 1AH
☎ 01485 600250
www.conghamhallhotel.co.uk**

Part of the exclusive Van Essen group of hotels, this is a seriously luxurious country house hotel in a Georgian manor with an amazing herb garden and surrounded by parkland.

Prices: from £135 for a double; occasional Sunday deals from £99 per person for dinner, bed and breakfast.

B&B

Crosskeys Riverside Hotel

**Bridge Street, Hilgay PE38 0LD
☎ 01366 387777
www.crosskeys.info**

As well as being a good base for exploring West Norfolk, this small country B&B has a large riverside garden on the River Wissey, and can lend guests a rowing boat and fishing rods.

Prices: from £55.

SELF-CATERING

The Granary

**Manor House, Churchgateway, Terrington St Clements, Norfolk PE34 4LZ
☎ 01553 828700**

A granary built in 1800 has been converted into a cottage which sleeps six (one double, one room with bunks and two singles) located next door to the so-called Cathedral of the Marshes. The village also has the African Violet Centre and access to the Peter Scott Walk. The house is set amidst paddocks, garden and orchard with a barbecue. Guests are encouraged to collect eggs from the hen house and seasonal fruit and vegetables from the walled garden.

Prices: £180 in low season, £350 in high season.

UNUSUAL

Appleton Water Tower

**near West Newton, Sandringham Estate
☎ 01628 825920
www.landmarktrust.co.uk**

The tower was built in 1877 to supply drinking water to the Sandringham estate and now gives exceptional views over the countryside. It sleeps four on three levels and has a garden full of wildlife.

Prices: three-night weekend: £800 to £1,094.

World Snail Racing Championship

According to the race's chief organiser, '**Congham** is to snail racing what Newmarket is to horse racing.' The annual event is part of the Church Fete held in the village of Congham 8 miles east of King's Lynn, on the third Saturday of July, and is the main fundraiser for the local St Andrew's Church. Separate adult's and children's races take place on a round table with a circumference marked at 13 inches from the centre, where all the labelled snails begin the race. The record set in 1995 stands at two minutes (www.snailracing.net). Anyone can enter.

During the 1960s a Congham man called Tom Elwes came across snail racing in France and recognised it instantly as a sport that would translate well to rural Norfolk, especially Congham with its ponds and low-lying land so popular with slimy gastropods. He instituted the annual world championships which now attract around 2,000 people including journalists who come from as far away as Sweden to cover the race.

The start of the race is heralded with the cry 'Ready, steady, slow' and trainers take different views on the best preparation, some swearing by British-grown lollo rosso rather than the more insipid iceberg lettuce. Neil Riseborough, president of the British Snail Racing Association and a farmer from Flitcham near Sandringham, is responsible for guarding against cheating and use of performance-enhancing drugs.

Other shops of note include the **Old Granary Antiques Centre** in King's Staithe Lane (☎ 01553 775509) and the **Old Curiosity Shop** at 25 St James Street (☎ 01553 766591). Another interesting shop (one of the few) on St James Street is **The Record Shop** (☎ 01553 691972), with appeal to anyone interested in 45-inch vinyl records and old LPs.

The best... FOOD AND DRINK

 ## Staying in

Head for the Tuesday or Saturday markets on their eponymous days to buy cheese, produce, fish, bread and pastries. The local butcher E H Prior & Sons has been trading since 1930 and can be found every Saturday on the market-place selling meat mostly sourced from local farms. They have taken over the next door bakery, now called **Priors Bakery.**

For generations, King's Lynn has been an important centre for agricultural production, so that one of its primary industries was Campbell's Soup until a

EATING OUT

RESTAURANT
Riverside Restaurant
27 King Street, King's Lynn PE30 1ET
☎ **01553 773134**
www.theriversiderestaurant.com

This town centre restaurant in a heavily timbered waterside barn is rated not just for its
river views from the terrace but for its
honest cooking. Mains such as roasted
monkfish or rack of lamb cost £14-17.
Hours are limited: 12pm-2pm and 6.30pm-
9.30pm, Monday-Saturday.

Andel Lodge
**48 Lynn Road, Tottenhill, PE33 0RH (on
the A10 5.5 miles south of King's Lynn)**
☎ **01553 810256**
www.andellodge.co.uk

This hotel welcomes non-residents to its
pleasingly old-fashioned dining room where
conventional British cooking is supple-
mented with more adventurous dishes. A
top-of-the-range starter would be steamed
Brancaster mussels in saffron & chive cream
(£7) and a sample main course, pan-fried
duck breast in a Chinese sauce (£10.50).

WINE BAR
Bradley's Wine Bar
10 South Quay, King's Lynn PE30 5DT
☎ **01553 819888**
www.bradleysbytheriver.co.uk

The quayside location of this bar is well
suited to an al fresco meal or sunset aperi-
tif. Light meals are served on the ground
floor while upstairs is a more formal

restaurant. Check out the Belvedere (ship
lookout) in this one-time Georgian merchant's house. Menu extends from fish and
chips with garlic mushy peas for £12.50 to
fillet steak and all the trimmings (£20).

Antonio's Restaurant & Wine Bar
Baxters Plain, King's Lynn PE30 1NP
☎ **01553 772324**

This decent Italian eatery in town is not far
from the attractive independent Majestic
Cinema on Tower Street. Bargain two-
course lunches might include mozzarella
and tomato salad followed by pizza, tagli-
atelli or gnocchi.

CAFÉ
Crofters Coffee House
27 King Street, King's Lynn PE30 1ET
☎ **01553 773134**

This daytime bolthole nestles in the vaulted
cellar of the ancient Guildhall, now Arts
Centre of King's Lynn. Although the building
is in the care of the National Trust, the café
and long-established Riverside Restaurant
upstairs isn't run by the Trust. Newspapers
are available to read, second-hand books to
buy and Fair Trade teas and good cakes
and pastries are served. The café is open
Monday to Saturday 9.30am–5pm.

company take-over resulted in the closure of the long-established factory in 2007. Despite an abundance of local fruit and vegetables, you will have to travel to Dents of Hilgay 4 miles south of Downham at West Fen beside the A10 (Downham Market, PE38 0QH; ☎ 01366 385661; www.dents ofhilgay.co.uk; open Mon to Sat 9am–5.30pm, Sun 10am–4.30pm). Dents operates a farm shop where you can buy all manner of good things from cheese to wine, home-baked pastries to readymade dishes.

King's Lynn has also long been a centre for the inshore seafood industry, primarily prawns, shrimps and cockles. However the catches are so small nowadays that no trading takes place down at the docks and you will have to visit a local fishmonger.

Drinking

As an important commercial port, King's Lynn was once awash with hostelries, many located around the market squares. Lots of pubs remain, though many are fairly ordinary and it's worth choosing with some care. **The Tudor Rose** on St Nicholas Street (☎ 01553 762824) is a picturesque inn built in 1500 that serves well-kept bitters in a dark wooden bar and can be accompanied by snacks such as chilli olives, feta and bread for £2.95.

The Crown & Mitre (☎ 01553 774669) on Ferry Street is a well-run traditional freehouse with a lovely terrace called the Vinery overlooking the river. The wooden floors and beams are suited to the maritime memorabilia which adorns the interior. As well as a good range of real ales, the pub serves a well chosen house wine and a very tasty house speciality, Croque Monsieur.

The backwards-running clock at the Live and Let Live (PE30 5PL; ☎ 01553 764990) at 18 Windsor Road has already been mentioned. This is a cosy Dickensian pub and the locals aren't at all hostile to visitors.

A more youthful crowd can be found at **Doctor Thirsty's** (22 Norfolk Street, Kings Lynn PE30 1AN; ☎ 01553 774445) especially on Sunday afternoons (5–7pm) when blues musicians come in for a session. Apparently this pub is used by skiving employees (who absent themselves for a 'doctor's appointment') and by groups of clubbers who like the neon bar and come here before heading to a late-night venue. On student nights (Mondays), pints cost £1.50.

Appleton Water Tower, Sandringham

Visitor information

Tourist Information Centres:
King's Lynn Tourist Information Centre, The Custom House, Purfleet Quay, King's Lynn PE30 1HP, ☎ 01553 763044, kings-lynn.tic@west-norfolk.gov.uk, open Apr to Sept 10am–5pm, Sun 12–5pm, Oct to Mar 10.30am–4pm, Sun 12–4pm; guided walking tours by Blue Badge Guide start from the Gaol House in Saturday Market. Tours last 90 minutes, take place at 2pm mainly at weekends and bank holidays May to Oct (adults £3, children £1).

Hospitals: Accident & Emergency, Queen Elizabeth Hospital, Gayton Road, King's Lynn PE30 4ET, ☎ 01553 613613, www.qehkl.nhs.uk, near the junction of the A149 and the B1145.

Supermarkets: Sainsbury's, Vancouver Shopping Centre, 15–23 St Dominic's Square PE30 1DS, ☎ 01553 772104; Morrison's, Coburg Street, King's Lynn PE30 1QB, ☎ 01553 768596, next to the railway station; Tesco, St Faiths Drive, Gaywood, King's Lynn PE30 4PU, ☎ 0845 6779392, open to midnight on weekdays.

Bike rental: Richardsons, 120 London Road, King's Lynn PE30 5ES, ☎ 01553 767014); Green Quay, The Marriott's Warehouse, South Quay, King's Lynn PE30 5DT, ☎ 01553 818500; Bircham Windmill, Bircham, Norfolk PE31 6SJ, ☎ 01485 578393; www.birchamwindmill.co.uk. Day hire costs adults £11, children £9 and for a tandem £22.

Taxis: King's Lynn Taxis, ☎ 01553 763636; Lynn Cabs, ☎ 01553 760600; A1 Cabs, ☎ 01553 772616; Haz's, ☎ 01553 777191/ ☎ 0800 197 8877

The nearest brewery is the new **Fox Brewery** near Hunstanton, and its beer is available only in the local pub and in bottles (see chapter on Coastal Norfolk). One of the largest ranges of bottled beers in the country is available from an unlikely place just outside King's Lynn. Beers of Europe Ltd (Garage Lane, Setchey, King's Lynn PE33 0BE; ☎ 01553 812000; www.beers ofeurope.co.uk), on the A10 about 4 miles south of King's Lynn, mainly operates as a mail-order business but welcome personal callers. It stocks more than 3,000 beers from Britain and around the world. There can't be many places where you can buy a bottle of Estonian beer (A Le Coq for £1.59), Tahitian beer (Hinano Tahiti for £1.99) and beers from 70 other countries. It's open daily until 6pm (4pm on Sundays).

FURTHER AFIELD

Castle Rising

This famous 12th-century stone castle is a hall keep like the castle in Norwich, as opposed to a tower keep, which means that it is broader than it is high. The powerful-looking walls with few windows are encircled by mighty earthworks, now grassed over, and children will enjoy running along the ramparts and down into the ditches. The keep was built about AD1140, though traces of an earlier Norman church can be seen on the south-east side of the site. The Norman gatehouse, wide staircase and rib vaulting are all very impressive.

CASTLE RISING, Norfolk PE31 6AH; ☎ 01553 631330; www.castlerising.co.uk; adults £4, children £2.20, families £12; open daily Apr to Oct 10am–6pm; Nov to Mar, Wed to Sun 10am–4pm.

Ouse Delta

A less obvious destination is the collection of quirky parish churches a few miles upriver along the Ouse Valley Way (www.ousevalleyway.org.uk). According to Simon Jenkins' *England's Thousand Best Churches*, these churches near the mouth of the Great Ouse contain the best late-medieval craftsmanship in the country. A cluster of four villages all starting with Wiggenhall just south of King's Lynn are full of charm and atmosphere:

- **Wiggenhall St Peter** is in picturesque ruins after a huge roof beam crashed to the ground not long ago.
- **Wiggenhall St Mary Magdalene** is infested with bats and has medieval stained glass and a visitors' book with entries from the early 1950s.
- **Wiggenhall St Germans** has richly carved pew ends representing the seven deadly sins, including a man clutching his money bags and another greedily pouring himself a drink.
- **Wiggenhal St Mary the Virgin** has even more wooden carvings of figures in Tudor dress, angels beheaded at the Reformation, St Agatha about to have her breast lopped off with what looks like a meat cleaver, and so on.

The 150-mile Ouse Valley Way which starts in Huntingdonshire, finishes at Green Quay in King's Lynn, and the final section takes you past these churches. It is easy to do the walk in one direction by using the train. The station in Watlington isn't far from the waymarked path and it is 8 miles by foot into King's Lynn.

Traditions at Castle Rising

The Castle's most famous resident was Queen Isabella. For having had a hand in the assassination of her husband Edward II, her son Edward dispatched her to Castle Rising, where she probably enjoyed a reasonably comfortable life. The excellent audio trail (available for an extra charge) embellishes the story of Isabella who some say was sent mad by her lonely exile and whose screams can occasionally be heard echoing across the countryside.

In the 1540s the castle passed to the powerful Howard family and Lord Greville Howard still owns and manages Castle Rising in partnership with English Heritage. In 1623 Henry Howard, Earl of Northampton, built some up-market red brick almshouses called Trinity Hospital beside the church to accommodate elderly women 'of honest life and conversation' and not 'haunters of alehouses'. This charity persists to the present day and currently manages nine flats set around a beautiful 17th-century courtyard, for women in financial or social need. On special occasions such as Founder's Day, the incumbents proceed to church wearing scarlet Jacobean cloaks and conical hats reminiscent of witches' hats.

Sandringham

Since 1862, Sandringham has been a favourite retreat for successive generations of the Royal Family. Queen Elizabeth and family spend Christmas and New Year here every year and remain officially in residence until February. Few visitors find the red brick house built in the 1870s a thing of surpassing beauty, though there are curiosities inside. However the vast grounds are lovely, with ancient trees, a landscaped lake surrounded by shady plants and a streamside walk. Visitor attractions have continually been added since Sandringham opened to the public for the 1977 Jubilee. For example in 2007, a maze was

Sandringham House

mown into the grass to amuse children, a farmers' market was introduced on the last Sunday of the month and a huge outdoor skating rink was installed under an illuminated canopy for the Christmas period (www.norfolkchristmasfestival.co.uk).

Each room on the ground level has a resident guide who will be delighted to talk about the house and the royal residents (though don't expect them to reveal anything scandalous). Apparently the staff keep photos of all the cabinets so that when their contents are removed for dusting, they can be put back precisely as they were before. The on-site museum is located beside the Stables Tea-room while the main restaurant is in the visitor centre outside the wall. Among the exhibits in the museum is the first motor car owned by the Royal Family, a 1900 Daimler Phaeton.

> **SANDRINGHAM HOUSE**, Museum and Gardens, The Sandringham Estate Office, Sandringham, Norfolk PE35 6EN; ☎ 01553 612908; www.sandringhamestate.co.uk; adults £11, children £5.50, family £27.50; museum and gardens only £7.50/£4/£19); open daily Apr to Oct (but closed the last week of July to prepare for the Sandringham Flower Show); house opening hours are 11am–5pm; gardens open at 10.30am.

Houghton Hall

> **HOUGHTON HALL**, Houghton Park, Near New Houghton, King's Lynn, Norfolk PE31 6UE; ☎ 01485 528569; www.houghtonhall.com; adults £8.80, children £3.50, families £22; open from Easter to Sept, Wed/Thurs/Sun and bank holidays only 1.30–5.30pm (grounds open at 11.30).

After spending time with the Royals at Sandringham, it will restore some balance if you go on to **Houghton Hall**, home of Britain's first de facto prime minister Sir Robert Walpole. In the 1720s, his power increased as King George I's diminished. Walpole was a huntin' and shootin' kind of man and the house and parkland retain that atmosphere. In fact Houghton Hall with its herd of white fallow deer is a working organic farm (and you can even buy barbecue packs of meat raised on the estate).

The grand and lavish **Palladian villa** is what most people come to see. The main entrance on the first floor is accessed by two external staircases sweeping up on either side to the *piano nobile*, while the more rustic ground floor was reserved for 'hunters, hospitality, noise, dirt and business'. The carved garlands, ornate fireplaces, friezes and painted ceilings all need to be admired.

The current owner Lord Cholmondeley (pronounced Chumley) proudly displays his father's intriguing collection of toy soldiers in the stable block. This isn't as boring as it sounds, since they are all arranged in tableaux to indicate battle formations, including wars in Africa.

Downham Market

Downham Market's attractions are unlikely to detain the casual visitor for very long. Some of its Dutch-influenced buildings made of the local reddish brown carrstone are attractive and the much vaunted black and white mock-Gothic cast iron town clock built in 1878 on the corner of the Market Place is a curious feature.

Downham Fryer at 38 Bridge Street regularly wins awards for its fresh fish from Grimsby and traditionally fried Lincolnshire potatoes. The picturesque **Castle Hotel** bedecked with flower baskets on the High Street is a welcoming place for a drink (PE38 9HF; ☎ 01366 384311; www.castle-hotel.com; from £75 for a double). Note the photo on the ceiling showing the stable yard (where traditionally horse fairs took place) covered by a glass roof that cracked in the terrible fire of 1910.

Collectors' World is a bizarre and entertaining collection of kitsch collected by a colourful character Eric St John-Foti. Since he had never thrown anything out over his long life, it was easy to set up a 1960s room with old TVs and LPs. As a great admirer of Barbara Cartland and Liza Goddard (who?), Dickens and Nelson, he has created displays devoted to all of them.

COLLECTORS' WORLD, Hermitage Hall, Bridge Farm, Downham Market, PE38 0AU; ☎ 01366 383185; adults £5.50, children £4.50, family £18; open daily 11am–5pm (last entry 4pm).

Stow Bardolph

This village 2 miles north of Downham is worth a visit for three things, the church, the pub and the farm. On the north side of the chancel in **Holy Trinity Church**, a memorial chapel holds the tombs of many generations of the Hare family, lords of **Stow Hall** up the road. Layered up the walls all around are hundreds of years, worth of baronets, some classically adorned, all looking powerful and imposing. In the corner is a wooden cabinet that you might overlook. The cupboard door swings open and you find yourself eyeballing a homely middle-aged woman. The waxwork of Sarah Hare from 1744 is as lifelike as anything at Madame Tussauds, and in fact their expertise was called upon in 1984 to conserve it.

The name Hare is everywhere in Stow Bardolph. The current mistress of Stow Hall, Lady Rose Hare, and her daughter Lucy open the hall's lovely gardens with cloisters, Victorian kitchen garden, and old Norfolk apple and medlar trees on Wednesdays in summer from 10am to 3pm (entry £3.50). **The Hare Arms** is open every day and is a superb hostelry whose steak and peppercorn pies were recently voted best in England (Stow Bardolph, PE34 3HT; ☎ 01366 382229; www.theharearms.co.uk).

Church Farm is the home of dozens of rare breeds of sheep, cattle, goats, pigs and poultry. Springtime is the best time to visit when baby animals are born every week. The sight of young lambs charging around en masse and 'stotting' (spring-jumping on all fours) is extremely comical. Much investment has gone into making this a full day out with adventure playground, nature walks and tearoom.

CHURCH FARM RARE BREEDS CENTRE, Lynn Road, Stow Bardolph, PE34 3HT; ☎ 01366 382162; www.church farmstowbardolph.co.uk; adults £7, children £6, families £24; open daily Mar to Oct 10am–5pm, open Nov to Feb, Thu to Sun.

Welney

The Ouse Washes are a huge storage area for flood-waters on the Cambridgeshire Norfolk border that are irresistible to water birds. Unfortunately the main A road through Welney is frequently closed because of flooding, as are some of the hides in the 1,000-acre nature reserve run by the **Wildlife & Wetlands Trust (WWT)**. From the large heated observatory, thousands of swans and ducks can be observed, especially at feeding time in winter.

WWT WELNEY WETLAND CENTRE, Hundred Foot Bank, Welney, Norfolk PE14 9TN; ☎ 01353 860711; wwt.org.uk; adults £7.10, children £3.50, families £18.95, open daily 9.30am–5pm.

Whooper and Bewick swans gather on their annual epic journey between Siberia and Iceland. In November and December, swan feeds take place daily at 3.30pm and floodlit evening feeds take place at 6.30pm Thursday to Sundays. At other times of the year, different birds can be seen, the reserve can be explored and children can go pond-dipping. A new sustainably built visitor centre has opened with a cheerful café called after one of the most common ducks seen at Welney, the widgeon.

THE BRECKS

Some people might dismiss the Brecks as a huge boring chunk of South Norfolk crossing into Suffolk. It consists of heath without the cliff and, on a blustery day, wuthering without the heights. But there is an appeal to this unsung area that most people rush past on their way to the bright lights of Norwich and the more accessible charms of the Broads. At the very least, stopovers are called for at lovely Castle Acre with its atmospheric ruined Norman priory, the Georgian market town of Swaffham, the prehistoric flint mines at Grimes Graves and the recreational forest of Thetford.

The underlying layer of chalk topped by windblown sand in this, the driest part of Britain, creates the Brecks, a 370-square-mile area that harbours wildlife not found elsewhere in Britain. The term breck refers to fields of poor soil that at one time were planted for a short period before being abandoned and allowed to revert to heather and gorse-covered heath. But without sheep and rabbits to graze the heath, it's soon overtaken by scrubby trees and thorns. Both the Norfolk and Suffolk Wildlife Trusts work hard to conserve this unique habitat. The dry, well-drained sandy soil seldom turns to knee-deep mud, which is useful for walkers and cyclists.

The number of 'Warrens' still marked on the Ordnance Survey maps of the Brecks (Beachamwell, Thetford, Wangford, etc.) is an indication of how important the rabbit industry was. Warrens were established in the Middle Ages to breed rabbits for food and fur, and this became an important and lucrative industry for centuries. The title of Warrener was one of high honour and came with a tied house or lodge. A single warren could provide 40,000 rabbits in a year, and at the height of the industry there were 20 warrens covering a vast area. It was not until the 20th century that rabbits were deemed a nuisance, especially from the 1920s when foresters were trying to establish Thetford Forest, and the disease myxomatosis was introduced in the 1950s. The rabbit population has recovered, so it's still common to see fields alive with hopping creatures, helping to keep down invasive vegetation. This together with the unusually chalky soil has resulted in the survival of rare orchids, lichens, insects and birds. Because of its rare populations of stone curlew, woodlark and nightjar, the Brecks have EU status as a Special Protection Area.

The national trail the Peddars Way starts in the Brecks heading due north as the crow flies (or the Romans build) once used by pilgrims bound for Walsingham. Other walks follow leafy river banks like the Nar along the northern edge of Breckland and the Little Ouse whose source is adjacent to the source of the River Waveney near the county boundary at Redgrave. Cycling is also rewarding along empty country roads and off-road tracks, lined with gnarled ivy-wrapped pine trees and past sleepy villages with thatched churches.

WHAT TO SEE AND DO

 Fair weather

Castle Acre

With the exceptionally fine ruins of an 11th-century Cluniac priory, the remnants of a castle at the other end of the village, pleasant tea rooms, pub and riverside stroll, Castle Acre is a great place for cyclists, walkers or motorists to pause. The Priory, which is run by English Heritage, is a short distance west of the main village. The graceful interlocking arches of the well-preserved free-standing west front prove that the Cluniac order of France was keen on architectural decoration. The prior's lodge is also in good condition considering its great age. You can also get a good view of the site from the riverbank, and can approach quite close to see the ancient long-drop privies. Take the lane off to the left just before the Priory where there is room to park a couple of cars by the Fords on the River Nar, a good place for children and dogs to play, and giving access to a footpath across the meadow to the ruins and to possible picnicking spots. From this place you can set off on a lovely 6-mile round walk incorporating sections of the Peddars Way and the Nar Valley Way (www.countrysideaccess.norfolk.gov.uk/pdfs/walk-14.pdf).

The less dramatic ruins of the Castle built by the same Norman family, the Warennes, who built the priory, are also in the care of English Heritage, but are freely accessible during the day.

> **CASTLE ACRE PRIORY**,
> Castle Acre, PE32 2XD; ☎ 01760 755394; www.english-heritage.org.uk; adults £5.30, children £2.70, family £13.30; open year round, summer daily 10am–6pm; winter Thurs to Mon 10am–4pm.

Castle Acre Priory

Local legends: the Swaffham pedlar

According to a well-known 15th-century folk tale, a Swaffham man dreamed a strange dream – that if he went to far away London Bridge he would discover how to become rich. Expecting to meet a wealthy man, John Chapman travelled to London and stood on the bridge, but to no avail. He began to think he had been a complete fool. Falling into conversation with a shopkeeper who had noticed him loitering, he confessed to the man that he had been an idiot for acting on a dream. This man said that he understood exactly what he meant, since he had just had a strange dream himself and had no intention of following up on it. He told John that he had dreamed that he had dug for treasure in the garden of a man called John Chapman who lived in Swaffham. John made his excuses, hurried home and began digging. Under a tree in his garden he found not just one but two chests full of gold and treasure. To show his gratitude he donated money to the church so that the north aisle could be built and a new spire erected. In fact records show that there was a churchwarden called John Chapman in 1462. He is now immortalised on the town sign for Swaffham and also in the carved bench ends in the church.

Swaffham

Like other towns in Breckland, Swaffham has benefitted from recent investment by the district council and the EU Regional Development Fund. Visible for miles around, two massive wind turbines have been built next to Waitrose on the edge of town, part of the Ecotech Centre dedicated to green technology and sustainability (see *What to do with children*).

The18th-century pillared, domed Butter Cross which once served as a town bandstand was built at a time when Swaffham was a fashionable Georgian town. It occupies the triangular space in the middle of the town, where the thriving Saturday market takes place (see *Shopping*).

The church of St Peter and St Paul, concealed from the Market Place by old trees, is built on a grand scale. Its greatest glory is its angel roof comprising 88 angels, wings spread and all different. It is said that the Puritans left them intact because Oliver Cromwell's grandmother was associated with the church. The interior also has some quirks like the charming 19th-century carving on a bench end in the north aisle of the Swaffham Pedlar with his wife and dog.

West of Swaffham

Within easy cycling distance of Swaffham is Cockley Cley, where a pleasant village green makes a convenient rest stop, especially if you have bought provisions in Swaffham Market for a picnic. The signposted **Iceni Village** is best

Gooderstone Water Gardens

avoided – there is an entry fee of £5 for a feeble reconstruction of a pre-Roman tribal Celtic village. A big black barn with a few farm implements and a graveyard for farm machinery awaiting restoration hold little interest. Their historical accuracy is called into immediate question by the sign on the road pointing towards a 7th century church, since the oldest church structures in the country are usually taken to be 10th century. Only ticket holders to the Iceni Village are officially allowed to look at the church and the 17th-century cottage next door.

Gooderstone Water Gardens, 3–4 miles further were a labour of love of the retired farmer who owned the waterlogged meadow. Four ponds and connecting waterways are crossed by 13 bridges, and a nature trail passes interesting natural history labels. Visitors congregate in the bird hide, cameras poised for the rare appearance of a kingfisher. Chances are much higher of seeing water boatmen skimming across the ponds and (in the early autumn) mallards displaying to potential mates.

A short distance along the B road brings you to **Oxburgh Hall**, a gem of a Tudor moated house now run by the National Trust. It was built in 1482 for the Bedingfield family who still occupy part of it. The waters of the wide moat lap at the foundations and there are excellent views from the crenellated roof of the barley-twist chimneys, the French parterre garden and the surrounding countryside. The most unusual features are a display of hangings embroidered by Mary Queen of Scots and Bess of Hardwick and the windowless hidey-hole for a priest who would have been in danger once the Protestants had outlawed Catholicism. Visitors are permitted to climb into the tiny closet in a turret of the gatehouse and lower themselves into the priest's hole. After that claustrophobic experience, you might feel in need of walking in the woods on the estate to visit the Catholic

GOODERSTONE WATER GARDENS, The Street, Gooderstone, PE33 9BP; ☎ 01603 712913; www.gooderstonewatergardens.co.uk; adults £5.50, children £2; open daily year round 10am–5.30pm (or dusk if earlier).

OXBURGH HALL, Oxborough, PE33 9PS; ☎ 01366 328258; www.nationaltrust.org.uk; entry: if gift-aided adults £8.20, children £4.10; families £20.50; open Feb to Oct, 11am–4pm Feb and Oct, 11am–5pm Mar to Sep, open daily in Aug, closed Thu/Fri otherwise.

EUSTON HALL, Estate Office, Euston, Thetford, IP24 2QP; ☎ 01842 766366; www.euston-hall.co.uk; house and gardens, adults £7, children £3, garden admission only £3; limited opening times: Thurs only between mid-June and mid-Sept, and a few summer Sundays, 2.30pm–5pm.

chapel dominated by an Antwerp triptych.

Privately owned **Euston Hall** south of Thetford has an important collection of paintings, including some by Van Dyck and Stubbs. Due to neglect by former proprietors, fires and financial problems, the house has been messed about with over the centuries, but the landscaped pleasure grounds are superb.

Thetford Forest

Thetford Forest is the largest lowland forest in the UK and is crisscrossed with walking and cycling tracks. The forest contains four colour-coded cycle routes covering a total of 18 miles, from gentle green routes for beginners to black routes for daring and experienced off-road cyclists. Bicycles can be hired from the **High Lodge Forest Centre** (see listing below) in the centre of the forest (free if you arrive by bike or Brecks Bus – see below, £6 for the Forestry Commission car park). There are adventure playgrounds, and walking and riding

Thetford Forest

trails. To avoid the parking toll, you can start at **Brandon Country Park** which has an impressive variety of unusual trees, good possibilities for mushroom-hunting in autumn or baby toad and dragonfly spotting in spring in the lake in front of Brandon Park House, and a restored walled garden with a well and a snake maze.

Grime's Graves

The alliterative name of this interesting site refers neither to dirt nor to burial places. Grim was an alternative name for the god Woden and graves were simply holes. Neolithic peoples discovered flint in the layers of chalk east of Brandon which they used for tools like axe heads. As long as four millennia ago, they used tools made of antler bone to dig more than 400 shafts to get at the flint. These prehistoric mines have been filled in by mine spoils and, later, drifting soil leaving behind a strange ridged and cratered area on which you can sometimes find large boulders of soft white chalk. English Heritage keeps open one of these excavated shafts so that visitors can descend 30ft via two ladders.

GRIME'S GRAVES, Lynford, Near Thetford, IP26 5DE; ☎ 01842 810656; www.english-heritage.org.uk; adults £3.30, children £2, families £8; open Mar to Oct daily, 10am–5pm (10am–6pm Jul/Aug) Apr to Sep; closed Tues/Wed in Mar/Oct.

Elveden Hall

Many movies have been filmed at Elveden Hall. For example, the 2001 film *Lara Croft: Tomb Raider* starring Angelina Jolie and Daniel Craig used the hall as the home of Lady Croft, and scenes from the James Bond film *Living Daylights* were also shot at the Georgian house. The TV production of *Gulliver's Travels* with Ted Danson and Mary Steenburgen used the place, as does the 2008 film *Dean Spanley* with a star cast that includes Peter O'Toole and Jeremy Northam. In Stanley Kubrick's *Eyes Wide Shut*, Tom Cruise's character gate-crashes a party filmed in the unusual Indian Hall at Elveden.

The reason for this architectural style in the middle of rural East Anglia is that Elveden Hall was owned by the Maharajah Duleep Singh in the 19th century. When the Maharajah of Lahore arrived in England in 1854 aged 16, he was taken up by Queen Victoria and eventually given the lease of the Elveden Estate where he turned himself into a high-living country squire. In the 1860s his home improvements included domes and marble decorations in an Indian style. Unfortunately the house is not open to the public, though you can see the Maharajah's simple grave in **Elveden Church** (a pilgrimage site for some Sikhs) and can visit the estate shops (see *Staying In*).

 ## Wet weather

Swaffham and Thetford both have interesting local museums, you can learn about the evidence (scant) for believing that Queen Boudicca is buried under platform nine of King's Cross Station, see the collection of treasures all found by one dedicated metal detector (Monique Slaven) over two decades from tiny medieval brooches to prehistoric tools made of flint from mines like Grime's Graves. Work is in progress on a new exhibition room dedicated to the Epyptologist Howard Carter who lived at Swaffham and discovered Tutankhamun's tomb in 1923.

The town of Thetford has long been associated with deprivation, so it's a surprise to find the smartly renovated museum occupying a fine timbered merchant's house. **The Ancient House Museum** serves as the main museum of Breckland life with fascinating displays about its role as rabbit capital of the country, its famous son Thomas Paine, author of *The Rights of Man* (published two years after the French Revolution and pre-cursor of the Declaration of Human Rights) and a less well-known character, Maharajah Duleep Singh.

SWAFFHAM MUSEUM, Town Hall, London Street, Swaffham, PE37 7DQ; ☎ 01760 721230; www.swaffhammuseum.co.uk; adults £2.50, children £1, family £6; open Feb to Dec, Tues to Sat 10am–4pm.

ANCIENT HOUSE MUSEUM, White Hart Street, Thetford, IP24 1AA; ☎ 01842 752599; £3.10, children £1.60; free Nov to mid-Mar; open Mon to Sat year round, 10am–4pm/5pm.

What to do with children ...

Go Ape

In Thetford, the **Go Ape** high ropes course is popular with adults and children who enjoy whizzing from treetop to treetop. Wearing safety harnesses, participants climb to dizzying heights and then scramble over rope bridges and down zip slides. Most people take about three hours to complete the course.

> **GO APE** Thetford, High Lodge Forest Visitor Centre, Near Brandon, Suffolk; ☎ 0870 458 9187 or 0870 444 5562; http://goape.co.uk; over-18s £25, under 18s £20. Minimum age 10, minimum height 4 ft 7 in; under 18s must be accompanied by an adult; advance booking required.

Banham Zoo

As it approaches its 40th year in business, **Banham Zoo**, north of the A1066 between Thetford and Diss, has just been crowned the 'Best Norfolk Attraction'. Its emphasis on breeding and conservation and its open-plan design means that its extensive collection of animals is well cared for from armadillos to zebras with lots of primates in between. A ride on the Safari Train allows you to get your bearings before wandering between the enclosures, the newest of which includes an elevated walkway through a giraffe house.

> **BANHAM ZOO**, The Grove, Banham, NR16 2HE; ☎ 01953 887771; www.banhamzoo.co.uk; depending on season adults £10.95–£14.95, children £7.95–£10.95; open all year round 9.30am–6pm in summer, 5pm in spring and 4pm in winter.

Ecotech Centre, Swaffham

For a fee, it's possible to climb the 300 steps inside one of the two wind turbines just near Swaffham at the Ecotech Centre (Turbine Way, Swaffham, PE37 7HT; ☎ 01760 726100; www.ecotech.org.uk/tourism. html) to a viewing platform. Entry is adults £5, children £3, family £15 and pre-booking is recommended. It's open weekdays 10am–4pm year round

Ecotech Centre, Swaffham

plus the last Sunday of May, June, July and August. Turbine tours run (weather permitting) at 11am, 1pm and 3pm plus extras if numbers require.

Activities

The **Breckland Leisure Centre and Waterworld** (Croxton Road, Thetford, IP24 1JD; ☎ 01842 753110; www.leisure-centre.com/centredetailsbrand.php ?ID=58) in Thetford with a flume and water cannon is a good standby if the weather turns nasty. If you have young children, hang on to them tightly near the rapids.

Anyone with a horse-mad child should consider Breckland as a riding destination with its miles of conifer-edged bridleways and off-road forest hacking. Some farms even permit you to stay on holiday with your horse, such as **Little Lodge Farm** (www.littlelodgefarm.co.uk), a working farm on the Little Ouse River that offers self-catering accommodation by the weekend or week. The **Brecks Countryside Project** encourages riding. Ancient droveways across Breckland follow pre-historic routes between pasture and market. For example a 10-mile ride along the Harling Drove can be enjoyed between East Harling and Weeting (www.visitnorfolk.co.uk/norfolk/horseriding.htm). At **Hall Farm** in Snetterton, the International League for the Protection of Horses houses up to 150 horses, and is open to the public on Wednesdays and weekends from 11am to 4pm (☎ 01953 498682; www.ilph.org) with a visitor centre and special events.

... and how to avoid children

The Peddars Way starts at Knettishall Heath Country Park and takes over from the Icknield Way coming in from Euston in the west, and the Angles Way from the east. The Nar Valley Way is a lovely 34-mile walk running from King's Lynn to Gressenhall mainly along the banks of the River Nar, though notoriously poorly signposted so not always easy to follow.

The Brecks have a number of breweries (see *Drinking*), some offering tours. Try the Car-Free Itinerary called 'Biking and Breweries' distributed by the Brecks Tourism Partnership or available online (www.brecks.org/ shared/pdfs/ Biking-and-Brewing.pdf).

Entertainment

Theatre and cinema

This lightly populated mainly rural part of the country can't offer much in the way of cultural entertainment, though the bright lights of Norwich are about 45 minutes by car from Thetford and the theatre in Bury St Edmunds less than half an hour. On the first Friday of the month, the enterprising Ecotech Centre in Swaffham puts on films (www.ecotech. org.uk/icenima.html).

The Westacre River Studios and Summer Theatre is an unexpected cultural centre in the countryside, with Stephen Fry as its patron. At a time when provincial theatre is under threat, it's

WESTACRE RIVER STUDIOS AND SUMMER THEATRE, River Road, West Acre, PE32 1UD; ☎ 01760 755800; www.west acreriverstudios.co.uk; ticket prices from £6 to £15.

The best... **PLACES TO STAY**

BOUTIQUE HOTEL

Strattons Hotel

Ash Close, Swaffham PE37 7NH
☎ **01760 723845**
www.strattons-hotel.co.uk

Unfazed by its popularity among celebrities, this hotel and restaurant remains loyal to its impressive green credentials. Fiercely original in its contemporary styling and exotic themed rooms, the hotel occupies a gracious Palladian building. Last year the hotel was short-listed for an award as the greenest place to stay in the UK.

Prices: £150 for a double to £225 for a suite with private garden; children £15

INN

The Ostrich Inn

Stocks Green, Castle Acre PE32 2AE
☎ **01760 755398**
www.the-ostrich-inn.co.uk

An appealing old coaching inn overlooking the village green of charming Castle Acre has two twin rooms, a double and a family room. The welcoming pub downstairs serves as the village local with live music, bingo and an unpretentious menu featuring a good selection of vegetarian food.

Prices: B&B from £65 for a double.

B&B/FARM

Colveston Manor

Mundford, near Thetford IP26 5HU
☎ **01842 878218**
www.colveston-manor.co.uk

This remote 18th-century farmhouse and working farm alongside the River Wissey offers guests complete peace and quiet and access to extensive gardens. Breakfasts are cooked on an Aga, and Norfolk farm dinners can be requested as well, using produce from the kitchen garden when possible. Children must be over 12.

Prices: From £27.50 to £32.50 per person.

Holly House

Snetterton South End, Snetterton NR16 2LG. ☎ **01953 498051**
www.hollyhouse-guesthouse.co.uk

Part of the exclusive Wolsey Lodges group, this thatched beamed country B&B is owned and run by a former restaurant chef, so the standard of gourmet breakfast and dinner is exceptional. Holly House recently won a 'Tourism in Norfolk award' for Best Guest House. Children must be over 12 to stay and you can bring your own wine.

Prices: £50 for single; £35 to £45 per person in a twin or double; including Norfolk breakfast and afternoon tea on arrival.

CAMPING

Dower House

Thetford Forest, East Harling NR16 2SE.
☎ **01953 717314**
www.dowerhouse.co.uk

Open from mid-March to the end of September, this secluded 20 acre site offers large roomy pitches for tents and caravans and extensive holiday facilities including an on-site pub and a heated pool. It has repeatedly won a David Bellamy Conservation Award. Because it tries to minimise light pollution, campers should bring torches.

Prices: from £11.50 to £23.25 per pitch.

SELF-CATERING

Old School Cottage

c/o Beechwood House, Wretham Road, Great Hockham, Thetford IP24 1NY
☎ **01953 498277, www.4starcottage.co.uk**

This brick and flint period cottage, characteristic of Breckland, features a private cottage garden and open fireplace, with a basket of logs provided free of charge. The pretty village of Great Hockham is only a mile from the Peddars Way and equally close to the Pingo Trail, a circular 8 mile walk past shallow water-filled craters left over from the ice age called pingos (from an Eskimo word).

Prices: £275–£475 per week.

extraordinary that a new 150-seater all-weather theatre marquee has opened with a four-month programme of tragedy, comedy and musicals. Jazz picnics are held out of doors in the lovely setting of the priory gardens.

Shopping

The market towns of Swaffham, Dereham, Thetford, Watton and Attleborough, are all worth a browse, especially on market day. Swaffham in particular has a thriving Saturday market that has continued since the Middle Ages and which includes an historic open-air auction. Bargain hunters will want to show up for the auction at the Town Pit Car Park on Pit Lane, but if you miss it the ordinary weekly market in the market place hosts an appealing range of food, flower, clothing and bric-a-brac stalls.

One of the biggest markets in Breckland is the Sunday market next to the Snetterton Racetrack near the A11. The market has one of the biggest model shops in the world together with a model car racetrack.

The best... FOOD AND DRINK

Staying in

Because of the historic rural nature of the Brecks, it has embraced the mantra of local produce with enthusiasm, and a number of farmers' markets are held: in Swaffham on the first Wednesday, Watton the first Saturday, Diss the second Saturday, Thetford the fourth Friday and North Lopham the fourth Saturday of every month. But plenty of local meat, fruit and vegetables, as well as Norfolk cheeses and food products are sold at normal weekly markets.

Up-market food shop (Elvedon Estate Fine Food Shop & Café Restaurant, Elveden, near Thetford IP24 3TJ ☎ 01842 898068; www.elveden.com) can be visited at **Elveden Hall** mentioned above, among a range of shops selling plants, cookery equipment, gifts. It stocks fruit and vegetables grown on the estate, and also has butchery, bakery and deli counters. Its own-label honey, chutneys, cakes and even wines can be purchased.

The **Mid-Norfolk Smokehouse** (Meadow Cottage, Cranworth IP25 7SH; ☎ 01362 820702; www.midnorfolksmokehouse.co.uk) between Dereham and Watton is another favourite place for foodies to head. Its smoked prawns, fish pâtés (£1.50 per pot) and fishcakes (costing only 60 pence) are particularly tempting, plus a full range of fish in season.

EATING OUT

FINE DINING
Brovey Lair
Carbrooke Road, Ovington IP25 6SD
☎ **01953 882706**
www.broveylair.com

This unusual restaurant near Watton calls itself a café but serves Michelin-standard food in a house party atmosphere. Guests are served a four-course menu (£47.50) that usually revolves around fish and spices, as chosen by the well-travelled chef.

RESTAURANT
Elveden Café Restaurant
Elveden, Thetford IP24 3TQ
☎ **01842 898068**
www.elveden.com/Cafe-Restaurant.php

Daytime menu indicates which dishes use ingredients from the 22,000 acre Elveden estate, such as roasted tomato and basil soup (£4.50) and which ones are local to East Anglia, such as warm pear and almond tart with homemade ice cream (£5). Tables are set out in the courtyard garden, and the house wine is available at the shop price of £7.

GASTROPUB
Chequers Inn
Griston Road, Thompson IP24 1PX
☎ **01953 483360**
www.thompsonchequers.co.uk

This thatched dining pub offers an extensive menu of pub classics like Stilton plough-man's, beef stroganoff and treacle sponge pudding. Main courses cost from £8 (lasagne) to £17 (fillet steak Rossini). The pub also offers accommodation.

CAFÉ
Willow Cottage Tearoom
Stocks Green, Castle Acre PE32 2AE
☎ **01760 755551**
www.broadland.com/willowcottage.html

In an idyllic village situation, this traditional tearoom serves cream teas, tea breads and light lunches. In good weather, outdoor tables overlook the village green. Closed Mondays.

 ## Drinking

Breweries

Several artisan breweries flourish in Breckland including the **Iceni Brewery** in Mundford just off the main Brandon-Swaffham road (www.icenibrewery.co.uk) which has a brewery shop, and a hop garden and offers pre-arranged guided tours (☎ 01842 878922). The people in charge love naming beers because Iceni has brewed 216 different ones since it opened in 1995, though now brew six regulars including Celtic Queen and Fine Soft Day (not to be confused with It's a Grand Day, which is stronger).

The daughter of Iceni's brewster set up a satellite brewery at the Elveden Estate in her gap year (www.icenibrewery.co.uk/elveden.asp) and now the Elveden Brewery brews an ale and stout which are both fairly potent. The Brandon Brewing Company occupies an 18th-century pink-washed cottage on the River Little Ouse. The shop is open six days a week selling intriguing bottled beers such as Rusty Bucket and Molly's Secret.

Pubs

In this forgotten corner of the country, there have been fewer pub take-overs and make-overs than in many other parts of the country, so most village pubs remain welcoming to visitors and unpretentious. One favourite is **The Olde Windmill Inn** in Great Cressingham between Swaffham and Watton (www. oldewindmillinn.co.uk). This old-world pub with many nooks and crannies serves a changing selection of real ales and honest food. It also has a small campsite in its garden. Another friendly pub is **The Stag** in West Acre, which serves good value meals, such as a bacon and mushroom baguette for £4.25 and well-kept ales.

In the forgotten-feeling village of Beachamwell just west of Swaffham, **The Great Danes Country Inn** serves Woodfordes Wherry and decent food in a cosy ambience. It overlooks a spacious village green on the other side of which is a picturesque church with a Saxon round tower and roofed with thatch in which noisy pigeons roost. If you can gain access, look for the graffiti of a demon on one of the columns.

Local knowledge

Ben Platts-Mills is an artist with a chain-saw, and specialises in creating sculptures from felled or damaged trees. His work can be seen around the region from the High Lodge visitor centre in Thetford Forest to the approach road to Sudbury where a carved tree sculpture depicts the history of the town's historic silk trade (www.treesculpture.co.uk). He lives in a home-made bender (wigwam) in a field called 'Heaven' in the Brecks.

Favourite walk: The Little Ouse Headwaters Project on the Suffolk/Norfolk border offers marvellous variety with four different wetland habitats. The project has been returning neglected land and farms to fenland.

Favourite shop: The Tool Shop on the High Street in Needham Market is run by a tool virtuoso, Tony Murland (tony@antiquetools.co.uk). I always love to browse through his selection of used tools from all over the world.

Favourite eatery: Every full moon we have a pizza party here at Heaven. I make a dough with spelt flour and everyone brings toppings. The pizzas are cooked in Lucio's wood-fired oven made of broken bricks, clay and earth using string and nails as measure.

Best view: A spot near Aylsham in Norfolk where for many years I have been involved with bender-building camps. I love wandering through the field at dusk to the Bure valley, after people of all ages and backgrounds have constructed their accommodation for the night from hazel branches and canvas.

Best local produce: I go to the organic Village Farm in Market Weston for their untreated whole milk made from their herd of Jersey cows.

Favourite event: Weird and Wonderful Wood is a wonderful two-day festival held on the third weekend of May every year in beautiful Haughley Park near Stowmarket (☎ 01359 240724). The festival celebrates everything to do with wood, and visitors can have a go at various activities like pole-lathe turning.

Visitor information

Tourist Information Centres:
The Shambles, Market Place,
Swaffham PE37 7AB, ☎ 01760
722255, www.aroundswaffham.co.uk
open Apr to Oct; 4 White Hart
Street, Thetford, IP24 1AD, ☎ 01842
820689, www.explorethetford.co.uk;
Brandon Country Park, Bury Road,
Brandon IP27 0SU, ☎ 01842
814955, www.forest-heath.gov.uk;
Visitor Centre, Wayland House,
Watton, IP25 6AB, ☎ 01953 880212,
www.wayland-tourism.org.uk, open
Easter to Oct.

Hospitals: 24-hour facilities available at Norfolk & Norwich University
Hospital A&E Department, Level 2,
East Block, Colney Lane NR4 7UY,
☎ 01603 287325, www.nnuh.nhs.uk,
4 miles south-west of the city centre,
near the University of East Anglia,
off the A47.

Websites: www.brecks.org –
The Brecks Partnership, Thetford
(☎ 01842 760116) website has a
marvellous range of leaflets suggesting car free itineraries on
themes such as brewing and with
cycling, walking and riding routes.
Some are downloadable here or
from the East of England Tourism
site, for example a detailed description of a 20 mile cycle route from
Swaffham (www.eetb.org.uk/doclib
/No.14%20The%20Brecks.pdf).

Supermarkets: Waitrose, Castle
Acre Road, Swaffham, PE37 7HT,
☎ 01760 336307, open until 8pm
(9pm Fri); Sainsbury's, London
Road, Thetford IP24 3QL, ☎ 01842
754580; Tesco, Kilverstone Road,
Thetford IP24 2RL, ☎ 0845 6779681,
open 24 hours in the week.

Transport: Brecks Bus ☎ 01842
816170 or Dial-a-Ride on ☎ 01638
608080 (www.brecks.org/travel-
details.aspx). Pre-bookable service
that operates around the region on
week days between 9am and 4pm,
for example from Brandon or
Thetford rail/bus stations to Thetford Forest High Lodge or to
Lakenheath Fen bird reserve.

Bike rental: Bike Art, High Lodge
Forest Centre, Thetford Forest IP27
0AF, ☎ 01842 810090; www.bike
art.com, daily hire charge £16 for
adults, £14 for children.

Taxis: A1 Cars, Thetford, ☎ 01842
755555; Home James, Watton,
☎ 01953 885966; Carters Brandon
Cars, Brandon, ☎ 01842 811430;
Cool Cabs, Swaffham,
☎ 01760 724988

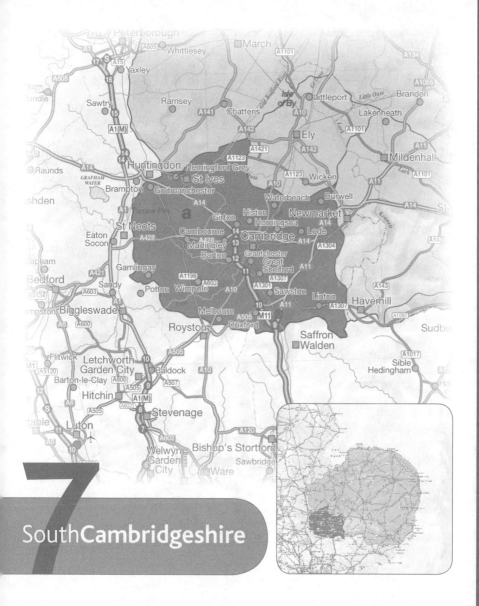

7

South**Cambridgeshire**

a. Cambridge and around

Unmissable highlights

01 Attend Evensong in King's College Chapel, p.307

02 Punt past the college Backs, p.306

03 Stroll to Grantchester for a pub lunch, p.309

04 Visit the hidden corners of colleges with free entry such as Clare, Christ's and Emmanuel, p.308

05 Admire the repair job done on the smashed Chinese vases at the Fitzwilliam Museum, p.310

06 Raise your glass in the Eagle pub where Crick and Watson first announced their discovery of DNA, p.320

07 Swim the 100-yard length of Jesus Green outdoor pool, a classic city lido, p.313

08 Admire the profusion of snowdrops – all 15 varieties – that carpet the grassy banks at Anglesey Abbey in January/February, p.323

09 Hire a bicycle and mingle with the thousands of students and residents to discover colleges, museums and attractions a little outside the city centre, p.322

10 See an eighth-century edition of St Paul's Epistles and the original manuscript of AA Milne's *Winnie the Pooh* on display in the magnificent Wren Library at Trinity College, p.308

SOUTH CAMBRIDGESHIRE

Not only does Cambridge top the list of must-see places in the East of England, the ancient university city is a world-class attraction that last year was included on a list of the 10 most unmissable sights worldwide, alongside the Eiffel Tower, Sydney Harbour Bridge and Shakespeares Globe. A lot of expectations ride on such a rating, but even on a rainy day, the architecture and green spaces, restaurants and shops of Cambridge never fail to reward. Too many people come on day trips and see nothing more than a couple of the greatest hits. A longer stay allows a glimpse of the subtleties of a spirited city that is much more than a theme park of ancient learning.

Predictably the city completely dominates the county of which it's the capital. Visitors with enough time to make day trips usually head to Ely or Bury St Edmunds (see separate chapters). But less well-known places of interest are concealed in the undulating countryside of South Cambridgeshire, from the sham ruined castle in the extensive grounds of Wimpole Hall to the bird-rich nature reserve at Paxton Pits alongside the River Great Ouse.

CAMBRIDGE AND AROUND

Cambridge is a place of parks, poetry and punts. While wandering among the streets, colleges and river paths of Cambridge the imagination easily conjures its famous alumni: Rupert Brooke and Virginia Woolf skinny dipping by moonlight at Byron's Pool; Sylvia Plath reciting Chaucer to the cows on nearby Grantchester Meadow, and Lord Byron keeping a bear on his staircase in his college Trinity. Despite the throngs of shoppers and the exasperating traffic, Cambridge retains its atmosphere of ancient learning, of withdrawal from the outside world. College gateways lead to a world of tranquil paved courtyards, velvety lawns and spectacular buildings designed by architects such as Wren and Gibbs.

All around central Cambridge, you can see magnificent buildings, equivalent to a dozen stately homes. It is often assumed that the university founded the city, but it was the other way round. The city of merchants was given its charter in 1201 and the first college, Peterhouse, was not founded until 1284 by the Bishop of Ely. Apparently it was a toss-up between Cambridge and Northampton (in which case an Oxbridge education would have been an Oxhampton education). Over the following centuries, more colleges were established and, cuckoo-like, the university colonised the town. At the other end of the historical spectrum, Robinson is the newest college founded in 1981 by a self-made millionaire who was born above his father's bike shop in Cambridge and who went on to make a fortune from Granada TV Rentals.

WHAT TO SEE AND DO

 Fair weather

The **River Cam** arcs around the north and west of the city centre with a series of lively and attractive green spaces inside its protective curve. Fingers of green nearly surround the city centre and also extend in all directions, from manicured gardens to commons on which cattle graze. It is incredible to be gingerly stepping over cowpats on Laundress Green and still be a 5-minute walk from Marks and Spencer. Similarly, once you are inside the hallowed gates of Trinity, St John's, Clare and King's Colleges, you forget that you are only a few minutes walk from the mobbed shopping thoroughfare of Sidney Street and St Andrew's Street.

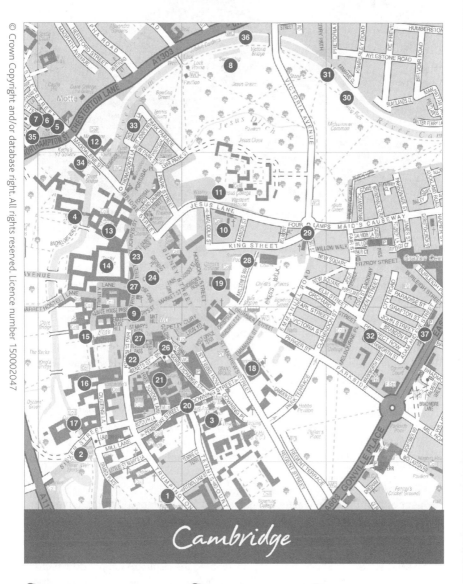

Cambridge

1. Fitzwilliam Museum
2. Mathematical Bridge
3. Museum of Archaeology & Anthropology
4. Bridge of Sighs
5. Folk Museum
6. Kettle's Yard
7. St Peter's Church
8. Jesus Green Swimming Pool
9. Great St Mary's
10. All Saints Church
11. Jesus College
12. Magdalene College
13. St John's College
14. Trinity College
15. Clare College
16. King's College
17. Queens' College
18. Emmanuel College
19. Christ's College
20. Museum of Zoology
21. St Bene't's Church
22. Eagle
23. Michaelhouse
24. Gardenia
25. Depot
26. First Class Teas
27. Indigo Coffee House
28. Clown's Café
29. St Radegund
30. Midsummer House
31. Fort St George
32. Free Press
33. River Bar + Kitchen
34. Thanh Binh
35. The Punter
36. Restaurant 22
37. Cotto's

The River Cam

It is the river and its bridges which make the back gardens (hence **The Backs**) of the famous old colleges so lovely. Punt guides will often tell gullible tourists that the wooden Mathematical Bridge at Queen's College was built without the use of nails, failing to mention that it was held together by iron pins at the joints, and later nuts and bolts. And apparently the Bridge of Sighs connecting two parts of St John's College is so-named not only because it's enclosed like its counterpart in Venice but because students en route to examinations can audibly be heard sighing.

Cycling is a way of life. Bicycles can be readily hired (see *Visitors Info*). If you feel a little nervous about weaving in amongst the Cambridge traffic, you can ride along the towpath beside the Cam (from Jesus Green footbridge away from town) or along the 3-mile cycleway to Grantchester.

Viewpoints

Just north of the river, **Castle Hill** is the best free vantage point for surveying the town. Having provided the city with impressive fortifications as recently as the Civil War, it's now not much more than a grassy knoll. For £2.50 you can climb the 123 steps inside the tower of **Great St Mary's**, the University Church off Market Square. It was originally designated the centre of Cambridge: technically undergraduates are still obliged to live within 3 miles of the church for at least 59 days of Michaelmas (autumn term), the same for Lent (Jan to Mar) and 52 days in the Easter term (Apr to June). Although a glorious view of rooftops and landmarks such as the thousand-year-old Saxon tower of **St Benet's Church** (the oldest building in Cambridge) can be had from the tower, you can't see the river (9am–4.30pm daily).

Green spaces

Jesus Green is an appealing destination for a gentle stroll under the vaulting canopy of plane trees, or for something a little more boisterous like a game of tennis or frisbee. Prior to 1496 the land occupied by Jesus Green was the site of the Nunnery of St Radegund founded in 1133, a name that survives in the excellent intimate pub called **The St Radegund Arms** nearby at 129 King Street.

From **Midsummer Common** it's a diverting 30-minute ramble along the towpath past the college boathouses to the riverside hostelries of Chesterton. You will pass picturesque houseboats with rooftop herb gardens, a derelict lifeboat and young couples on benches gazing into each other's eyes, before coming to **Stourbridge Common**. From 1211 this was the venue for what at its height was one of the biggest trading and entertainment fairs in Europe, with puppet shows, rope dancers and wrestling matches, said possibly to have inspired John Bunyan's Vanity Fair. Walking away from the river across Stourbridge Common, you come to the charming ancient **Leper's Chapel**, just a stone's throw from the busy Newmarket Road, lined with multiple superstores like Comet and B&Q.

A tranquil hour or two should be spent in the Cambridge University **Botanic Garden** which incorporates fragrant borders, mature trees and a duck-enhanced water garden. The glasshouses contain a wealth of exotica, including the spec-

> **CAMBRIDGE UNIVERSITY BOTANIC GARDEN**, £4; under-16s free; open 10am–6pm Apr to Sep, 10am–5pm Feb, Mar and Oct, 10am–4pm Jan, Nov and Dec.

tacular jade vine, whose bright turquoise flowers are designed to attract bats to carry out pollination and there is a pleasant café serving Fairtrade tea and coffee.

The famous philosopher Ludwig Wittgenstein is buried in the overgrown **Ascension Burial Ground** off Huntingdon Road, though it's tricky to locate his grave even using the map provided on the chapel wall. He died in the home of his doctor at neighbouring 76 Storey's Way.

Colleges

The glorious late Gothic towers of **King's College Chapel** create the iconic image of Cambridge. The college founder Henry VI compulsorily purchased riverfront land and the main street was blocked; in fact a fifth of Cambridge was demolished to build the college. At the time the cathedral-sized chapel was built, there were

> **KING'S COLLEGE CHAPEL**, Adults £6, children £4.50 but free to attend services such as Evensong (5.30pm most days in term-time); Recorded information on times of services; ☎ 01223 3311 55 or visit www.kings.cam.ac.uk/ chapel/services/index.html.

only seven students in the college. Henry VI wanted to keep the decoration simple to glorify God, but by the time it was finished under Henry VIII, the king's taste ran to lots of royalist symbolism such as Tudor Roses, which can be seen on the screen.

Trinity College is another superb college that owes much of its wealth to the Tudor monarch who founded it. Its Great Court is the largest of all

Oxbridge colleges and is the site of the annual Chariots of Fire run (on which the film was based) in which undergraduate runners try to get round the 367m circumference of the court in the 43 seconds that it takes to strike 12 o'clock. One of the glories of the college is the Wren Library fronting the river. There is a delicious incongruity in seeing laptops left on tables in ancient carrels adorned with intricate carvings by Grinling Gibbons. But it's the priceless collection of manuscripts that impresses, mostly of old boys of the college – notes made in the crabbed script of Sir Isaac Newton, a poem by Wordsworth, and A A Milne's *Winnie the Pooh*.

Great Gate, Trinity College from inside Great Court

Colleges charging no admission include **Trinity Hall** and **Clare College,** both with its lovely gardens overlooking the river, **Magdalene** with the Pepys Library occupying an impressive 17th-century building (open 2.30–3.30pm in term time), **Emmanuel** opposite the brand new John Lewis store in town, with a Wren

> **WREN LIBRARY**, included in the £2.20 admission charge to the college; open to the public in term time, weekdays 12–2pm, Sat 10.30am–12.30pm.

Chapel, and **Jesus College** a little off the beaten track with carved Gothic arches in the cloister. One of the best college gardens is the Fellows' Garden at **Christ's** where the legendary Milton's Mulberry can be seen (open weekdays 2–4pm in term time, 9.30am–noon in vacations), though the story that Milton composed poetry under it is probably apocryphal.

Kettle's Yard

Just a few steps up Castle Hill brings you to a Cambridge treasure. Kettle's Yard was the home of Jim Ede, a curator at the Tate, whose life's project was

> **KETTLE'S YARD**, Castle Street, Cambridge CB3 0AQ; ☎ 01223 352124; www.kettlesyard.co.uk; free; house open Tues to Sun afternoons only; the gallery is open Tues to Sun 11.30am–5pm.

to create an artistic home environment out of several workers' cottages knocked together. The muted colours and exquisite arrangements of 20th-century furniture, paintings and *objets trouvés* achieve its founder's aim superbly well as a haven of harmony (open 1.30–4.30pm, free admission after pulling the bell cord). Jim Ede's simple memorial tablet (1895–1990) can be seen in the picturesque redundant church of **St. Peter's** next door. Note the unusual 11th-century font adorned with four mermen with bifurcated tails. Confusingly Kettle's Yard also refers to a cutting-edge modern art gallery in an adjacent building.

Punting

Punting on the River Cam

Punting goes on throughout the year with or without chauffeurs. The cost of hiring one of these flat-bottomed craft which were so useful on the pre-drained fens for catching eels and cutting reeds is £14–£16 for one hour, £10 per hour for two or more hours provided you are prepared to punt yourself. Scudamore's (www.scudamores. com) owns a fleet of 150 pleasure punts operating out of four punt stations along the River Cam. A slightly lower hourly rate of £12 is charged at the Trinity College punt station.

You can also hire a rowboat or Canadian canoe at the Mill Pond. The Granta Punt & Boat Company (☎ 01223 301845; www.puntingincambridge.com) charges £14 an hour for up to four people. Chauffeur punters (who can make touting Venetian gondoliers seem bashful) will make themselves known as you pass Magdalene Bridge and Silver Street.

Wall outside King's College

Grantchester

Cycle, walk or punt through the meadows to Grantchester – or if necessary just drive the four miles – to have morning coffee or afternoon tea and sustenance at the venerable **Orchard Tea Gardens** (☎ 01223 845788) where the deckchairs in the vast and lovely garden have seated many Cambridge luminaries over the 100 years since the place opened to the public. This quintessentially English retreat has associations with the poet Rupert Brooke whose famous lines about Grantchester were written when he was in Berlin and feeling nostalgic: 'Stands the church clock at ten-to-three/ And is there honey still for tea?'

The owner of the Old Vicarage where Rupert lodged after he left Orchard House kept bees and provided fresh honey to the tea garden.

Grantchester has no fewer than four pubs, most close to the river but none with river views. The popular **Red Lion** (big garden, good for families, not much atmosphere indoors), **Rupert Brooke** (more up-market food) and **The Green Man** are often mobbed by day trippers on a warm summer's day. The Blue Ball Inn further from the river is a no-nonsense but historic pub preferred by locals.

 ## Wet weather

Fitzwilliam Museum

The Fitzwilliam is one of the nation's great (under-rated) museums with a marvellously varied collection: drawers full of detailed Roman minia-tures and Korean ceramics as well as Old Masters. You can admire the handiwork of the conservator who pieced together the precious Chinese vases smashed by a clumsy visitor in

> **FITZWILLIAM MUSEUM,** Trumpington Street, Cambridge CB2 1RB; ☎ 01223 332900; www.fitzmuseum.cam.ac.uk; entry: free; open Tues to Sat 10am–5pm, Sun 12am–5pm.

2006 (now safely behind glass). After a major facelift a couple of years ago, the museum now has a very pleasing café and shop.

Cambridge and County Folk Museum

The Folk Museum at the bottom of Castle Street has also benefitted from a major recent redevel-opment. Once an inn, its higgledy-piggledy rooms contain thousands of fascinating local artefacts like a trap for bedbugs. Newly installed panels tell entertaining stories of the university

> **FOLK MUSEUM,** 2–3 Castle Street, Cambridge CB3 0AQ; ☎ 01223 355159; www.folkmu seum.org.uk; adults £3.50. children £1 or free with adult; open daily 10.30–5pm, Sun 2–5pm.

and city's colourful and sometimes venal past that make you glad that today's academics are on the whole a committed hard-working bunch.

Fitzwilliam Museum

Cambridge and County Folk Museum

Local knowledge

Felix Turner is a 19-year-old student and punt chauffeur who has lived in Cambridge all his life.

Favourite restaurant: Dojos Noodle Bar on King Street serves big bowls of tasty noodles, with a good choice for vegetarians like me.

Secret tip for lunch: On a sunny day order a big bowl of salted edamame beans for £4.20 at the Japanese restaurant Teri-aki, and share them with a friend at an outdoor table overlooking Quayside.

Favourite takeaway: The 'Trailer of Life' in the Market Square is thronged with late-night clubbers buying kebabs up until 3am.

Favourite café: I like the friendly studenty atmosphere and the home-cooked food at Clowns on King Street.

Favourite pub: The Rathmore Club has pool tables, darts, a juke box and because it's Irish it's a great place to go whenever there is an Irish football match or on St. Patrick's Day.

Best off-licence: Cambridge Wines on King's Parade (I have to say that because my father runs it).

Favourite activity: Having a kick around on Jesus Green on a Sunday afternoon.

Best kept secret: The historical commentary offered by punt chauffeurs should not always be trusted.

Favourite view: It has to be the view you get from a punt of the grand symmetrical New Court of St John's College.

Favourite walk: Since I'm usually on a bike or a punt, I don't walk much, but sometimes it's fun to walk up Castle Hill for a late-night view of the city.

Quirkiest shop: Talking-T's (owned by the daughter of Cambridge's former MP) does witty T-shirts and will print your own slogans including on belts – lots of scope for gifts.

Best thing about living here: I am planning to do Spanish at university and I often bump into Spanish speakers (and not just tourists I take out on the river).

Favourite hangout: Chilling late at night on the low wall outside King's College which we call 'Foreigners' Wall', a great place for people-watching.

Specialist Museums

Because of the university, Cambridge has more specialist museums than probably anywhere else of similar size, from the Whipple Museum of the History of Science to the University Library which mounts small but perfectly formed exhibitions. These are all free, but tend to have opening hours limited to afternoons on weekdays.

The **Scott Polar Museum** traces courageous and foolhardy expeditions to the Arctic and Antarctic. Particularly impressive is the section relating to Sir Ernest Shackleton's vessel the *Endurance* which became trapped in Antarctic ice – forcing him to make an 800 mile journey in an open boat to seek rescue for his crew, all of whom survived.

> **SCOTT POLAR RESEARCH INSTITUTE**, Lensfield Road, Cambridge CB2 1ER; ☎ 01223 336540,www.spri.cam.ac.uk/museum; free; open Tues to Fri 11am–1pm/2–4pm, Sun 12–4pm.

The **Archaeology and Anthropology Museum** on Downing Street (http://museum.archanth.cam.ac.uk) has an astonishing collection from prehistoric weapons to a Solomon Islanders' canoe. The cast gallery of the **Museum of Classical Archaeology** (☎ 01223 335153, www.classics. cam.ac.uk/ark.html) has a colossal Herakles and an alarming Gorgon among many beautiful plaster casts of Greek and Roman statues.

Less well-known points of interest in the university include **New Hall**, one of the two remaining single sex women's colleges, which has one of the largest collections of women's art in the world (after Washington and Berlin). You can wander round the college between 10am and 6pm to look at the paintings and drawings which are scattered around the many corridors of the architecturally striking college on Huntingdon Road (www.newhall.cam.ac.uk/womensart). Look out for Maggi Hambling's startling painting of 1986, *Gulf Women Prepare for War*.

What to do with children

Newnham Playground is a delightful place and, from May to September, the large Lammas Land paddling pool is full of shouting children. There is a popular little playground next to the river on Jesus Green as well.

Glaze to Amaze near the Grafton Centre (54 Burleigh St; ☎ 01223 319600; cost about £25) allows children from as young as two to decorate their own ceramic plate, mug or piggy bank, which is then fired (to be collected a couple of days later). The shop provides stencils, sponges, patterns and non-toxic paints.

In summer, a favourite destination for older children is **Jesus Green**, which has free tennis courts, a skatepark, impromptu games of football and frisbee and a wonderful outdoor lido, Jesus Green Swimming Pool. On a hot day, families and groups of young people spend more time sunbathing on the ample banks than in the unheated pool, which lies alongside the River Cam. An alternative swimming venue is Parkside Pool which has a flume and three graduated diving boards.

Every Wednesday evening in winter, Cambridge University's **Institute of Astronomy** invites the public in for stargazing sessions accompanied by an optional talk. Children with an interest in the stars will enjoy seeing Mars through a massive old-fashioned telescope housed in its own mini-observatory, with astronomers on hand pointing out stars of interest with laser beams and focusing giant binoculars on the Milky Way.

> **JESUS GREEN SWIMMING POOL**, Off Chesterton Road, Cambridge; ☎ 01223 302579; open May to Sept until 8pm weekdays, 6pm weekends.

> **INSTITUTE OF ASTRONOMY**, Madingley Road, Cambridge CB3 0HA; ☎ 01223 337548; www.ast.cam.ac.uk/public/public_observing; free; Wed 7.15pm for the talk, 7.45pm for the stargazing (weather dependent).

Entertainment

Music and theatre

For a city of just 120,000 citizens, the range of cultural offering, in Cambridge is impressive. From Afro-Cuban jazz at the **Junction Shed**, an interesting venue in the soul-less Cambridge Leisure Park near the Hills Road Railway Bridge (box office ☎ 01223 511511; www.junction.co.uk) to magnificent concerts of sacred music in **King's College**, from storytelling evenings downstairs at the laid-back CB2 Bistro-Café on Norfolk Street to mainstream touring theatre productions at the **Cambridge Arts Theatre** near the market square. Tickets to many venues are available from the **Corn Exchange** Box Office next door to the Tourist Office (☎ 01223 357851). Student theatrical and musical events can be of an astonishingly high standard, so watch for posters in college lodges and on railings.

Special events

The River Cam is at its loveliest in the spring when the punts are coming out of hibernation and the crocuses and daffodils are out in profusion. **Boat races** are always entertaining. The Lent Bumps take place in the first week of March and the Summer Bumps are in late June. If you want to watch from the large riverside garden of the Plough pub in Fen Ditton, bag your spot early. Training activity on the river near the boathouses is feverish in the run-up in March to the Boat Race Season.

The green spaces of Cambridge come alive in July when the City Council mounts a programme of **Fun in the Parks** including a French Market on Parker's Piece, an outdoor cinema, and puppet shows and storytelling events for children. July has many competing events, such as the annual film festival based at the Arts Picturehouse Cinema in early July, Open Studios when local artists and craftspeople open their homes to show off their wares during all the weekends of July, and then the famous Cambridge Folk Festival at the end of the month (for which it's almost as difficult to get tickets as it is for Glastonbury). One of the summer highlights is the **Cambridge Shakespeare Festival** where performances are of a professional not a student standard. The college gardens are an idyllic place to crack a bottle of fizz on a balmy summer's evening in anticipation of seeing Oberon and Titania appear from under a giant willow tree. Tickets are £14 from the City Centre Box Office (☎ 01223 357851).

Shopping

King Street has an eclectic mixture of shops, from the ultra chic (**Blu Max** for designer shoes and clothes) to the well-stocked **Heffers Art and Graphics Shop**. To find a hidden treasure, visit the cluster of antique shops at the lower end of Gwydir Street in the old Dale's Brewery, including **Hive Antiques and Collectibles** open seven days a week.

Books

Cambridge used to have a more interesting range of bookshops than it does now. The old Cambridge family firm of Heffers was bought up by Blackwell's some years ago, in an attempt to compete with Waterstone's and Borders, all located within a stone's throw of one another.

For antiquarian books, browse in **G David Bookseller** on an obscure lane running off Market Square towards King's. Unusually, the bargain shelves outside contain a few books you might actually want to read. **The Haunted Bookshop** nearby (www.sarahkeybooks.co.uk) is a small antiquarian shop, specialising in 19th- and 20th-century children's and illustrated books, very few of which are about ghosts.

Crafts

The stalwarts who erect their stalls every Thursday, Friday and Saturday in All Saints Market off Trinity Street deserve to have their wares browsed. Potters, photographers and wood carvers are all approachable.

The Visitors' Book

Things to do in Lyme Regis

'We've just spent a delightful few days of a balmy September in Cambridge. At first we were worried that there wouldn't be much for young children since college buildings and courts aren't very appealing to pre-schoolers especially where it's forbidden to walk on the grass. But we found several of the university museums grabbed 5-year-old Freddie (and his younger brother was happy to go along for the ride). They loved the giant finback whale skeleton outside the Zoology museum and found lots to marvel at inside.'

'The helpful woman in the tourist office recommended the unglamorous-sounding Sedgwick Museum of Earth Sciences which provided what all little boys seem to like, a big dinosaur, in this case an Iguanodon which we were interested to learn was a gift from the King of Belgium a hundred years ago and one of the first dinosaur skeletons assembled for public view.'

'It was great that all the university museums were free because it meant we could drop in for a short while on our afternoons to see a few highlights without feeling guilty.'

'Anyway, the weather was so fine we didn't want to spend our whole time in museums. We had a lovely outing to the gardens of Anglesey Abbey and all enjoyed visiting the working water mill since it happened to be one of the two milling days a month. We would love to go back to Cambridge when the boys are a little older and explore some of the colleges and other treasures.'

Simon and Ruth Willoughby, Fred (5), Tim (3)

The best... PLACES TO STAY

BOUTIQUE HOTEL

Hotel du Vin

15–19 Trumpington St, Cambridge CB2 1QA (across the road from the Fitzwilliam Museum), ☎ 01223 227330/1 www.hotelduvin.com

This ultra-stylish hotel which opened in 2007 is designed for spending time in rather than just using as a touring base. Intelligent understated service is combined with luxurious yet quirky design including several suites with two elegant free-standing baths near the eight-foot wide bed. The hotel has a library, a wine tasting room and a bistro serving superb food.

Prices: from £145 for a double.

HOTEL

Arundel House Hotel

Chesterton Road, Cambridge CB4 3AN ☎ 01223 367701 www.arundelhousehotel.co.uk

A standard provincial Victorian hotel, the Arundel House is saved by its location overlooking Jesus Green and easily accessible on foot to central Cambridge, by the ease of parking and by the traditional English breakfast. Try to ignore the carpets and muzak.

Prices: B&B from £70 for a standard double; some special deals e.g. three night mid-week break for £175.

INN

The Castle

37 St Andrews Street, Cambridge CB2 3AR, ☎ 01223 307477 www.thecastlecambridge.co.uk

This is a rare example of a city centre pub that offers bed and breakfast. The six rooms upstairs have been recently refurbished (no en suite) along with the pub downstairs that has been hauled up-market. At the same time it acquired a late licence, so the Castle is recommended only for night owls.

Prices: B&B £55 for a single; £65 for a double or family room.

Crown & Punchbowl

High Street, Horningsea, Cambridgeshire CB25 9JG (5 miles north of Cambridge) ☎ 01223 860643 www.thecrownandpunchbowl.co.uk

This 17th-century country pub next to the church has five contemporary, spacious rooms. Wireless internet connection makes it popular with business people as well as tourists. The pub has a highly regarded restaurant and serves City of Cambridge ales including the tasty Hobson's Choice.

Pricse: B&B £75 for a single; £95 for a double.

ORGANIC B&B

Lynwood House B&B

217 Chesterton Road, Cambridge CB4 1AN, ☎ 01223 500776 www.lynwood-house.co.uk

This friendly guesthouse north of the River Cam is near the footbridge to Midsummer Common. Breakfasts include organic bread and eggs, and local free-range sausages and bacon. Children must be over 12 to stay.

Prices: from £75 for a en suite double/twin; from £90 for a family triple.

GUEST HOUSE

Byron's Lodge

63 High Street, Grantchester, Cambridge CB3 9NF, ☎ 01223 841003 www.byronslodge.co.uk

With thatched roof and 17th-century features, Byron's Lodge boasts Lord Byron as a past patron and is situated just a few minutes from the delightful Grantchester Meadows. The gardens are open to the public for afternoon teas. Children may be allowed to stay.

Prices: B&B from £80 to £140 for double and luxury bedrooms.

The best... FOOD AND DRINK

 ### Staying in

With a sophisticated consumer base, good quality food is never far away. Demand for organic local produce has been rising faster in Cambridge than anywhere. As an illustration, a branch of Burger King in the city centre has recently been replaced by **Origin8 Farm Shop & Café** with the motto 'Herding the Farmyard into the High Street'. Nevertheless supermarkets seem to have a powerful grip on Cambridge and there has long been a shortage of good

CELEBRITY CONNECTIONS

All the great and the good come to Cambridge at some point, whether it's Prince Charles coming to open a new environmental centre or Hans Blix coming to participate in a Cambridge Union debate about the Iraq war. Cambridge is also a favourite setting for film-makers, so that not long ago Cate Blanchett was spotted floating on the river while filming *Elizabeth: The Golden Age* about the Queen's relationship with the adventurer Walter Raleigh, played by Clive Owen. Celebrity spotters loitered around Midsummer Common where all the film trailers were parked, hoping to catch a glimpse of a star.

Sooner or later celebrities visiting Cambridge hire a chauffeured punt. In a single summer week, punts were boarded by Jamie and Jules Oliver and their daughters, Stephen Fry visiting his alma mater and Scarlett Johansson who was filming *The Other Boleyn Girl* in Ely.

Fame has brushed Grantchester many times. The World War I poet Rupert Brooke lived first in Orchard House and then up the road at the Old Vicarage. He would often go skinny-dipping in Byron's Pool, named after the poet, who also frequented the pool for swimming parties. It can still be visited on a pleasant walk through woods (signposted from the road to Trumpington), but is a little too overgrown and muddy to tempt many swimmers these days. Jeffrey Archer and wife Mary bought the very same Old Vicarage in 1979, and this has been their home ever since apart from the two years (2001–2003) that Jeffrey spent in prison for perjury and perverting the course of justice.

delicatessens. At least Waitrose now has a special East Anglian produce section which might sell fenland celery in season, local apple juice and New-market Powters sausages. **Balzano's** (204 Cherry Hinton Road, CB1 7AW; ☎ 01223 246168) is a great Italian deli but its location isn't very convenient.

The daily open market in the city centre has fruit and vegetable stalls, a cheese stall, fishmonger, and the excellent **Earth's Crust bakery**. Vendors change from day to day, but all provide excellent fodder for a punting picnic or for home cooking. The weekly farmers' market takes place on Sundays with stalls selling everything from olives to coffee beans to ostrich burgers. Among the least resistible is **Tom's Cakes** selling cakes made with free-range eggs, locally grown fen carrots and Bramley apples. If you miss them in Cambridge on a Sunday you can buy them at other markets (mentioned later in this chapter) or visit the bakery shop in the village of Somersham (West Newlands Industrial Estate, Somersham, Cambridgeshire PE28 3EB; ☎ 01487 842200; www.tomscakes.co.uk. It's open Thursday to Saturday mornings till 1pm.

The well-heeled flock to the **Cambridge Cheese Company** in All Saints Passage for their posh nosh. Fitzbillies at 51 Trumpington Street has been famed for its Chelsea buns since the 1920s and will also provide picnics that have been pre-ordered (☎ 01223 352500; www.fitzbillies.com). **Al-Amin food** store on Mill Road has a marvellous range of exotic foodstuffs including tubs of home-made curry. For the best sourdough bread in Cambridge, make the short trek from Mill Road to **Cotto's** at 183 East Road where they bake organic breads on the premises in a wood-burning stove.

Five miles south-west of Cambridge, **Burwash Manor Farms** (New Road Barton, Cambridge CB3 7BD, near Junction 12 of the M11; ☎ 01223 262600; www.burwashmanor.net) is a delightful complex of individual shops including **The Larder** which sells a range of upmarket deli items and organic produce. Its asparagus in season is locally renowned.

Smoked fish, meat and cheese as well as lots of deli goodies such as olives, cheeses and frozen meals are available from the traditional **River Farm Smokery** in Bottisham off the A1303 (CB25 9BU), a location with no river and no farm. Fresh fish is also available Wednesdays to Saturdays.

Takeaways
A student favourite for kebabs and souvlaki is **Gardenia's** (known as Gardies) in Rose Crescent, just off Trinity Street. Thousands of students plus a few celebrities such as Michael Portillo and Stephen Fry fought tooth and nail to keep this institution open when the landlords (Gonville and Caius College) wanted to change it into student accommodation. Its lease has been renewed till 2011. **Tommy Tucker** at the city end of Milton Road serves the best chips in Cambridge.

EATING OUT

FINE DINING
Midsummer House
**Midsummer Common, Cambridge
CB4 1HA, ☎ 01223 369299
www.midsummerhouse.co.uk**

Off-the-planet cuisine has resulted in two
Michelin stars. The superior staff know
exactly where every ingredient has been
sourced. A three-course dinner-cum-work of
art costs £76, with wines from £16 to £1,800.

Alimentum
**152–154 Hills Road, Cambridge CB2 8PB
☎ 01223 413000
www.restaurantalimentum.co.uk**

This high-end restaurant serves exquisite
dishes that use only ethically sourced ingredients. The owner claims to have visited all
his meat suppliers to check rearing conditions, and only fish from sustainable
sources appears on the menu. The menu
has Spanish influences since the chef is
from Spain, and has worked in several
famous restaurants. Main courses cost
£15–20.

Restaurant 22
**22 Chesterton Road, Cambridge CB4
3AX. ☎ 01223 351880
www.restaurant22.co.uk**

This long-established and very civilised
restaurant regularly wins plaudits. Seasonal
menus change monthly, and the wine list is
extensive. A three-course menu costs
£29.95, wine is from £17.95.

RESTAURANT
Brasserie Gérard Cambridge
**27-28 Bridge Street, Cambridge, CB2 1UJ
☎ 01223 448620
www.brasseriegerard.co.uk/location/
cambridge**

Positioned right in the heart of Cambridge
this relaxed brasserie offers a traditional
menu day and night. Typical mains include
beef bourguignon for £12.95 and crispy
maison lafitte duck leg for £13.50. Of
course, it wouldn't be a French restaurant
without a great range of steaks too and the
rump steak can be enjoyed as part of a
reasonable fixed price three course menu
for £20.

Al Casbah
**62 Mill Road, Cambridge CB1 2AS
☎ 01223 579500
www.al-casbah.com**

This rather unusual Mediterranean restaurant
is immediately eye-catching. Passers-by are
greeted by a huge grill, with even bigger
flames, as the freshly-prepared meat and fish
are cooked for everyone to see. Inside the
restaurant, a great Bedouin tent completely
covers the ceiling creating an authentic
Algerian atmosphere. Dishes are traditional
with a house speciality of couscous royale –
tagine cooked lamb chop and chicken
served on couscous with vegetables and
charcoal grilled merguez.

The Oak Bistro
**6 Lensfield Road, Cambridge, CB2 1EG
☎ 01223 323361
www.theoakbistro.co.uk**

Open since March 2009, this local bistro
offers two stylish bistro settings inside and a
walled garden for al fresco dining. The bistro
is open for lunch and dinner Monday through
to Saturday but is closed on Sundays. The
lunch menu is particularly reasonable and
appealing offering an interesting selection
of three courses for £15.

Thanh Binh
**17 Magdalene Street, Cambridge CB3
0AF (opposite Madgalene College just
north of the River Cam). ☎ 01223 362456**

Tasty and authentic Vietnamese dishes are
served with aplomb at this well-run peaceful
establishment, which has the advantage of
being BYO (bring your own). But if you
forget, you can indulge in a fresh lime juice
drink.

GASTROPUB
Punter
**Northampton Street, corner of Pound Hill,
Cambridge CB3 0EA, ☎ 01223 363322**

This is the newest gastropub in Cambridge
with a changing blackboard menu displaying particularly inventive starters. Casual
tables fill rooms with different characters
including a refurbished barn with a stone
floor and a courtyard terrace.

EATING OUT

Three Horseshoes
High Street, Madingley, Cambridgeshire CB3 8AB, ☎ 01954 210221, (about three miles west of the city, off A1303)
www.threehorseshoesmadingley.co.uk

Privileged undergraduates often persuade their parents to take them here at the end of term. A classy contemporary menu is served in the conservatory dining room, though a simpler menu is available in the bar-grill area or garden, e.g. two courses for £11, five courses for £21.

CAFÉ
Michaelhouse Café
Trinity Street, Cambridge CB2 1SU
☎ 01223 309147
www.michaelhouse.org.uk/html/the_cafe.html

This wholesome café housed in a sensitively renovated 14th-century church on Trinity Street attracts ladies who lunch plus shoppers and visitors with its excellent fresh vegetarian food, lovely cakes and local art exhibited on the walls.

Indigo Coffee House,
8 St Edward's Passage, Cambridge CB2 3PJ, ☎ 01223 295688

This independent gem serves good bagels and cakes as well as coffee. It is treated like an alternative common room by the students and fellows of nearby colleges. With only eight or nine tables, it's usually difficult to find space.

Clown's
54 King Street, Cambridge CB1 1LN
☎ 01223 355711

Good for lingering over a newspaper, this bohemian place is run by an Italian family who take the coffee they serve seriously.

Aunties Tea Shop
1 St Mary's Passage, Cambridge, CB2 3PQ
☎ 01223 315641
www.auntiesteashop.co.uk

Aunties is a Traditional English Tea Room set up by the current owner, Yvonne Prevett, in 1979. The home-made cakes and scones are a particular treat although it also serves baguettes and sandwiches. Being close to the Arts Theatre, Aunties has been host to a number of celebrity guests and claims to have regular customers who visit from as far afield as Japan.

 # Drinking

The historic **Eagle** on Bene't Street near King's Parade is a well-preserved coaching inn. New arrivals from London in the 18th century would be shaken up and dirty, and the sign 'Bath' is still visible on the back wall. Of the three dormer windows above the outside drinking area, it's said that the one on the right is always kept open ever since a serving girl found herself unable to open it and perished in a fire. Try a pint of the excellent Speckled Hen at the place where Crick and Watson had their eureka moment and in 1951 announced to startled patrons nearby that the double helix structure of DNA carries genetic information.

    The Free Press pub on Prospect Row is a fine back-street hostelry serving wholesome good value food (and bans mobile phones). For a riverside recommendation, head to the **Fort St. George,** though it can get very crowded on a hot evening. The 'snug' has an eccentric game called 'Ringing the Bull' whereby you have to swing a loop onto a wall-mounted hook which looks (and is) impossible.

The Live & Let Live on Mawson Road off Mill Road is an untarted-up wooden-floored treasure beloved of locals. Its impressive range of real ales complements its English menu, especially popular for Sunday lunch.

Hovering on the edge of a council estate, **The Carlton Arms** is many locals' favourite pub. The energetic landlord has transformed the big rough pub into a gem with an illuminated garden terrace, comfortable chairs, a hearty menu and, best of all, a rotating series of excellently kept real ales.

The only local breweries within range of Cambridge are the **Milton Micro-Brewery** (www.miltonbrewery.co.uk) and the **City of Cambridge** in Chittering off the A10. But these beers are almost never available locally because virtually all Cambridge pubs are tied to other breweries. The only genuinely free house in the city is **The Cambridge Blue**, an excellent hostelry on Gwydir Street off Mill Road, which sometimes carries City of Cambridge brew Hobson's Choice.

Cambridge is home to one independent cider-maker who blends unsprayed cider apples with locally grown dessert types to produce a mouth-puckeringly dry scrumpy-style cider (7%). **Cassels Cider** is available on tap at several pubs including the Live & Let Live and the St Radegund, and in bottles at local farmers' markets and quality off-licences like Bacchanalia on Victoria Road.

Moving from pubs to bars, **The River Bar + Kitchen**, overlooking Magdalene College across the river (☎ 01223 307030, www.riverbarkitchen.com), is a stylish Conranesque bar where cocktails cost £5.50 and innovative food is served. Another trendy place is **The Depot** at 46 Trinity Street. They do two cocktails for £6 early evening on most days.

FURTHER AFIELD

Madingley

You don't have to be an American to be moved by the curved rows of identical crosses covering a vast sloping field at the **American Cemetery**. The site was developed on land donated by the university in the decade following the Second World War and was chosen because so many US servicemen were based in East Anglia. Nearly 4,000 Americans are buried here and more than 5,000 whose remains were never found are commemorated on the Wall of the Missing. The usual way for tourists to reach the cemetery is on the open-topped bus; however it can also be reached by a pleasant 3-mile walk from the University Library to the village of Coton and across a field to the Cemetery. You could then return to the city from the Madingley Park & Ride site about a mile away.

Visitor information

Tourist Information Centres:
The **Cambridge Tourist Information Centre** is located on Wheeler Street near the Market, ☎ 0906 586 2526, 60p a minute, www.visitcambridge.org, the Cambridge Visitor Card (£2.50) gives discounts to attractions, punt hire, cinema, restaurants, etc. The website

Hospitals: 24-hour A&E, Addenbrooke's Hospital, Hills Road. An out-of-hours service is run by CamDoc at the Chesterton Hospital, Union Lane, Cambridge CB4 1PT (☎ 01223 464242).

Websites: Localsecrets.com – carries reviews of restaurants, pubs, etc. and readers' feedback about these places, complete with dates so you can tell what is current; Shape Walks (www.stridedesign.net/shape walks/home.aspx) describes six themed tours covering historic highlights, contemporary architecture, Victorian Cambridge, Tudor Cambridge, clocks and sundials, and green spaces; www.plcane.clara.net – see for *Cambridge Corners* 'Walks and Rides Away from the Crowds'.

Supermarkets: Sainsbury's, St. Andrew's Street is the only supermarket in the city centre (no car access). The large Coldhams Lane Sainsbury (Brooks Road, CB1 3HP) was the first out-of-town Sainsbury's in the country; Waitrose, 50 Hauxton Road, Trumpington, CB2 2LQ, near Junction 11 on the M11; Tesco, Newmarket Road, plus branches in Milton, Fulbourn and further afield the Tesco Extra store in Bar Hill (CB23 8EL) 7 miles along the A14.

Tours: Tours with Blue Badge guides can be joined via the Tourist Office; try to join one by local historian Allan Brigham who offers fascinating offbeat information about the city. As a man of the people, he is proud of his day job as a council-employed street sweeper (www.colc.co.uk/cambridge/tours).

Bike rental: Cambridge Station Cycles located at the station, ☎ 01223 307125, www.stationcycles.co.uk; City Cycle Hire, 61 Newnham Road CB3 9EY, ☎ 01223 365629, www.citycycle hire.com); hire price from £8 a day.

Taxis: Panther, ☎ 01223 715715, biggest company in Cambridge with automated telephone system; AMC, ☎ 01223 566858; Camtax, ☎ 01223 242424; Nighttime taxi ranks can be found on the main street (Sidney Street outside Boots).

Local legend: Alice and Charles

In 1848, a young astronomer named **Charles Todd** got a job at the Cambridge University observatory and moved from Greenwich. Soon he met and fell in love with Alice Bell who lived in a picturesque cottage on Free School Lane (still standing just behind the Eraina Taverna). The only problem for Charles and Alice was that she was only 12 years old, but he agreed to wait until she was of marrying age. Later he was offered an exciting job in the colonies as Observer and Superintendent of Telegraphs in South Australia. Before accepting, he consulted Alice, whom he married when she was 17. In 1855 they sailed to Australia together where they had a long marriage and produced three children. Perhaps because he was able to imagine the suffering of being out of communication with his sweetheart, he expressed his intention of trying to forge a telegraphic link between Australia and England. Sure enough his best known and most famous achievement was the Overland Telegraph, which in 1872 for the first time connected Adelaide and the rest of Australia, through Darwin, with England by a single wire. While burying the wire in the outback, the workmen discovered a dry riverbed with waterholes and springs, one of which was the spot where they built a key telegraph station. Today this is just outside Alice Springs, named by the chief surveyor after the girl from Cambridge. And Alice Springs is now situated on the River Todd, mainly dry and the scene of the annual mock Henley-on-Todd Regatta, which consists of teams running along the dry sandy river race carrying mock boats and tubs.

Anglesey Abbey

Six miles north-west of Cambridge, the estate of Lord Fairhaven is better known for its gardens and mill than for the Jacobean house. Nearly 100 acres of landscaped garden, now in the care of the National Trust, are full of interest and colour at any time of year. Although 18th century in inspiration, they were laid out in the 1930s. Unusually, one of the highlights of the calendar is winter when masses of snowdrops bloom. At the furthest corner of the property, the 18th-century Lode Mill is open to the public and has milling days every other Saturday.

The house was subject to an unfortunate scandal in 1999 when a long-serving butler,

ANGLESEY ABBEY, Gardens and Lode Mill, Quy Road, Lode, Cambridgeshire CB25 9EJ; ☎01223 810080; http://www.angleseyabbey.org; www.angleseyabbey.org; if gift-aided £8.45 adults, £4.20 children; free to National Trust members; reduced prices for entry to gardens only; seasonal gardens open Wed to Sun year round, 10.30am–4.30/5.30pm), house open late Mar to late Oct, Tues to Sun 1–5pm.

Domingo Bermudez, stole 65 heirlooms from his employer. He removed items from the main house to the house on the estate where he lived. While he was in his native Spain trying to recover from depression, the theft was discovered and Lord Fairhaven sent a note sacking him. The strange sequel to the story is that when the butler discovered this, he sued his employer (unsuccessfully) for unfair dismissal.

Two great walks from Cambridge

The **Fen Rivers Walk** follows the River Cam all the way to Ely 16 miles to the north. The walk combines both scenic and historic interest. For many centuries the River Cam formed a crucial transportation route for trade and cargo. The Cambridge coat of arms is flanked by two seahorses and shows a bridge over the Cam with several boats, indicating that the city's early prosperity came from its river trade.

The route follows drained floodbanks on both sides of the rivers linking Cambridge and Ely, and is well-signed with an eel symbol. Black fields of peat are broken by rivers and streams edged with willow and reed, the same reeds that used to be collected by fenmen to make baskets. The eastern route from Cambridge to Clayhithe via Fen Ditton and Horningsea crosses fields and may be more muddy than the towpath along the river. The watery landscape and famous big skies of eastern England can be savoured out in the Fens with names such as **Adventurers' Fen**, named after the 'Gentleman Adventurers', 17th-century versions of venture capitalists who helped the Earl of Bedford in his great drainage project to drain the Fens.

It is possible to do part (to Waterbeach or Stetham) or all of the walk to Ely and return to your starting point by train or bus. You can also do it over two days and break your journey at a pub charmingly named **Five Miles from Anywhere No Hurry Inn** in Upware (☎ 01353 721654). An information packet with a route map with suggested detours and wildlife guide is available for £2 from the Cambridge Information Office.

Walking the Devil's Dyke

Those without cars aren't excluded from the following suggested walk, which can be done making use of the train from Cambridge to Dullingham or a local bus from Drummer Street Bus Station in the centre of Cambridge. The half-hourly service to Newmarket stops near the Newmarket racecourse at a roundabout on the A1303 marked by a huge equestrian statue (fare £3.50). Immediately past the bus stop, a marked footpath leads left onto the **Devil's Dyke**, a 7-mile embankment created in Saxon times for defence purposes and considered one of the finest Dark Age earthworks in Britain. According to a local legend, the Devil's tail formed the dyke as he retreated in fury at having been turned away from a wedding he tried to attend in Reach church.

On your left you are looking down on the National Stud and your right on beautifully maintained gallops running parallel to the dyke where you might see racehorses being trained. The dyke continues for 4–5 miles into the picturesque village green at Reach where the homely Dyke's End pub offers a perfect lunch stop with its two beers brewed on the premises and a good menu. You can then either walk a gentle mile and a half to catch a bus in Swaffham Prior back to Cambridge or proceed along tracks and banks along a lode (canal) a further 5 miles to the River Cam. From Waterbeach there are frequent trains to Cambridge and an hourly bus service.

Wimpole Hall

Far more visitors come to Wimpole to walk in the grounds than to sightsee in the house. **The Home Farm** has rare breeds of sheep, pigs and cattle, and the thatched **Great Barn** houses a collection of farm implements contemporary with the creation of the farm at the turn of the 19th century. The most popular seasonal event is lambing in March and April. The farm is well set up for children with a good adventure playground and mini pedal tractors.

WIMPOLE HALL, Arrington SG8 0BW, 10 miles south-west of Cambridge; ☎ 01223 206000; www.wimpole.org; free to National Trust members, gift-aided to home farm adults £6.95, children £4.70, combination ticket to all attractions £12.60/£6.80, family £33; parking £2; home farm open weekends year round, plus some weekdays Mar to Oct; hall is open Mar to Oct (both always closed on Fri).

The Hall itself is the largest country house in Cambridgeshire but its history has been chequered. After vast sums had been spent on improving the house and park in the 1840s, the estate passed to the 5th Earl of Hardwicke who barely ever visited. True to his sobriquet, 'Champagne Charlie', he squandered his inheritance within 15 years and had to pass Wimpole to his main creditor, who owned a bank. By the time the last owner, Rudyard Kipling's daughter Elsie Bambridge and her husband acquired it in 1938, it was run down and devoid of furniture. They worked hard to restore and furnish the house which they then bequeathed to the National Trust.

The landscaped parkland is truly vast and also free to explore by foot. By following the main track you will come to a Chinese bridge over a lake and then a ruin which from a distance looks like a Suffolk round-towered church. In fact it's a sham Gothic castle built in 1771 to provide a satisfying view from the house down in the valley.

Duxford Aviation Museum

As an outpost of the Imperial War Museum in south London, **Duxford Museum** has an important national collection of aircraft from the past 100 years displayed in vast hangars. The aerodrome at Duxford was built during the First World War, later becoming a flying school and a fighter station. During the Second World War, Duxford was handed over to the US 8th Air Force who lost thousands of planes and men. The sleek Norman Foster building at Duxford today, visible from the M11, has displays of historic American aircraft and also serves as a war memorial.

IMPERIAL WAR MUSEUM DUXFORD, CB22 4QR, Near junction 10 of the M11, 11 miles south of Cambridge ; ☎ 01223 835000; http://duxford.iwm.org.uk; adults £16, under-16s free; air shows £25/£10; open daily, summer 10am–6pm, winter 10am–4pm.

There are examples of planes that flew in the First World War in the **British Aircraft Collection**. Duxford's annual air show takes place in September and various other vintage fly-bys and aerobatic air shows are held in the summer months.

If you travel further south and leave the motorway at junction 9 you will be in Essex and within easy reach of two first-class destinations, the picturesque and affluent market town of **Saffron Walden** and the lavish country house and park at **Audley End**, now in the care of English Heritage but with a sweet miniature steam railway personally overseen by the last owner, the 10th Lord Braybrooke.

The Great Ouse

This waterway rises in Northamptonshire and goes through much of Cambridgeshire flowing from St Neots through the Paxton Pits Nature Reserve, on to Godmanchester, once a Roman crossroads, to the National Trust mill at Houghton, across the river from the lovely villages of Hemingford Grey and Hemingford Abbots. A short distance downstream is pretty **St Ives**, once the scene of a huge annual cloth fair attended (perhaps) by men with seven wives, hence the rhyme. St Ives developed around the furthest navigable point on the river, so that hundreds of years ago goods could be conveyed all the way to and from The Wash at King's Lynn. When the mill at Houghton ceased milling commercially in 1930, the river's history as a working river came to an end and now is reserved for pleasure craft.

St Ives' best feature is its 15th-century stone bridge with a chapel built into it and five low arches. Visible from the bridge is the Holt Island Nature Reserve which can be accessed via a bridge from Church Street. It was once a source of thatching reeds taken from osier beds. The reserve is open on summer weekends.

About 10 miles upriver, **Paxton Pits** is an extensive bird reserve built round a labyrinth of lakes left over from decades of gravel extraction. The site is ideal for wildlife because the artificially formed islands are free of predators and suitable for ground-nesting birds. The website http://paxtonpitssightings. blogspot.com records all sightings of oystercatchers, little egrets, barnacle geese, etc.

Hemingford Grey

The oldest continuously inhabited house in England is in this riverside village. The garden gate to Hemingford Manor gives directly onto the riverside path in a perfect setting. In fact this stretch of the Great Ouse is so idyllic with spire and cottage, reeds and lily pads, it's almost Constablesque. The moated Manor is reputed to have been built under the Normans in the 1130s, and if you join a tour you will be shown the oldest part of the house which is through the owner's bedroom. Diana Boston is the daughter-in-law of Lucy Boston, author of the *Green Knowe* series of children's books set in the house, and for her creative gardening and quilting. Although Lucy died in 1990 (aged 98), the garden is still maintained beautifully and open to the public daily, whereas the house is open strictly by appointment.

THE MANOR, Hemingford Grey, Cambridgeshire PE28 9BN; ☎ 01480 463134; www.green knowe.co.uk; house tour/garden, adults £6/£3; garden open 11am–5pm.

A visit to this cultivated corner of Cambridgeshire could be suitably rounded off with a meal at the village gastropub on the High Street The Cock (☎ 01480 463609; www.cambscuisine.com).

A pleasant six mile circular walk can be constructed linking the Hemingfords, Houghton and St Ives. Similarly Paxton Pits can serve as the starting point for a long walk that loops up to Offord Cluny.

8

Ely&theFens

a. Ely

b. Wisbech and North Fenland

Unmissable highlights

01 Join a tour of the Octagon Tower of Ely Cathedral and survey miles of fens from the roof, p.332

02 Tour the old family-run Elgood's Brewery in Wisbech and its acres of landscaped gardens, p.345

03 Buy smoked eel or an ostrich burger from the farmers' market in Ely or marsh samphire in Wisbech, p.340, 350

04 Explore Woodwalton Fen and gaze out at farms which may soon be flooded in pursuit of the Great Fen Project, p.352

05 Have tea and scones in the garden of the quaint Peacocks Tearoom by the river in Ely, p.341

06 See how a simple fenman would have lived in the renovated Fen Cottage at Wicken Fen, p.343

07 Admire the double hammerbeam angel roof of the large church in the market town of March, p.351

08 Indulge in the excellent cuisine served at the Anchor in Sutton Gault, an historic inn in the middle of nowhere, p.341

09 Visit the Wisbech and Fenland Museum to discover the story of Thomas Clarkson (a Wisbech native) and his role in abolishing the slave trade, p.347

10 Take a cruise on the River Great Ouse, p.337

ELY AND THE FENS

The Fen country consists of 1,300 square miles of treeless, hedgeless flatlands stretching away to the horizon in every direction. The fertile soils have been cultivated for centuries so that at first it might seem a thoroughly tamed and monotonous area of fields of potatoes, sugar beet and wheat. Yet it's an atmospheric place, a lost and empty land in the middle of nowhere.

Beneath such infinite skies, men can feel dwarfed and in need of human society which can be found in the civilised cathedral city of Ely or in the underrated Georgian market town of Wisbech.

Were it not for the ongoing efforts of man, the Fens would consist of water and marsh not habitable land. The prospect of learning about the 'Fen Drainage Story' might not quicken your pulse, but it's a remarkable one. Many places are below sea level and would be flooded by the first winter rains if there weren't endless pumping stations and sluices and dykes to control the water. In the 17th century, the eminent Dutch engineer Cornelius Vermuyden was headhunted to oversee the drainage of the Fens, the most ambitious civil engineering project of the time. Prisoners of war from Scotland and Holland were forced to labour, creating dykes and drains so that former marshland could be turned into ultra-productive farmland.

The work was at first carried out in the face of violent opposition from local Fenmen who saw their traditional livelihoods of eel-catching, reed-cutting and fishing as under threat. But the drainage continued nonetheless with an unforeseen consequence, that the extraction of water from the land would shrink the peat soils. Striking proof of this can be seen at Holme Fen Post south of Peterborough: a huge post made of cast iron was driven into the peat in 1851 so that the top was level with the ground. Now it stands a full 15ft clear of the ground. While driving round Fenland roads, be prepared to be unnerved by noticing that the rivers on one side of the raised road are noticeably higher than the fields on the other. Many rivers are surrounded by washlands which are designed to 'store' flood waters, and sometimes cars are re-routed away from flooded roads in these areas.

For a vivid evocation of life in the Fens before the war, Graham Swift's 1983 novel *Waterland*, later turned into a powerful film with Jeremy Irons, can't be bettered.

ELY

Before the great drainage, Ely stood in splendid isolation surrounded by swamps and pools. Flat-bottomed barges, precursors of the Cambridge punt, were used as transport and in winter it was sometimes necessary to lace on skates. Although the surroundings are now dry land, the region is still referred to as the 'Isle of Ely'. Some translate Ely as 'Isle of Eels' though it probably refers simply to a 'place of eels'.

Nowadays, the majestic towers of Ely Cathedral sail on the Fenland skies in a way that St Paul's-next-the-Gherkin or even Durham-on-the-Cliff can't rival. Ely is like an architectural oasis in the level expanses of the southern fens. With its Oliver Cromwell associations, flourishing markets and pleasant waterside area, Ely isn't just a one-hit wonder. Some choose to make calm and peaceful Ely their base for visiting Cambridge, a quarter of an hour away by a frequent train service.

WHAT TO SEE AND DO

 Fair weather

Ely Cathedral

Whatever the weather, Ely Cathedral is the main attraction in town. The magnificent building is matched by its setting amidst meadows and grazing parkland right in the middle of Ely, with the remnants of a Tudor orchard within the Cathedral precincts. Access can be through the great arch of **Ely Porta** (now part of the King's School Ely) or from the bottom of the hill nearer the railway station. The largest collection of domestic monastic buildings in the country is located in the Cathedral grounds.

Construction work began in 1081 and Ely soon acquired cathedral status, although the city never had a large population. The Norman nave retains its original proportions, though the great Victorian architect Sir Gilbert Scott restored and altered the floor and roof. The glory of Ely Cathedral is its stone Octagon Tower topped with a wooden lantern which was built in the early 14th century to the designs of an architecturally gifted monk. A tour of the **Octagon Tower** allows you to marvel at the four massive oak timbers brought from Bedfordshire in the 1320s on which the unique

> **ELY CATHEDRAL**, Chapter House, The College, Ely, CB7 4DL; ☎ 01353 667735; visits.tours@cathedral.ely.anglican.org; www.elycathedral.org; open to visitors summer 7am–6.30pm, winter 7am–6.30pm Mon to Sat, 7am–5.30pm Sun; admission including general guided tour £6.50, admission and a tour of the Octagon Tower £12.00; booking advisable.

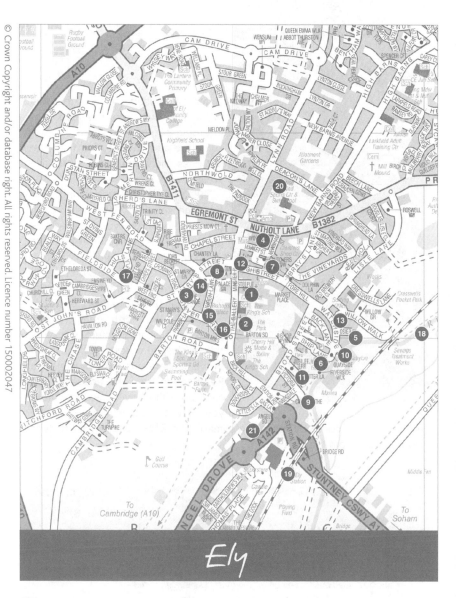

Ely

1. Ely Cathedral
2. Ely Porta
3. Oliver Cromwell's House
4. Ely Museum
5. Babylon Gallery
6. The Maltings
7. Market Place
8. Old Fire Engine House
9. Boathouse Restaurant
10. Peacocks Tearoom
11. Cutter Inn
12. Lamb Hotel
13. Waterside B&B
14. Cathedral House
15. Prince Albert
16. The Fountain
17. West End House
18. River Great Ouse
19. Station
20. Paradise Swimming Pool
21. Planet Zoom

Ely Cathedral's Octagon Tower

lantern was constructed. The tour also takes you out onto the lead roof affording superb 360 degree views. Tours are also available up the taller but less architecturally impressive **West Tower.**

The interior is awe-inspiring, and from the spacious entrance through the Galilee Porch, your eye will be drawn to the vast length of the nave lined with round arches.The cathedral's oldest relic from Saxon times is Ovin's Stone. The light-drenched **Lady Chapel** can be reached via a passageway from the north transept. The perpendicular architecture is breathtaking (despite widespread mutilation of the carvings and tracery during the Reformation) and the acoustics are amazing with a seven-second echo if you dare to test it. Note that one window is sponsored by Tesco, presumably the 21st-century equivalent of royal patrons from the past.

Local legends: tales of the Fenlands

A land of uncertain ground, frequent mists and remote communities is bound to give rise to tales of supernatural occurrences. Phantom monks are heard singing, female figures vanish over the horizon and mysterious will-o'-the-wisp lights have been associated with the Fens for centuries. The most dangerous are the Jack o' Lanterns which appear as glowing flickers out over the swamplands, beckoning those that see them to step out in pursuit and to a certain death in the bogs. According to superstition, those following the treacherous Fen pathways at night should avoid whistling at all costs so as not to summon the dancing Lantern Men. If one was spotted, the advice was to hit the ground and hide your face until the danger had passed. It is now thought that these mysterious lights were due to rotting vegetation that gave off marsh gases which occasionally ignited by themselves.

According to an ancient Fenland custom, showing a grey goose feather split

Waterside

The regenerated waterside of the River Great Ouse is just a 10-minute walk from the great west door of Ely Cathedral along the High Street, which turns into Fore Street and then into Waterside. This picturesque lane leads down to the river where Muscovy ducks and pleasure boats foregather. This car-free hive of activity and magnet for visitors has a pleasant collection of restaurants, pubs and an antique shop plus the trendy, publicly funded Babylon Gallery right on the waterfront. The mood is usually a happy one here, especially if you pause to buy an organic ice cream from the barrow near the Cutter Inn. You can sit on a bench to watch the waterside activity which might include a boat crew training for a forthcoming race. As a nearby plaque commemorates, the 1944 Oxford–Cambridge Boat Race took place here rather than on the Thames since large gatherings were banned in London during the war.

The newest addition to the area is a controversial new stainless steel artwork called *Sluice,* which celebrates the creation of the Denver Sluice about 15 miles further down the River Great Ouse.

Oliver Cromwell's house

At a time when Cromwell's fortunes had been flagging and he even gave some thought to emigrating to Puritan New England, in 1636 he inherited from an uncle a comfortable half-timbered house and promptly moved his family to Ely. He took up the job of collector of tithes for the Cathedral, a position which seems to have

OLIVER CROMWELL'S MUSEUM, 29 St Mary's Street, Ely CB7 4HF; ☎ 01353 662062; http://visitely.eastcambs.gov.uk/cromwell/oliver-cromwells-house; adults £4.50, children £3.10, families £13, open daily Apr to Oct 10am–5pm, Nov to Mar 11am–4pm Mon to Fri and Sun, 10am–5pm Sat.

almost in two down the quill signified that you were in need of help, and could claim the protection of a fellow Fenman. Oliver Cromwell, who was born on the edge of the Fens, was well acquainted with the secret signal and made liberal use of it when recruiting his army. But it wasn't a well-guarded secret because Charles I seems to have made use of the same technique. When on the run from Cromwell across the Littleport Fens, the king and his Cavaliers managed to escape by showing split goosefeathers to the Roundhead guards. Even as Charles was captured and sentenced to be executed, he thrust a feather at Cromwell, who spent a sleepless night tormented by the thought that he was about to break a sacred Fenland tradition. After the king was beheaded and the news got round of Cromwell's action, many of his men sent back feathers he had given them and returned to their homes where they could be sure of living among people who would never betray fenland customs.

radicalised him and pushed him to embark on his famous path of godly reformation. Two years after the Civil War had started, Cromwell and his mounted Ironsides charged through the Porta Gate during an Evensong service at the Cathedral, arrested the dean and proceeded to knock heads off carved angels and saints before locking the doors of the Cathedral for over a decade.

Now serving as the tourist information centre, the ancient house where the Cromwell family lived is next door to St Mary's Church. In subsequent times it has been a pub and a vicarage, and now also serves as a museum with reconstructions of 17th-century domestic life and audio-visual displays about the Lord Protector of the Commonwealth. One of the bedrooms is said to be haunted (though the Cambridge Paranormal Society could find no evidence when it spent a nigh there a few years ago; see www.cprs.co.uk/cromwell house.html).

Ely Museum

Telling the story of the ordinary folk rather than lofty ecclesiastics, the local museum is full of interest. It is housed in one of the city's oldest buildings, formerly a gaol, and displays in the cells bring to life the sorry plight of 18th-century prisoners. One of the galleries focuses on life in the Fens in the early 20th century and archive film shows skating competitions and traditional eel catching.

ELY MUSEUM, The Old Gaol, Market Street, Ely, CB7 4LS; ☎ 01353 666655; www.elymuseum. org.uk; £3.50; accompanied children free; open Mon to Sat 10.30am–5pm, plus Sun afternoon in summer; winter earlier closing time and closed all day Tues.

Wet weather

Stained Glass Museum

Near the main entrance, the cathedral houses a separate museum of stained glass with examples from 1240 to the present. Many narratives from the Bible were incorporated in the glass for the benefit of illiterate parishioners over the centuries. One more modern piece was done by Moira Forsyth when she was an art student in the 1930s and puts a comic spin on the story of *The Prodigal Son*. While the grieving father is delighted when his errant son returns, the lower panels indicate that his brother was not best pleased 'and neither was the fatted calf'.

STAINED GLASS MUSEUM, The South Triforium, Ely Cathedral, CB7 4BL; ☎ 01353 660347; www.stainedglassmuseum.com; entry: adults £4, families £8, joint ticket available with cathedral admission; open daily, summer Mon to Sat 10.30am–5pm, Sun 12pm–6pm, winter Mon to Sat 10.30am–5pm, Sun 12pm–4.30pm.

Babylon Gallery

BABYLON GALLERY,
Waterside, Ely, CB7 4AU;
☎ 01353 616375; http://adec.org.
uk/babylon-gallery.co.uk; free
admission; open from 10am (11am
on Sun) to 4pm (5pm summer
weekends); closed Mon
wheelchair accessible.

The Babylon Art Gallery is housed in a converted malthouse and brewery warehouse right on the water. It takes its name from the area of land on the other side of the river, equivalent to the wrong side of the tracks, where poor boat builders, basket weavers, potters and eel catchers lived.

As well as promoting contemporary local and digital art, the Babylon has links with the Hayward Gallery and sometimes mounts impressive touring exhibitions.

 ## What to do with children

A Children's Trail Guide in the cathedral contains the usual quiz, and there is a floor labyrinth near the main door, installed by the Victorians. Some say it's based on an old custom of confusing evil spirits trying to enter the holy place; others that it's an image of the maze of life leading to God at the centre. The Dean's Meadows on the other side of the Cathedral are often grazed by horses and sheep, and there is a playground at the bottom of the hill.

River cruises operate from the Waterside are on summer weekends and in school holidays. You can hire narrow boats and motor cruisers from Bridge Boatyard, usually by the week. A scheme is underway to enhance recreational boating in the Fens and to link the waterways of the three cathedral cities of Ely, Peterborough and Lincoln by 2014.

- **Fenland River Cruises**, Ship Lane, Ely, CB7 4BB; ☎ 01353 777567; river launch makes half-hour tours of the Great Ouse around Ely; tickets: adults £4, children £3.
- **Maritime Leisure Cruises**, Boston, Lincolnshire PE20 2NU (☎ 01205 460595; www.maritimecruises.co.uk). Converted tugboat *Marianne* operates lunchtime cruises in season from the Maltings on Ely's Waterfront.
- **Bridge Boatyard**, Bridge Road, Ely CB7 4DY (☎ 01353 663726; www.bridgeboatyard.com).

If you are desperate there is a leisure complex off Nutholt Lane with a swimming pool or you can resort to Planet Zoom, an indoor play centre near the station in Ely, alongside a bowling alley, Stikes Bowl Multiplex, for older children (☎ 01353 668666). 'See also Denny Abbey Farmland Museum below.'

Entertainment

With a tiny population of 14,500, Ely isn't big enough to support much theatre or a cinema. However, films are regularly shown in the Maltings on the riverside at the ADEC Cinema (Arts Development in East Cambridgeshire), The Maltings, Ship Lane, Ely CB7 4AU (24-hour cinema information line ☎ 01353 666388; www.adec.org.uk/what/cinema.html).

Special events

The Cathedral is the venue for regular concerts and other special events. In the city, the main annual festivity aimed squarely at visitors is **Ely Eel Day** held on the last Saturday of April, a recent innovation to celebrate Ely's heritage. The prospect of an eel-throwing contest might bring to mind the barbaric ritual (now defunct) of throwing cats off church towers, but it's more akin to the Yorkshire 'wellie wanging' since the 'eels' are made from bunched up socks.

 Shopping

As it has been for centuries, Ely is an important market town. Market Square within view of the cathedral has a produce market on Thursdays and a busy collection of stalls selling crafts and curiosities as well as food on Saturdays.

For collectables and assorted junk/treasures try the **Waterside Antiques Centre** inside the converted Maltings building by the quay (The Wharf, Ely CB7 4AU; ☎ 01353 667066; www.ely.org.uk/waterside.html; open every day). It isn't always easy to identify some of the objects and ephemera for sale, such as old agricultural tools, but you might find an unusual souvenir such as an antique bottle, lantern or map.

Topping & Company Booksellers at 9 High Street (CB7 4LJ; ☎ 01353 645005) is an energetic bookshop with staff who can advise from first-hand reading experience.There are frequent author events, and the shop is open every day. From the summer of 2008, a third storey containing more hand-built wooden bookcases wil permit a view of the Octagon Tower.

The best... PLACES TO STAY

HOTEL

Lamb Hotel 🏠 ✍ 🛏 🍴

Ely CB7 4EJ. ☎ 01353 663574
www.thelamb-ely.com

Although this historic hotel has suffered from poor reviews, its location rescues it, just a stone's throw from Ely's cathedral tower. It aims to retain the traditional atmosphere of a coaching inn, with its hardwood floor and oak-hued interior.

Prices: B&B from £80 to £125.

INN

Anchor Inn ✍ 🛏 🍴

Bury Lane, Sutton Gault CB6 2BD (8 miles west of Ely), ☎ 01353 778537
www.anchor-inn-restaurant.co.uk

The 17th-century Anchor Inn in the middle of nowhere is an acclaimed foodie haunt (see restaurant listing below), emphasising seasonal and traditional British ingredients such as fish from the River Farm Smokery in Bottisham. The family-run Anchor has won recognition from the *Good Food Guide* and the *Michelin Guide* and offers four comfortable guest rooms.

Prices: B&B from £79.95 for a double.

FARM/ORGANIC

Hill House Farm ✍ 🐄

9 Main St, Coveney CB6 2DJ (4 miles west of Ely), ☎ 01353 778369
www.hillhousefarm-ely.co.uk

This beautifully converted barn at Hill House Farm, the Old Granary, offers luxury five star self-catering accommodation for up to six people. Children must be over 15 to stay.

Prices: £350 to £650 for a week.

B&B

Waterside ✍

29 Waterside, Ely CB7 4AU
☎ 01353 614329/ ☎ 07785 730429
www.29waterside.org.uk

Comprising two workers' cottages, the original deeds from 1763 are on display. Some of the original laths and beams are retained while the bedrooms have a Victorian flavour with old wine and beer jars. Guests can breakfast in the walled cottage garden where herbs and ferns are grown (the latter are a favourite of the New Zealander proprietor) and where a bird table attracts wrens and thrushes.

Prices: from £60 for a double.

SELF-CATERING

Cathedral House ✍

17 St. Mary's Street, Ely CB7 4ER
☎ 01353 662124
www.cathedralhouse.co.uk/coach house.html

At the bottom of a walled garden, the original Coach House has been imaginatively restored and converted into a holiday cottage of character that sleeps 4/5. Many of the property's original features, complement modern facilities, while extras such as a well-stocked bookcase and games add a homely touch.

Prices: from £500 for a week low season.

UNUSUAL

The Old Hall

The Old Stuntney, Ely, CB7 5TR
☎ 01353 663275
www.theoldhallhotelely.co.uk

This intriguing and grand house is steeped in history and has been owned by the Steward family since 1897. Elizabeth Steward, the mother of Oliver Cromwell, was born there. Set on the southern edge of the Fens, the house has spectacular views across farmland to Ely Cathedral. Despite its grandeur, there are only two rooms available for bed and breakfast, but the antique décor and stunning surroundings make for a rather special stay.

Prices: from £110 per night for a double, including breakfast and afternoon tea.

The best... FOOD AND DRINK

Staying in

The fortnightly farmers' market comes to Ely on the second and fourth Saturdays of every month and bristles with interesting regional products. It isn't always easy to find Ely's most famous foodstuff, though delicious smoked eel is often available from one of the stalls. Only one traditional eel catcher remains. Peter Carter still makes his willow traps by hand and sets them in likely positions as generations have before him. He usually demonstrates this dying art at Ely's Eel Day.

Although the Thursday market is the main produce market, food stalls also set up on Saturdays. An enticing selection of stalls sell home-baked goods including pies and breads, as well as other staples like cheese.

Drinking

Ely and Fenland have a long and honourable tradition of brewing. Two small breweries have recently moved within a few miles of Ely, and yet neither's products are served in any of Ely's pubs. But you can buy the range of oaked beers bottled by the Fenland Brewery in Little Downham (www.elybeer.co.uk), just north of Ely, at the farmers' market.

Several old-fashioned beer-drinkers' locals can be visited in Ely, for example on genteel Silver Street. **The Prince Albert** (62 Silver St, CB7 4JF; ☎ 01353 663494) near the Barton Street long-stay car park, keeps its Green King ales well and has a simple menu, snug garden and friendly service. On the corner of Silver Street and Barton Square in the lee of the Cathedral, **The Fountain** ☎ 01353 663122, remains relatively free of tourists, mainly because it doesn't serve food.

A few minutes' walk west but off the beaten track brings you to **West End House** (West End, Ely CB6 3AY; ☎ 01353 662907), a prettily decorated white pub with red trim, where the welcome is warm and the pints are reasonably priced.

EATING OUT

FINE DINING

The Old Fire Engine House Restaurant & Gallery
25 St Mary's Street, Ely CB7 4ER
☎ **01353 662582**
www.theoldfireenginehouse.co.uk

This Ely institution prides itself on its unwavering devotion to traditional English cuisine using seasonal vegetables grown on the Fens plus game, meat and fish. You might get an eel stew made to a local recipe. The building retains the layout of rooms as it would have been when it was a farmhouse, but the fireman's pole, if there ever was one, is long gone, (most starters £5.50, mains £15–17). Cream tea in the lovely walled garden is another possibility (£7.20).

Boathouse Restaurant
5 Annesdale, Ely CB7 4BN
☎ **01353 664388**
www.theboathouseely.co.uk

This is the only restaurant in Ely to be included in the *Good Food Guide*. The interesting menu might feature a salad of marsh samphire, radish and berries. Signature starter dish is baked duck parcels with Asian greens (£7); mains cost £10–15. Pleasant outdoor terrace on the river.

PUB/RESTAURANT

Cutter Inn Waterside Restaurant
42 Annesdale, Ely CB7 4BN
☎ **01353 662713**
www.thecutterinn.co.uk

After years of relying on its fantastic quayside location to guarantee a stream of customers, new owners have dragged the food up-market. The menu is still cut of traditional cloth (gammon steak and pineapple, breaded plaice), but it's now better cooked. It has a good children's menu and friendly service. Naturally the outdoor terrace is full to bursting on a sunny day.

GASTROPUB

The Anchor Inn
**Bury Lane, Sutton Gault, Cambridgeshire
CB6 2BD (8 miles west of Ely)**
☎ **01353 778537**
www.anchor-inn-restaurant.co.uk.

Prize-winning country pub in remote fenland location, originally built in the 1650s to house men working for Vernaigden digging the Hundred Foot Drain (or New Bedford River). Gourmet menu and presentation, though with informal pub service. Average price of a three-course dinner is £26–30 before wine.

CAFÉ/TEAROOMS

Peacocks Tearoom
65 Waterside, Ely CB7 4AU
☎ **01353 661100**
www.peacockstearoom.co.uk

This superb tearoom has a pretty cottage garden filled with wisteria. Since Peacocks was voted 'Top Tea Place 2007' by the Tea Guild, it has become even busier and early arrival is recommended (no bookings are taken). Light lunches, snacks and proper cakes are served as well as cream teas (£5.50) with clotted cream and option of gooseberry jam in addition to the usual strawberry and raspberry. Range of country teas such as elderflower are available. The tearoom is open 10.30am–4.30pm on Wednesdays to Sundays plus bank holiday Mondays. It's closed in January.

Inside Peacocks Tearoom

ⓘ Visitor information

Tourist Information Centre:
29 St. Mary's Street, Ely CB7 4HF,
☎01353 662062,
tic@eastcambs.gov.uk/
http://tourism.eastcambs.gov.uk;
shares building with Oliver Cromwell
Museum; parking – despite endless
debates, car parking in Ely is still free
of charge.

Hospitals: The Princess of Wales
Hospital, Lynn Road (☎ 01353
652000) doesn't have A&E facilities.
The nearest emergency department
is at Addenbrooke's Hospital, Cambridge, Hills Rd, Cambridge CB2
0QQ (☎ 01223 2451510.

Websites: www.eastcambs.gov.uk –
map of the short and long-term car
parks can be downloaded here.

Supermarkets: Waitrose, Bray's
Lane, Ely CB7 4QJ; Tesco, Angel

Drove, Ely CB7 4DJ. Note that the
best view of the Cathedral is
reputed to be from the Stuntney
Causeway (the A142), a little
beyond the Tesco superstore. The
discount supermarket Lidl is in the
process of applying for permission
to open a store across the road
from Tesco.

Local newspaper: The Ely Standard
is a daily paper with a website
(www.ely-standard.co.uk) that
covers 'What's On' and local campaigns and issues.

Transport: Every 15 minutes from
the junction of the A10 and
Downham Road.

Taxis: Alan's Taxis, Ely, ☎ 01353
665050; Fencabs of Ely, Queen
Adelaide, Ely, ☎ 01353 669966,
www.fencabsofely.co.uk.

FURTHER AFIELD

Stretham

At one time the Fens were littered with steam-powered pumping stations, most
now demolished. Without their incessant pumping of rainwater from the low
level of shrunken peat up to the rivers at a higher altitude, the Fens would have
reverted to their pre-17th-century swampy state.

Without volunteer enthusiasts, the **Stretham Old
Engine** would not figure on the tourist map. This
fine old drainage station with its commanding
brick chimney just alongside the River Great Ouse
is worth a small detour from the A10 between Ely
and Cambridge. The massive scoop wheel that
was used into the 20th century to move water from

STRETHAM OLD ENGINE,
a mile south of Stretham (follow
signposts) and 5 miles south of Ely;
☎ 01353 648578;
www.strethamoldengine.org.uk; adults
£3, children £1; open Apr–Sept
certain afternoons (check website).

Denny Abbey

drainage channels back safely into the river.

On the west side of the A10, the spacious and attractive village of **Haddenham** has a turn-of-the-19th-century windmill that is open on the first Sunday of the month. In the centre of the village Haddenham Galleries has changing exhibitions for potential buyers of creative art.

Denny

DENNY FARMLAND MUSEUM, Denny Abbey, Ely Road, Waterbeach, Cambridge CB25 9PQ; ☎ 01223 860988/489; www.english-heritage.org.uk,www.denny farmlandmuseum.org.uk; adults £4.50, children £2.50, families £12 (more on an event day); open daily Apr to Oct 12pm–5pm.

Another stopping place of interest on the A10 is at Denny where **Denny Abbey** is unusual for having played host to three separate monastic orders since its foundation as a satellite of Ely Cathedral in 1160. The refectory building remains in a good state of preservation. Most families come to Denny for the **Farmland Museum** (7–8 miles north of Cambridge and south of Ely) which has been developing lots of hands-on exhibits about fenland farming targeted at visiting children.

Wicken Fen

WICKEN FEN NATIONAL NATURE RESERVE, Lode Lane, Wicken, Ely, Cambridgeshire CB75XP; ☎ 01353 720274; www.wicken.org.uk; adults £5.99, children £2.99; families £14.99; open daily year round dawn to dusk.

Billed as the last undrained fragment of fen, Wicken is a National Trust nature reserve that serves as a tranquil retreat. This ancient land may be undrained but it's certainly not unmanaged – otherwise visitors would quickly sink into the reedy bog. Instead they can follow gentle boardwalks and footpaths through this wetland past a squat windmill to a tower bird hide beside the lode (artificial waterway leading into the Rivers Cam and Ouse). If you are there on a summer Sunday afternoon, you could visit Fen Cottage, built from traditional local materials and furnished as a humble fenman's family might have lived in the early 20th century.

The National Trust is pursuing a breathtakingly ambitious plan over the next century to buy up nearly 15 square miles of farmland to the south in order to return it to wetland. You can take a walk skirting the edges of Wicken Fen between the villages of Upware and Wicken. There is little habitation in Upware apart from the amusingly named public house, **Five Miles from Anywhere No Hurry Inn** (Old School Lane, Upware CB7 5ZR; ☎ 01353 721654; www.fivemilesinn.co.uk). **The Maid's Head** in Wicken (12 High Street, Wicken CB7 5XR; ☎ 01353 720727) is a proper local with a large grassy garden and good food.

WISBECH AND NORTH FENLAND

The borderlands of north Cambridgeshire and Norfolk aren't a glamorous part of the region. There is nothing tame or twee about this landscape. In the recent words of Stephen Fry, 'the Fens stand as one of the most misunderstood, neglected and extraordinary features of the British landscape. Not to mention beautiful ... They are a remarkable part of our (agri)cultural, historical and engineering history.'

The year after Magna Carta, the treacherous flood-prone lands north of Wisbech swallowed up King John's entire retinue and much treasure because they were in too much of a hurry to wait for local guides to direct them along a causeway at low tide, or so the legend goes. Wisbech, capital of the northern Fens, was a prosperous Georgian market town and retains much of its gracious layout and handsome architecture. The city expanded around its port on the River Nene. In its trading heyday, hundreds of ships arrived and departed each week for ports around the North Sea.

Before the great drainage projects, these northern Fens covered vast areas of reedy swamp where mosquitoes bred and malaria was rife. The people lived off the fish, eels and birds, and depended on peat and willow for their primitive industries. The now obsolete term 'fen slodgers' referred to half-amphibious men who manoeuvred their way through the bogs by using stilts or punt poles in summer and skates in winter. Traditional jokes about the people having webbed feet still circulate. The picture this calls up is a far cry from the elegant sweep of houses along the banks (called 'brinks') of the River Nene which were built by wealthy Wisbech merchants and landowners.

WHAT TO SEE AND DO

 Fair weather

If it weren't for the traffic, you could imagine that you had stepped into the set of a BBC costume drama, and indeed television productions of *Martin Chuzzlewit* and *David Copperfield* have been filmed in Wisbech. There aren't just isolated buildings to admire but uninterrupted stretches of unspoiled Georgian architecture on either side of the river, and on town streets. The Crescent, on which the town museum is located is especially pleasing with its array of fashionable homes, now mainly offices, with their matching white sashed windows

Local legends: the Wisbech Giant

In the time of the Norman invasion, superstition held that a vicious giant inhabited the bogs north of Wisbech. Traders and travellers always took a long detour to avoid him, but not Tom Hickathrift. Tom was your classic idle teenager who lounged by the fire while his widowed mother worked her fingers to the bone. One day a neighbouring farmer in Wisbech offered Tom's mother two bundles of straw on condition she could arrange for them to be collected. She implored Tom to bestir himself, which he did. Instead of carrying the usual load, he came back carrying on his back 20 hundredweight of straw and his great strength was revealed. His services were suddenly in demand and he was hired to deliver barrels of beer from King's Lynn to Wisbech. Tiring of the long way round, he decided to cut through the giant's territory and was instantly berated in a booming voice. Undaunted, he stood his ground which sent the enraged giant to collect his weapons. Meanwhile the unarmed Tom removed a wheel and axle from his cart to use as shield and club. At first the two combatants were evenly matched. But the giant had so successfully cowed the locals that he hadn't had to fight for a long time and was out of shape. When he fell to his knees and begged for mercy, Tom chopped his head off, helped himself to all the silver and gold in the giant's cave, and became the hero of the Marshland. Just over the Norfolk border in Walpole St Peter, a small stone effigy of Tom can be seen supporting the north stairs in the impressive 14th-century church.

and fan lights above the doors; sometimes the symmetry is achieved by painting windows onto brick, though these 'blind windows' aren't easy to spot.

Clarkson Memorial

In a prime spot overlooking the main Town Bridge stands an impressive Victorian monument to the town's most famous son, Thomas Clarkson. At a young age Clarkson became passionately opposed to slavery and doggedly collected manacles and thumbscrews from slave ship captains, evidence of the inhumanity of the slave trade to try to shock the British public. He toured the country with his famous box (now in the Wisbech Museum) containing African handicrafts and objects to persuade people he met on his campaign that merchants should be trading in goods not human beings.

Elgood's Brewery

The 130-year-old family brewery of Elgood's has an attractive, peaceful 4-acre garden which is open to the public. It includes Georgian and Victorian features such as a maze, herb garden and rockery. Like so much of Wisbech, the brewery buildings date from the Georgian period and overlook the River Nene.

Elgood's Brewery

There are brewery tours at 2pm on days when the gardens are open. Many of the brewing techniques are just as traditional as the architecture and some of the brewing vessels have been in use for five generations. River water is used to cool the ale and the spent hops are used to enrich the soil in the gardens.

Peckover House

Built in 1722, Peckover House is considered a contender for the finest Georgian townhouse in England. Its imposing pedimented frontage with Italianate columns draped in wisteria bespeaks great prosperity (the Peckovers were the first banking family of the region). The Friends' Meeting House next door has a small cemetery full of Peckovers as well as the grave of Jane Stuart, illegitimate daughter of Catholic King James II (not generally open to the public).

From the front of Wisbech's showpiece house, you wouldn't guess that hidden behind is a 2-acre walled garden with many features such as a summer house, 300-year-old orange trees and many exotic plants collected by the Peckovers on their travels. There is also a reed-thatched barn now a tea shop (see *Eating Out*)

Peckover House

Octavia Hill Birthplace Museum

Wet weather

Wisbech and Fenland Museum

This is one of the oldest museums in the UK and hasn't been altered or updated much. The charming wooden display cases are full of geological collections so beloved by the Victorians. Inside you will learn that malaria, often referred to as 'ague', was not uncommon as late as the 20th century. Fenland locals resorted to drinking 'poppy tea' or smoking opium or hemp (i.e. cannabis), all grown locally. The museum also has an exhibition about Clarkson's role in the abolition of the slave trade.

WISBECH AND FENLAND MUSEUM, Museum Square, Wisbech PE13 1ES; ☎ 01945 583817;info@wisbechmuseum.org.uk; www.wisbechmuseum.org.uk; entry: free; open year round Tues to Sat from 10am–4pm.

Octavia Hill Birthplace Museum

Wisbech seems to specialise in producing social reformers. Octavia was the eighth daughter of James Hill, who built an infant school for poor children next to the church. She was inspired by John Ruskin's work in the area of housing reform and worked in London to transform slum areas around Marylebone into decent family neighbourhoods. She also campaigned to save Hampstead Heath and Parliament Hill and for ordinary people to have access to parks and gardens. She was also one of the founding mothers of the National Trust in the 1890s. The exhibits about Octavia's life and work include animated models and interactive activities, for example the cellar has a mock-up of Victorian slum living, bringing to life the privations endured by the poor (including a display on bedbugs).

OCTAVIA HILL BIRTHPLACE MUSEUM, 1 South Brink Place, Wisbech PE13 1JE; ☎ 01945 476358; www.octaviahill.org.uk; £2.50, children free; open mid-Mar to end Oct (and all year by appointment) on Wed/Sat/Sun/ bank holidays 1–4.30pm

What to do with children

A colony of rabbits has taken over a key roundabout in Wisbech which young children might enjoy seeing. The Freedom Bridge over the River Nene downstream from the Town Bridge leads to a rabbit-populated roundabout, not as unusual as Chicken Roundabout in Bungay mentioned elsewhere in this book, but still remarkable. As in Bungay, a suggestion that the animals be removed met with strenuous local opposition and now the council is creating a colourful habitat for the rabbits. Troughs will be added from which the rabbits can eat and drink. Taking its cue from the nearby quay, site of the proposed Nene Waterfront Regeneration project, three disused river cruisers are being installed and planted with flowers; these have been named Nutmeg, Hazel and Bright Eyes after characters in *Watership Down*.

 ## Entertainment

Theatre
For a town of not much more than 20,000, Wisbech is fortunate to have a professional theatre called **Angles Theatre and Arts Centre** (Alexandra Road, Wisbech PE13 1HQ; ☎ 01945 474447; www.anglestheatre.com) with a resident company. Seating only 112 people, it was built in 1793 (a quarter of a century earlier than the Regency Theatre Royal in Bury St Edmunds) making it one of the oldest surviving theatre buildings in the country. It is now owned by the Christian Spiritualist Church and the programme includes the usual pantos, musicals, youth productions and concerts.

Special events
The annual Rose Fair (www.wisbech-rosefair.co.uk) in early July is centred on the Church of St Peter and St Paul but sees the whole town decorated with floral displays and with a parade encircling the town from Queens Road. The Fens stretching into Lincolnshire are important for flower production so there are plenty of local supplies for the fair.

At the opposite end of the calendar Wisbech has recently introduced a **Christmas market** a week or so before Christmas, which takes over the town and attracts thousands of visitors. Attractions include a hog roast, costumed historic characters strolling around town and plenty of fenland meat and produce.

The best... **PLACES TO STAY**

HOTEL

Rose and Crown Hotel

23 Market Place, Wisbech PE13 1DG
☎ **01945 589800**
www.roseandcrownwisbech.co.uk

The premises of this, the oldest hotel in Wisbech, have been used as a hostelry for more than 500 years and have a few original features left over from the 15th century. Maintaining its old world atmosphere, the Rose and Crown isn't for the faint-hearted since it's reportedly home to ghosts. With three bars including Tidnam's Tipple Inn, social butterflies will find no shortage of places to steady their nerves.

Prices: B&B from £50 for a double.

INN

Oliver Twist Country Inn

High Rd, Guyhirn, near Wisbech PE13 4EA, ☎ 01945 450523
www.theolivertwist.com

As well as offering accommodation, the Oliver Twist Inn is also a restaurant of local renown. The owners are committed to serving good ale with the food and have to date served an impressive 749 different beers.

Prices: B&B double from £85.

FARM

Bodgers Farm

Howard and Kate Phillips, Bodgers Farm House, Black Drove, St Johns Fen End PE14 8JU, ☎ 01945 430880
www.bodgersfarmpottery.co.uk

A quiet rural retreat offering bed and breakfast in the middle of Marshland Fen, Bodgers Farm aims to defeat guests with the 'Bodgers challenge', polishing off a country English breakfast. Located on a working farm, Bodgers is surrounded by open countryside with a chance of spotting badgers in the garden. Pottery courses for beginners and improvers are given by the proprietor in the on-site studio.

Price: from £27.50 per person per night; pottery classes begin at £12 per hour.

CAMPSITE

Virginia Lake

Virginia Lake, Smeeth Road, St Johns Fen End PE14 8JF, ☎ 01945 430167
louise@virginialake.co.uk

Virginia Lake comprises a 100-pitch caravan park, tent site and 2-acre fishing lake. An on-site shop sells groceries and fishing equipment and the site has its own bar and clubhouse. Virginia Lake is open all year and dog walks and cycle routes can be found close by.

Prices: from £10 to £20 per night.

SELF-CATERING

Bank Cottage Holiday Cottages

Mouth Lane, North Brink, Near Wisbech PE13 4UQ, ☎ 0800 804 6498
enquiries@bank-cottage.co.uk
www.bank-cottage.co.uk

A group of three rural cottages just 100 yards from the River Nene is surrounded by farmland. The area offers an abundance of flat lanes for cyclists and quiet walks including a picturesque stroll along the riverbank to the recommended local pub and restaurant in Guyhirn (see Oliver Twist above). The garden includes a barbecue and seating area.

Prices: from £40.

UNUSUAL

Fenland Self Catering Holidays

Railway Carriage and Ivywood Carriage, Mandalay, Station Road, Wisbech St. Mary PE13 4RY, ☎ 01945 410680
www.fenlandselfcateringholidays.co.uk

Two Victorian railway carriages have been converted to holiday accommodation. Railway Carriage and Ivywood Carriage are set in their own gardens, and can sleep up to four people each. Access to a 3 acre apple orchard, local fishing opportunities and pleasant walks combine to make this a true fenland experience.

Price: from £150 to £240 for a week for Railway Carriage; from £180 to £300 for a week for Ivywood; short breaks start at £80 for two nights.

349

The best... FOOD AND DRINK

 ## Buying in

As a market town since medieval times, Wisbech has two market locations. The Market Place leading into the High Street in the main town has lots of pleasing glass and timber shopfronts on buildings adorned with gables and parapets. Wisbech isn't a delicatessen kind of town so you need to go to one of the regular open-air markets, held every Thursday and Saturday, as well as a fortnightly farmers' market on Friday mornings, where you can buy herbs and honey, fruit and game. During Rose Fair Week (first week in July), you will find local produce, cakes and flowers, among many other things.

On the north side of the river and to the right of the Town Bridge, is the Old Market where once dozens of ships tied up at the quayside and unloaded their wares. Originally this is where farmers bought and traded tools and seed, and sold their cattle and corn. Now on Saturdays you can buy local cheeses, seasonal produce such as samphire and fast food. Meanwhile the old traditional auction market for flowers and produce still takes place daily (except Tuesdays) at 4pm not far away on the site of the old Cattle Market at the Chase Auction Hall on Chapel Street (PE13 1RF).

If you are approaching Wisbech from the south on the A1101, you will pass several farm shops around Upwell and Outwell, which are well worth a stop; try for example J B Russell at 133 School Road in Upwell.

A one-woman company called Fascinating Food (Alison Sloan, Pear Tree Cottage, River Road, West Walton PE14 7EX; ☎ 01945 467238; www.fascinat ing-food.co.uk) puts on occasional short cookery courses at a cottage near Wisbech specialising in traditional fenland recipes such as Norfolk Vinegar Cake and Beer Bread.

 ## Drinking

Many pubs and hotels serve the local tipple **Elgood's**. Especially if you can't tour the brewery, try to sample one of its tasty prize-winning ales either at the brewery café or at one of the eight or so pubs in town that carry it. Elgood's Cambridge Bitter won the 'Champion beer of Britain' award recently and their Golden Newt has a pleasing floral taste. Both Black Dog mild and the stronger Black Shuck have an interesting treacly tarry taste which you either love or hate. (The demon dog Black Shuck has been the subject of legends throughout East Anglia; one of his visitations is described in the section on Blythburgh at the end of *Coastal Suffolk*.)

EATING OUT

RESTAURANT

Chameleon Restaurant
55–57 West Street, Wisbech PE13 2LY (on edge of town centre past St Peter and St Paul Church)
☎ **01945 474198**

Intimate bar restaurant with a changing menu of appealing dishes and real ale. Choices might include melted goat's cheese salad with olive tapenade and red mullet fillet with citrus couscous and a pesto dressing. Note early closing time of 9pm Mondays to Wednesdays, 9.30 Thursdays to Saturdays. The restaurant is closed on Sunday evenings.

CAFÉ

Peckover House Café
North Brink, Wisbech PE13 1JR
☎ **01945 583463**
peckover@nationaltrust.org.uk

You can usually count on the National Trust (at least between March and October) to provide a bowl of wholesome homemade soup and some yummy cakes. The attractively converted 17th-century barn café in the gardens of Peckover House is no exception.

PUB

The Marshland Arms
47 School Road, Marshland St James, Wisbech PE14 8EY
☎ **01945 430319**
www.marshlandarms.co.uk

Located 4 miles east of Wisbech in the remote Fens, this pub is known for its well-kept beer, good home-cooking and homely service. It even has one double bedroom which costs £50 bed and breakfast for two.

The Rose Tavern (53 North Brink, Wisbech, PE13 1JX; ☎ 01945 588335) is favoured by real ale drinkers wanting a change from Elgood's range. This small, riverside hostelry serves various guest beers such as Fuller's London Pride and Shepherd Neame Spitfire and Norfolk's Woodford's Wherry. And if you walk along North Brink between Peckover House and the Elgood's Brewery you will pass several other inviting pubs, such as the Red Lion and the Hare and Hounds.

FURTHER AFIELD

March

Another fenland market and railway town, March was never as grand as Wisbech and doesn't have any comparable architecture, except the roof of **St Wendreda's Church** (21 Wimblington Road, March PE15 9QW; ☎ 01354 653377; www.stwendreda.co.uk/index.html). Named after the 7th-century princess whose remains were venerated here for centuries, it managed to preserve its double hammerbeam angel roof from the Puritan looters by plying

Visitor information

Tourist Information Centres:
Fenland District Council, 2–3 Bridge
Street, Wisbech PE13 1EW, ☎
01945 583263; tourism@
fenland.gov.uk; www.fenland.gov.uk;
open Mon to Sat 9.30am–5pm.
Because Wisbech is often neglected
by tourists, the staff are usually
eager to advise and assist.
Hospitals: Nearest Accident &
Emergency is Queen Elizabeth Hospital, Gayton Road, King's Lynn PE30
4ET, ☎ 01553 613613,
www.qehkl.nhs.uk, near the junction
of the A149 and the B1145.
Websites:
www.strideguides.com/wisbech/ind

ex.html – an excellent up-to-date
podcast to accompany a walking
tour of Wisbech which can be downloaded to your iPod or MP3 player
and used with an accompanying
map that can be printed off from the
website; www.visitthefens.co.uk –
useful links to places of interest.
Supermarkets: Tesco, Cromwell
Road, Wisbech PE14 0SD, ☎ 01945
671400.
Bike rental: Little Ranch Leisure,
Begdale, Elm, Wisbech PE14 0AZ,
☎ 01945 860066
Taxis: Fenland Cabs, Wisbech,
☎ 01945 474554.

them with drink and bribing them with church silver. The church is usually closed, although you can sign out the key from the nearby **Seven Stars** pub and while you do so, enjoy the friendly ambience, the Greene King bitter and food cooked on the premises at better than fair prices. Market days in March are Wednesdays and Saturdays.

Great Fen Project

Just off the A1 between Huntingdon and Peterborough, an amazing experiment is going on at
Woodwalton Fen. The Wildlife Trust is acquiring
surrounding farms in order to flood them and
return them to their original pre-drainage habitat,
hugely increasing the area to 9,000 acres of what
is the oldest nature reserve in Britain. Even now it's a magical place with sedges and scrub crowding the boardwalks, and rare species like fen violets. Moths, dragon-flies and birds abound, and the hope is that in time rare birds such as marsh harriers and bitterns might return. About 20km of walks lead out from the Rothschild Bungalow, the thatched verandahed building built on stilts by

GREAT FEN PROJECT, Office
in Cambourne, Cambridgeshire
(☎ 01954 713500; www.great
fen.org.uk; free.

Charles Rothschild in 1910, and originally used as a research base by scientists from Cambridge University. Access to Woodwalton Fen National Nature Reserve is from Ramsey Heights, 1km east of the reserve.

Holme Fen is situated about 5km north-west of Woodwalton Fen (as the crow flies) and on the south-western shore of what was once the largest lake in southern England, Whittlesey Mere, drained only since 1851. Holme Fen is the largest silver birch woodland in lowland Britain, and has several lakes and bird hides.

Flag Fen

Flag Fen does for the Bronze Age what Sutton Hoo does for Anglo-Saxons, that is it brings the period to life. As is well known from the various 'bog people' that have been unearthed in Europe by archeologists, waterlogged bogland is capable of preserving organic material for vast periods of time. In normal conditions, wood would have disintegrated and vanished centuries ago, but here you can see gigantic timbers that have been carbon-dated to 3,000-plus years old, still showing tool marks. They were part of a massive palisade, possibly erected for ritual purposes. Visible traces of a Roman road survive, as does the oldest wheel in the country.

FLAG FEN, The Droveway, Northey Road, Peterborough, Cambridgeshire PE6 7QJ; ☎ 01733 313414; www.flagfen.com; adults £5.50, children £4.25, family £15.25; open 1 Mar to 31 Oct.

The museum and visitor centre are low-impact buildings that almost seem to float on the bog. A guided tour will show you why crafted metalwork vessels were purposely broken before being placed in the water. The theory that they were sacrificial offerings seems less plausible than that the settlement didn't want a conquering tribe to loot their goods. Excavations and theorising are ongoing.

Index

Y

Z

This edition published in Great Britain, in 2011 by

Crimson Publishing, a division of Crimson Business Ltd
Westminster House
Kew Road
Richmond
Surrey
TW9 2ND

© Crimson Publishing, 2008. Reprinted with amendments, 2011.

A catalogue record for this book is available from the British Library

ISBN: 978 1 78059 039 4

The author and publishers have made every effort to ensure that the information in *The best of Britain: East Anglia* is up-to-date and accurate. However, the publishers shall not be liable for any loss, injury or inconvenience sustained by any traveller as a result of information or advice in this guide.

Printed and bound by Ashford Colour Press Ltd., Gosport, Hants.

Series editor: Guy Hobbs
Layout design: Nicki Averill, Amanda Grapes, Andy Prior
Typesetting: Amanda Grapes
Cover design: mccdesign ltd and Andy Prior
Picture editor: Lianne Slavin
Production: Sally Rawlings
Proofreader: Cheryl Paten
Town map design: Reproduced by kind permission of Codair Design and Publicity Ltd, using source material from Ordnance Survey, see pages 119, 149, 229, 269, 305 and 333. Reproduced by permission of Ordnance Survey on behalf of HMSO. © Crown copyright, 2008. All rights reserved. Ordnance Survey Licence number 150002047.
Inside cover design: Tom Hulatt
Regional map design: Tom Hulatt
Regional map source material: © Maps in Minutes™/Collins Bartholomew, 2008

Acknowledgements
Author acknowledgements: Of the many friends and family who have shared their East Anglian secrets with me, I would especially like to thank Alex Buxton, Roger Hardie, Rosalie Kerr and Steve Chadwick. For many years, a group of friends and I have gone for a weekly walk in the Fens and on occasional longer trips to the coast. I owe a huge debt to their knowledgeable and enlivening conversation (and to Claire's coffee). Without the hundreds of excursions made from my home in Cambridge over the past two decades, many of them masterminded by Philip Hardie, this book could not have been written. I have benefitted from his boundless enthusiasm for country and coastal walking, off-the-beaten-track pubs, medieval churches and even the Fen drainage story.
Series editor acknowledgements: I would like to thank the many fellow East Anglians who have been badgered into helping with the preparation of this book, especially Sarah Wilkinson, Veronica and Mary Anne Woolf, Ellen and Esther Paige, Rupert Taylor, Cheryl Paten, John and Steve Swanbury, Dani Church, Ruth Watson, Mike Fenwick, Martin and Lyn Ayres, Ben Platts-Mills and Felix Turner.

Help us update
While every effort has been made to ensure that the information contained in this book was accurate at the time of going to press, some details are bound to change within the lifetime of this edition: phone numbers and websites change, restaurants and hotels go out of business, shops move, and standards rise and fall. If you think we've got it wrong, please let us know. We will credit all contributions and send a copy of any Best of Britain title for the best letters. Send to: Best of Britain Updates, Crimson Publishing, Westminster House, Kew Road, Richmond, Surrey TW9 2ND.

Norfolk and Suffolk picture credits

Front cover: Going Home (Norfolk Broads), © Laurence Gough/Shutterstock; **Inside flap**: Poppies at Leiston, John Swanbury; **Back cover**: Constable Country, Britain on View; Holkham Beach, Britain on View/Rod Edwards; **Inside cover**: Martello Tower at Sunrise, Suffolk; iStockphoto; **Contents**: Punting on the River Cam: Britain on View/ Ingrid Rasmussen; **Introduction**: Field: Sue Kington; **Title Page**: The Frith: Little Ouse Headwaters Project; **Introduction**: King's College Chapel: Britain on View/ Eric Nathan; **Introduction**: Boat on Aldeburgh Beach: Mykel Nicolaou; **Unmissable Highlights**; 1 Holkham Beach: Britain on View/ Rod Edwards; 2 King's College Chapel: Britain on View; 3 Butley Oysterage: Butley Orford Oysterage; 4 Norfolk Broads: Britain on View; 5 Blythburgh: John Swanbury; 6 Wicken Fen: Sue Kington; 7 Blickling Hall: National Trust/ Nick Meers; 8 Constable Country: Britain on View; 9 Elm Hill: Britain on View; 10 Coastal Walks: Roger Hardie; **Local Recommendations**; 1. Norwich Puppet Theatre: Norwich Puppet Theatre; 3. Blakeney Hotel: Blakeney Hotel; 5. Fish Shacks: Britain on View/ Rod Edwards; 7. Betty's Fen, Arthur Rivett; **Factfile**: John Swanbury; **p.55**: Shutterstock/ Len Green; **p.56**: Steve Swanbury; **p.58**: Shirley Wentworth; **p.61**: Dani Church; **p.62**: Sue Kington; **p.63**: Scarlet Page; **p.67**: Britain on View; **p.70**: Philip Hardie; **p.72**: National Trust/ Paul Wakefield; **p.73**: Britain on View; **p.74**: Philip Hardie; **p.74**: Britain on View; **p.75**: Landmark Trust; **p.77**: Jeremy Young; **p.83**: Robert Jackson, Chapel Books; **p.85**: Ruth Watson; **p.86**: Britain on View; **p.87**: National Trust/ Joe Cornish; **p.91**: National Trust/ Joe Cornish; **p.97**: Sue Kington; **p.100**: Britain on View; **p.102**: John Swanbury; **p.103**: John Swanbury; **p.108**: Guy Hobbs; **p.118**: Britain on View; **p.122**: Colchester and Ipswich Museum Service; **p.123**: Sue Kington; **p.125**: Landmark Trust; **p.130**: Pictures courtesy of Babergh District Council; **p.132**: Susan Griffith; **p.133**: Pictures courtesy of Babergh District Council; **p.135**: Pictures courtesy of Babergh District Council; **p.136**: National Trust/ Rupert Truman; **p.137**: Kentwell Hall; **p.138**: Gainsborough House; **p.150**: English Heritage; **p.151**: St Edmundsbury Borough Council; **p.157**: Philip Hardie; **p.159**: National Trust/ Ian Shaw; **p.159**: St Edmundsbury Borough Council - West Stow Anglo Saxon Trust; **p.162**: Mildenhall Museum; **p.165**: English Heritage; **p.167**: Easton Farm Park; **p.180**: Sue Kington; **p.181**: Sue Kington; **p.182**: www.english-nature.org.uk; **p.186**: Jim Tilcock; **p.194**: Sue Kington; **p.195**: Susan Griffith; **p.197**: Sue Kington; **p.199**: iStockPhoto; **p.202**: Extreeme Adventure; **p.202**: North Norfolk Railway; **p.206**: Philip Hardie; **p.212**: Sue Kington; **p.214**: Shirley Wentworth; **p.215**: Shirley Wentworth; **p.217**: National Trust/ Rupert Truman; **p.230**: English Heritage; **p.233**: Martin & Lyn Ayres; **p.236**: Britain on View/ East of England Tourism/ Visit Norwich/ Rod Edwards; **p.245**: Delia's Restaurant and Bar; **p.252**: Sue Kington; **p.254**: Shutterstock/ David Hughes; **p.254**: John Swanbury; **p.257**: BeWILDerwood; **p.263**: Shutterstock/ David Hughes; **p.274**: King's Lynn Museums; **p.275**: The Green Quay; **p.280**: Landmark Trust; **p.283**: By gracious permission of H.M. The Queen; **p.288**: English Heritage; **p.290**: Gooderstone Water Gardens; **p.291**: Forestry Commission; **p.293**: Ecotech Centre; **p.299**: Marion Leeper; **p.306**: Britain on View; **p.308**: Britain on View; **p.309**: Britain on View; **p.309**: Susan Griffith; **p.310**: The Fitzwilliam Museum, Cambridge; **p.310**: Cambridge and County Folk Museum; **p.311**: David Hardie; **p.334**: Britain on View; **p.341**: Peacocks Tearoom; **p.343**: English Heritage; **p.346**: Elgood's Brewery and Garden; **p.346**: Britain on View; **p.347**: Octavia Hill's Birthplace House; ; **Colour Section: Suffolk**; Marram grass-covered sand dunes behind Southwold Beach: Sue Kington; Oulton Broad at sunset: John Swanbury; Beach huts and lighthouse, Southwold: Sue Kington; Old half-timbered cottages, Lavenham high street: iStock photo; Fields near Blythburgh: John Swanbury; Hen Reedbeds Nature Reserve: Sue Kington; Lowestoft South Beach: John Swanbury; Metfield Church: John Swanbury;
Colour Section: Norfolk; Holkham Beach, Holkham Hall Estate: Britain on View/Rod Edwards; Thurne Dyke Wind Pump, Norfolk Broads: Britain on View/Rod Edwards; Norwich city centre Christmas lights: Britain on View; Brancaster Beach: John Swanbury; Blakeney harbour: Britain on View; Castle and Market Square, Norwich: Britain on View; Boats moored outside a pub, Norfolk; Broads: Britain on View/ ANPA/ McCormick-McAdam;
Colour Section: Cambridgeshire; Reed-lined drove footpath, Wicken Fen: Sue Kington; Christ's College, Cambridge: Britain on View; Cottage in Little Wilbraham, Cambridgeshire: John Swanbury; The nave and ceiling of Ely Cathedral: Britain on View; Ely at sunset: Britain on View.

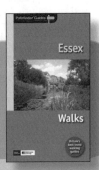